INSIDERS' GUIDE® SERIES

D1538441

INSIDERS' GUIDE® TO

MYRTLE BEACH
AND THE GRAND STRAND

TENTH EDITION

JANICE McDONALD

INSIDERS' GUIDE

GUILFORD, CONNECTICUT
AN IMPRINT OF GLOBE PEQUOT PRESS

All the information in this guidebook is subject to change. We recommend that you call ahead to obtain current information before traveling.

INSIDERS' GUIDE®

Copyright © 2001, 2003, 2005, 2008, 2010 Morris Book Publishing, LLC
A previous edition of this book was published by Falcon Publishing, Inc. in 1999.

Project Editor: Lynn Zelem
Layout Artist: Kevin Mak
Text design: Sheryl Kober
Maps: XNR Productions, Inc. © Morris Book Publishing, LLC

ISSN 1544-4015
ISBN 978-0-7627-5344-4

Printed in the United States of America
10 9 8 7 6 5 4 3 2 1

CONTENTS

Directory of Maps

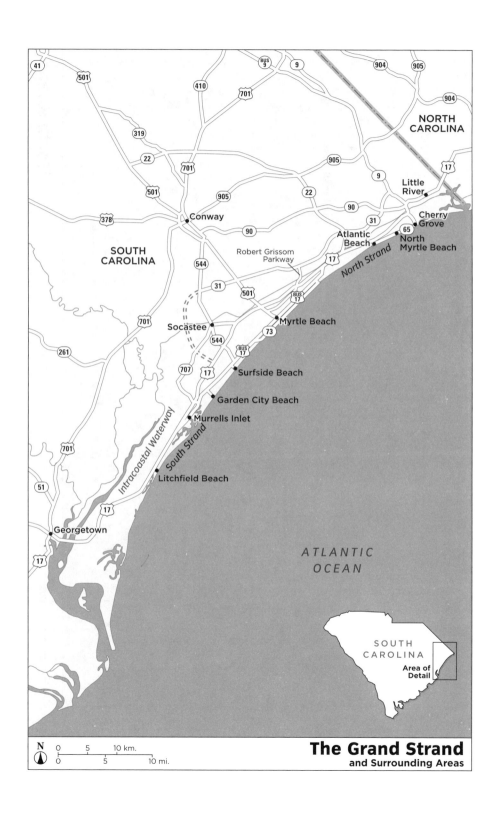

The Grand Strand
and Surrounding Areas

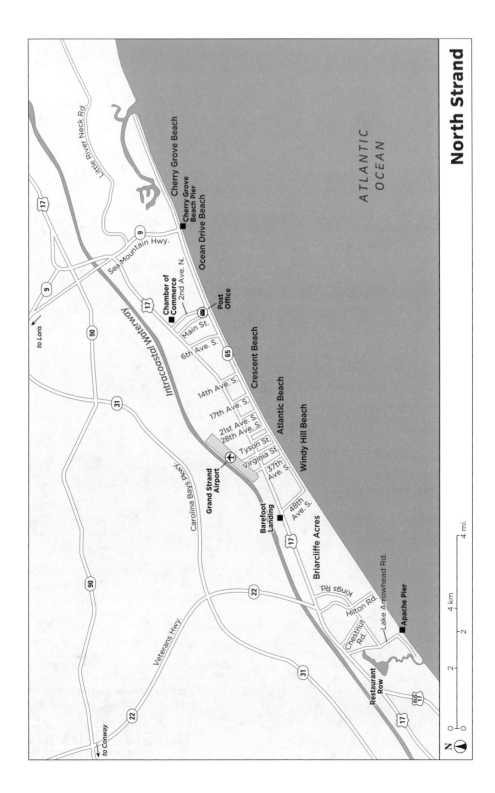

North Strand

ATLANTIC OCEAN

Cherry Grove Beach
Cherry Grove Beach Pier
Ocean Drive Beach

Little River Neck Rd.

Sea Mountain Hwy.

Chamber of Commerce
2nd Ave. N.
Post Office
Main St.
6th Ave. S.
Crescent Beach
14th Ave. S.
17th Ave. S.
Atlantic Beach
21st Ave. S.
28th Ave. S.
Tyson St.
Virginia St.
37th Ave. S.
Windy Hill Beach
Grand Strand Airport
Barefoot Landing
48th Ave. S.
Briarcliffe Acres
Kings Rd.
Hilton Rd.
Lake Arrowhead Rd.
Chestnut Rd.
Apache Pier
Restaurant Row

Intracoastal Waterway

Carolina Bays Pkwy.

Veterans Hwy.

to Loris
to Conway

N

0   2   4 km
0   2   4 mi.

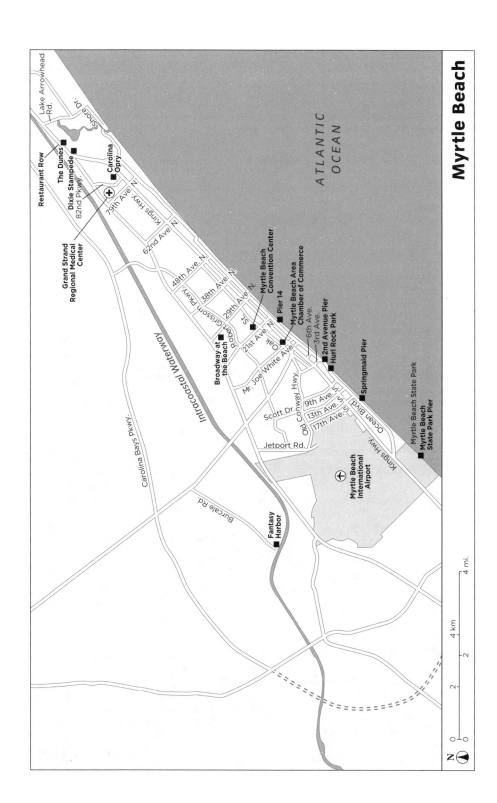

Myrtle Beach

Restaurant Row
Lake Arrowhead Rd.
Shore Dr.
The Dunes
Dixie Stampede
82nd Pkwy.
Carolina Opry
79th Ave. N.
Kings Hwy.
Grand Strand Regional Medical Center
62nd Ave. N.
Intracoastal Waterway
48th Ave. N.
Robert Grissom Pkwy.
38th Ave. N.
29th Ave. N.
Myrtle Beach Convention Center
Pier 14
St.
21st Ave. N.
Oak
Myrtle Beach Area Chamber of Commerce
6th Ave.
3rd Ave.
2nd Avenue Pier
Hurl Rock Park
Broadway at the Beach
Mr. Joe White Ave.
Old Conway Hwy.
Scott Dr.
9th Ave. S.
13th Ave. S.
17th Ave. S.
Springmaid Pier
Jetport Rd.
Carolina Bays Pkwy.
Myrtle Beach International Airport
Kings Hwy.
Ocean Blvd.
Myrtle Beach State Park
Myrtle Beach State Park Pier
Burcale Rd.
Fantasy Harbor

ATLANTIC OCEAN

N

0   2   2   4 km
0   2   2   4 mi.

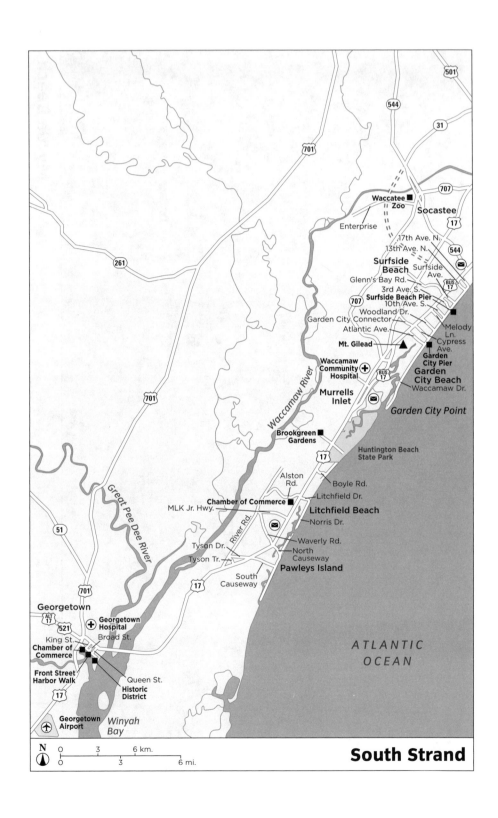

South Strand

PREFACE

Don't think of your trip to Myrtle Beach in terms of how long it will take you to get here—the few hours from Columbia or the all-day drive from Pennsylvania. Rather, think of what you are gaining on this sandy adventure: incomparable ocean views and sultry breezes, mounds of all-you-can-eat crab legs, your highest score on a video game or lowest in golf, a perfect memento to wear back home, or (and probably most of all) a touch of that Southern sunshine that will slow you down to the comfortable pace of the local drawl.

As you've probably heard by now (with nearly 14 million visitors annually, word can't help but spread), the Grand Strand has a lot more to offer than its wide, fun-filled beach. You should definitely spend your afternoons there, lying out, reading, crabbing, shelling, and swimming—you know, all the traditional beach things Myrtle Beach provides so well. But what should you do in the cool mornings? What if it's raining? What if your child asks about the area's flora and fauna or history? Which golf courses allow walking? With your special tastes in consideration, where should you stay? And, where should you eat?

When you arrive, you'll see plenty of signs pointing you in many different directions; the multitude of businesses along US 17 compete with each other in everything from price to visibility. But with *Insiders' Guide to Myrtle Beach and the Grand Strand,* you'll be prepared for, if not knowledgeable of, the new surroundings. As Insiders, we have crafted a guide to the Grand Strand specifically for people who want to enjoy themselves; even though we're not necessarily on vacation here, we heartily agree the Grand Strand is about enjoying yourself.

There are many ways to accomplish this, from strolling the beach and eating grilled meals to playing the most exclusive golf clubs and experiencing fine dining. With this Insiders' look at the Grand Strand, we hope we are helping you come up with the right combination and ensuring that you'll come back to try out a new one next year.

We looked at all the possibilities, trying to think of the most significant Insiders' tip to make your excursion as comfortable as possible, and this is the one that leapt to our minds first: Do not underestimate the value of a good sunscreen!

ACKNOWLEDGMENTS

I don't care where else I may travel or live, I will always be a "beach girl." My earliest memories are of squatting in the sand and letting the waves come in and roll over me. Childhood memories are filled with wandering the beach, hunting for sharks' teeth, combing the piers, and going to the Pavilion.

While everyone says their childhood memories are great, I can't imagine anyone's could top the ones I have of growing up in a community that cared so much about one another and had a beach in the backyard to play in as well.

My wonderful mother still lives in the home where I lived as a child, and although Myrtle Beach has grown up as well, it's still a place I call home and love dearly. Working on this book helped me realize just how much where I grew up and who I grew up with shaped me, and how all of those people I loved so much then are still there for me when I need them.

I want to thank my mom, Dorothy McDonald, for still being the person I can run things by and for going with me on some of my fact-finding expeditions. You really are the reason I love doing what I do. To my sisters, Anna McDonald Boyce and Paula McDonald Miles—thanks, you guys, for being my sounding board and for helping me laugh during deadline times. For my friends Trish Brocklesby and Lesta Sue Hardee—thanks for keeping me entertained and helping me relive some of those old beach memories and fill in some of the blanks.

I'm also thankful for all of the patient, faceless people who answered my questions when I called on them to get information.

—Janice McDonald

HOW TO USE THIS BOOK

This incredible 60-mile stretch of beach from Little River to Georgetown, appropriately dubbed the Grand Strand, is a vacationer's mecca. There's so much going on in any given area that, oftentimes, people need not wander beyond a 2-mile radius from their hotel to keep busy all day and night. We hope that this guide to South Carolina's favorite coastal resort will help you effectively plan your next visit here, your relocation, or your retirement. One thing is sure: This guide will give you a true Insiders' view of the Grand Strand from those of us who live, work, and play here.

In producing the *Insiders' Guide to Myrtle Beach and the Grand Strand*, we have tried to lead you through the dizzying options of things to see and do. The chapters on Shopping, Restaurants, Nightlife, Annual Events, Entertainment, Attractions, Kidstuff, and Arts and Culture should be good starting points for planning your activities. If you still have time and energy, the chapter on Day Trips can direct you to nearby sites of interest. The last thing we want is for you to get lost around here, so we've provided a Getting Here, Getting Around chapter as well as a variety of maps of the overall area, including main arteries and roadways.

We also have used the regional headings of the North Strand, Myrtle Beach, and the South Strand in the chapters to orient you and save you travel time. By breaking out these areas, you can pinpoint people, places, and things closest to you. Basically, the North Strand is anywhere from the village of Little River to Myrtle Beach proper. Lake Arrowhead Road and the Restaurant Row section of the Grand Strand will be your landmarks of note that you have passed from the North Strand into Myrtle Beach proper.

The Myrtle Beach section of the Strand continues southward until you see the signs denoting Surfside Beach. Surfside marks the starting point of the South Strand entries in this book, encompassing Garden City Beach, Murrells Inlet, Litchfield Beach, Pawleys Island, and Georgetown. Road signs let you know that once you've hit the Murrells Inlet area, you've traveled from Horry County into Georgetown County.

This guide contains several listings from sister regions, which we call Beyond the Strand. As a geographical heading, Beyond the Strand lends itself to areas within Horry or Georgetown Counties that are considered inland and usually denote areas west of the Intracoastal Waterway.

Whether you're staying for a weekend, a week, or permanently, this guide will help you find suitable accommodations or a roof over your head; check out the Accommodations and Real Estate chapters.

To make financial planning easier, we've coordinated a dollar-sign key to give you a price range for places to eat and stay. However, prices quoted in this guide are subject to change, and each establishment reserves the right to make those changes without prior notice. Also, we do apologize here and now if you should contact any place mentioned in this guide only to find it out of business. As is typical of a resort area, there is so much new market competition here that it's not unusual for a certain percentage of businesses to close their doors each year.

Other chapters provide vital information on child care, education, local laws, retirement, and medical care.

When using the Insiders' Guide, you'll come across a lot of cross-referencing. We do this to give you the most complete information possible. For example, you may be reading an entry in the Attractions chapter that refers you to the Kidstuff chapter for more information. The Kidstuff chapter may include the same entry, but it's written from the perspective of relating to children's interests. In this way you'll be able to get the whole scoop on a place, what there is for adults and for children.

Scattered throughout the various chapters are special Insiders' tips (indicated by **i**) for quick insights. Our guide is written by longtime South Carolina residents, and the tips are our way of sharing our insider information. You will also find more lengthy Close-ups with information that is particularly interesting, unusual, or distinctly Myrtle Beach. There is also a table of contents and an index to help you find what you are looking for.

Please note that the area code for the Coastal and Pee Dee regions of South Carolina is 843 (which replaced an 803 code in 1998).

This (843) area code includes the South Carolina counties of Beaufort, Charleston, Chesterfield, Colleton, Darlington, Dillon, Florence, Georgetown, Horry, Jasper, Marion, Marlboro, and Williamsburg. It will also take in most of Berkeley County and parts of Clarendon, Dorchester, and Lee Counties.

We hope *Insiders' Guide to Myrtle Beach and the Grand Strand* will give you a real feel for this area and the opportunity to experience it to the fullest. With this information in hand, you'll fit right in as if you've been beachcombing all your life.

AREA OVERVIEW

It's only appropriate that a place best known for its beaches is actually an island. The Grand Strand of South Carolina stretches for 60 miles along the northern Atlantic coast of the state, with Little River Inlet to the north and Winyah Bay to the south. Separated from the mainland by the Roosevelt-era shipping lane known as the Intracoastal Waterway, the area is connected to the mainland by four highways, including US 17, which runs the entire north-south length of the coast. In fact, the entire region can be cut off from vehicle traffic by closing seven bridges.

The Grand Strand is named so for a reason: The wide strand accommodates people of every type at various activities, including swimming, sunbathing, seashelling, volleyball playing, Sea-Dooing, fishing, parasailing, boating, and more. The communities are first and foremost beach oriented. All the houses and buildings are designed for optimum views of the water. One street inland, Myrtle Beach goes beyond sand in your shoes and provides restaurants, shopping, golf, and many other diversions.

Considered one of the nation's top vacation destinations, the Grand Strand hosts nearly 14 million visitors annually. The increasing number of attractions, theaters, outlet malls, shopping centers, ecotourism opportunities, and golf courses attracts visitors throughout the year. The Myrtle Beach area has received these positive national reviews:

- The Travel Channel has named Myrtle Beach one of the best family beaches in the U.S.
- Yahoo! Travel named Myrtle Beach the top beach destination in the United States for 2007.
- For two consecutive polls, *National Geographic Traveler* magazine has voted Myrtle Beach one of the Top Ten Beaches in the United States.
- AAA listed Myrtle Beach in its "Top 10 Driving Destinations" for four consecutive years.
- In 2009, Forbes.com listed Myrtle Beach in its top 100 places in the United States for Business and Careers. Forbes also named the Fun Plaza as one of America's 10 Best Arcade Boardwalks.
- Readers of *Southern Living* consistently choose the Myrtle Beach area as both a favorite "Beach Town" and destination for "Family Vacation" in their Reader's Choice Awards.
- Myrtle Beach has been labeled by many as the Seaside Golf Capital of the World, and *Sports Illustrated* and the National Recreation and Park Association have also bestowed on Myrtle Beach the title of Sportstown USA.
- In the past several years, both the *Wall Street Journal* and *Money* magazine have listed Myrtle Beach among America's top spots for retirement.

NORTH STRAND

Tourist development of the North Strand began around 1937 with a log cabin–type motel. Except for some serious destruction from Hurricane Hazel in 1954, these little beach communities have maintained their individual identities while creating a greater presence as North Strand entities.

Although minimal but steady erosion has prompted an ongoing renourishment project on a 25-mile stretch of beach between North Myrtle Beach and Garden City Beach (see the related Close-up in the Beach Information chapter), many folks who call the North Strand home boast that they still have the world's widest beach.

While the claim is disputable, no one will deny that their beach is remarkably wide—especially when the tide is at low ebb. Unlike many South Carolina beaches, this section of sand still offers plenty of room to bask in the sun, take long walks, mastermind sand castles, and play volleyball and paddleball, even when the tide is high.

The sand of the North Strand is packed firm; driving cars on the beach used to be popular but is now prohibited. But bikes are allowed and make for an enjoyable ride. Bicycles and a three-wheeled, low-riding style of bike can be rented along the North Strand, so avoid the hassle of bringing your own. The three-wheelers are a comic and attention-getting mode of travel; you sit in a semi-reclined position and pedal with your feet out front. It's awkward at first, but with a little concentration, you'll get the idea. Although these big trikes have handgrips, you steer using your feet and the sway of your body. Attachments allow you to pull the kids along.

i While you may see numerous offices labeled "Visitor Center" or "Tourist Information Center," only the ones bearing the chamber of commerce emblem are officially associated with the convention and visitors bureau. These places can be good sources for information, but they are often operated by real estate companies who will try to encourage you to visit their properties.

Little River

At the northernmost tip of the Grand Strand is a community that was first settled centuries ago by Native Americans who called it "Mineola" or "Little River."

Once an unspoiled fishing village, Little River is now the fastest growing community in Horry County. The population has all but doubled since the 2000 census as people try to escape the hustle and bustle of North Myrtle Beach, just a few miles south. US 17 through town is now a busy thoroughfare of restaurants and businesses, but the original waterfront section of the community still hosts cruises down the Intracoastal Waterway, fishing charters, and deep-sea excursions. It also hosts the Grand Strand's two gambling cruises.

Each spring, thousands make the pilgrimage to the waterfront for the extremely popular Blue Crab Festival (see the Annual Events chapter). In addition to fabulous fresh seafood, the daylong event features live music and an array of arts and crafts. If you miss that, the Shrimp and Jazz Festival over Columbus Day weekend is gaining a similar reputation for good food and fun.

North Myrtle Beach

North Myrtle Beach, home of the state's shimmy-in-your-well-worn-Weejuns dance, the shag, makes up the largest section of the North Strand. The city was established in the 1960s when legendary South Carolina congressman John Jenrette (then a state legislator) argued that the four smaller communities of Cherry Grove, Ocean Drive, Crescent Beach, and Windy Hill would prosper if they merged into a single municipality.

Condominiums and small motels are typical oceanfront accommodations, but you can still find front-row cottages. Their suitability for house parties, coupled with North Myrtle Beach's long-standing party-hearty reputation, make it a mainstay for shaggers, collegiate men and women, and arcade-loving kids.

From mid-May, when exams end at many institutions, until mid-June, you'll find North Myrtle overflowing with celebrating students from far and wide. On Easter weekend alone, an estimated 75,000 to 90,000 kids flock to the beach for dancing and romancing. Over the years police have been forced to become especially strict about public drinking. Consequently, many college kids have found themselves singing the jailhouse blues instead of dancing on the Strand. Jenrette, who served as the first town judge, still enjoys telling of his escapades trying not to jail many a young drinking party-seeker in the early days of North Myrtle. Even today, for those willing to demonstrate a little self-control, one visit will confirm an irrefutable truth: There's no better place on the eastern seaboard to celebrate the end of another school year.

Cherry Grove, just south of Little River, is one of several communities that compose North Myrtle Beach. Highway 9 or Sea Mountain Highway is the only way into Cherry Grove from US 17, so watch the signs carefully. Cherry Grove has its share of oceanfront condominiums and motels, but away from the ocean you'll find rows of houses on pilings lining serpentine channels and inlets. Many Cherry Grove residents and tourists handpick this section of the Strand because they relish the joys of catching, cleaning, and cooking their own seafood.

From dawn to dusk, Cherry Grove's Hogg Inlet bustles with folks shrimping and fishing, crabbing with chicken necks, and dutifully tending their fish pots. Patient anglers troll, seeking out the day's best fishing spots. At night they gig for flounder. You'll be glad to know Hogg Inlet has a public boat landing, so you don't have to own a home on the creek to partake of the inlet's bounty. In recent years Hogg Inlet has also become a late-night hangout and parking spot for young locals wanting a secluded smooching area.

Along US 17 the communities known as Ocean Drive, Crescent Beach, Atlantic Beach, and Windy Hill run together in a hard-to-distinguish blur. In fact, if you're not a local, it's nearly impossible to know when you've passed from one community into the next. On the ocean you'll find more motels and condominiums in Ocean Drive and Crescent Beach. Ocean Drive is best known as the place where the world-famous dance the shag originated. Accordingly, Main Street Ocean Drive boasts several clubs where beach music will never go out of style.

Although not technically a part of the city of North Myrtle Beach, Atlantic Beach sits between the Windy Hill and Crescent Beach communities. Historically, Atlantic Beach was known as the "black beach" because during Jim Crow years it was the only beach on the southern Atlantic seaboard open to African Americans. Separated for years from the rest of North Myrtle Beach

by oceanfront chain-link fences, today Atlantic Beach has a few small motels, nightspots, and lots of cottages, and it is still primarily an African-American community.

Where North Myrtle ends Briarcliffe Acres begins, sheltered by a wall of tall pine trees. Moderately upscale and almost solely residential, this tiny town is easy to miss if someone doesn't point it out. The easy way to find it is to look for Colonial Mall on the west side of the highway.

One of the North Strand's many delights is Barefoot Landing, a top-ranked tourist attraction. On US 17 and inland from Windy Hill Beach, this charming variation of a shopping center includes shops nestled around a 27-acre freshwater lake. Barefoot Landing is home to more than 100 specialty and retail shops, factory direct stores, more than 1,100 feet of floating dock, a boardwalk, and a handful of waterfront restaurants. Attractions include the Barefoot Carousel, T.I.G.E.R.S. Preservation Station, Alligator Adventure, the Alabama Theatre, and the House of Blues.

The North Strand wraps up with the Grand Strand's famed Restaurant Row. Like a string of fine pearls, an impressive selection of restaurants lines either side of US 17. Seafood, of course, is the natural specialty, but hearty steaks, spicy ribs, Italian favorites, Japanese options, and even down-home country cooking can be found along this renowned strip. During summer dinner hours, nearly every restaurant sports a long line of eager patrons, but you're sure to find the food worth the wait. Highway traffic is especially heavy during that dinner rush, which starts as early as 4:30 p.m. and continues until around 9 p.m.

Closest to Myrtle Beach is the unincorporated Shore Drive community. Highly developed and densely populated, this is an area of high-rise hotels and condominiums, retiree homes, a nearly constant flow of renters and time-share purchasers, and a couple of upscale residential communities.

MYRTLE BEACH

While some may be unfamiliar with the term "Grand Strand," just about everyone knows the name "Myrtle Beach." The chamber of commerce has started referring to it simply as "My Beach" in its promotional materials, but the locals call it "the Beach." Native pride virtually assures this is the only beach where they will admit to laying a towel.

To look at the string of high-rise hotels and condominiums, it's hard to believe the community first began its love affair with the tourism industry as a vacation spot for mill workers in the 1930s. The buildings that still exist in downtown proper show signs of those early boom days before "the Beach" became a full-fledged resort destination.

As Myrtle Beach is billed as the Seaside Golf Capital of the World, it's evident that golf reigns supreme here. But the flip side is that it is also the Miniature Golf Capital of the World, so it's evident that good old-fashioned family fun is equally important.

ⓘ Pay attention to North and South indicators on numbered street names. For example: Not only is 30th Avenue North 60 streets north of 30th Avenue South in Myrtle Beach, but there is also another set of 30th Avenues, North and South again, in North Myrtle Beach.

More and more, the area is becoming a year-round destination, but the summer season kicks off with the annual Sun Fun Festival. While a mainstay had always been sand castle building contests, the festival got serious in 2006 and started a habit of trying to maintain its status as home of the world's largest sand castle. That same year it made its way into the *Guinness Book of World Records* by bringing in 160 dump-truck loads of sand to create a 32.5-foot-tall behemoth. Not satisfied, in 2007 festival organizers opted to outdo itself with another castle 2.5 feet taller.

The tourism experts say that Myrtle Beach's greatest attractions are still the Atlantic Ocean and the beautiful beaches. But in the past few years so many other things have sprung up that

it is hard for even Insiders to keep track of the latest attraction. In addition to shopping, amusement parks, miniature golf, water parks, waterway cruises, live-entertainment theaters, and golf, there is a constant quest among promoters to find even greater ways to satisfy visitors and residents alike. Whether it's the family beach, golfer's paradise, the country music and live-entertainment haven, the food, the shopping, the amusements, the attractions . . . whatever the draw, Myrtle Beach seems to provide something for everyone.

Even old-timers are amazed at the development that has transformed Myrtle Beach.

The *Wall Street Journal* declared that the state bird of South Carolina is evolving into the "construction crane" because of Myrtle Beach. Myrtle Beach once was a summer vacation resort catering to blue-collar factory workers primarily in North and South Carolina and Tennessee. In fact, even Generation-X locals can remember when the only real tourist season was during July when the textile mills closed for vacation. But the face of Myrtle Beach has rapidly changed, becoming a mixture of blue-collar workers, northern mid-management retirees, upscale golfers, families, and a whole new demographic of white-collar vacationers.

During the past several years, the Strand's 104-plus golf courses have helped expand the spring and fall shoulder seasons in the tourism industry to make Myrtle Beach a nine-month resort. More than four million rounds of golf are played in the area each year.

Still, the average visitor to the Myrtle Beach area is an ocean-seeking vacationer. Almost 40 percent of nearly 14 million annual visitors live within a day's drive to the beach. Myrtle Beach is approximately halfway between New York City and Miami.

Myrtle Beach's streets are laid out on a grid system, so it's easy to find your way around once you establish parameters. Everything is based on proximity to "the Beach" and "the Boulevard." Ocean Boulevard runs along the oceanfront for virtually the length of Myrtle Beach proper. Avenues connect it with US 17 Business—known locally as "Kings Highway"—which transects the entire Grand Strand. The avenues' numbers start near the heart of the old downtown and work north and south, so you have both a First Avenue North and a First Avenue South, and so on. Southward, the numbers only reach to 30th, while to the north is goes to 82nd.

The term "the Avenues" has become synonymous with the residences that occupy the land east of Kings Highway from 30th Avenue North to 82nd. A mixture of permanent and part-time residents, old homes and rebuilds, these homes are either oceanfront or within walking distance of the water and are the most desired real estate in Myrtle Beach. While there is a stretch of hotels mixed in with beachfront homes from 52nd Avenue to 79th, most visitors will turn their attention to the beach south of 30th Avenue North. From there to 30th Avenue South, the beach is taken over by a virtual solid stretch of hotels and condominiums.

The legendary Myrtle Beach Pavilion and its host of amusements were located almost midway between. In 2006, the Pavilion was demolished to make way for a new development, but many of the surrounding businesses, including Ripley's Believe It or Not! Museum and the arcades, continue to draw visitors. Those wanting to ride amusement-park rides can still do so at Family Kingdom on Ocean Boulevard.

The city used to almost end to the west at Oak Street, which parallels Kings Highway north of the heart of downtown. Now, between Oak and US 17 Bypass is the Robert Grissom Parkway and a host of shopping centers and businesses, including Coastal Federal Field, where Myrtle Beach's Atlanta Braves Class A baseball team and the Pelicans play.

Less than a mile from the beach, between 21st and 29th Avenues North, you will also find Broadway at the Beach, a massive development that includes stores, restaurants, theaters, and even a lake with paddleboats. Broadway at the Beach is now home to some of the Pavilion's most popular attractions, including the Carousel and 1900 Pipe Organ.

The beaches of the Grand Strand are public; in fact, law specifically designates how many feet apart public access areas must be, based on development density. Thanks to the vision of Myrtle Beach officials, many of the city's public access areas have parking available. The city has erected blue and yellow signs along the Boulevard to help visitors recognize these access sites. Wheelchair access to the beach is also provided; through the efforts of several area civic clubs, beach services now offer specially designed wheelchairs that are easy to maneuver on the sand.

Myrtle Beach hosts many annual festivals. Two of the most popular are the Sun Fun Festival, usually held the first full weekend in June, and the Canadian-American Days Festival, held in March to coincide with spring break for Canadian students.

Established in 1951, the Sun Fun Festival originally served as an official kickoff for the summer season. Even now that Myrtle Beach is a year-round tourist destination, the traditional Sun Fun Festival continues to offer four days of nonstop fun in early June. The famous festival frequently attracts national media attention to the beauty and bikini contests, sand castle building, celebrity appearances, children's games, musical and theatrical performances, cookouts, sailing regattas, and much more.

Canadian-American Days offers a jam-packed agenda, too. "Can-Am," as locals call it, was developed in recognition of thousands of Canadian tourists who were already visiting the beach every spring. In 1961 the chamber of commerce decided to launch a Canadian advertising campaign to extend the beach season by encouraging even more northern visitors during the otherwise slow time. During this nine-day festival, banks willingly exchange currency, and some businesses even offer an exchange rate at par. Radio, television, and newspapers headline Canadian news.

See the Annual Events chapter for details on both of these events.

SOUTH STRAND

The South Strand includes Surfside Beach, Garden City Beach, Murrells Inlet, Litchfield Beach, and Pawleys Island. Compared with the rest of the Grand Strand, the South Strand subscribes to a more leisurely pace and lifestyle, with less neon and glitter as well as a low-key nightlife with just as much allure. Many praise this stretch of land, with its rich marshland, uninhabited beaches, bountiful inlets, and maritime forest, as the Carolina coast's finest treasure. For those same reasons, South Strand residents cherish their privacy and work vigilantly to protect the area's resources.

The town of Surfside dates back to the 1800s, when it was known as Roaches Beach and was home to a timber plantation. The land changed hands and names a few times but was renamed Surfside Beach in 1952 and incorporated in 1964 with 881 residents. Today, billing itself as "the family beach," the town's year-round population is more than 4,500. Immediately adjacent to Myrtle Beach and most like it in nature, Surfside Beach has become a destination unto itself—mostly for RV park visitors and hotel guests who like a little more solitude than Myrtle Beach offers.

US 17 in Surfside is lined with restaurants, beach shops, and attractions, including the Legends in Concert show of celebrity impersonators. Accommodations along Surfside's oceanfront differ somewhat from those in Myrtle Beach. Fewer high-rises tower above the sun-drenched beaches, and cottages and condominiums treasure comfort.

Directly south of Surfside Beach, Garden City Beach is a family-oriented retreat sporting hundreds of residential homes, summer cottages, and condominiums. Surf fishing reels in many participants along this beach, which is also a favorite retreat for beachcombers. Garden City Beach is also one of the Grand Strand's most popular retirement destinations, with large controlled-access senior-citizen communities dominating the area.

The point where Atlantic Avenue punctuates Ocean Boulevard is the only area in Garden City that resembles the glittery expanses of Myrtle Beach. Here you'll find arcades and carnival-style food vendors. As for quieter pursuits, walking Garden City's pier is a popular pastime, particularly when a silvery Carolina moon is riding high.

The North Jetty of Garden City was built in 1979 with rocks weighing up to 200 pounds each. It extends 3,445 feet from the shore and stabilizes the inlet across the ocean so commercial and recreational boats won't bog down. The jetty ensures ideal boating conditions, regardless of tidal action, which is especially important for those who fish commercially and rely on the sea's bounty to make a living.

South of Garden City is Murrells Inlet, the oldest fishing village in South Carolina. Murrells Inlet is home to anglers, writers, poets, and more legends and ghost stories than any other part of the Grand Strand. Mickey Spillane, who created the detective character Mike Hammer, lived in the Inlet for 50 years until he passed away in 2006. Many other nationally known novelists, poets, and musicians live here, all of whom love the small-town atmosphere of being able to walk into a fish market or an antiques shop without being mobbed.

Fishing in the creeks and waterways of Murrells Inlet has been a way of life for generations, and the quiet community trumpets itself as the Seafood Capital of South Carolina. Best known to tourists for dozens of seafood restaurants in a 3-mile stretch, Murrells Inlet also is home to numerous antiques shops, fresh seafood markets, and Captain Dick's, one of the Grand Strand's best marinas (see the Boating chapter).

The journey south on US 17 from Murrells Inlet to Litchfield is a quick, pretty trip. Densely wooded areas line the highway and give a sense of traveling back in time, a sensation deliberately cultivated by locals. Carefully manicured landscapes adorn the median along the main highway. Once known as Magnolia Beach, the popular resort of Litchfield Beach takes its name from Litchfield Plantation, a rice plantation on the Waccamaw River. The manor house is one of the few still-standing plantation homes surrounded by majestic oaks. Open as a country club and a bed-and-breakfast, Litchfield Plantation is now classified as a small world-class luxury hotel.

Litchfield's quaint shops, outstanding restaurants, and various accommodations are reasonably new compared to the historic resort of Pawleys Island, slightly south of Litchfield. The beaches of Litchfield and Pawleys are among the widest, most litter-free, and best-preserved on the South Carolina coast; however, much of the property is private, and you'll find only a few points of public beach access. Though the points are clearly marked, parking is limited.

Pawleys Island proclaims itself the oldest resort area in America. Even in the 1700s the tiny barrier island was a summer retreat for wealthy plantation owners and their families. Despite storms and the ravages of time, many of their cottages, weatherworn and rustic looking, still remain. Hence, for many years, locals have termed their island "arrogantly shabby." As a matter of fact, bumper stickers, T-shirts, and tourism brochures for Pawleys Island all have adopted that description.

Today Pawleys is known for its low-key lifestyle, handmade hammocks, and sightings of the Gray Man, a friendly ghost who warns of impending hurricanes. The cherished lifestyle is carefully protected by islanders. The 2-mile island was incorporated as a town in 1984 and in recent years has made for one of the most colorful political stories in South Carolina's history, with their struggle to restrict local building codes and prevent construction of high-rise condominiums and hotels. They have been successful. A few bed-and-breakfast inns flourish, offering a taste of beach living as it used to be: simple, unassuming, and perfectly tranquil.

South of Pawleys Island and at the foot of the Grand Strand is Georgetown, a shipping community that was once called Little Charleston. With a Revolutionary War–era flavor; the narrow, brick streets; and its well-preserved, two-centuries-old churches and homes, the flavor of the town really is colonial. A bell-towered Rice Museum dominates the center of town and features exhibits that track the antebellum history of the plantation heyday.

In recent years the little community has grappled with pollution problems stemming from wastewater discharge from International Paper and a steel mill that have long replaced the shipping, slaving, and rice industries. Still, there is enough flavor left of the old colonial town and enough old-style bed-and-breakfast residences that the visitor seeking to step back in time will find a paradise in Georgetown.

Myrtle Beach and the Grand Strand Vital Statistics

Nicknames: "The Grand Strand"—the extra-wide beach and grouping of all the beach towns, such as Little River, Windy Hill, Myrtle Beach, Garden City, and Pawleys Island. "The Independent Republic"— Horry County, because of historical events such as the signing of secession papers in Conway (the county seat), and Horry County's geographic separation, with rivers and marshes separating it from the rest of the state.

Mayor of Myrtle Beach: John Rhodes

Population: (Horry & Georgetown County) 318,011 (permanent residents)

Area: The Grand Strand—60 miles of coast, from Little River to Georgetown

Average temperatures: July—air 88, water 80; January—air 56, water 50

Average days of sunshine: Sunny, 216; rainy, 72; average humidity at 1 p.m., 57 percent

Major university: Coastal Carolina University

Important dates in history:

> 1730: The city of Georgetown is planned
> 1779: South Carolina joins Union
> 1900: Burroughs and Collins Company constructs a railway to the beach
> 1901: First hotel, the Seaside Inn, is built
> 1927: Myrtle Beach's first golf course, Pine Lakes Country Club, is opened
> 1936: Intracoastal Waterway is opened to boaters
> 1938: Myrtle Beach is incorporated
> 1954: Hurricane Hazel
> 1989: Hurricane Hugo
> 1997: Beach Renourishment Project begins; area's first museum of art opens
> 2009: The second largest fire in South Carolina history burns 20,000 acres of the Grand Strand

Major area employers: Burroughs and Chapin, AVX, Horry County School District

Famous sons and daughters: Vanna White, Alabama (started as Wild Country at the Bowery), Nancy O'Dell

Major airport: Myrtle Beach International Airport

Major roadways:

- Ocean Boulevard: runs parallel to ocean throughout most of Grand Strand.
- US 17 Business (Kings Highway) and Bypass: also runs parallel to the ocean a little farther inland.
- US 501: from Florence, into Conway and on into the heart of the Grand Strand. To get to the North Strand, leave US 501 after Aynor and take either Highway 22 to U.S. Highway 17 between Myrtle Beach and North Myrtle Beach or take the smaller Highway 90 after Conway to the more northern sections of the Beach.
- I-40 East (to US 17 South): for travelers coming from eastern North Carolina.
- I-95 and I-20: for those coming from the west into Florence.

Driving laws: South Carolina issues both five-year and ten-year licenses. Drivers over the age of 65 receive five-year licenses. To obtain a driver's license, you must be at least 18 years of age; to obtain a permit, age 15; new residents may use old licenses for up to 45 days. Seat belts and child safety restraints required. Headlights must be on when use of wipers is necessary.

Alcohol laws: Drinking age is 21. Sale of alcohol is permitted on Sunday. Beer and wine available at grocery stores; liquor sold at liquor stores, package stores, and ABC stores (marked with large red dots).

Sales tax: 6 percent South Carolina sales tax plus 1 percent local tax within Myrtle Beach city limits; 35.2 cents per gallon gasoline tax; maximum of $300 tax on purchase of vehicles.

Hospitality tax: 2.5 percent hospitality fee charged on prepared food, admissions, and overnight accommodations of less than 90 days.

Tourism information:

Myrtle Beach Area Chamber of Commerce (main office)
1200 North Oak St.
Myrtle Beach, SC
(800) 356-3016, (843) 626-7444

Myrtle Beach Area Chamber of Commerce
Airport Welcome Center
1100 Jetport Rd.
Myrtle Beach, SC 29577
(800) 356-3016, (843) 626-7444

North Myrtle Beach Chamber of Office
270 US 17 N.
North Myrtle Beach, SC 29582
(877) 332-2662, (843) 281-2662

South Strand Office
3401 US 17 S.
Murrells Inlet, SC 29576-0650
(800) 356-3016, (843) 651-1010

Georgetown Chamber of Commerce
1001 Front St.
Georgetown, SC 29440
(800) 777-7705, (843) 546-8436

GETTING HERE, GETTING AROUND

Just the smell of salt air can make that vice that has had a grip on your chest start to unwind. Imagine yourself with your toes buried deep in the warm sand and the salty breeze on your face as you listen to the gentle crashing of the waves. Those thoughts can put you in a hypnotic trance that will have those around you wondering what's behind that silly grin on your face.

Ahhhh, vacation on the Grand Strand!

We'd all like to be able to just transport ourselves magically without having to actually go through the trouble of getting there. But since that's not going to happen, this chapter is designed to help make the trip a little easier.

There's no real magic here—just some practical and helpful information from those of us who have brought getting around the area with as little hassle as possible to an art form.

GETTING HERE

By Automobile

The popularity of the Grand Strand has soared, with an estimated 14 million visitors pouring in every year. Dramatic road improvements have helped eased congestion on the major thoroughfares in recent years and new projects are under way. But take it from those of us who have lived here for years: It's easy to avoid traffic snarls if you travel at the right times of day and night. Plan your trip so that you will be driving US 501 into Myrtle Beach before 7 a.m. or after 7 p.m. Monday through Thursday. Also, stay off beach exit roads right after hotel checkout time on Saturday and Sunday. You will be much better off to check out of your room, put the bags in the car, and hang around town until late afternoon. That way you can also get in one extra afternoon on the beach, which is far more pleasant than bumper-to-bumper driving.

If you're coming to the Grand Strand from eastern North Carolina, you might want to try I-40 east or US 17 south to Wilmington, North Carolina. At Wilmington, head southbound on US 17. You should expect traffic to be moving pretty slowly along that stretch, unless you heed our previous advice and travel it early morning or late evening.

From Charleston take US 17 north. It could be crowded at peak traffic times.

If you're traveling north on I-95, take exit 170 (clearly marked Myrtle Beach), near Florence. Take US 76 to US 501 and follow it the rest of the way.

US 501 is the main thoroughfare from all points west into Myrtle Beach. It's called "Holiday Highway," but it can be anything but a holiday because of all of the congestion. Traffic is heavy under the best of circumstances, but it is especially trying between 11 a.m. and 4 p.m. on Saturday during the summer.

Vacationers heading to the North Strand beaches—Little River, North Myrtle Beach, and Atlantic Beach—now have two options to miss the US 501 traffic. If you've come from I-95, cross US 501 near Marion and continue on US 76 to Nichols. Then take a right onto Highway 9, which takes you almost to Little River. That route is mostly two-lane roads, so you may want to continue about 30 miles farther on US 501 past Marion. After Aynor, take the four-lane Highway 22 or Veterans Highway.

Completed in 2001, the Veterans Highway project was seven months ahead of time and $300,000 under budget. The South Carolina Department of Transportation estimates 70,000 vehicles will use the route daily, but it's still relatively undiscovered and offers a straight shot north to US 17. The highway ends just south of Myrtle Beach Mall (formerly Colonial Mall) near Barefoot Landing.

If you miss either of these roads, the bad news is that you will have had to endure the traffic on US 501 between Conway and Myrtle Beach. But you can still avoid having to go all the way to US 17 by taking the Carolina Bays Parkway, or Highway 31, east of Conway. Also four-lane, this highway intersects both Highway 9 and Highway 22. A new connector on the north end opened in August 2009 and allows quick access to the Ocean Drive end of North Myrtle Beach. Named for the first mayor of North Myrtle Beach, the Robert Edge Parkway allows traffic from Highway 31 and Highway 90 to connect directly to Main Street in Ocean Drive.

If you're traveling I-20, follow the signs toward Florence. The road will merge into I-95 north and bypass Florence. Then take exit 170, same as if you'd come the whole way on I-95. If you're traveling south on I-95, take exit 193 at Dillon. Head toward Latta, then take US 501. If you're going to North Myrtle Beach, you can take Highway 9 all the way from Dillon.

If you're going to the South Strand, you might want to take Highway 544. You'll turn to the right off US 501 about 4 or 5 miles out of Conway. If you opt to continue on US 501, you will connect with the US 17 Bypass at the overpass about 10 miles out of Conway, just after the bridge over the Intracoastal Waterway. US 501 and the US 17 Bypass are much easier roads to travel than Highway 544, but they'll add a few miles to your trip, and traffic is usually bad between 7 a.m. and 7 p.m. or when it's raining. It's a toss-up. The route you pick will probably depend on what kind of road you prefer.

Coming South via I-77

Coming to the Grand Strand via I-77 from western North Carolina, West Virginia, Ohio, western Pennsylvania, Michigan, and, possibly, Canada can be a trying time. We've consulted a couple of travel-service offices for their best directions, but when we tried those routes, we wound up spending a lot of time sitting in traffic. So here's a favored route of some transplanted northerners who call Myrtle Beach home: Travel I-77 South through Charlotte, North Carolina, to Rock Hill, South Carolina. Just past Rock Hill, take exit 77 onto US 21 South. Stay on US 21 for about 5 miles and exit east onto Highway 5. Stay on Highway 5 for about 5 miles until you reach US 521. Head south on US 521 to Lancaster. Outside of Lancaster take Highway 9 for about 3 miles to Highway 903. Take Highway 903 east for about 20 miles to Highway 151 and turn right. Stay on Highway 151 for about 40 miles to Darlington. Just outside of Darlington, take US 52 toward Florence until it junctions with I-95. Take I-95 north and follow the instructions included in this chapter (see previous section) from that point.

It sounds confusing, we know, but pull out your map and highlight the route in advance. Even though the roads look like two-laners on most maps, you actually will travel four-laners most of the way, with the exception of the 60-mile or so stretch between Lancaster and McBee, South Carolina. Following these directions it should take about three and a half hours to get from Charlotte to Myrtle Beach. If you don't want to bother with the back roads, we understand. If you prefer interstate highways, stay on I-77 to Columbia, South Carolina, then take I-20 to Florence and follow the directions included in this chapter from that point. The advantage is traveling all interstates, but it might take a little longer.

Some relief possibly is in sight: Long-term plans call for the building of I-73, which will eventually run from Sault St. Marie, Michigan, to Myrtle Beach. It's expected to become a major thoroughfare for northern tourists traveling to the Grand Strand. (I-73 will share some common corridors with I-74, which will connect Davenport, Iowa, to Lumberton, North Carolina.) But don't get your hopes up yet; only North Carolina has sections of I-73 open, and even though most of the routes would incorporate existing roads that were scheduled for upgrades, there is still no definite timeline for completion. I-73 would connect to the Grand Strand by joining Highway 22 (Veterans Highway) west of town and end on

Kings Highway north of Briarcliff. The South Carolina Department of Transportation has approved making its 80-mile stretch of I-73 a toll road.

By Plane

In addition to services offered at the Myrtle Beach International Airport and the Grand Strand Airport (listed subsequently), private planes and corporate jets can access the Conway-Horry County Airport (843-397-9111), off U.S. Highway 378, outside Conway. The airport is home of the North American Institute of Aviation, an international pilot training school. Overnight tie-down is $3. (See the Child Care and Education chapter for more information.)

MYRTLE BEACH INTERNATIONAL AIRPORT
1100 Jetport Rd., Myrtle Beach
(843) 448-1589
www.flymyrtlebeach.com
The Myrtle Beach International Airport continues to grow to meet the increasing demands of those choosing to fly to their favorite vacation destination. There are currently two terminals with one security checkpoint, and the first phase of a $130 million airport expansion is under way. Plans call for creating a state-of-the-art facility as well as increasing the number of gates from 7 to 12. In addition, under the 2009 American Recovery and Reinvestment Act, the Myrtle Beach Airport was awarded two grants for expansion. The nearly $7 million of stimulus money will allow for terminal ramp reconstruction and new airfield lighting.

Flights are offered by US Airways, Delta Airlines, Continental Airways, Northwest, Spirit, United Airlines, and Myrtle Beach Direct Air. After years of being serviced largely by commuter planes, most airlines flying into the Beach utilize full-size jets.

Direct flights to and from Myrtle Beach are available for Atlanta, Charlotte, Chicago O'Hare, Detroit, New York–LaGuardia, Newark, Niagara Falls, and Washington Dulles International Airport.

Airline reservation numbers include: Delta, (800) 221-1212; Continental, (800) 525-0280; Myrtle Beach Direct, (877) 432-3472; Northwest, (800) 225-2525; United, (800) 241-6522; and US Airways, (800) 428-4322.

For private or charter aircraft, Myrtle Beach Aviation, the general fixed-base operator at Myrtle Beach International Airport, can be reached at (843) 477-1860.

You should be able to get to Myrtle Beach by air from just about anywhere in the United States. Unless you can book an express flight, you'll have to take a smaller commuter flight, probably from a major air terminal in Charlotte, North Carolina, or Atlanta, Georgia.

GRAND STRAND AIRPORT
33rd Avenue S. and Terminal Avenue,
North Myrtle Beach
(843) 272-5337
Horry County operates the Grand Strand Airport, where private aircraft and corporate jets can land. You don't have to notify anyone that you're coming, but be aware that all services close for business at 10 p.m.

You can leave your craft for several days while you enjoy the beach. The airport is about 1 block west of US 17, pretty much in the heart of North Myrtle Beach.

The fixed-base operator at Grand Strand Airport is Ramp 66, which can be reached by telephone at (843) 272-5337 or (800) 433-8918, or by e-mailing Bob McGoarty at bob@ramp66.com. More information is available at www.ramp66.com. Overnight tie-down starts at $10 per night. Fuel is also available. If Ramp 66 staffers have time, and your accommodations aren't too far away, they will take you to your motel.

Ramp 66 also has its own car rental service, featuring all new cars, including compacts and SUVs. Customers can use a car for an hour for free. After that, it's $8 per hour. It also has weekly rates. If you're coming into the airport at odd hours, you need to take care of your car rental ahead of time. Ramp 66 is at your service seven days a week.

LORIS–TWIN CITIES AIRPORT
US 701
This is a public and unattended airport for training and landings for private aircraft.

Rental Cars

Nine companies rent cars and vans on-site at Myrtle Beach International Airport. They include: Alamo, (800) 462-5266; Avis, (800) 331-1212; Budget, (800) 527-0700; Dollar, 800) 800-4000; Enterprise, (800) 261-7331; Hertz, (800) 654-3131; National, (800) 227-7368; Thrifty, (800) 847-4389; and US Save, (800) 272-8728.

By Bus

You should be able to get to Myrtle Beach on a Greyhound bus from just about any point in the United States. You'll find it easier during the summer, when more buses are scheduled. The station, at Oak Street and Seventh Avenue North, Myrtle Beach, is open from 9 a.m. to 5 p.m. and closed holidays. Call (843) 448-2472 or (800) 231-2222 for details.

By Train

Don't count on riding the train to your Grand Strand vacation destination; Florence and Dillon are the two closest places Amtrak serves. The problem is getting to Myrtle Beach from either of those cities. There is bus service from both on Greyhound, but there is only one bus each day. During slow months, the route is subject to cancellation if there are not enough bookings, so make sure you check prior to booking your train ticket.

i If you're traveling with your dog, your furry companion must be kept on a leash. In North Myrtle Beach the only beach access restrictions for pets are during the summer days, from 9 a.m. to 5 p.m. But in Myrtle Beach and in Surfside, entire sections are out of bounds for four-footed friends year-round.

By Boat

The most scenic and perhaps most peaceful way to get to the Grand Strand is by boat. The Intracoastal Waterway generally parallels the Atlantic Ocean for 1,200 miles from Boston to Key West, Florida.

In 1932 the Army Corps of Engineers dug a 20-mile canal, connecting Little River to the Waccamaw River. This portion goes right through the Grand Strand.

Boaters can tie up at Barefoot Landing for a day of shopping and dining, and an evening of country music at the Alabama Theatre. There are numerous marinas along the waterway and the Waccamaw River, where boaters can spend the night, eat in a nice restaurant, buy groceries, or have their motors tuned up.

Many of the marinas have signs along the waterway telling you what CB radio channel to tune in to contact them.

Marinas along the Grand Strand include Hague Marina, just before Socastee, (843) 293-2141; Bucksport, a very popular docking spot, (843) 397-5566; Wacca-Wache at Wachesaw Landing, (843) 651-2994, (843) 651-7171, or (800) 395-6694; and Cedar Hill Landing, in the Murrells Inlet area, (843) 651-8706. (See the Boating chapter for details about these and other marinas.)

There is a city-owned marina in Conway, (843) 248-1711, on the Waccamaw River. If you're traveling south on the waterway, turn right at Enterprise Landing at Channel Marker 25. Then head north for about 9 miles. Some boaters choose this course to enjoy the river's beauty. It winds and has some sharp turns, so if your boat's length is 40 feet or more, you might not want to try it.

To navigate the waterway, it's a good idea to have a nautical chart. Such charts point out dangerous spots, marinas, and buoys and describe available services at the marinas.

You won't find the waterway as crowded as US 501, but it is a popular artery for travelers, recreational boaters, and water-skiers. Water routes can get crowded on weekends—especially the Waccamaw River.

The stretch between Conway and Bucksport is especially charming—a wonderful place to get back in touch with nature. Egrets build nests on the channel markers, and beautiful old trees overhang the water. If you're fortunate enough to travel at night, the moon glistens on the water, and you can spot campfires back in the woods. At times campers come to the riverbank and shout hearty hellos to the boaters.

ℹ **Thanks to milepost markers along the length of US 17 Business and Bypass, finding businesses and landmarks along the Grand Strand has gotten easier. The markers begin on the southern end of the Grand Strand with milepost marker number 185 at the Georgetown County line. They end with number 221 at the North Carolina line.**

GETTING AROUND

Navigating the Strand Like a Local

Trying to navigate the Grand Strand can be a frustrating venture at first because there seem to be so many names for the same routes. You'll hear "17 Bypass," "Kings Highway," "the Boulevard," and a host of others. We're going to try to make sense of all this for you.

The first thing to remember is that all main arteries along the Grand Strand parallel the Atlantic Ocean. Closest to the beach is Ocean Boulevard (aka "the Boulevard" or "the 'Vard"). Ocean Boulevard officially runs from Garden City Beach northward, breaks for 5 to 7 miles of private land and state park, and ends at Dunes Golf and Beach Club, 9000 Ocean Blvd. It picks up again at 48th Avenue South, at Windy Hill beach, and continues northward to Cherry Grove beach.

Westward from Ocean Boulevard, the next main roadway is Kings Highway—commonly referred to as US 17 or Business 17 (in Myrtle Beach). Kings Highway is the proper name for this road in Myrtle Beach. To make a mental note, just remember that Kings Highway is also called "Business 17" because shops, restaurants, and attractions galore line both sides of this main artery. Kings Highway (US 17) stretches the length of the Strand to Georgetown, then southward all the way through South Carolina. (*NOTE:* For this guide, we only use Kings Highway to refer to US

17 Business in Myrtle Beach; otherwise, we defer to US 17.)

Still moving west, you'll come across the racing traffic of US 17 Bypass or Alternate 17. True to its name, this highway's purpose is to bypass traffic from Kings Highway. The Bypass reaches from Murrells Inlet northward until it merges with Kings Highway at Dixie Stampede just south of the Restaurant Row district. Once you've merged here, the road becomes US 17.

If you really want to skip through town like a true native—anywhere from the Myrtle Beach International Airport to 48th Avenue North, in Myrtle Beach—here's how:

Leaving the Myrtle Beach International Airport, take the first right turn onto South Broadway (road signs read S.C. HIGHWAY 15). As you proceed, South Broadway will turn into West Broadway at the stoplights. Keep in the center lanes that allow you to travel straight through this original downtown section of Myrtle Beach until you reach the third set of stoplights; then get in the left-turn lane. Turning left will put you on Oak Street; you'll wind through town to 38th Avenue North. Go straight through the 38th Avenue stoplights onto Pine Lakes Drive and pass through a lovely old residential section of Myrtle Beach all the way to 48th Avenue North.

ℹ **If you have car trouble or are in an accident while traveling in the Grand Strand area, just hit *HP on your cellular phone and ask for SCDOT Incident response. The State Department of Transportation will dispatch an emergency roadside response unit to help.**

Getting around in Myrtle Beach is easier thanks to the widening of 21st Avenue North between Kings Highway and US 17 Bypass. Another project widened Oak Street to five lanes—four travel lanes and a turn lane—from 21st Avenue North at the Myrtle Beach Convention Center to 29th Avenue North. From 29th Avenue North to 38th Avenue North, the road was widened to three lanes—two travel lanes and a turn lane. The project also included the addition of curbs, gutters, and sidewalks. The Robert M. Grissom Parkway is a four-lane route from 48th Avenue North in Myrtle Beach to Harrelson Boulevard near the airport.

Several years ago the state pledged more than half a million dollars for road construction in Horry County. Veterans Highway, or Highway 22, was completed in 2001. Among the other road-construction highlights:

- A frontage road from Forestbrook Road to the Intracoastal Waterway
- Carolina Bays Parkway, which adds four lanes from Highway 9 to a bridge across the Intracoastal Waterway near 62nd Avenue North
- Conway Perimeter Road between US 378 and US 501
- A cloverleaf bypass from US 501 to US 17 Bypass
- Highway 544 converted to five lanes from Socastee to Conway
- Intersection improvements on US 501, Highway 90, and Secondary Roads 31 and 66
- Overpass above US 501 at the turnoff for Freestyle Music Park

The wishes of residents and visitors who have long hoped for new and better roads along the Grand Strand are clearly being granted. The $900 million worth of road construction means the process of traveling from one place to another is changing faster than a speeding bullet. For detailed and current project information, visit www.cityofmyrtlebeach.com.

Taxis

For easy, accessible travel it's always best to have an automobile when exploring the Grand Strand. Let's face it, to cover 60 miles of territory, any other mode of transportation will take considerable time. But there's nothing more expedient than a cab to simply get from point A to point B in good time. We warn you that taxi fares are not cheap around here. The meter will read $1.50 from the start and fares are $2.40 per mile. Extra passengers will run $1. To give you an idea of the usual cost, a trip from Myrtle Beach International Airport to a Myrtle Beach destination around 21st Avenue North costs approximately $15, which includes a $6 airport surcharge. Try any of the following companies for service: Airport Cab, (843) 222-2222; Airport Taxi, (843) 444-4000; Beachside Taxi, (843) 361-2464; Taxi Tropical, (843) 267-7778; or Yellow Cab, (843) 444-0444. Shuttle service through www.MyrtleBeachTransportation.com, (843) 449-4445, provides transportation to from the airport to any location along the Grand Strand and will even take you as far south as Charleston if needed.

Public Transit

Once you're in Myrtle Beach, you might want to walk or catch a ride on the Coastal Rapid Public Transit Authority, (843) 488-0865. Consisting of 35 vehicles, the company offers bus service 8 a.m. to 8 p.m., Monday thru Friday, 364 days a year. The Coastal RTA serves the coastal Carolina region, including Myrtle Beach, North Myrtle Beach, Surfside Beach, Georgetown, and Conway. Schedules and fares are listed at http://RideCoastRTA.com.

HISTORY

Even though the name Myrtle Beach has been around for less than 100 years, people have been enjoying the Grand Strand area for a few centuries, from the original Native American inhabitants and visiting dignitaries such as George Washington to today's vacationers. Despite all the new development that obscures much of this history, you could say we're keeping up a historic seaside tradition by maintaining the Grand Strand as one of the East Coast's favorite getaways.

EARLY HISTORY

Long before Europeans landed on these shores, what is now US 17 and the section of it known as Kings Highway began as an Indian trail. It then evolved into a stagecoach route from northern colonies (eventually states) to Charleston and Savannah. After his election, George Washington used the route and lodgings along the way. (For more details about his journey, see the Close-up in this chapter.) The Waccamaw and Winyah Indians were the area's first inhabitants and the rivers and bays here are named after them. Native Americans called this area *Chicora,* which means "the land." The Horry County Museum in Conway (see the Attractions chapter for more details) has exhibits detailing their way of life. Additionally, a burial mound is on Waites Island near Little River. In fact, Native American artifacts have been unearthed all along the Carolinas' coast.

As early as the 1520s, Europeans were attempting to settle this area, but it wasn't until the 1700s that things got exciting. Even before the American Revolution, pirates made good use of the bays and inlets of the Grand Strand. To this day locals relish stories about Blackbeard marauding local shippers and rumors that Captain Kidd buried treasure somewhere around Murrells Inlet. Edgar Allan Poe's novella *The Gold Bug* is a fantastic account of good old South Carolinian treasure hunting.

Georgetown is the state's third oldest port city. The city was planned by English colonists in 1730 and quickly became the center of America's colonial rice empire. *A Woman Rice Planter* is a fascinating personal account by Elizabeth Allston Pringle of her struggles to maintain her rice plantation after the Civil War ended and changed the plantation system irrevocably. The colonial spirit of Georgetown is preserved in many still-standing plantations; Hopsewee Plantation is the birthplace of Thomas Lynch Jr., a signer of the Declaration of Independence.

Pawleys Island, just north of Georgetown, is the original vacation spot for this area and one of the first resorts in the United States. A half mile wide and 4 miles long, the island is abundant with oleander and oak trees pressed in between the old summer cottages. Pringle wrote of Pawleys Island, "To me it has always been intoxicating, that first view each year of the waves rolling, rolling, and the smell of the sea, and the brilliant blue expanse."

Also on the south end of the Grand Strand, Murrells Inlet is the oldest fishing village in the state. It is home to anglers, writers, poets, legends, and ghost stories. The area's history, much like a Southern romantic novel, recounts stories of pirates patrolling the seaside, aristocratic plantation owners accumulating immense wealth, the daughter of a U.S. vice president being forced to walk the plank of a pirate ship, phantom lighthouses steering ships from storms, and cemetery-walking ghosts searching for lost lovers. The Spanish moss–laden oak trees do nothing but encourage these stories.

The story of Alice Belin Flagg is probably the most romantically tragic. Alice was caught in the traditional dilemma of the upper-class belle in love with a beau her family did not approve of. Her beau presented her with an engagement ring, but since she couldn't wear it on her finger, she wore it on a ribbon around her neck, where it was eventually discovered by her brother, who ripped it off and threw it into the creek on their plantation. Of course, Alice pined away for the ring of her forbidden beau and died for want of true love.

Until the 1900s the beaches north of Murrells Inlet were practically uninhabited because of geographical inaccessibility and the poor economy. Still, a few fairly large salt-milling operations existed there prior to the Civil War. During the separate skirmishes, all were destroyed. The largest was in the Little River Neck region and had more than 50 buildings. A second was located in the area that is now the exclusive Dunes Golf and Beach Club, somewhere around the 18th hole. Salt pots can be found on display at the Strands Civil War Museum, located at the Myrtle Beach Indoor Shooting Range on the US 17 Bypass.

20TH-CENTURY MYRTLE BEACH

The creation of Myrtle Beach as we know it began during the first part of the 20th century when F. A. Burroughs bought some timberland several miles inland from the South Carolina coast. In a story that rings with as much irony as buying Manhattan Island for beads and trinkets, the owners of the timberland would only agree to sell if Burroughs would agree also to buy the "worthless" coastal land as part of the same deal. So Burroughs was stuck with that property, too. Confounded at the worthlessness of the area, called Long Bay, Burroughs sought to find a way to add value to the sandy strip.

Meanwhile, the towns of Cherry Grove and Windy Hill had been well established. In an effort to find funding to develop the beach area into a resort to outclass Pawleys Island, Burroughs contacted a New York stockbroker named S. G. Chapin. To help with the effort, Burroughs's wife gave the area a more attractive name: Myrtle Beach, for the rows of myrtle trees growing along the coastline. Chapin was at first interested, but his wife was so adamant about not wanting to live in the wilderness that he was prepared to reject the idea outright. But after meeting, the two men became such good friends that they decided to go forward with the project. Thus, in 1912 Myrtle Beach Farms Inc.—and the future of the Grand Strand—was born.

Although the area's first motel, Seaside Inn, was constructed in 1901 (under the direction of F. A.'s son, F. G. Burroughs), the rich and famous were not flocking to the beach. In fact, except for members of the Burroughs or Chapin extended families, there were very few visitors; Burroughs did convince some relatives to buy lots from him (at $25 each) to build resort cottages.

Following the Pawleys Island lead, the two entrepreneurs coaxed a wealthy textile magnate, John Woodside, to build a resort playground hotel for the rich and famous. In 1925 Woodside bought 65,000 acres from Myrtle Beach Farms and began building his dream. First to come was the luxurious Ocean Forest Hotel. A classic high-rise for its time, the wedding-cake-style hotel was resplendent with marble floors, crystal chandeliers, an enormous ballroom, and even a lighthouse on top—as if it weren't already visible enough on the virtually barren coastline.

Woodside also built the area's first golf course, the 36-hole Ocean Forest Golf Club, and was in the process of expanding his resort when the stock market crashed in 1929. He lost his dream back to Myrtle Beach Farms, which maintained the Ocean Forest Hotel until 1974, when it was demolished. The Ocean Forest Golf Club was renamed Pine Lakes and downsized to 18 holes. Its clubhouse is on the National Register of Historic Places.

The corporation continued to operate small hotels and cottages, rent and sell land, and develop beachfront attractions until the 1954 destruction wrought by Hurricane Hazel, and the dream to attract the rich and famous went on a back shelf in favor of survival . . . a survival that was supported by becoming an inexpensive beach for working-class families.

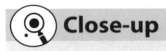 **Close-up**

George Washington Tours the Grand Strand

Just as millions of people do every year now, George Washington toured the Grand Strand in 1791. Two years after he was elected president, George Washington wanted to visit the new states "to become better acquainted with their principal characters and internal circumstances as well as to be more accessible to numbers of well-informed persons who might give useful information and advice on political subjects." He also wished "to acquire knowledge of the face of the country, the growth and agriculture thereof; and the temper and disposition of the inhabitants toward the new government."

As you read Washington's comments, note that many of the family names he mentions are still in use today: Mrs. Horry (Horry County), Vereen (Vereen Marina and Vereen Park), Pawley (Pawleys Island). Also, we've preserved the president's spelling for historical flavor.

Washington followed the same road we take almost every day; in fact, the section of US 17 that runs through Myrtle Beach is known as Kings Highway in his honor (the former colonists weren't quite comfortable with the new title of president). While he toured the coast, he saw the condition of the people at all levels of society, staying at public houses when possible and paying for his accommodations when allowed. When William Washington of South Carolina offered him use of a Charleston town house, President Washington declined. "I cannot," he wrote, "without involving myself in inconsistency; as I have determined to pursue the same plan in my Southern as I did in my Eastern visit, which was not to incommode any private family by taking up my quarters with them during my journey. It leaves me unencumbered by engagements, and by uniform adherence to it, I shall avoid giving umbrage to any, by declining all such invitations."

Even though it's the same road, the Carolina coast was much different for Washington: " . . . the country from Wilmington through which the road passes . . . is pine barrens with very few inhabitants . . . a perfect sameness seems to run through all the rest of the Country. On [the rivers] especially the swamps and low lands on the rivers, the soil is very rich; and productive when reclaimed. . . . " Obviously this president did not need to travel with a motorcade.

His accommodations were equally as rural. "Excepting the Towns (and some Gentlemens Seats along the Road from Charleston to Savanna) there is not with in view of the whole road I travelled from Petersburgh to this place, a single house which has anythh. [sic.] of an elegant appearance—They are altogether of Wood and chiefly of logs—some indd. [sic.] have brick chimneys but generally the chimneys are of split sticks filled with dirt. . . . "

Washington's first stop in South Carolina was at James Cochran's house, which stood in what is now the town of Little River near the intersection of Minneola Avenue and US 17. Of course, most of the places where Washington stopped at are now gone, but a few in the South Strand do remain.

"April 27 . . . lodged at Mr. Vareens [sic.] 14 miles more and two miles short of the long bay. To his house we were directed as a Tavern, but the proprietor of it either did not keep one, or would not acknowledge it. We were therefore entertained (& very kindly) without being able to make compensation."

The house of Jeremiah Vereen Sr. stood near the intersection of what is now US 17 and Lake Arrowhead Road in Restaurant Row. The Vereens kept a public house for many years—possibly the progenitor of all the restaurants to follow?

"April 28, Mr. Vareen [sic.] piloted us across the Swash (which at high water is impassable, & at times, by the shifting of the Sands is dangerous) onto the long Beach of the Ocean; and it being at a proper time of the tide we passed along it with ease and celerity to the place of quitting it which is estimated at 16 miles. . . . "

This swash referred to by Washington is probably Singleton's Swash, which enters the ocean just north of Myrtle Beach at the Dunes Golf and Beach Club.

"April 28 . . . Five Miles farther we got dinner & fed our horses at a Mr. Pauleys a private house, no public one being on the road. . . . "

George Pawley was also a government official; he had been in the First and Second Provincial Congresses (1775, 1775–1776) and in the First General Assembly (1776). He served as justice of the peace in 1765 and 1774 and as a colonel in the militia around 1775.

"April 28 . . . being on the Road, & kindly invited by a Doctor Flagg to his house, we lodged there; it being about 10 miles from Pauleys & 33 from Vareens."

Dr. Henry Collins Flagg (1746–1801) married Rachel Moore Allston, the widow of William Allston of Brookgreen Plantation on Waccamaw Neck, in 1784. The site of the house in which Washington stayed is now occupied by the Alligator Pool fountain at Brookgreen Gardens.

"April 29 . . . We left Dr. Flagg's about 6 oclock and arrived at Captn. Wm. Alstons' on the Waggamaw [sic.] to Breakfast."

Clifton Plantation, the home of William Alston (1756–1839), stood on the banks of the Waccamaw River on Waccamaw Neck. Now part of Arcadia Plantation, Clifton then "looked like fairyland" to Washington. "His house which is large, new, and elegantly furnished, stands on a sand hill, high for the Country, with his Rice fields below; the contrast of which with the lands back of it . . . is scarcely to be conceived."

Thirteen rounds of fire, one for each state of the Union, saluted his arrival across the river by "an elegant painted boat," and he was escorted to his lodgings, reportedly the house of Benjamin Allston on Front Street. Locals now maintain that this is the same Adam-style brick house with a hipped roof that stands on a raised basement and faces the Sampit River at 1019 Front Street in Georgetown.

"May 1 . . . Left Georgetown about 6 Oclock, and crossing the Santee Creek [Sampit River] at the Town and the Santee River 12 miles from it . . . we breakfasted and dined at Mrs. Horry's about 15 Miles from Georgetown. . . . "

This is Hampton Plantation, which is open to the public. The home of Daniel Horry II, it was a working rice plantation at the time of the president's visit. Harriott Pickney Horry and her mother, Eliza Lucas Pickney, greeted Washington in 1791 when he stopped at Hampton for breakfast. The ladies "were arrayed in sashes and bandeaux painted with the general's portrait and mottoes of welcome."

From there Washington continued this inaugural journey to Charleston and Savannah. The South Carolina Department of Archives and History in Columbia has a more detailed record of this momentous journey.

VACATION TIME

From 1954 through the 1980s, a rebuilt Myrtle Beach—with a new boardwalk and modernized pavilion replacing the 1909 bathhouses and 1912 amusements building—remained a small summer beach resort for a few hundred thousand blue-collar families from North and South Carolina. Myrtle Beach was a minor destination dotted with small mom-and-pop hotels, amusement parks, and small regional attractions. Myrtle Beach had indeed grown into a modest and pleasant resort.

Hurricane Hugo hit in 1989, but again the Grand Strand rebounded. Building and rebuilding has become more than a hobby around here, and dozens of ambitious projects are always under way. The number of golf courses has reached 105. Barefoot Landing, formerly Village of the Barefoot Traders, expanded over a scenic marsh and set the precedent for a new, natural Myrtle Beach as opposed to the harsh neon that glowed in the 1980s. Broadway at the Beach opened in 1995 and successfully combines both glitzy and charming features for an all-day experience. This growth has anchored the Strand even more solidly as a major tourist destination and has been accompanied by many smaller and just-as-worthwhile establishments opening up throughout the Grand Strand area.

Currently, roughly 14 million visitors relax here annually. People still come to get away from their busy, landlocked lives just as generations before have. Though we now have all the modern conveniences (some days you just can't do without air-conditioning) and distractions (using up a roll of quarters at the arcade can be so satisfying), we're still here for the same reason: those rolling, rolling waves.

ACCOMMODATIONS

onsidering that the Grand Strand offers literally thousands of accommodations for visitors, we have tried to narrow the scope to those establishments that consistently get positive reviews from the public. That's not to say that all others are dank tenements, but the numbers are far too vast to bring all the players into this arena. Lodging is in such demand along the Grand Strand that new facilities are being built as fast as you can turn these pages, and smaller mom-and-pop hotels are abundant here.

It's safe to say that 95 percent of the hotels, motels, and condominiums on the Grand Strand line both sides of Ocean Boulevard, the road that parallels the Atlantic Ocean from North Myrtle Beach to Surfside Beach and becomes Waccamaw Drive in Garden City. Don't be confused if you're riding along, in awe of the hundreds of lodging marquees, and the road suddenly jogs west to US 17 Business. A couple of miles of private property separate North Myrtle Beach from Myrtle Beach, and you'll find several campgrounds between Myrtle Beach and the end of the South Strand.

A ROOM WITH A VIEW

Properties closest to the beach are considered oceanfront. Properties with an ocean view refer to rooms that have a view of the ocean but do not directly face it (on the side of the building) or, in some cases, rooms not on the east side of Ocean Boulevard. Rooms with a balcony or walkway are referred to as rooms with a side view. You might also run across terms such as poolside or streetside, which denote a room's location within the property. Be sure to ask specific questions about the location of your room when confirming your reservation.

ABOUT PETS

Those of you who travel with your pets might find it difficult to rent a room.

The City of Myrtle Beach passed an ordinance that prohibits animals of any kind in the area on the beach or Ocean Boulevard between 21st Avenue North and 13th Avenue South. It seems there was a problem over the years with folks bringing their pets and other exotic animals (boa constrictors, ferrets, iguanas) down to the heavily populated Pavilion area, causing quite a stir

with other pedestrians. The law was passed to help prevent any accidents or incidents caused by the animals. The Pavilion is gone but the law remains. Dogs are not allowed anywhere on the beach from 9 a.m. to 5 p.m. May 15 through September 15.

REGARDING RESERVATIONS

As in most resort areas, be prepared to make a deposit when calling in your reservation. It is required by the majority of properties and will be credited to your bill. Generally, a deposit equals a day's rent. To avoid hassles, use credit cards, cash, or traveler's checks to pay for everything; most local banks will not cash out-of-town personal checks unless you have an account with them or enough picture identification to satisfy the FBI on a manhunt. Vital reservation information includes the time you plan to arrive, the number in your party, the length of your stay, and the date you plan to depart.

Although rooms are plentiful, the Strand's population swells to almost four times its year-round size in the heat of summer, and all of these people need a place to lay their weary heads. Think twice about driving to the beach and "finding" a room, especially in the middle of the night. The tourism season blooms like the flowers each spring and peaks like the hot noonday sun each summer. As the autumn leaves fall, so do lodging rates; in wintertime, snowbirds flock to the beach for cheap, cheap rates. In the 1960s and 1970s, most businesses rolled up the sidewalk from Labor Day until Easter. That is a practice of the past. As the Grand Strand is quickly becoming a year-round resort, the majority of properties remain open throughout the year.

HOTELS AND MOTELS

These accommodations are listed according to location, beginning on the North Strand and ranging southward through Myrtle Beach and the South Strand. In accordance with the Americans with Disabilities Act, all of these properties should be wheelchair accessible; establishments must comply to stay in business. Keep in mind when making reservations that most accommodations offer at least a 10 percent discount if you're staying a week or longer. Most also offer senior citizen, travel club, and group discounts as well. Always ask about any special rates or entitlements.

On any given evening, there are approximately 89,000 rooms available on the Grand Strand—ranging from hotels, motels, and condos to time-share units. But even with so much capacity, there's apparently still room for more growth in the market. Annual occupancy rates are still on the rise, and new accommodations continue to climb skyward.

Unless otherwise indicated, all accommodations listed in this chapter accept at least Visa and MasterCard as methods of payment. Inquire about alternative options when you make your reservation.

Please note that we have also indicated establishments that provide babysitters or referrals for such services.

Have a pleasant and comfortable stay.

Price Code

The dollar-sign key used with each listing is based on the average room rate for two people (at least two double beds) per night in the middle of July, when hotel and motel rates are at their highest. This average rate was determined by taking into account all the types of lodging available at each property. Weekends and holidays always command a higher room rate.

$.	$68 to $93
$$	$94 to $120
$$$	$121 to $145
$$$$	$146 to $171
$$$$$	$172 and up

North Strand

AVISTA RESORT   **$$$**
300 North Ocean Blvd.,
North Myrtle Beach
(800) 968-8986, (843) 249-2521
www.avistaresort.com

The Avista Resort is a full-scale condominium resort with twin towers and 378 rooms from which to choose. Avista has one-, two- or three-bedroom condos available, each with full kitchen as well as a private balcony. There is a full-service restaurant on-site, as well as a poolside grill and a lounge. There are three pools, two lazy rivers, a kiddie pool, and three hot tubs. It also has a state-of-the-art fitness club and wireless Internet access. Centrally located, Avista is within walking distance to North Myrtle Beach's dance clubs, restaurants, and shopping.

BAY WATCH RESORT   **$$**
2701 South Ocean Blvd.,
North Myrtle Beach
(866) 270-2172
www.baywatchresort.com

Located in North Myrtle Beach's Crescent Beach section, Bay Watch is part of Oceana Resorts. It accommodates groups of all sizes, from meetings to family getaways. Each of the 523 rooms has its own fully equipped kitchenette, and there are two-, three-, and four-bedroom units available. Bay Watch features a 600-foot oceanfront pool deck as well as an indoor pool and lazy river, four four-person spa tubs, kiddie pool, game room, and fitness center. There is a business center with Internet access.

The hotel's restaurant, the Blue Room Cafe, is an ideal dining spot for families, golfers, or just friends. Even locals have been known to frequent the Fishtails Beach Bar for dining and dancing or the Sandtrap Lounge & Sports Bar. Both have a running calendar of planned activities or drink specials to help draw a crowd.

While Bay Watch does cater to group meetings, the resort is large enough that you don't feel like you are intruded upon by large gatherings. Bay Watch is part of a locally owned group of resorts, so the staff is well versed on local activities, including fishing and golf excursions.

BLOCKADE RUNNER MOTOR INN $
1910 North Ocean Blvd.,
North Myrtle Beach
(843) 249-3561
www.blockaderunner-sc.com
On the oceanfront in the popular Ocean Drive section of North Myrtle Beach, the Blockade Runner offers 72 two-bed units, including efficiencies, all overlooking the ocean. In addition to an oceanfront pool and kiddie pool, guests can also enjoy the Jacuzzi and a delicious meal in the on-premises restaurant, the Sea Oats Cafe. The restaurant is open from 6 a.m. to 2:30 p.m. every day, and from 5 to 9 p.m. in the summer months. Golf specials are offered from Labor Day through June 1.

LAKE SHORE MOTEL $
1443 US 17, Little River
(800) 500-8508, (843) 249-1653
www.lakeshoremotelsc.net
The Lake Shore Motel has 20 spacious rooms featuring double and king-size beds. Each room is equipped with a refrigerator and cable TV. Championship golf, deep-sea fishing, excellent restaurants, and the beautiful beaches of the Grand Strand are all just minutes away. After enjoying the activities and attractions, you can relax by the motel pool or try the fishing on the lake.

OCEAN CREEK PLANTATION
RESORT & CONFERENCE CENTER $$
10600 North Kings Hwy.,
North Myrtle Beach
(800) 845-0353, (843) 272-7724
www.oceancreek.com
Ocean Creek Plantation is one of the grandest resorts along the beach. The luxurious accommodations (435 in all) include studios and one-, two-, and three-bedroom condominiums in six separate complexes. The 57-acre resort's oceanfront beach club features a large outdoor pool, sundecks, and a poolside bar. The resort's beach club includes a kiddie pool, playground, and volleyball court.

Guests can enjoy fine dining at the Four Seasons restaurant if they don't want to leave the property. Supervised activities for the kids are available in summer months, freeing parents for a little private vacation time. The resort also features seven on-site lighted tennis courts and extends guest privileges at a majority of area golf courses. Ocean Creek staff consider the finest details, whether hosting a family of four or a conference for hundreds.

SAN-A-BEL RESORT $$
1709 South Ocean Blvd.,
North Myrtle Beach
(800) 458-9945, (843) 272-2079
http://sanabeltowers.com
San-A-Bel offers 97 two-bedroom, two-bath condominiums. Each unit has a full kitchen with microwave and dishwasher, as well as a washer and dryer adjoining the kitchen area. All of the balconies have recently been remodeled. The beautiful indoor heated pool features expansive skylights and glass walls for unobstructed views of the ocean. Outside, a large wooden sundeck surrounds the whirlpool—a relaxing haven after a workout in the fitness room.

THE SEASIDE INN $$
2301 South Ocean Blvd.,
North Myrtle Beach
(800) 433-5710, (843) 272-5166
www.seasideinnmb.com

The Seaside Inn is a recently renovated condominium complex that has been transformed into a luxury boutique resort. There are 69 spacious, one-, two- and three-bedroom units, each with an ocean view. They include all the comforts of home: full kitchens, dining rooms, washer/dryer, a Jacuzzi tub, and high-speed Internet access. Most rooms include a continental breakfast in the resort's restaurant. There are two pools on-site, a lazy river, two hot tubs and a state-of-the-art fitness facility.

Myrtle Beach

ANDERSON OCEAN CLUB AND SPA $

2600 North Ocean Blvd.,
Myrtle Beach
(866) 576-8494, (843) 213-5340
www.andersonoceanclubonline.com
Long a family favorite in Myrtle Beach, the Anderson Inn replaced its quaint old hotel a few years back with a luxury high-rise. The 304 condominiums feature studios and one-, two-, and three-bedroom units as well as a full-service day spa called the Awakening. There are two outdoor and one indoor pool, a lazy river, an indoor heated kiddie pool, and a hot tub. Anderson Ocean Club is in the center of Myrtle Beach, close to grocery stores, malls, entertainment, and restaurants.

ATLANTICA RESORT $$$

1702 North Ocean Blvd.,
Myrtle Beach
(800) 248-0003, (843) 448-8327
www.atlanticaresorts.com
Formerly known as the Poindexter, this resort caters to families and couples only. The Atlantica, set on 300 yards of white, sandy beachfront, is within walking distance to the arcade area. Ocean-view and oceanfront rooms and efficiencies are available. Atlantica offers guests the use of 10 pools (both indoor and outdoor), whirlpools, a gigantic kiddie pool, and a lazy river. There is an on-site restaurant for all meals, a meeting room, and exercise facilities.

Special package plans run the gamut from golf and amusement park to honeymoon and entertainment. Supervised children's activities are planned every day during the summer.

BEACH COLONY RESORT $$$

5308 North Ocean Blvd.,
Myrtle Beach
(800) 222-2141, (843) 449-4010
www.beachcolony.com
This resort has everything you'll need for a great vacation. Beach Colony is home to 218 vacation units that include oceanfront suites; two-, three-, and four-bedroom condominiums; and ocean-view studios. There are also 77 additional two-bedroom, ocean-view condominiums in a separate tower. Guests may dine in the restaurant or relax in the lounge. For water other than the ocean, the resort has a kiddie pool, two outdoor pools, an indoor pool, and indoor and outdoor whirlpools for winding down. An exercise room, saunas, and a racquetball center offer you options for working up a sweat. The Carolina Room at Beach Colony can accommodate up to 180 people for meetings or events, and the Azalea Room can take in up to 60 guests. The resort also has a multilevel, covered parking garage; an outdoor lazy river water ride; and an arcade.

This resort is home to Fusco's, a wonderful Italian restaurant that serves one of the area's only Sunday brunch buffets. The folks at Beach Colony can refer guests to reputable babysitters.

i All of the public beaches on the Grand Strand have lifeguard services to help ensure the safety of visitors. During high winds and rough seas, if riptides are in the area, lifeguards will fly red caution flags that warn guests to stay out of even the shallows of the surf. If caught by a riptide, swim parallel to the beach to escape.

BERMUDA SANDS $

104 North Ocean Blvd.,
Myrtle Beach
(800) 448-8477, (843) 448-8477
http://myrtlebeachinns.com

Located only a few yards from the Second Avenue Fishing Pier and just blocks from the Family Kingdom amusement park, Bermuda Sands is a family-friendly hotel that is a great value for those who want to be in the heart of it all. One of the Beach's older hotels, it has just 150 units. Still, if being right on the beach isn't enough, it has an indoor and outdoor pool, kiddie pool, as well as a Jacuzzi and lazy river. One-, two-, and three-bedroom units are available, and all have a kitchen or at least a kitchenette.

The hotel offers both family specials and getaways for couples. They are also among the few pet-friendly hotels on the beach.

BEST WESTERN GRAND STRAND INN AND SUITES $$
1804 South Ocean Blvd.,
Myrtle Beach
(800) 433-1461, (843) 448-1461
www.myrtlebeachbestwestern.com
This Best Western is located across the Boulevard from the ocean and is a property that caters mainly to families and couples. Grand Strand staff takes pride in the cleanliness and value of their property.

Ninety-six units are available, ranging from single rooms to one-, two-, three-, and four-bedroom efficiencies, on up to luxury penthouse suites. There's even a three-bedroom, fully equipped cottage, which can be perfect lodging for an extended family vacation.

A large sundeck beckons guests to partake of the renowned Carolina sunshine—take a quick dive into the swimming pool for an instant cool-off. Just ask the front desk, and they will be happy to arrange a scuba, golf, or entertainment package for you. Laundry facilities are available.

BREAKERS RESORT HOTEL TOWER $$$$
2006 North Ocean Blvd.,
Myrtle Beach
(800) 952-4507, (843) 444-4444
www.breakers.com
Staying at the Breakers has been a family tradition for generations; now the Breakers has an adjoining North Tower to accommodate even more

vacationing families and golfers in two- and three-bedroom abodes. This property boasts more than 470 units based on more than 20 room plans. Typical rooms feature two beds facing the ocean, or you can choose from two- or three-room suites with fully equipped kitchens. Honeymoon, golf, and family packages are house specialties. During the summer season kids can take part in various planned activities. Paradise Tower is adjacent to the resort, with one-, two-, and three-bedroom condos, parks, shops, and restaurants, as well as an oceanfront water park that's enclosed for year-round use. Guests enjoy two indoor pools, one outdoor pool, and a 418-foot lazy river.

Near downtown Myrtle Beach, the Breakers is accessible to numerous shops, restaurants, and attractions. Ample parking is available, and that's hard to come by at most uptown places. Wheelchair-accessible facilities are provided in the main tower only.

CABANA SHORES $$
5701 North Ocean Blvd.,
Myrtle Beach
(800) 277-7562, (843) 449-6441
www.cabanashores.com
Cabana Shores' name says it all. Located in the quiet Cabana section of Myrtle Beach, this small, family-run resort offers 74 single and double rooms and fully equipped condominiums. Winter rates are outrageously low for the caliber of accommodations and amenities offered here, and it's an especially appealing lodging option for many senior citizens. Cabana Shores offers its guests an expansive outdoor pool and is just across the street from the beach.

CAPTAIN'S QUARTERS RESORT $$
901 South Ocean Blvd.,
Myrtle Beach
(800) 695-8284, (843) 448-1404
www.captainsquarters.com
Although the Captain's Quarters Resort has been around for many years, the management continues to keep up with the times by expanding and renovating the property when needed. There are 373 units: efficiency apartments, and one-

bedroom and two-room suites. The family can splash about in one of 11 pools and whirlpools or the lazy river. The resort's recreation center features an extra-large arcade, so bring lots of quarters. The on-site Captain's Restaurant serves breakfast, lunch (until 2 p.m.), or dinner. Guests also have access to laundry facilities. Adjacent to the resort is the Ocean Inn, a quaint inn with its own pool and lazy river. The Inn offers oceanfront and ocean-view rooms and efficiencies. Golf privileges are offered at more than 70 championship courses in the area, so pack your clubs.

i During the winter months traffic on Ocean Boulevard is especially light, making it a pleasant and more scenic option to Kings Highway.

CARAVELLE RESORT HOTEL & VILLAS $$
6900 North Ocean Blvd.,
Myrtle Beach
(800) 785-4460, (843) 918-8000
The Caravelle started out as a small resort and over the years has grown to include nine properties with a total of 614 rooms and suites. The resort offers a great mixture of rooms, efficiencies, and deluxe executive suites to accommodate just about any need. Amenities include several pools, a game room, an exercise room, and a restaurant. Adults and children love the lazy river pool, where you grab an oversize inner tube and glide along the course of the ride. The complex has two kid-friendly lazy rivers and a kiddie pool. Golf and entertainment packages are available.

CARIBBEAN RESORT $$$
3000 North Ocean Blvd.,
Myrtle Beach
(800) 552-8509, (843) 448-7181
www.caribbeanresort.com
The longtime locally owned Caribbean has undergone some major changes in recent years. In addition to the Dominican Tower, the Cayman Towers opened its doors in June of 2008. The towers feature two-, three-, and four-bedroom luxury units. And for those who prefer a quieter

atmosphere, two other properties are located across the street from the main resort. The Ibis has two-bedroom condos, while the Chelsea House has two- and three-bedroom condos.

Known for its water features, the Caribbean's motto is "More, more, more!" Already boasting one of the most spacious and beautiful oceanfront pool decks in Myrtle Beach, it has several new water amenities that can be enclosed in the winter months. These include a second 200-foot lazy river, a 48,000-gallon swimming pool, a 750-square-foot children's splash deck, and two large hot tubs. If that's not enough, there is also a new oceanfront Water Park, which includes a large swimming pool and hot tub, a Silly Sub children's interactive water play attraction, and a 60-foot tube slide.

The Caribbean also specializes in golf packages and boasts the ability to book more than 400,000 rounds of golf each year.

CAROLINA WINDS $$$
200 76th Ave. N., Myrtle Beach
(800) 523-4027, (843) 449-2477
www.carolinawinds.com
Carolina Winds is known for its fine condominiums and guest suites—147 units in all. This oceanfront property is away from the hustle and bustle of downtown and features everything you'll need for a luxurious visit. Guests can take a dip in the 120-foot-long oceanfront pool and wind down in the lazy river. An on-site sauna is available for visitors. Jacuzzis and hot tubs are added attractions, as are golf packages in fall and winter.

COMPASS COVE OCEANFRONT RESORT $$$
2311 South Ocean Blvd.,
Myrtle Beach
(800) 331-0934, (843) 448-8373
www.compasscove.com
Located near the center of Myrtle Beach, the famous Compass Cove Oceanfront Resort has more than 530 luxurious units, including one-, two-, and three-bedroom condominiums and 720 feet of oceanfront beach. Compass Cove is one of the area's largest resort hotels and offers such

amenities as 22 pools, including 6 indoor and outdoor pools, 3 indoor and outdoor lazy rivers, Jacuzzi hot tubs, and kiddie pools. A variety of golf, entertainment, and family packages are available.

CORAL BEACH RESORT $$$$
1105 South Ocean Blvd.,
Myrtle Beach
(800) 843-2684, (843) 448-8421
www.coral-beach.com

With 301 units and plenty of amenities, Coral Beach is definitely one of the trendiest and largest resorts on the beach. Accommodations include standard rooms, efficiencies, and two-room suites.

Named "Best Family Accommodations" in Myrtle Beach in 2003 by the Travel Channel, Coral Beach is one of the only resorts on the beach that houses an arcade, complete with a bowling alley. Children are entertained with supervised activities offered from June through Aug. Other amenities include in-room safes, complete kitchens in all efficiencies and suites, a steam room, saunas, and three whirlpools.

Did we say pools? How about two outdoor heated pools, kiddie pools, a lazy river ride, and a pool bar. In addition to a full-service restaurant, guests may enjoy cocktails at the Sandbunker Beach Bar or a good laugh at MacDivot's Comedy Corner.

COURT CAPRI $$
2610 North Ocean Blvd.,
Myrtle Beach
(800) 533-1338, (843) 448-6119
www.courtcapri.com

If for no other reason, we had to include this motel since it's the only one along the Grand Strand with a rooftop heart-shaped whirlpool and sundeck! Needless to say, Court Capri offers honeymoon packages. Rooms and one- or two-bedroom efficiencies can be booked year-round, as well as extensive golf packages. The Capri also offers guests an indoor pool, indoor whirlpool, Jacuzzi, kiddie pool, exercise facilities, and a full-service restaurant.

CROWN REEF RESORT $$$
2913 South Ocean Blvd.,
Myrtle Beach
(800) 405-7333, (843) 626-8077
www.crownreef.com

All 514 units in this beautiful motel are oceanfront, with balconies overlooking 125 feet of beach and the Atlantic. Efficiencies, rooms, deluxe suites, and Jacuzzi suites are for let. The property offers 20 pools and whirlpools, convention facilities, a fitness center, a game room, 575 feet of lazy river (the largest on the beach), Jacuzzis, hot tubs, three full-service restaurants, and an express restaurant. During the summer there are lots of activities for kids—fitness walks, arts and crafts, face painting, seashell searches—keeping the younger set busy so grown-ups can lounge by the pool or indulge in an afternoon nap. Entertainment packages can be booked from this resort.

DAYTON HOUSE $$$
2400 North Ocean Blvd.,
Myrtle Beach
(800) 258-7963, (843) 448-2441
www.daytonhouse.com

For more than 30 years, the Thomas family has been rolling out the red carpet for families, senior citizens, and vacationing couples. In the last decade four new buildings have been added to the property—now offering 328 units, including 96 two-room oceanfront suites. Amenities include a large outdoor spa, an oceanfront lawn and sunning area, a lazy river, indoor and outdoor pools (including the beach's first walk-in, overflow pool), whirlpools, an exercise room, and golf packages at more than 90 courses. Beginning Jan 2007, all rooms at the Dayton House are smoke-free.

Before going out on the town, check with the front desk of your hotel or motel about free passes or discount coupons. For promotional purposes many Grand Strand clubs and attractions supply accommodation properties with thousands of these to give to guests. There's no harm in asking!

DRIFTWOOD ON THE OCEANFRONT $$

1600 North Ocean Blvd.,
Myrtle Beach
(800) 942-3456, (843) 448-1544
www.driftwoodlodge.com

The Driftwood prides itself on being one of the beach's first oceanfront hotels, opening its doors almost eight decades ago. Back then, it was a group of oceanfront cottages, and today it offers three modern buildings in that same location. All of the 90 accommodations at Driftwood have updated furnishings as well as refrigerators and microwave ovens, whether you're staying in a room or efficiency unit. Just 6 blocks from the arcade area, this hotel offers two outdoor pools.

ECONO LODGE INN & SUITES $

1401 South Ocean Blvd.,
Myrtle Beach
(800) 992-0269, (843) 444-0346
www.atlanticparadise.com

Formerly the Atlantic Paradise Inn, this hotel joined the Econo Lodge franchise in 2008. Nothing fancy, but the 74 two-room apartments and efficiencies offer your family an affordable vacation at the beach. Amenities include an oceanfront pool with deck, a kiddie pool, and an indoor whirlpool. Golf and country-music packages are available.

FAIRFIELD INN
MYRTLE BEACH–BRIARCLIFFE $$

10231 North Kings Hwy.
Myrtle Beach
(800) 369-8033, (843) 361-8000
www.fairfieldinn.com

At Fairfield Inn you can always count on a comfortable room and friendly service. The hotel has 86 rooms, all with remote-controlled TVs, free local calls, and wireless Internet. Cribs and in-room safes are also available. Amenities include an indoor heated pool with heated spa, outdoor sunning deck, a complimentary deluxe continental breakfast with 24-hour coffee and tea, laundry valet, and self-service laundry facilities. The Fairfield Inn is located just a short drive from area golf courses, beaches, attractions, and restaurants.

FOREST DUNES RESORT $$$

5511 North Ocean Blvd.,
Myrtle Beach
(800) 845-7787, (843) 449-0864
www.forestdunes.com

This resort, across the Boulevard from the beach in the Cabana section, houses 108 oceanfront or ocean-view units, which are one-bedroom and three-bedroom condominiums. Once you've unpacked, take advantage of the wide, sandy beach in front of this resort, or float along the lazy river. (The lazy river is enclosed during the winter months, so it's always available to guests.) Other features include indoor and outdoor pools, a kiddie pool, whirlpool, exercise room, video-game room, and an independently leased bar and grill. Comforts of home include laundry facilities and spacious rooms. Golf and entertainment packages are available.

GRAND ATLANTIC OCEAN RESORT $$$

2007 South Ocean Blvd.,
Myrtle Beach
(800) 852-7032, (843) 448-7032
www.grandatlanticresort.com

The Grand Atlantic Ocean Resort opened in the spring of 2007, replacing the old Firebird Motor Inn. It offers one-, two-, three-, and four-bedroom oceanfront condominiums, the largest of which can accommodate up to 12 people. The 18-story oceanfront resort has a wide array of swimming and splashing facilities, including two kiddie pools and play pools that have water jets, waterfalls, and mushroom falls. There is a spacious, sun-chair-lined pool deck; a winding indoor lazy river; and an indoor and outdoor pool. The wide lawn area offers a chance to allow you to relax and enjoy the view of the Atlantic.

Conference facilities can accommodate any size meeting, and the Grand Atlantic offers a wide array of golf packages. Just south of the busy downtown area, the Grand Atlantic is close to restaurants and attractions.

GRAND STRAND DAYS INN $
806 South Ocean Blvd.,
Myrtle Beach
(800) 448-8261, (843) 448-8261
www.myrtlebeachmotels.com
This modest property could be perfect for a family looking for bargains. Only 18 blocks to the arcade area, the Days Inn rents 57 double rooms and efficiencies. It's across the street from the ocean and offers guests an outdoor pool as well as a kitchenette and cable television in each room. A free continental breakfast is available each morning.

HAMPTON INN $$
4709 North Kings Hwy.
Myrtle Beach
(800) 833-1360, (843) 449-5231
www.hamptoninn.com
At the Hampton Inn, a family-oriented hotel with 150 units, children stay free with parents. A couple of blocks from the ocean, this Hampton Inn is somewhat of a landmark around these parts and is a favorite of local seniors. Guests may start the day with a free continental breakfast, and then you're on your own to explore the area. This Hampton Inn also houses a huge indoor swimming pool and a fitness room.

HAMPTON INN NORTHWOOD $$$
620 75th Ave. N., Myrtle Beach
(800) 543-4286, (843) 497-0077
www.hamptoninn.com
Like its sister on North Kings Highway, the Northwood is within walking distance of the beach and serves guests a complimentary deluxe continental breakfast. Among its 122 rooms are 21 two-room suites, four with Jacuzzis. Guests can enjoy a pool, exercise room, and sauna here.

HILTON MYRTLE BEACH RESORT $$$$
10000 Beach Club Dr.,
Myrtle Beach
(843) 449-5000
www.hilton.com
Get ready for a one-stop vacation experience at the Hilton, which offers 374 ocean-view guest rooms and 11 full suites. Each has a private balcony, refrigerator, microwave, and coffeemaker.

The hotel is set on the 18-hole Arcadian Shores championship golf course, and guests are privy to reduced greens and cart fees at this course. You'll also find four on-site lighted tennis courts exclusively for guests. Tennis clinics and lessons are available for a fee. Other recreational options include volleyball, a fully equipped fitness room, and, when you've had enough exercise, a resident masseuse.

The Hilton is home to Café Amalfi, an oceanfront restaurant that serves lunch daily. It also features Beachcomber's, a small seasonal cafe that whips up sandwiches, finger foods, and pizza.

Hilton's popular pool deck usually pays tribute to beach music, with live bands playing favorite shagging and dance tunes from 1 to 5 p.m. daily all summer. The Hilton shares many amenities with Kingston Plantation, which is right next door.

JONATHAN HARBOUR $$
2611 South Ocean Blvd.,
Myrtle Beach
(800) 448-1948, (843) 448-1948
www.jhoceanfront.com
Two- and three-room efficiency units with fully equipped kitchens and laundry facilities are what you'll find here. With the hotel located right on the beach, you can enjoy recreation or relaxation in the indoor or outdoor pool, one of two whirlpools, the kiddie pool, and exercise room. Guests have ample parking facilities across the street.

KINGSTON PLANTATION $$$$$
9800 Queensway Blvd.,
Myrtle Beach
(800) EMBASSY, (843) 449-0006
www.kingstonplantation.com
Kingston Plantation is a multimillion-dollar resort with more than 700 hotel rooms (including 255 ocean-view suites), condominiums, townhomes, and villas set in a richly designed atmosphere. The grounds span 145 oceanfront acres east of Restaurant Row. The resort features two conference centers, wireless Internet, several pool

decks, a Caribbean family water playground, and a new lazy river. In addition, there is a year-round bar and seasonal pool bar, and two seaside restaurants, including an Omaha Steakhouse Restaurant and Café Amalfi (located at the Hilton). A visit here isn't complete if you don't take advantage of the 50,000-square-foot Sport and Health Club that includes racquetball courts, aerobics classes, state-of-the-art tennis courts, cardiovascular and weight-training machines, and massage services. With an on-site golf department, arranging a round is easy here.

All of the suites have been redecorated with art deco furnishings, and Caribbean accents have been added to the exterior. The 20-story hotel is an Embassy Suites property, and the price code listed for the Kingston Plantation towers reflects their rates. Other units are privately owned and rented separately.

This is more than a place to store your luggage; it's a vacation destination and group-meeting attraction—an exceptional choice as evidenced by nine years of Gold Key Awards.

LANDMARK RESORT HOTEL $$$
1501 South Ocean Blvd.,
Myrtle Beach
(800) 845-0658, (843) 448-9441
www.landmarkresort.com

Everything you need for a great vacation is right here at this oceanfront property. The 570 hotel rooms include penthouse and tower suites as well as single and double rooms. This hotel is the only Grand Strand property to have a covered pedestrian bridge across Ocean Boulevard that links its accommodations with the parking lot across the road.

Entertainment includes an English-style pub and dining in the Gazebo restaurant. Families can play in the video-game room, relax in the sauna, or splash about in the water park, which has a wading pool with waterfalls, barrel dumps, and jet tunnels as well as a lap pool and Jacuzzi. The Landmark also specializes in hosting group tours and conferences. Golf packages are available. The Landmark also has full laundry facilities and a nine-hole putt-putt course.

LA QUINTA INN & SUITES $$
1561 21st Ave. N., Myrtle Beach
(800) 687-6667, (843) 916-8801
www.lq.com

If you're not particular about staying near the ocean, then you might try this prototype La Quinta. This is one of the chain's first hotels to feature two-room suites and extended-stay facilities.

Across the street from Broadway at the Beach, this 128-room hotel treats guests to a continental breakfast every morning and accepts small pets. Amenities include an outdoor pool, exercise room, free wireless Internet, refrigerators, microwave ovens, and coffeemakers. Each room sports a 25-inch television and Super Nintendo games.

MERIDIAN PLAZA RESORT $$$
2310 North Ocean Blvd.,
Myrtle Beach
(800) 323-3011, (843) 626-4734
www.meridianplaza.com

The Meridian Plaza is a tall, sleek building that rents out 94 ultramodern one-bedroom suites, each with a fully equipped kitchen, two televisions, and ocean views. Parking in the downtown area is normally crowded; however, the Plaza provides spaces for its guests in the five-level garage. Amenities include indoor and outdoor pools, whirlpools, and free wireless Internet. Special golf packages are available from Sept through May.

MONTEREY BAY $$$
6804 North Ocean Blvd.,
Myrtle Beach
(888) 255-4763, (843) 449-4833
www.montereybaysuites.com

This newly renovated boutique hotel includes all oceanfront suites. Luxurious decorations include granite countertops and raised oak cabinets. Guests enjoy a free breakfast each morning and free wireless Internet. The resort has indoor and outdoor pools and partners with Cinzia Spa at North Beach Plantation for spa services.

OCEAN DUNES RESORT & VILLAS $$$$
201 75th Ave. N., Myrtle Beach
(800) 845-0635, (843) 449-7441
www.sandsresorts.com

The twin towers of this huge resort provide 400 rooms; suites; one-, two-, and three-bedroom villas; plus three-bedroom oceanfront penthouses. On-site features include oceanfront pools with bars, indoor pools and whirlpools, a steam room, saunas, massage therapy, weight room, game room, gift shop, and convenience store. But wait, there's much more: Entertainment options include nine restaurants, several bars, and a water park that includes a lazy river, waterslides, and a bubble pool.

During the summer, supervised programs are offered for children, and kids get a free T-shirt and identification bracelet. The Ocean Dunes staff can also refer you to reputable babysitters.

Children younger than 18 also stay free in the same room with an adult. Golf, entertainment, and specialty packages are available. Courtesy airport pickup is provided.

OCEAN FOREST VILLA RESORT $$$$
5601 North Ocean Blvd.,
Myrtle Beach
(800) 845-0347, (843) 449-9661
www.sandsresorts.com

All of the Forest's 243 two-bedroom villas face oceanfront, ocean-view, or poolside. Each villa is conveniently designed to house two full baths, an equipped kitchen, a living room, dining room, and balcony.

This is a vacation place with children in mind. On-site are two outdoor pools and two heated whirlpools. On top of that, special programs for kids and babysitting services run from Memorial Day through Labor Day.

Golf packages at 100-plus area courses can be arranged, plus entertainment tours. Privileges to an off-site fitness center and tennis courts can be had for the asking. Ocean Forest provides airport shuttle transportation.

OCEAN REEF RESORT HOTEL $$$$
7100 North Ocean Blvd.,
Myrtle Beach
(800) 542-0048, (843) 449-4441
www.oceanreefmyrtlebeach.com

The motif might be called "Come to the island, mon," but the beach is definitely Myrtle. Near the northern end of a Myrtle Beach residential section, the Ocean Reef exudes a sense of exclusivity. The Ocean Reef opened a new condominium tower in 2006, adding 52 one- to four-bedroom units to the already existing 205 hotel rooms. Each has a view of the Grand Strand.

Ocean Reef also includes an Island Oasis kiddie park, featuring bucket drops, water streams, and fountains. That's in addition to the already existing lazy river and sundeck whirlpool outdoors, as well as indoor swimming pool and whirlpool.

Ocean Reef has two restaurants and a lounge, as well as a fitness room and wireless Internet throughout. Banquet and meeting facilities are large enough to accommodate 400 people. Golf packages and referrals to bonded babysitters are coordinated through the staff.

THE PALACE RESORT $$$
1605 South Ocean Blvd.,
Myrtle Beach
(800) 334-1397, (843) 448-4300
www.palaceresort.com

The Palace condominiums are fit for kings and queens. You'll feel like royalty in any of the 298 suites at this plush resort that towers over the ocean. Featured amenities include Jacuzzis, hot tubs, enclosed pools, putting greens, a sauna, and a steam room. Although many of the condominiums are privately owned, there are numerous units available for weekly rentals. The Palace rents only to couples and families.

PATRICIA GRAND RESORT HOTELS $$
2710 North Ocean Blvd.,
Myrtle Beach
(800) 255-4763, (843) 448-8453
www.patricia.com

From the moment you step into the plush setting of the Patricia Grand, you'll know you're someplace special. The 501 luxurious accommodations include double rooms, efficiencies, and executive suites designed to pamper those with the most discriminating tastes. The Patricia Grand completed a full renovation of all of its rooms for the 2007 season. The oceanfront restaurant and lounge are relaxing retreats after you've had enough of the pool, whirlpool, lazy river, or sauna. When it's time for more active pursuits, arrange a golf outing through the front desk. Hotel staff are happy to arrange golf and entertainment packages as well as group tour and travel excursions. The Patricia Grand's central location means shopping malls, attractions, and restaurants are within easy reach.

PLANTATION INN $

9551 US 17, Myrtle Beach
(800) 222-5783, (843) 449-5348
www.plantationinnmyrtlebeach.com

Guests receive a free continental breakfast each morning. You'll find 85 rooms plus five Jacuzzi suites and an outdoor heated pool. Special packages include golf, entertainment, romance, Christmas, and New Year's options. Room rates are considered low during peak season but are relatively high during the winter months, as the hotel aims for consistent pricing rather than extreme fluctuations from one season to another. This hotel is 1.5 miles from the beach.

THE REEF

2101 South Ocean Blvd.,
Myrtle Beach
(800) 845-1212, (843) 448-1765
http://reefmyrtlebeach.com

This longtime family beach favorite offers choices of recently remodeled single units, two-bedroom units, one- and two-bedroom suites as well as a penthouse. Located on the ocean on the south end, the Reef has an indoor/outdoor pool, a kiddie pool, video-game room, and a sauna. Check out the delightful Creek Ratz restaurant.

i If you are strolling on the beach and see yellow tape around a mound of sand, it's not a buried body! It's likely a sea turtle nest. If you encounter a turtle at night, turn off any flashlight and keep your distance, especially if they are nesting. Also, never try to assist a hatchling in its effort to get to the sea. Let it follow its natural path.

RIPTIDE BEACH CLUB $$

2806 North Ocean Blvd.,
Myrtle Beach
(843) 448-1486
www.riptidebeachclubs.com

The Riptide offers 88 one- and two-bedroom condos, most of which are rented out with permission of the owners. All have sleeper sofas or a set of twin or bunk beds for plenty of places to rest weary heads. Amenities include two oceanfront pools, hot tubs, and an exercise facility. During the summer there are activities planned for the entire family, including wine and cheese get-togethers, craft workshops, and trips to a water park.

SANDCASTLE RESORTS $$$
SANDCASTLE AT THE PAVILION

1802 North Ocean Blvd.,
Myrtle Beach
(800) 910-5368 (reservations only),
(843) 448-7101
www.sandcastleatthepavilion.com

SANDCASTLE SOUTH BEACH

2207 South Ocean Blvd.,
Myrtle Beach
(800) 626-1550, (843) 448-4316
www.sandcastlesouthbeach.com
www.sandcastleresorts.com

The Sandcastle people run two properties in Myrtle Beach, both of which offer 240 accommodations. Sandcastle at the Pavilion is within 9 blocks of the action-packed Myrtle Beach arcade area. Here guests can choose from oceanfront and oceanview rooms, suites, and efficiencies, many of which have separate sleeping and living quarters.

Amenities abound with a winding river, oceanfront pool, kiddie pool, plus another swimming pool and whirlpool inside. There is also an on-premises cafe.

Sandcastle South Beach was brand new in 1998. All of its units are oceanfront. Here you'll find rooms, suites, and efficiencies offering two queen-size beds. This newer Sandcastle has all the amenities of its northern cousin, but it has added Jacuzzis, a lounge, a gift shop, and a seasonal cabana bar. Both locations arrange an extensive array of golf packages.

SAND DUNES RESORT HOTEL $$$$$
201 74th Ave. N., Myrtle Beach
(866) 845-1011, (843) 449-3313
www.sandsresorts.com

Once you've checked into the Sand Dunes, you'll have to leave the hotel only to sightsee. The 400 accommodations here range from double rooms and efficiencies to two-bedroom executive suites and oceanfront penthouses.

Overlooking the Atlantic Ocean are the River City Cafe and a lounge called Mango's. For a quick bite there's a sidewalk pizza shop, ice-cream parlor, and beach bar and cafe.

This is an arena of activity with a full-scale water park including indoor and outdoor pools and a lazy river. Also available are a fitness facility and Bogey's Back Alley game room and entertainment center. When you're ready to truly unwind, Sand Dunes now has a full day spa called Atlantis. From Memorial Day through Labor Day, the hotel coordinates programs for children and offers babysitting services. The Sand Dunes also treats its guests to courtesy airport pickup. Golf and entertainment packages can be arranged at any time.

SANDS BEACH CLUB
ALL-SUITE RESORT $$$$$
9400 Shore Dr., Myrtle Beach
(800) 565-4094, (843) 449-1531
www.sandsresorts.com

This centrally located resort is on a point of land at the end of Shore Drive, overlooking both the Atlantic Ocean and the Dunes Club marsh. It's in the middle of everything, yet secluded. With 125 units, Sands Beach Club gives guests the option of a two-bedroom oceanfront suite or a one-bedroom unit with views of the ocean and marsh. Regardless of the number of bedrooms, each Sands suite is spacious and includes a separate living room, dining room, and full kitchen.

Topper's at the Pointe Oceanfront Restaurant and Lounge, on the premises, is totally encased in glass to take advantage of the spectacular seascape. A gourmet pizza shop, game room, and mini–convenience store are also on-site. Meetings for up to 200 people can be arranged by the staff.

For recreation Sands Beach Club offers a sports deck with hoops and nets for impromptu basketball and volleyball matches. Here you'll also find two lighted tennis courts, indoor and outdoor pools, and whirlpools for guests. Supervised programs for the kids and a child-care service for toddlers are available from Memorial Day through Labor Day. A roster of specialty packages includes golf, entertainment, and honeymoon options. Sands also offers a free shuttle service from Myrtle Beach International Airport.

SANDS OCEAN CLUB RESORT $$$$$
9550 Shore Dr., Myrtle Beach
(888) 999-8485, (843) 449-6461
www.sandsresorts.com

Treat yourself to a one-, two-, or three-bedroom suite or efficiency along the oceanfront at the Sands Ocean Club Resort. This upscale facility offers numerous on-site amenities, including several pools, a lazy river, lounges, Ocean Annie's Beach Bar, restaurants (including a delicatessen), gift and golf shops, an exercise room, and golf privileges at more than 100 area courses. During summer months children's programs and a toddler child-care service are available to guests. Kids will be happy to know that a lazy river flows at the Sands Ocean Club Resort. Courtesy airport transportation is always available to the guests of Sands.

SEA CREST OCEANFRONT RESORT $$
803 South Ocean Blvd.,
Myrtle Beach
(800) 845-1112, (843) 913-5800
www.myrtlebeach-resorts.com

While this is a Holiday Inn property, it has chosen to rebrand itself and go for a more resort feel than other Holiday Inn properties. It offers a complete resort atmosphere right in the heart of Myrtle Beach. In addition to the Sea Crest's numerous pools, it has opened an expansive water park, complete with a submarine and a shipwreck. But there is much more to this property than just splish-splashing. The property boasts one and a half acres of oceanfront lawn for lounging and playing. The new Malibu Beach Bar and Oceanfront Grill offers daily entertainment and theme nights during the summer.

There are 380 units in all, with 28 different room types to choose from. Relax in the lounge or get a workout in the exercise room. The Sea Crest is also just blocks from the Family Kingdom amusement park and within walking distance to the Second Avenue Pier.

SEA DIP MOTEL AND CONDOMINIUMS $$
2608 North Ocean Blvd.,
Myrtle Beach
(800) 334-1467, (843) 626-3591
www.seadip.com

Sea Dip is a family-friendly establishment that specializes in family vacations. With 100 units available, reservation options include single rooms, efficiency apartments, two-room suites, and efficiency suites with three double beds. Sea Dip offers guests two oceanfront pools, two whirlpools, a sundeck, a kiddie pool, a lazy river, and laundry facilities. The ever-smiling staff is always happy to arrange golf, entertainment, honeymoon, or motor-coach packages. This motel is about a 12-block walk from the arcade and amusement areas.

SEAGLASS TOWERS $$
1400 North Ocean Blvd.,
Myrtle Beach
(843) 286-1100
www.bluegreenonline.com

The SeaGlass's name says it all. The gleaming glass-enclosed 19-story tower reflects the ocean and can be seen for miles down the Grand Strand. The condominium complex was originally part of the Yachtsman Resort but was sold as a separate entity in 2006. Its freshly updated accommodations feature fully equipped kitchens with dishwasher and microwave, comfortable bedrooms, and whirlpool baths.

The SeaGlass has both indoor and outdoor pools and minigolf on-site. The Pier 14 restaurant is located right out the back door, but an on-site restaurant is also available.

SEA MIST RESORT $$
1200 South Ocean Blvd.,
Myrtle Beach
(800) SEAMIST (793-6507), (843) 448-1551
www.seamist.com

The Sea Mist is a complete world within itself, sprawling along both sides of Ocean Boulevard. The resort houses more than 823 rooms, efficiencies, suites, town houses, and bungalows for families and tour groups. As if that weren't enough to choose from, the Sea Mist turned some of its units into Jacuzzi suites. And if you stay six paid nights at standard rates, the seventh night is free.

This expansive complex features 10 pools and a large on-site water park with an innertube slide, an activity pool, and a lazy river that stretches more than 500 feet. And that's not all. Guests can putter around on the resort's miniature golf course, work out in the health club, or dine in one of several restaurants. The kids really seem to go for the ice-cream parlor, doughnut shop, and video arcade. Organized activities focus on keeping the kids occupied. Adults enjoy golf privileges and the glorious Carolina sunshine.

The Sea Mist is smack-dab in the middle of downtown Myrtle Beach, and parking and traffic can be hectic. But once you've parked the car, you won't have to leave until it's time to pack up and go home; just about anything you'll need can be found in the resort complex.

SUPER 8 MOTEL $
1100 South Ocean Blvd.,
Myrtle Beach
(800) 448-7577, (843) 448-8414
www.super8.com

Across the street from the ocean, you'll find this humble motel offering 41 one-room efficiencies with refrigerators, and three two-bedroom units. An outdoor pool, picnic area, and shuffleboard are available to guests. Golf packages can also be arranged by the staff. Recently renovated, the Super 8 offers a good value for those on a budget who don't mind doing without some of the frills of a resort hotel.

WESTGATE MYRTLE BEACH $$$$
415 South Ocean Blvd.,
Myrtle Beach
(800) 230-4134, (843) 448-4481
www.wgmyrtlebeach.com

Located right in the middle of all the action, the Westgate Myrtle Beach Oceanfront resort hosts one of the liveliest, continuous pool-bar parties—it lasts all season. Formerly a popular Holiday Inn, the hotel was completely renovated in 2008 and has raised the bar for its guests. Completely non-smoking and pet friendly, the Westgate appeals to the whole family. There are 306 rooms, and all oceanfront units boast private balconies to watch either the poolside happenings or the ocean. Amenities include a poolside bar, lazy river, and an on-staff golf director.

THE YACHTSMAN RESORT HOTEL $$$$
1304 North Ocean Blvd.,
Myrtle Beach
(800) 955-2627, (843) 448-2214
www.gold-crown.com

The longstanding twin towers of the Yachtsman are now separated by a gleaming tower called the SeaGlass, which is an entirely separate condominium resort. It can be a bit confusing, but the two entities are friendly to one another and recognize that Yachtsman guests may be going back and forth across the SeaGlass property.

The Yachtsman's twin towers house more than 142 all-suite condominium units in the very heart of the downtown area. Exclusive packages cater to golfers, honeymooners, and tour groups. One of the closest attractions to the resort is Pier 14, a restaurant that extends over the ocean.

The studio and one-bedroom suites feature fully equipped kitchens and whirlpool baths big enough for two people. Inside you'll find one pool; outside are two pools, Jacuzzis, hot tubs, a miniature golf course, and shuffleboard. The Yachtsman was voted one of South Carolina's favorite getaways by *The State* newspaper.

South Strand

DAYS INN SURFSIDE PIER RESORT $$$
15 South Ocean Blvd.,
Surfside Beach
(800) 533-7599, (843) 238-4444
www.daysinnsurfside.com

The Days Inn Surfside Pier offers the same affordable rates as most area Days Inns. This hotel overlooks the Surfside Pier (hence the name), which was restored after sustaining severe damage during a 1995 storm. This area tends to be more crowded than others on the South Strand because of the pier. Guests enjoy sampling the restaurant's home-style cuisine and sipping their favorite beverages at Scotty's Beach Bar on the property's oceanfront. All 158 units offer a side view of Surfside Beach. There's an outdoor heated pool and a Jacuzzi, too.

LITCHFIELD BEACH & GOLF RESORT $$$$$
14276 Ocean Hwy. Pawleys Island
(888) 766-4633, (843) 237-3000
www.litchfieldbeach.com

There is no other resort in the historic Lowcountry that compares to Litchfield Beach & Golf. Set amid 4,500 acres of marshlands and oceanfront property, the complex features an array of accommodations, including villas, condominiums, and cottages. The grounds are enhanced with avenues of century-old oaks, flowering gardens, and uncrowded beaches. Although the resort is about 15 minutes from Myrtle Beach, there is no hint of either neon or a hectic pace.

Ranked one of the top-50 resorts in the country by *Tennis* magazine, Litchfield's 17 on-site clay courts attract tennis lovers from far and wide. Three signature golf courses grace this resort: River Club, Willbrook Plantation, and Litchfield Country Club. Litchfield appeals to many families looking for accommodations a cut above those at traditional resorts. Children's activities are provided "as needed." In addition to the spa, indoor and outdoor pools, and racquetball courts, the resort offers a sauna, beauty salon, and the ever-popular restaurant and lounge known as Webster's.

OCEAN VIEW MOTEL $

131 North Ocean Blvd.,
Garden City Beach
(843) 651-2500
www.gardencityinns.com

The Ocean View is a small motel in one of the quieter beach communities of the Grand Strand. While the 39-unit motel is not on the beach, it does have an unobstructed view of the ocean and is just 100 yards from the sand.

The Ocean View caters to families, offering two- and three-bedroom efficiencies and some connecting rooms. They also have laundry facilities and are happy to refer babysitters. It has a large pool and is a clean and friendly stop for those on a budget who still want to be able to enjoy a beach vacation.

ROYAL GARDEN RESORT $$$$

1210 North Waccamaw Dr.,
Garden City Beach
(800) 446-4010, (843) 651-1929
www.royalgardenresort.com

In the midst of the weatherworn beach houses and cottages of Garden City Beach is the Royal Garden Resort, with more than 206 condominium units and suites. The oceanfront property features golf packages. Enjoy Royal Garden's indoor and outdoor pools, a Jacuzzi, sauna, game room, and gift shop. Restaurants and attractions are within walking distance, and there's a seasonal snack bar, too.

WATER'S EDGE RESORT $$$$$

1012 North Waccamaw Dr.,
Garden City Beach
(800) 255-5554, (843) 651-0002
www.watersedgeresort.com

With 135 spacious condominiums boasting one, two, and three bedrooms, this resort is larger than its neighbor, the Royal Garden Resort, but offers the same features, including pools, Jacuzzis, and an oceanfront lounge and deck with a perfect view of the beach. Golf, entertainment, and honeymoon packages are offered. Supervised activities for the kids are available during the summer months.

Other Featured Accommodations

DAYS INN BEACHFRONT $$

1403 South Ocean Blvd.,
Myrtle Beach
(800) 826-2779, (843) 448-1636
www.myrtlebeachmotels.com

If you're looking for an affordable, convenient stay for the family, Days Inn is just the ticket. This oceanfront inn rents 54 side-view and oceanfront efficiencies and double and king-size rooms. All have private oceanfront balconies. Continental breakfast is included.

The property offers a swimming pool and kiddie pool. It's located about 11 blocks from the popular Family Kingdom amusement park and 1 mile south of the arcade area.

Entertainment and golf packages are available with reservations.

MYRTLE BEACH RESORT $$$$

5905 US 17 S., Myrtle Beach
(888) 627-3767
www.myrtle-beach-resort.com

Myrtle Beach Resort is an all-in-one vacation destination, sprawling along more than 33 acres of oceanfront property. Condominium and villa-style accommodations can be found here, ranging from studios to one-, two-, and three-bedroom units.

Here you'll discover a recreational wonderland that offers six swimming pools (two indoors), a 375-foot lazy river, four whirlpools, three saunas, basketball, volleyball, shuffleboard, and tennis courts. The resort also sports arcade games and a kiddie playground. Twenty-four-hour security keeps all of Myrtle Beach Resort's guests safe and sound.

Staff members are always happy to arrange great golf packages for visitors.

NORTH BEACH PLANTATION $$$$$
4825 South Hwy. 17,
Windy Hill
(877) 361-3165
www.northbeachtowers.com
North Beach Plantation is the Grand Strand's newest luxury resort. Located on 66 acres of oceanfront property, North Beach combines old Southern charm with modern conveniences. The first thing you will notice is the striking twin-tower configuration of the main building. This self-contained residential resort will ultimately feature 750 oceanfront condominiums, town houses, and single-family homes. While North Beach includes acres of pools, many visitors may choose to relax at the world class Cinzia Spa. The 17,000–square-foot facility offers integrative medical and holistic treatments and is an all-encompassing destination for optimal health, fitness, and well-being. Also on-site are upscale boutique shopping and gourmet dining.

RV AND CAMPING FACILITIES

Myrtle Beach–area campgrounds offer more than 9,000 individual campsites with all the comforts of home for a perfect family vacation. Each campground offers basic services plus a variety of recreational activities.

Summer is the area's most popular camping season; most children are out of school, and families can plan their vacations together. However, camping is quickly becoming a year-round activity along the Grand Strand, so don't roll into town during October through March and expect to find accommodations easily. The fall and winter seasons attract many campers due to the mild climate and off-season rates. All of the campgrounds are within walking distance of grocery stores, restaurants, and attractions.

North Strand
BRIARCLIFFE RV RESORT
10495 North Kings Hwy., Myrtle Beach
(843) 272-2730
www.briarcliffervresort.com
Camping at Briarcliffe RV Resort is hardly a camping experience. Located on the south end of North Myrtle Beach, it is considered one of the premier RV resorts on the East Coast. Briarcliffe has more than 180 sites, all with full hookups. Beautifully landscaped, it caters to the active, featuring an 18-hole miniature golf course, shuffleboard, horseshoes, basketball court, and a playground. An 85-foot, oversize Olympic swimming pool overlooks the Intracoastal Waterway. The resort also has two bathhouses and two laundry facilities.

The popular Barefoot Landing shops and several restaurants are within walking distance, and the Tanger Outlets are nearby, as are several theaters. Beach access is just 1 mile away. Because of the popularity of the resort, reservations are recommended.

Myrtle Beach
APACHE FAMILY CAMPGROUND
9700 Kings Rd., Myrtle Beach
(800) 553-1749, (843) 449-7323
http://apachefamilycampground.com
You can select from 277 rental sites from the total inventory of more than 700 spacious campsites (the remainder are annual rentals or permanently booked) nestled beneath towering pines and oaks at Apache Family Campground.

All sites have sewage hookups, free cable TV, and picnic tables. Amenities include a large swimming pool, laundry facilities, and a fully stocked trading post. Apache Campground is home to the longest and widest fishing pier on the East Coast—Apache Pier (see the Fishing chapter)—complete with a restaurant and seasonal live entertainment.

Depending on site location, the summer daily rates are as low as $48.

KOA KAMPGROUND

613 Fifth Ave. S., Myrtle Beach
(800) 255-7614, (843) 448-3421
www.myrtlebeachkoa.com

Nestled in this densely wooded area, campers at the KOA might have trouble believing that the heart of Myrtle Beach is just 700 yards away.

More than 500 campsites are available in this 60-acre complex that offers log cabin–style rentals—called Kamping Kabins—in addition to its large, shaded tent sites. Free cable TV is included with utility hookups, and KOA provides bathhouses with showers. You and the family can splash about in the two pools or rent bicycles. Other amenities include a convenience store with gas station, game room, and Laundromat. They also keep guests entertained with an outdoor cinema, the Kampfire Theatre, and hay wagon rides.

Depending on site location and hookups, the summer daily rate ranges from $32 to $66. Kabins run from $48 to $62.

LAKEWOOD CAMPING RESORT

5901 South Kings Hwy.,
Myrtle Beach
(800) 258-8309, (843) 238-5161
www.lakewoodcampground.com

Lakewood celebrated its fiftieth year in 2009. It is among the largest oceanfront campgrounds in the Myrtle Beach area, with more than 1,900 campsites complete with utility hookups. It is also home of *High Steppin' Country,* a musical and variety show featuring professionally trained talent, local to the community. Each summer from June to Aug the entertainers perform three nights a week before packed houses, singing and dancing country favorites mixed with a few contemporary numbers.

The three-acre recreation complex provides a variety of activities, including an 18-hole miniature golf course. Five freshwater lakes are stocked with fish just begging for a hook. When it's time to cool down, kids of all ages will love rushing into the Olympic-size pool from the sliding board built into a tropical rock formation. Campers can also enjoy a heated pool and a Jacuzzi or take

a ride down the Hippo Slide, the world's largest inflatable waterslide.

Beach Villa rentals are available in addition to camper storage and annual leases. Depending on site location, the summer daily rate ranges from $36 to $41.

MYRTLE BEACH STATE PARK

4401 South Kings Hwy.,
Myrtle Beach
(843) 238-5325
www.discoversouthcarolina.com

The Myrtle Beach State Park is just 3 miles south of downtown Myrtle Beach and is one of the most popular public beaches in the area. Opened in 1935, it was the first state park opened to the public in South Carolina; it's also the site of the first campground and fishing pier on the Grand Strand.

The park offers 350 campsites, five cabins, two apartments, picnic areas with shelters, a swimming pool, nature trails, playground equipment, a park store, and snack bar. Each site has water and electrical hookups and is convenient to hot showers and restrooms.

The summer daily rate is $23 per site, $25 for reserved spots, and there is an additional $4-per-person (age 16 and older) admission charge to enter the park.

MYRTLE BEACH TRAVEL PARK

10108 Kings Rd., Myrtle Beach
(800) 255-3568, (843) 449-3714
www.myrtlebeachtravelpark.com

Only 10 miles north of downtown Myrtle Beach, the Travel Park offers more than 1,100 campsites in a variety of locations: oceanfront, wooded, or lakeside, all complete with utility hookups. Furnished villas and 35-foot travel trailers are also available for rent. Campers can enjoy a variety of swimming activities, including an indoor/outdoor pool and a lazy river, or fish for freshwater game from surrounding lakes. There is a full-time recreation director to make sure you don't run out of things to do. There is a three-night minimum stay in the off-season and a seven-night minimum stay June 6 through Aug 15. The summer daily rate starts at $55.

OCEAN LAKES FAMILY CAMPGROUND
6001 South Kings Hwy.,
Myrtle Beach
(800) 722-1451, (843) 238-5636
www.oceanlakes.com

Like many Grand Strand campgrounds, Ocean Lakes is a world within itself, providing campers with everything from convenient shopping, meeting rooms, and laundry facilities to a chapel, a book-exchange library, a post office, and telephones. Daily programs for children are available during the summer months.

Ocean Lakes is the largest campground facility on the East Coast. Of nearly 3,500 sites, less than 1,000 are transient sites. Ocean Lakes offers 250 rental units (ideal headquarters for an affordable vacation), and the remaining sites are permanently leased.

A four-time winner of the National RV Park of the Year award by the American RV Club, Ocean Lakes also received the 2006 South Carolina Governor's Cup, awarded to businesses that benefit their community, both economically and through improvement of quality of life. In addition to a beachfront location, Ocean Lakes boasts an indoor pool and an observation deck that enables a breathtaking view of the Atlantic. There is a nature center, game center, and minigolf course, and bicycles are available for rent. Depending on site location, the summer daily rate ranges from $57 to $62.

PIRATELAND FAMILY CAMPGROUND
5401 US 17 S., Myrtle Beach
(800) 443-CAMP, (843) 238-5155
www.pirateland.com

Set among 140 acres of stately oak trees, private lagoons, and oceanfront property, PirateLand is a real treasure. More than 30 years of business has garnered PirateLand several generations of family vacationers whose visits turn into neighborhood block parties. Each of the 1,400 oceanfront and lakeside campsites is fully equipped with a picnic table, hookups for utilities, and free cable TV. Trailer storage space is also available. Keep in mind that you don't have to be a camper to enjoy the surroundings at PirateLand. The campground also offers fully furnished, two- and three-bedroom lake-view villas for weekly and monthly rental.

Campground amenities include a 510-foot lazy river, a heated indoor pool and spa, an Olympic-size outdoor pool, playgrounds, tennis courts, a miniature golf course, and an arcade. The staff organizes activities including beach volleyball, deep-sea fishing, golf, Bible school, arts and crafts, and neighborhood cookouts. The campground's general store is stocked with practically everything you can imagine or forgot to pack. There is also a coin-operated laundry facility.

Depending on site location, the summer daily rate ranges from $58 to $62.

South Strand

HUNTINGTON BEACH STATE PARK
US 17 S., Murrells Inlet
(843) 237-4440
www.discoversouthcarolina.com

Huntington Beach State Park, about 3 miles south of Murrells Inlet, is a nature lover's dream come true. The diverse natural environment of the South Carolina coast awaits at the freshwater lagoon, salt marsh, and nature trail. The view of the beach from Huntington Beach State Park is one of the most breathtaking you'll find along the Grand Strand. The park is also the site of the historic castle Atalaya, the former winter home and studio of American sculptress Anna Hyatt Huntington.

Park facilities include about 135 campsites, 53 of which can be reserved in advance; the rest are rented on a first-come, first-served basis. There are picnic areas with shelters, a boardwalk, a park store, and nature programs directed by park staff. Each site has water and electrical hookups, and hot showers and restrooms are nearby. Sewage hookups are available at about 24 sites. The summer daily rate, from Apr through Oct, is $25 to $28; from Nov through Mar, $23 to $25.

VACATION RENTALS

Want to take the whole gang, be it family or friends, on a little extended vacation? You may want to consider renting a large condominium or beach house. The kids, young and old, can be entertained by the sand and surf. The grown-ups looking for true rest and relaxation can pull a chair and a glass of lemonade on to the deck for a little wave watching and snoozing. These accommodations combine the comfort, convenience, and semi-privacy of home with the carefree existence of vacation. These short-term rentals have their own kitchens, but some have restaurants on-site for the evening when you just don't feel like cooking. Others are equipped with laundry facilities.

The vacation-rental option is great for large parties and events (such as family reunions), and it's often more affordable than resort hotels once the cost is divided. The option of bringing and preparing your own food helps the cost factor, as well as catering to the all-day snackers of all sizes!

With so many of the hotels in the Grand Strand going condominium, it's a tough decision on whether to go high-rise, resort, villa, or beach house. And it can be even tougher finding the right vacation rental to suit your needs. Group accommodations tend to be rather elusive, since most are under the thumb of rental management companies or real-estate firms. Still, you can expect a wide variety of design, decor, and amenities. It's wise to try to book a group accommodation well in advance of your stay, again depending greatly on which season you plan to visit. Have a good idea of the amenities you'd like to have, whether you're looking for a cabin without phones or the full suite with recreation center and Jacuzzi, or maybe your needs are more along the lines of a playpen and crib. We've uncovered a few that might be worth looking into.

NORTH STRAND

BAREFOOT RESORT & GOLF
4980 Barefoot Resort Bridge Rd., North Myrtle Beach
(888) 556-4972, (843) 390-7900
www.barefootgolfresort.com
Between all of the businesses called Barefoot along the Grand Strand, its easy to get confused, but the Barefoot Resort is in a class by itself. Located just across the Intracoastal Waterway from Barefoot Landing shops, the resort is considered an ultimate coastal vacation destination. Rental properties include three- and four-bedroom condominiums in the tower, as well as one, two-, three-, and four-bedroom villas. Some of these villas are located in communities surrounding the four golf courses, while others overlook the yacht club, which opened in 2006. Rates range from $812 to $2,394 a week during peak season.

i As you're reserving your vacation rental, be sure to ask if bed linens and towels are provided or if you need to bring your own. If linens are not included, most agencies can make them available for a fee.

BEACH VACATIONS
4403 Hwy. 17 South, North Myrtle Beach
(800) 449-4005, (843) 449-2400
www.myrtlbeachcondorentals.com

The staff of Beach Vacations promises to accommodate any size group, anywhere along the Strand. This company has a large inventory of one-, two-, three-, and four-bedroom units, efficiencies, condos, cottages, and golf-course villas. All of the properties have access to swimming pools, and golf packages can be arranged. Peak season prices start at $700 per week and range to $2,500.

CENTURY 21 THOMAS
625 Sea Mountain Hwy., North Myrtle Beach
(800) 249-2100, (843) 249-2100
www.century21thomas.com

Serving strictly the North Myrtle Beach and Little River areas, this company maintains more than 400 units, condos, houses, and oceanfront or channel homes and has been honored with Century 21's prestigious Centurion and Grand Centurion Awards numerous times. One- to seven-bedroom accommodations can be rented, and as many as 20 people can stay in one of the larger homes. Ninety-five percent of the condos offer pools, and all of the homes are oceanfront or second row from the Atlantic. Staff can arrange golf and entertainment packages for guests. Prices start at $725 per week for a one-bedroom unit and range all the way up to $10,500 for an eight-bedroom oceanfront beach house.

SHORE CREST VACATION VILLAS
4709 South Ocean Blvd., North Myrtle Beach
(800) 456-0009, (843) 361-3600
www.bluegreenrentals.com

Beautifully decorated and outfitted, Shore Crest Villas offers one- and two-bedroom condo units with full kitchens, two baths each, and extra sofa beds. The one-bedroom villa accommodates four people easily; the two-bedroom can sleep six guests. The property sports an indoor pool and Jacuzzi, exercise room, and video-game arcade. On the oceanfront is another pool, a Jacuzzi, and a lazy river. Shore Crest is part of the Bluegreen Vacation Club and members are given priority for rental. A week's stay at Shore Crest in the middle of July costs about $179 to $318 a night depending on the unit size.

MYRTLE BEACH

BAREFOOT VACATIONS
3405 North Kings Hwy., Myrtle Beach
(800) 845-0837, (843) 626-7457
www.barefootvacations.info

Spanning the length of the sunny Grand Strand, Barefoot, not to be confused with Barefoot Resort & Golf, manages 100-plus properties, including one-room suites, one-, two-, and three-bedroom condos, plus annual rentals. Barefoot Vacations has an excellent staff of experienced coordinators for family reunions, honeymoon accommodations, shopping trips, and holiday vacations. Most properties have swimming pools available to guests, and some include a clubhouse for events. The staff can also arrange dining, show, and golf packages. The weekly cost of a Barefoot Vacations property in mid-July is $850 to $2,500.

BOOE REALTY
7728 North Kings Hwy., Myrtle Beach
(800) 845-0647, (843) 449-4477
www.booerealty.com

Booe's inventory of more than 200 rental properties consists of condominiums, houses, and townhomes that sleep 4 to 8 persons and beach houses that accommodate 9 to 21 guests. Except the condos, no other units include swimming pools. But keep in mind that most beach houses are oceanfront or just across the street from the blue Atlantic. In mid-July condos and town houses start at $650 per week, and oceanfront beach houses range from $1,495 to $6,000 weekly. Booe specializes in winter rentals and golf packages.

LITUS* TO LET
1551 21st Ave. N., Suite 24, Myrtle Beach
(888) 449-9000, (843) 449-9000
www.litus.com

A state-of-the-art reservation and customer-service center at LITUS* can put you in touch with a huge inventory of rentals all over the Grand Strand, from efficiencies to luxurious oceanfront homes suitable for 25 people. Prices range from $50 per night to $6,000 for a week's stay. The staff encourages potential guests to call their customer-service center at any time, since last-minute cancellations often provide visitors with the perfect place at big savings.

MYRTLE BEACH VACATION RENTALS
603 Briarwood Dr., Myrtle Beach
(800) 845-0833, (843) 272-7070
www.mb-vacationrentals.com
All along the Grand Strand, Myrtle Beach Vacation Rentals manages hundreds of vacation villas, condos, and cottages. Studios, efficiencies, and up to four-bedroom accommodations are available, most of which are within comfortable walking distance to the beach or offer an on-site pool. Formerly known as Chicora, Myrtle Beach Vacation Rentals also arranges golf, tennis, and entertainment packages for guests. During peak season, rentals run anywhere from $675 to $2,085 a week. A four-bedroom, three-bath oceanfront villa costs about $2,545 for a week's stay.

THE NOBLE COMPANY
1125 48th Ave. N., Myrtle Beach
(800) 358-6625, (843) 449-6625
www.thenoblecompany.com
Since 1980 the Noble Company has arranged vacation packages for families in some of the nicest condominium properties in North Myrtle Beach and Myrtle Beach. One- to four-bedroom condos can be rented, along with a limited number of large beach homes. Garnering a select group of vacation properties over the years, Noble prefers to rent to families, married couples, and singles older than 25. No house parties are permitted in any of the company's rental units, so look elsewhere if you want to have a beer bash. Prices in mid-July range from $675 a week for a two-bedroom, two-bath unit across the street from the ocean to $2,000 a week for a four-bedroom, three-bath oceanfront condo.

OCEANFRONT VACATION RENTALS, INC.
1551 21st Ave. N., Suite 12, Myrtle Beach
(800) 247-5459, (843) 626-2072
www.oceanfrontvac.com

Oceanfront Vacation Rentals represents more than 100 properties throughout Myrtle Beach, including one-, two-, and three-bedroom condominiums with fully equipped kitchens boasting microwaves, color cable TVs, VCRs, and laundry facilities. Most properties are only minutes from shopping, swimming, amusement parks, world-class family music shows, and other attractions. Prices range from $600 for one-, two-, and three-bedroom condos that overlook the salt marsh and golf course, are a short walk to the beach, and have indoor and outdoor pools, to $9,900 for a sprawling oceanfront home with eight bedrooms, seven baths, a pool and Jacuzzi, a large oceanfront porch, a fireplace, and a large back porch overlooking the ocean.

SLOAN REALTY AND MANAGEMENT AND ENDLESS SUMMER VACATIONS
9662 N. Kings Hwy., Myrtle Beach
(800) 476-1760, (843) 449-0835
www.sloanrealty.com
Approximately 200 units, efficiencies, cottages, and penthouse suites are available for rent through this company. Some of the properties are large enough to accommodate 10 people under one roof. All include access to swimming pools. Summer rentals begin at $620 per week for an efficiency and $3,000 to 4,000 a week for a fancy beach house.

SOUTH STRAND

DUNES BEACH VACATIONS
128 Atlantic Ave., Garden City Beach
(888) 621-4194, (843) 651-2116
www.dunesbeachvacations.com
All up and down Surfside Beach and Garden City Beach, along canals, inlets, and channels, Dunes Realty manages a large inventory of condominiums, cottages, and beach houses. This company rents almost exclusively to family groups. The smallest accommodation starts at $725 a week in mid-July, and a seven-bedroom beach house will cost from $3,500 to $7,700. Dunes Beach Vacations accepts MasterCard and Visa.

GARDEN CITY REALTY INC.
608 Atlantic Ave.,
Garden City Beach
(800) 395-5930, (843) 651-2121
www.gardencityrealty.com

Staying in its own neighborhood, this company handles about 555 rental properties in the Garden City Beach and Surfside Beach areas. Garden City Realty offers one-, two-, and three- bedroom condos, homes, and oceanfront beach houses. Most units sport pools, and some offer hot tubs. In mid-July a three-bedroom condo starts at $1,340 per week; a six-bedroom oceanfront home, $7,700.

GOLF COLONY RESORT
1841 Colony Dr., Surfside Beach
(800) 654-6522, (843) 650-6363
http://beachstarproperties.com

Golf Colony offers 11 colonies of three to five buildings each. Each has its own pool and barbecue area. Some have Jacuzzis.

The Colony offers guests 588 condos that range from studios to one- and two-bedroom accommodations, which can sleep up to 10 people. All have fully equipped kitchens and washers and dryers. The resort is just 1.5 miles from the ocean.

From May to Aug weekly rates run from $511 to $721; nightly stays are $75 to $105. There is a three-night minimum, six-person maximum for all reservations and a onetime cleaning charge of $55 to $108, which includes linen service.

PAWLEYS ISLAND REALTY COMPANY
88 North Causeway, Pawleys Island
(800) 937-7352, (843) 237-4257
www.pawleysislandrealty.com

With properties concentrated in the Pawleys Island and Litchfield Beach areas, this family-owned company offers all sizes of cottages and homes in a variety of price ranges. On the average, Pawleys Island Realty handles accommodations for groups of about eight people. It does not accept credit cards. In business since 1962, Pawleys Island Realty knows the area better than many of the larger firms.

PLANTATION RESORT
1250 US 17 N., Surfside Beach
(800) 845-5039, (843) 913-5000
www.plantationresort.com

Although a little way from the beach, this resort is nestled in the heart of a protected bird sanctuary, home to Canada geese, American woodcocks, and an abundance of wildlife. Two- and three-bedroom villas are available with two and three bathrooms, towels and linens, fully equipped kitchens, and washer and dryer. Staying here entitles you to free summertime shuttle service to and from the beach and access to a 70,000-square-foot health and swim club. The club includes a heated pool, lazy river, sauna, steam rooms, weights, and aerobics. The staff can arrange golf and entertainment packages. Mid-July rates run $120 to $250 per night, with discounts applied to reservations of at least seven nights.

SURFSIDE REALTY
213 South Ocean Blvd.,
Surfside Beach
(800) 833-8231, (843) 238-3435
www.surfsiderealty.com

If you're looking at Surfside Beach or Garden City Beach as your vacation destination, this company maintains nearly 500 apartments, condos, duplexes, cottages, and houses. This company has been arranging vacations since 1962 and has a strict policy of booking families only. Golf packages can also be arranged through Surfside Realty.

During the summer a one-bedroom apartment rents for $600 to $1,000 per week, and a house with a pool runs about $2,800 to $5,700. Special off-season discounts apply from post–Labor Day through May.

BED-AND-BREAKFASTS

Besides the burgeoning number of hotel and motel suites springing up all over the Grand Strand, bed-and-breakfast establishments have also been making their mark. Most likely due to the incredible amount of competition from other accommodations from Little River through Garden City Beach, you'll find the majority of bed-and-breakfast inns have put down roots south of Murrells Inlet and especially in Georgetown.

It's not surprising that Georgetown should become the region's hub of bed-and-breakfast lodging, since the area is home to its fair share of sprawling, historic homes that lend themselves perfectly to the concept. Georgetown, founded in 1729, is a woman with a past—fascinating and mysterious—and is known as the "Ghost Capital of the South." By 1840 Georgetown was not only an ideal port for shipping vessels but also produced more than half of all the rice grown in the United States.

As the rice plantations flourished, so did the townspeople and antebellum life. Culling incredible wealth in a relatively short period of time—from 1840 through the 1850s—some residents built well-appointed homes along the oak-shaded tunnels of streets in town. Gracious plantations served as hubs for entertaining and farming along the shores of Winyah Bay, and the Waccamaw, Black, and Pee Dee Rivers.

Georgetonians have worked hard to preserve their heritage, and their town remains a lovely step back in time with an intact historic district, preserved homes, and original churches and storefronts. Today historic tour companies run a brisk business by boat, by tram, or by horse-drawn carriage.

Each of the bed-and-breakfast inns we have listed in this chapter has a distinct personality that seems to have evolved from the property itself and its proprietors. The owners also operate their bed-and-breakfasts, taking great pride in what they consider to be their labor of love.

Price Code

This price code indicates the average one-night rate for two people during peak season.

$.................... $70 to $95
$$ .... $96 to $120
$$$ .... $121 to $145
$$$$ .... $146 and up

MYRTLE BEACH

THE CHESTERFIELD INN $$$
700 North Ocean Blvd.,
Myrtle Beach
(866) 213-9534, (843) 448-3177
Sitting in the heart of Myrtle Beach, the Ches-

terfield Inn is listed on the National Register of Historic Places. Originally built in 1926, the inn is a gentle oasis in the midst of this busy section of the beach. There are 52 rooms available. Family operated, it is located right on the beach and has a pool on the premises

SERENDIPITY INN $$
407 71st Ave. N., Myrtle Beach
(800) 762-3229, (843) 449-5268
www.serendipityinn.com
A short, 300-yard walk from the beach, Serendipity is completely enclosed by dense foliage and a wraparound wall. This decades-old property was built to offer guests separate entrances and baths.

Fifteen appointed rooms are available; a few are noted as king suites with three rooms. Visitors are treated to a private pool and hot tub in the central courtyard, shuffleboard, table tennis, and bicycles.

Breakfast is served fresh every morning. The menu changes daily but always includes a large fruit tray and steaming baked goods.

Owners Kay and Phil Mullins are happy to coordinate and cater special events, such as family reunions, gatherings, and weddings. They can also make provisions for babysitting services. Smoking is permitted outside in the courtyard only. Free wireless Internet is available anywhere on the property.

SOUTH STRAND

ALEXANDRA'S INN $-$$$
620 Prince St., Georgetown
(888) 557-0233, (843) 527-0233

Surrounded by manicured gardens, flower beds, and scented magnolia trees, Alexandra's Inn was built in 1880 as an overflow for guests of the Winyah Inn (now the Masonic Lodge). The main house was dramatically restored. Special detail was given to enhancing the gracious home's original pine floors, moldings, 11-foot ceilings, and fireplaces that come with every room.

Because the home resembles Tara from *Gone with the Wind,* each bedroom is named after a character in the famous story and decorated with that person in mind. Here you'll find Scarlett's, Bonnie's, Ashley's, Melanie's, and Rhett's rooms. Each room has cable TV and telephone, as well as a private bath with shower, tub, or Jacuzzi. The main-house rooms are designed for two people only; young children cannot be obliged.

Standing poolside, the carriage house is a private accommodation with two bedrooms, a large bath, living room, dining room, and full kitchen. Decorated in light, breezy colors, it is a favorite for families or the business traveler looking for longer stays.

A gourmet breakfast is served every day for guests staying in the main house. The front porch hosts a full army of rockers. Innkeepers Rob and Sandy welcome small weddings or other special events. They can even coordinate and cater functions for you.

> **i** The owners of local bed-and-breakfasts usually know a lot about local history, activities, and events. Be sure to spend some time talking with your hosts.

DUPRE HOUSE BED & BREAKFAST INN $$-$$$$
921 Prince St., Georgetown
(877) 519-9499, (843) 546-0298

This charming bed-and-breakfast inn has not only won the hearts of its regulars; it has earned a spot on the National Trust of Historic Preservation because of its historical significance.

Records of the house date from 1734 when Elisha Screven first laid plans for her dream home on town lot 53 in Georgetown. The home changed ownership several times, the last surviving chronicle showing that Susannah Gignilliat lived there and filed a claim in 1776 for reimbursement for supplies given to American troops during the American Revolution. The inn is named after Susannah's mother, Mary Magdalen DuPre. Unfortunately, all other documents of ownership for the next 60 years were destroyed by Sherman's Advance during the Civil War.

DuPre House has been extensively altered over the course of the 20th century, but its second-floor wall overhang on the northwestern facade remains a rare example of an old building technique, uncommon to the southeastern states.

Each of DuPre's five rooms boast queen-size poster beds and private baths. Three of the suites include fireplaces. A full breakfast is served every morning to guests and includes a private roast coffee, blended especially for the DuPre House. Afternoon and evening refreshments are also served. Without leaving the grounds of the inn, you can take a refreshing dip in the pool or bubble away in the hot tub.

In July 2003 the property was purchased by Sam Murphy, formerly of the Colonial Williamsburg Foundation, and Karen Komar, a retired U.S.

Army officer. Both are committed to preserving the inn and its history for future generations to love and admire.

DuPre House accepts bookings for receptions, small meetings, and family gatherings. Business travelers are accepted. Smoking is allowed outside only.

HARBOR HOUSE INN $$
15 Cannon St., Georgetown
(843) 546-6532
www.harborhousebb.com

Harbor House Inn (circa 1765) is located directly on Georgetown's working waterfront. It is, in fact, Georgetown's only historic, waterfront B&B. Sailors say its distinctive red roof is visible 3 miles out across the bay. Harbor House has welcomed seafarers from across the globe for more than two centuries. The imposing three-story Georgian house is listed on the National Register of Historic Places, gracing the banks of the Sampit River from a bluff amid magnolia trees, camellias, and venerable live oaks. Harbor House is within walking distance to main-street stores. restaurants, and the historic district of Georgetown.

The house is accompanied by another monument of South Carolina history—the Red Store. This circa-1740 shipping warehouse formerly stored silks, indigo, and imported wines. From shaded rockers on the inn's porch, visitors can view sailing ships and the blue waters of Winyah Bay—a view that has remained unchanged for centuries.

Innkeeper Meg Tarbox runs the immaculately restored house, keeping the original heart pine floors gleaming and dust off family antiques, eight fireplaces, and Oriental carpets. Meg is a Georgetown native with an intimate knowledge of her area.

The inn offers four beautifully appointed rooms with private baths and waterfront view. In addition to the popular porch rockers, guests can share the joggling board, piano, bicycles, games, and books. Smoking is permitted on the open-air porches.

LITCHFIELD PLANTATION $$$$
Kings River Rd., Pawleys Island
(800) 869-1410, (843) 237-9121
www.litchfieldplantation.com

At the end of a quarter-mile avenue lined with live oaks draped in Spanish moss, you'll find the stately Litchfield Plantation Manor House (circa 1750). The home overlooks fields where Carolina long-grain rice flourished in the early 1800s.

The inn tariff includes lodging in one of the four gracious rooms, a daily full breakfast, use of the private heated pool and cabana, a private beach club at Pawleys Island, on-site tennis courts, and access to the award-winning, on-site Carriage House Club Restaurant. The Plantation boasts additional suites and villas for a total of 35 rooms and suites to accommodate couples, families, and small groups. Nonsmoking rooms are available.

Litchfield Plantation is a member of the prestigious Small Luxury Hotels of the World Society.

MANSFIELD PLANTATION $$
1776 Mansfield Rd., Georgetown
(866)717-1776, (843) 546-6961
www.mansfieldplantation.com

A National Historic Landmark on the site of many archaeological digs, Mansfield is an authentic antebellum plantation of the Old South, offering bed-and-breakfast stays and historical tours. The plantation dates back to 1718, but Civil War buffs will enjoy retracing of the footsteps of Dr. Francis S. Parker, a signer of the South Carolina Ordinance of Secession, who planted rice here from 1842 to 1862. Parker was forced to leave his beloved Mansfield in April 1862 when federal gunboats crossed into Winyah Bay and raided plantations along the Black River. The Parkers were forced to sell Mansfield in 1912, but in 2004, after a 92-year absence, it returned to the hands of the Parker family. Sallie and John Parker have committed themselves to running a bed-and-breakfast like no other and have restored both the manor and guesthouses.

Situated on 1,000 idyllic acres of pine forest, rice fields, and dikes, Mansfield retains the original plantation house, avenues of 220 live oaks draped with Spanish moss, more than 100 blooming camellia bushes, the antebellum slave village, chapel, schoolhouse, winnowing tower, and parts of the rice threshing mill. The unspoiled environment plays host to alligators, beavers, fox, deer, otters, and birds, including an occasional bald eagle.

Eight charming and comfortably outfitted rooms in historic guesthouses, featuring hand-carved woodwork and mantelpieces, are for let. Private baths and air-conditioning keep each room comfortable. A full breakfast is served every morning in the elegant dining room of the plantation house.

Guests have the opportunity to fish for bream and bass or play golf on the adjacent 18-hole Wedgefield Plantation course. Weekend getaway packages are also offered at the plantation. Smoking is permitted outside on the grounds.

SEA VIEW INN $$$–$$$$
414 Myrtle Ave., Pawleys Island
(843) 237-4253
www.seaviewinn.com

This place is a Pawleys Island tradition. Sea View's 20 rooms overlook the ocean and the salt marshes of the inlet. As bed-and-breakfast inns go, this is among the most rustic. For more than 65 years, families have dined on authentic Lowcountry cuisine and have relaxed in the privacy of the traditional wraparound porch. This is the ideal vacation destination for anyone who wants to get away from it all and have it all at the same time.

Owners Brian and Sassy Henry took over operation in 2002 and have continued the Sea View's reputation for friendliness and pride in its natural setting. During the spring and fall months, the Sea View offers special events with a myriad of themes, including weeklong artist workshops, spa weeks, nature and historical retreats, and even a "girl's getaway."

In addition to your swimsuit, shorts, and T-shirts, the other things you'll need are a good book and a fishing pole. Your stay includes three meals daily. From Memorial Day through Labor Day, Saturday to Saturday reservations are required. During other times of the year, a two-night minimum stay is required. Smoking is not permitted. No credit cards are accepted.

THE SHAW HOUSE BED-AND-BREAKFAST $
613 Cypress Court, Georgetown
(843) 546-9663

Mary and Joe Shaw operate this refuge that overlooks Willowbank Marsh, considered by many to be a bird-watcher's paradise. Getting to the Shaw House requires a jog through town since it's set off the beaten paths of Georgetown, yet it's within walking distance of its historic district, shops, and restaurants.

Three spacious rooms can be rented here, all furnished in antiques and offering a king- or queen-size Rice bed. Bicycles, games, and an extensive library are extended to guests. Nightly turndown and chocolates are mainstay luxuries at the Shaw House.

A Southern home-cooked breakfast that includes fresh baked bread and pots of rich coffee is served each morning. Many guests of Shaw House have written that Mary is the ultimate hostess and personification of Southern hospitality.

Smoking is permitted on the outside porches.

BEYOND THE STRAND

THE CYPRESS INN $$
16 Elm St., Conway
(800) 575-5307, (843) 248-8199
www.acypressinn.com

Just 12 miles from the heart of Myrtle Beach in the charming town of Conway, this AAA Four Diamond bed-and-breakfast offers a welcome change of pace. Overlooking the Waccamaw River, it boasts 12 guest rooms, each with its own personality. The Carolina Room offers a king-size mahogany four-poster bed, fireplace, and a two-person Jacuzzi with a 12-inch French showerhead above. The Miss Marple Room, featuring English country decor, is home to more than 60 Agatha Christie novels. Other amenities found in the rooms are plush bathrobes, luxurious bed linens, herbal soaps and shampoos, and comfortable beds. The business traveler will find the amenities and comfort of a luxury hotel—in-room desk, Wi-Fi, TV/VCR, private baths, fax and copier on-site—along with the personal service a bed-and-breakfast provides.

Each morning, breakfast is served in the sunny breakfast room. Wonderful, specially blended coffee, teas, homemade breads and muffins, fruit, and a hot entree are presented to the guests. Some guest favorites include sweet potato pancakes, Cypress Eggs, and peachy French toast.

The inn is ideally located on Conway's River-walk. Guests can spend a leisurely afternoon rocking on the porch, renting a boat and cruising the Waccamaw River, biking around town, or playing tennis just across the street.

The Cypress Inn partners with a local day spa to offer create-your-own spa packages that include relaxation massages, manicures and pedicures, and facials.

The inn is available to accommodate groups for business retreats, women's retreats, church retreats, and team-building gatherings. They also offer workshops on cooking, quilting, and flower arranging.

RESTAURANTS

We all work hard to have a good time, strolling the beach in that soft sand, fighting the waves, spiking volleyballs, spotting and picking up all those pesky shells, stretching out on beach towels and working on a tan. Whatever you do here on the Grand Strand, you're going to work up an appetite whether you like it or not.

Nearly 1,600 restaurants accommodate our various palates. If you want to try every one of them on your next visit, plan on staying and eating three square meals a day for one year, five months. With this many restaurants from which to choose, this chapter can't begin to do justice to all the area's offerings. So we've opted to highlight a handful of favorites—mostly individually owned restaurants unique to the Strand. Of course, there are lots of good places we don't have room to cover, so our best advice for you is to explore!

One caveat: You might have to look a little harder to find a selection of exotic ethnic cuisine. Grand Strand restaurants have easy access to fresh seafood and therefore rightly emphasize the fresh catch and local nettings; you'll definitely find more family-style seafood buffets here than any single genre, followed closely by pancake houses. But as Myrtle Beach grows, so do our tastes, and restaurant owners are branching out into Thai, Fusion, Australian, and Mediterranean, establishing some of the finest restaurants in America right in our biscuit-and-country-ham kind of town. Sushi? We are on the ocean after all.

And the number of restaurants is growing almost weekly. The village of Murrells Inlet, on the South Strand, is billed as the "seafood capital of South Carolina" with its several dozen restaurants; the town of Calabash, North Carolina (on the North Strand), is credited with inventing Southern-fried seafood; and the stretch of US 17 between Myrtle Beach and North Myrtle Beach has been dubbed Restaurant Row because of its historical concentration of eateries. The opening of Broadway at the Beach and downtown Myrtle Beach establishments and their efforts to be competitive have brought even more restaurants into the mix.

OVERVIEW

What to wear? What to wear! Yes, you can dine in long dresses and dark suits in some of the Strand's establishments, but you can also wear shorts and even bathing suits in others. From candlelight elegance to beer bashes in flip-flops, it's all here.

Don't think even for a minute that the phenomenal number of restaurants or the incredible choices of cuisine are Johnny-come-lately ventures for tourism's sake. The dining heritage of the Grand Strand goes back 200 years and is deeply entwined with the ghost stories, pirate adventures, and folklore of this historic strip.

Hush puppies, the deep-fried and seasoned dollops of cornmeal served with most Southern seafood dishes, are delivered as baskets of delicious little Ping-Pong-ball-size treats. The tasty morsels were invented more than 150 years ago, when it was fashionable for families to let dogs sleep under the table while they were eating. It was at one particular Murrells Inlet plantation that the cook decided to do something about the dogs that weren't sleeping as much as they were begging for treats from the table—especially when the meal was full of the aroma of fresh-cooked fish. This cook decided to take some leftover breading, add a little sugar, and make some quick-fried dough balls to set in baskets on the table. The idea was that when the dogs began begging, diners would toss a couple of dough balls under the table to "hush" the puppies. Of course, it wasn't long before the humans at the table took a taste, and soon the dog pacifiers were "hushing" people, too.

Over the years many seafood restaurants nationwide have offered hush puppies, but it is only in Murrells Inlet that the original sweet-flavored treats retain that unique plantation recipe. The cook at one Inlet restaurant today claims that his hush puppy recipe was handed down through eight generations. Even restaurants along the North Strand are often baffled by the South Strand flavor that seemingly no one has been able to duplicate; most Calabash-style restaurants serve hush puppies with onions in place of the sugar-sweet flavor.

Calabash is a word you'll see a lot when you go cruising for restaurants along the Strand. Calabash is a little fishing village in North Carolina, just across the state line, where Myrtle Beach vacationers have driven the 25 or so miles north on US 17 to enjoy the delicious fresh seafood meals since the 1930s. But in the past decade or so more than half the seafood buffet restaurants in Myrtle Beach have incorporated the word Calabash into the menus or signs describing their seafood. It has come to refer to the style of cooking that made tourists flock to the town: oily seafood dipped in a light cornmeal batter, deep fried and smothered with seasoned butter, then delivered to your table golden brown and piping hot.

Also in the Grand Strand's gastronomic mix are plenty of regionally and nationally known restaurants whose quality you can always count on: Cracker Barrel, Shoney's, Quincy's, Red Lobster, the Olive Garden, Pizza Hut, Fuddrucker's, T.G.I. Friday's . . . the list is nearly endless. And we haven't even considered the fast-food regulars, all of which are present here.

Please note that many Grand Strand restaurants don't accept reservations, and long lines are common at the more laid-back walk-in places. The best bet here is to call before going or just drop in and see. As Insiders, one thing we have learned is that half the fun of eating at the beach is the adventure of finding a new favorite.

Price Code

The following key indicates the price range for a dinner for two, excluding cocktails, tax, and tip. Lunch fares usually run a third to a half less than the dinner prices. All prices, of course, depend on what you choose as an entree, so this key uses the price of an average meal (based on both the restaurant's response to our questions as well as our own computation from menu entrees).

Unless we note otherwise, all restaurants in this chapter accept at least Visa and MasterCard as methods of payment.

$...................... Less than $20
$$ .... $21 to $35
$$$ .... $36 to $50
$$$$ .... $51 and more

NORTH STRAND

BENITO'S BRICK OVEN PIZZA $$
1596 US 17 S., North Myrtle Beach
(843) 272-1414
www.benitosnmb.com

Benito's New York–style pizzeria and pasteria offers a variety of traditional Italian specialties. The hand-tossed pizza is prepared with homemade care in an authentic wood-fired brick oven and is among the Strand's finest. Many of Benito's pizza selections are inspired by locations from around the world. From the Tropical Tahiti Island special to tempting choices that hint at locales from Barcelona to Mexico, there is a wealth of choices for every palate. Benito's offers more than 20 toppings—from artichoke hearts to chunks of fresh pineapple. Although the undisputed specialty is pizza, fresh salads and a handful of pasta dishes round out the menu.

THE BRENTWOOD RESTAURANT $$
4269 Luck Ave., Little River
(843) 249-2601
www.thebrentwoodrestaurant.com

The Brentwood is a feast for all your senses. The first floor of this remodeled Victorian-style restaurant, built in 1910, is reserved for dining. Upstairs there is a European "salon" where guests can retire after dinner for dessert and drinks, including espresso and cappuccino. It's also the perfect place to relax and leisurely enjoy a bottle of wine with cheese. Toss in a game of backgammon, and you've got the makings of a splendid interlude.

The food is, quite simply, excellent. Chef Eric Masson, a French native, moved here with his wife and children after running successful restaurants in Saratoga Springs, New York. Chef Eric holds three degrees from the prestigious Ferrandi Culinary School in Paris. His approach is fresh, local, and simple. In addition to homemade desserts, the gourmet menu includes fresh veal, rack of lamb, fresh local seafood (the crab-crusted grouper is extraordinary!), beef, pork, and chicken. Entrees come with fresh-baked bread, a crisp salad, and a guaranteed-tasty vegetable of the day. The Brentwood is open for dinner Monday through Saturday. Seatings begin at 4:30 p.m., and reservations are suggested but not required.

DAMON'S GRILL $$$
Barefoot Landing, 810 US 17 S.,
North Myrtle Beach
(843) 272-5107
www.ribsribsribs.com

One sample is all it takes to understand why Damon's is best known for its award-winning ribs. Even so, those who prefer something lighter or with less mess will be more than satisfied with a menu that also offers excellent grilled steaks, numerous chicken selections, fresh seafood, and giant salads. Whatever you order, do not miss the opportunity for a side of onion rings. A thick, amazingly tender stack of the sweetest kind always arrives hot and golden. Damon's has mastered the art.

Those in search of a lighter meal should opt for the Honey-Lime Salad. Chicken is scattered atop tossed greens and tomatoes, but what makes this salad a real standout is the fruit—loads of mandarin orange slices as well as fresh pineapple and strawberries. The honey-lime dressing is unique and uniquely delicious. All the desserts are worthwhile, but the Triple Chocolate Truffle Cake is sure to bring you back for more.

Guests can choose between the restaurant's quiet and understated dining room or a high-

i Horry's Restaurant by the Waccamaw River is a "Family Tradition Begun in 1957." Located on Highway 9, 6 miles out in the country from North Myrtle Beach, Horry's specializes in oysters and fresh catch. This is the epitome of a locals' place, and going by the only true measure of culinary excellence (a full parking lot), also one of the best places in the Grand Strand for local seafood. Breaking with Grand Strand tradition, they call their hush puppies corn dodgers.

energy clubhouse atmosphere that showcases DTV—a proprietary state-of-the-art, multiscreen entertainment system that delivers sports, network programming, and interactive games.

DUFFY STREET SEAFOOD SHACK $$
202 Main St., North Myrtle Beach
(843) 281-9840
319 Sea Mountain Hwy.,
North Myrtle Beach
(843) 249-7902
202 Maison Dr., Myrtle Beach
(843) 281-9840
www.duffystreetseafood.com

Part tavern, part restaurant, and true local hang-out, Duffy's Seafood Shack started out on Ocean Drive in 1992 and has expanded to three locations, including the Cherry Grove section and Myrtle Beach proper. They are known for their raw bar but also serve everything from burgers and po'boys to steak and lobster. Make sure to try the fish, corn, and crab soup. You'll need to get there early if you want a spot at the bar.

GREG NORMAN'S AUSTRALIAN GRILLE $$$
Barefoot Landing, 4930 US 17 S.,
North Myrtle Beach
(843) 361-0000
www.shark.com/australiangrille

This exceedingly popular restaurant's namesake is the same Greg "the Shark" Norman of golfing fame who designed the Norman Course, which you can view from your table at his Australian Grille.

The flavors and seafood-heavy selection of the Australian Grille perfectly complement a stay on the Carolina coast, and the lively, aboriginal decor of the Grille goes well with our own Low-country stylings. The menu is amazing: pan-fried lobster dumplings, Tasmanian sea mussels, miso and cane sugar–marinated sea bass, habanero-rubbed tenderloin, yellowfin tuna, and all sorts of Australian-inspired nightly specials. Tables are hard to get, and reservations are recommended. The Shark Pub is just as spacious and elegant as the dining rooms and includes a few TVs for sporting events (hmm, wonder which ones?). It has its own satisfying menu: fried calamari tossed in a sweet-and-sour chili glaze, Queensland cut fries, and famous pizza baked in an authentic wood-burning oven.

JOE'S BAR & GRILL $$$
810 Conway Ave., North Myrtle Beach
(843) 272-4666
www.dinejoes.com
Owner and chef Joey Arakas wanted to give the Grand Strand a restaurant that would make diners feel as though they never left the comforts of their own homes. Fine dining in a rather rustic atmosphere is what has kept Joe's one of the busiest establishments in town for more than a decade.

Joe's is not the place to go if you have a craving for something fried: There is no such thing on this menu. The cuisine is definitely continental, including steak, seafood, veal, and poultry dishes. All marinades, sauces, soups, and dressings are made fresh daily. Fish lovers should

i Off the beaten path but worth the search is the old fishing village of Little River. Turn east off US 17 onto Minneola Avenue, and you'll find yourself at the Intracoastal Waterway. Small waterfront restaurants with names such as Captain Juel's Hurricane, Crab Catchers, and the Cockney Cheddar serve "just off the boat" fresh fish. During warm-weather months, you can dine on their decks and watch not just fishing boats, but pleasure craft.

try the whole boneless rainbow trout coated in cornmeal, stuffed with crabmeat, and laced with a Southern Comfort mushroom cream sauce. Joe's is open for dinner only, with happy-hour and early-bird specials.

THE PARSON'S TABLE $$$$
US 17 N., Little River
(843) 249-3702
www.parsonstable.com
Ed Murray Jr., executive chef and owner, brings more than a quarter century of culinary experience to the Parson's Table. He has been selected one of the Best Chefs in America, putting him in illustrious company that includes Wolfgang Puck, Alice Waters, Jeremiah Tower, Lydia Shire, Louis Osteen, Jean-Louis Paladin, and Elizabeth B. Terry. With credentials like these, you can rest assured you will enjoy a truly world-class meal.

Mouthwatering entrees run the gamut from prime rib and tender filet mignon to veal, pork, lamb, roast duckling, and plenty of fresh seafood. One favorite is the lump crab cakes. Lightly sautéed and served with a distinctive dill mustard sauce, this crab cake stands out in a region where almost everyone has a favorite crab cake recipe. Sautéed in lemon butter, the Little River Shrimp and Scallops, featuring fresh local shrimp and tender scallops, boasts an unexpected Southern touch—chopped pecans. It's a different twist you won't soon forget.

A longtime favorite of locals and returning visitors, the Parson's Table is ranked among the Top 50 Best Overall Restaurants in the United States by the Academy Awards of the Restaurant Industry. It was ranked No. 1 in Historic Restaurants of South Carolina Mobil Travel Guide and in 2009 received both a coveted Golden Fork award from the Gourmet Diners Club of America and a Triple Diamond rating from AAA. If you're looking for elegance and a sure bet, this is your winner.

PRESTON'S $$
4530 US 17 S., North Myrtle Beach
(843) 272-3338
www.prestonsrestaurant.com

Located at the entrance to Barefoot Landing, Preston's combines both seafood and country cooking at an enormous buffet. You better bring your appetite when you come. Its expansive menu includes baby back ribs, fresh vegetables, both broiled and fried seafood, and, of course, desserts such as cobbler. The large dining room is equipped to handle groups and often does, so try to get there early.

T-BONZ GILL & GRILL $$
Barefoot Landing, 4732 US 17 S.,
North Myrtle Beach
(843) 272-7111
US 17 Bypass and 21st Ave. N.,
Myrtle Beach
(843) 946-7111
www.tbonz.com

T Bonz's big ol' menu and spacious (if noisy) interior is fun, fun, fun. Hearty portions of beef, grilled chicken, vegetarian entrees, seafood, and more are standard fare. For the Southern born 'n' bred, we think you'll be particularly fond of the shrimp-and-grits specialty—a creamier dish of the snowy stuff has never been created to our knowledge. We sometimes choose T-Bonz just because the folks there are so environmentally conscious. They recycle all their glass and cardboard, and avoid the use of plastic foam. The atmosphere is casual, the price is affordable, and kids are welcome.

Open from 11 a.m. until late night, T-Bonz also offers light lunches and an after-hours social scene. Stop in at either location.

TONY'S ITALIAN RESTAURANT $$
1407 Old Hwy. 17 N.,
North Myrtle Beach
(843) 249-1314

Tony's is the oldest Italian restaurant along the Grand Strand and has been in operation since 1953. The recipes for Tony's dishes have been handed down from generation to generation, and the kitchen never compromises its homemade quality. Nothing on your plate at Tony's is prepackaged or frozen; even the herbs are freshly picked from the restaurant's very own garden.

Homemade Ice Cream on the Beach

Painter's Homemade Ice Cream has been churning out the best homemade ice cream on the Grand Strand since 1952. Located in the Crescent Beach section of North Myrtle Beach, it beats out the national chains as Best of the Beach year after year. It's nothing fancy: You still park on a dirt driveway and walk up to the screened window to place your order. (You pick up at the window a few feet over.) Picnic tables are there for you to sit and savor the experience—and then go back for more. In addition to the cones, sundaes, and shakes, Painter's also makes some pretty impressive ice-cream sandwiches.

Flavors include all the ones you'd expect, although the strawberry has huge hunks of fresh fruit you'd never find in a grocery store. Try the black cherry, banana nut, maple walnut, bubblegum, or even watermelon. If you fall in love with a flavor, they will happily pack up a quart or two for you to take home. Rest assured, it will never be enough.

The founders started the business at the site and even lived here. Relatives still stay from time to time, and most of the ice cream is made on-site. There are now three locations on the Grand Strand, but the family still maintains that personal touch. Bring cash; they don't accept credit cards.

Our perfect Tony's dining experience starts with the Clams Posillipo (steamed clams draped with marinara sauce) as an appetizer followed by the Terri Lynn Veal Scallopini, featuring fresh mushrooms and artichoke hearts in a brown brandy sauce.

For dessert we heartily recommend the chocolate Godiva cake, a wicked seven-layer cake laced with Godiva liquor. Tony's is open Monday through Saturday for dinner.

MYRTLE BEACH

US 17 Business is known as Kings Highway throughout Myrtle Beach. The Kings Highway address is used for most of the establishments listed in this section.

AKEL'S HOUSE OF PANCAKES $
6409 North Kings Hwy., Myrtle Beach
(843) 449-4815
For local color don't miss Akel's; it's a Myrtle Beach landmark. In an area known for its stellar lineup of pancake houses, Akel's rates right up top. Whether for the food, the service, or the all-night hours, we're not sure. The atmosphere is friendly and surprisingly familiar. Gossip, laughter, and local news travel from one table to another; a meal here is as good as reading the local paper!

Open 10 p.m. to 2 p.m., Akel's is everybody's favorite way to wrap up a night on the town. Needless to say, it's a great way to start your morning, too. Come watch the locals in their element! While breakfast fare is the house specialty, Akel's offers lots of sandwiches, salads, burgers, and even steaks as well.

ANGELO'S STEAK & PASTA $
2011 South Kings Hwy., Myrtle Beach
(843) 626-2800
A staple in Myrtle Beach since 1980, Angelo's is the home of an all-you-can-eat Italian buffet that includes lasagna, chicken cacciatore, pizza, spaghetti, stuffed shells, tortellini Alfredo, stuffed ravioli, and Italian sausage. Every meal at this restaurant is accompanied with a big bowl of crisp salad served family-style and wonderful garlic rolls.

A full-service menu is available as well, and Angelo's claims to serve "the greatest steaks in the universe." If you're like us, you'll spend a good amount of time mulling over whether to head for the buffet or try a sirloin. Both are mouth-watering.

Angelo's opens for dinner at 4 p.m. every day of the week. The Italian buffet closes at 8:30 p.m.

A bit farther north, where US 17 Business and Bypass meet, Dolly Parton's *Dixie Stampede* has proved itself one of the Grand Strand's most spectacular dinner shows. With nearly three dozen horses, dozens of talented cast members, and cozy seating for a thousand situated around a 35,000-square-foot arena, *Dixie Stampede* is a Dolly Parton creation. A one-price ticket includes the show, a satisfying four-course feast, and entertainment in the nonalcoholic saloon prior to the show.

i Just about any seafood restaurant worth its salt will list she-crab soup on its menu. While recipes vary greatly, she-crab soup gets its name because crab roe (eggs) are added to the rich blend of cream, crabmeat, and sherry.

BONEFISH GRILL $$
7401 North Kings Hwy., Myrtle Beach
(843) 497-5292
www.bonefishgrill.com
Bonefish has become a fast favorite among locals for its fresh fish and inventive salads. The first Bonefish started in St. Petersburg, Florida, and founders Tim Curci and Chris Parker have worked to take the mystery out of fish for people who don't eat it very often. The staff is trained to answer questions about any seafood selection, and the descriptions will make you want to try it all. There are fun spices and great combinations in dishes that you would swear were just pulled from the water hours ago. Even the bar has become a hangout for those who want to

sample some of the appetizers, such as the Bang Bang Shrimp, a spicy, crispy shrimp, or the bacon-wrapped sea scallops.

Bonefish opens for dinner at 4 p.m. Mon through Sat and at 3 p.m. on Sun.

CAGNEY'S OLD PLACE $$$
Restaurant Row, 9911 US 17 N.,
Myrtle Beach
(843) 449-0288
www.cagneysoldplace.com

For three decades Cagney's Old Place has been a favorite local dining and dancing spot—and tourists have discovered our secret. There's ambience aplenty and great food, too. Many of the antiques that enliven Cagney's decor came from the Ocean Forest Hotel, a fabulous oceanfront accommodation that was demolished in 1974.

Cagney's specialty has always been prime rib, but everything is perfectly delicious. A children's menu is also available. *Southern Living,* a magazine reputed for its high standards, recommends this classic.

Only dinner is served at Cagney's.

CAROLINA ROADHOUSE $$
4617 North Kings Hwy., Myrtle Beach
(843) 497-9911
www.centraarchy.com/carolinaroadhouse.php

Carolina Roadhouse is owned by the same folks who manage the equally successful California Dreaming, Frank ManZetti's, and Joey D's, to name a few located across the South. But don't consider this a "chain restaurant." Carolina Roadhouse displays unusually beautiful architecture and interior design. Soaring ceilings, arched windows, skillfully positioned mirrors, and an abundance of recessed lighting establish a mood that is intimate without a hint of stuffiness. The sweet, spicy scent of cedar abounds, as does a medley of exquisite smells from the wide-open kitchen.

The service is outstanding; so is the food. From tender barbecue chicken to melt-in-your-mouth ribs, steaks, and seafood, the portions and variety are impressive. Salads, sporting an

incomparable hot bacon and honey-mustard dressing, are enormous and otherworldly. A plain ol' croissant takes on a new dimension served hot, dripping with warm honey. Seafood gumbo, brimming with okra, shrimp, and crawfish, is anything but ordinary. And leaving without sampling a bowl of baked potato soup would be an absolute injustice. For dessert try the Key lime pie. It tastes "straight from the grove."

Open daily for lunch and dinner (same menu), Carolina Roadhouse is one of the most happening restaurants in Myrtle Beach, so don't miss out. Dress is casual, and reservations are accepted. Go quickly.

CHESTNUT HILL $$$
Restaurant Row, 9922 US 17,
Myrtle Beach
(843) 449-3984
www.chestnuthilldining.com

In an area saturated with fine-dining options, Chestnut Hill distinguishes itself. Smack-dab in the heart of Restaurant Row, Chestnut Hill sits beneath age-old oaks and overlooks a small, quiet lake. Its location is worlds removed from the resort hustle-bustle and sets the stage for a dining experience that's out of the ordinary.

From the pasta sauces to the cheesecakes, absolutely everything is made from scratch, and 80 percent of the fresh seafood served here was caught on Chestnut Hill's own boat—just hours before. The menu is filled with gourmet dishes, and the service is friendly and accommodating.

Owners Chris and Greg Lee have several extremely popular restaurants along the Strand, and they know more than a thing or two about feeding hungry people.

Dinner is served every evening. Chestnut Hill serves an outstanding Sunday brunch.

COLLECTORS CAFE AND GALLERY $$$$
7726 North Kings Hwy.,
Myrtle Beach
(843) 449-9370
www.collectorscafeandgallery.com

Everybody has their own concept of a great res-

 **Close-up**

Theme Restaurants

From outlandish architecture to glass-encased collections to celebrity owners, quite a few restaurants along the Grand Strand are rewriting the recipe for a fun, new-experience-filled, and bedazzling dining experience.

House of Blues, Hard Rock Cafe, KISS Coffeehouse, Caddyshack, Planet Hollywood, and Jimmy Buffett's Margaritaville are the best examples of this restaurant trend. They're also among the most popular, so they are easy to recognize and find, but then again, parking might not be. They put on an elaborate show, though, and work hard for their money.

House of Blues in Barefoot Landing, North Myrtle Beach, is visible from US 17, but you might mistake it for a massive barn that someone forgot to tear down. The 43,000-square-foot elegantly shabby structure looks like it is one of the originals in Myrtle Beach, but it has been open just a few years. To achieve this effect, the House of Blues went around the country buying not only the art and artifacts that fill the place, but also actually used and worn architectural and construction material, then carefully pieced it all together into the 700-capacity restaurant, outdoor "Sugar Shack" deck, and 1,800-capacity concert hall that stands today.

The restaurant, with its Southern pit-cooking smells and ceiling embossed with portraits of blues legends, will draw you in. Every time we go, much as we try to order something else, we can't stay away from the Mississippi Cat Bites and the mashed sweet potatoes.

But even more irresistible is the House of Blues' Sunday gospel brunch. Every Sunday morning gospel groups from around the South perform at the House of Blues concert hall. It is an invigorating, soul-stirring experience. The elaborate banquet of grits, biscuits, roast beef, shrimp and rice, sausage, and delicious bread pudding almost gets in the way of all the napkin waving, foot stomping, and hallelujah-ing.

For more information on the musical talent that appears at the House of Blues, see the "kicks!" entertainment section of every Friday's *Sun News*.

Hard Rock Cafe at Broadway at the Beach is probably the most recognized and picturesque; at any sunny moment, the sphinxes that guard the Hard Rock entrances are a favorite snapshot point. This international pharaoh of restaurants occupies a huge pyramid surrounded by palm trees along the US 17 Bypass. It's hard to miss; at night it is lit up with spotlights, and around the clock it blares good old rock 'n' roll. The Hard Rock Cafe in Myrtle Beach—with its pyramid shape—is the only Hard Rock Cafe in the world built in this distinctive shape. The spectacular lighted fountain that graces its entrance is also one of a kind. When you enter the structure, you're a floor above the dining room—from this vantage point you get a bird's-eye view of everyone else's meals and the cafe's collection of historic rock memorabilia.

The interior is covered with a stone finish, more hieroglyphics, and mementos of rock 'n' roll. The walls vibrate with echoes from the guitars of Hank Williams Jr., the Who, Joe Walsh, the Allman Brothers, the Black Crowes, Black Sabbath, Pearl Jam, Guns N' Roses, Jimi Hendrix, Bob Dylan, and Jerry Garcia. These instruments were once in the hands of legends, and now they're out in the open to enjoy as you dine. A myriad of displays fill every nook, even at the phone booth and in the restrooms.

Of course, the menu can't be outdone by the elaborate interior, and you have your choice of almost 50 items. The Hard Rock, with its "Love All, Serve All" philosophy, has cooked up a selection for every lifestyle, from the Hard Rock Veggie Burger to the Hickory Chicken & Ribs Combo.

For more theme-time fun, back in Celebrity Square at Broadway at the Beach, is Caddyshack. Murray Brothers Caddyshack is one of the more recent additions to Broadway at the Beach.

The restaurant is designed to look and feel like a country club gone awry. Comedian Bill Murray and his five brothers—actors Brian, Joel, and John and businessmen Andy and Ed—encourage guests to "Eat, Drink and Be Murray." The concept is accredited to Andy Murray, longtime chef and restaurateur, and cofounder Mac Haskell. Here the brothers' love of golf runs headlong into their side-splitting sense of irreverence. The Caddyshack name recalls the brothers' teenage years, when all of them worked as caddies and in other golf-related jobs to earn tuition for Catholic school. And it is, of course, the name of one of Bill Murray's hit movies, which was cowritten by Brian Doyle-Murray.

The 8,500-square-foot restaurant opens onto a 3,000-square-foot deck that overlooks Broadway at the Beach's lake. Nearly 300 guests can be accommodated easily. The Bunker Bar, featuring specialty drinks and televisions aplenty to cover multiple sporting events, seats a few additional dozens. Looper's Lounge, which doubles as a billiards room, provides a spacious area to accommodate large groups. And "The Shed" sells Murray Brothers merchandise, including T-shirts, hats, glasses, golf attire, and miscellaneous golf gadgets.

The restaurant's interior highlights the brothers, the sport of caddying, and that classic Murray trait—humor. More importantly for hungry patrons, the restaurant features a full-service continental menu that includes everything from wings and peel 'n' eat shrimp to oversize salads, all sorts of sandwiches and signature clubs, as well as steaks, barbecue, fresh seafood, chicken, ribs, and pasta. Murray Brothers Caddyshack is open seven days a week for lunch and dinner.

You'll also find yourself able to have a KISS moment at Celebrity Square's KISS Coffeehouse. Think of it as Starbucks on platform shoes with some heavy makeup thrown in.

It's easy to spot with its 20-foot replica of the KISS-style platform boots on the exterior. Inside is the real thing—a pair of authentic Gene Simmons shoes. Simmons is owner of the establishment, which is decorated with memorabilia and sells plenty of merchandise along with its coffee and sweets. As the managers put it, it is "a stimulating environment to drink a stimulating beverage."

Planet Hollywood sits just across 25th Avenue from Broadway at the Beach. A meal here will leave you feeling like you've broken bread with your favorite luminaries. The building itself is a blue and green planet, and the cement foundation is imprinted with the handprints and signatures of Bruce Willis, Demi Moore, Sylvester Stallone, Arnold Schwarzenegger, Melanie Griffith, Don Johnson, Jean Claude Van Damme, and others.

Inside Planet Hollywood is a panorama of blockbuster movie hits. Throughout all the display cases, between booths, around pillars, and covering an entire two-story wall is a collage of superstar faces a la the *Sgt. Pepper's Lonely Hearts Club Band* album cover. George Clooney looks mischievous; Elvis croons; Melanie hugs Don; Demi looks captivating in an evening gown, as does Bruce in his muscle T; and, for some reason, Antonio Banderas is bowling but still manages to look smooth as can be.

So settle in and unfold the 4-foot-long menu. Start off with a cocktail—a Ghost or a Cliffhanger or, if you're brave, the Terminator (catch that pattern?). As an appetizer we recommend the Chicken Crunch, which is tender chicken strips coated with Cap'n Crunch cereal and served with Creole mustard. For the main course the menu offers a fusion of West Coast, Italian, and Asian.

Singer Jimmy Buffett's Margaritaville at Broadway at the Beach is a mecca for Parrotheads and just about anyone who wants to have a good time. Whether you're hanging in the Tiki Room or chillin' on the Euphora boat docked outside, it's a great place to grab a bite and soak in the atmosphere of the beach. The menu is very Caribbean and plays off the titles of many of Buffet's songs. You can have a Cheeseburger in Paradise or Volcano Nachos, as well as conch fritters or coconut shrimp—all while calypso music (and Buffett) plays in the background. The restaurant transitions to a nightclub after 9:30 p.m., so hang around and do a conga line as the drinks flow.

taurant. Some enjoy the casual, comfortable, and unpretentious. Some like the blue-blood feeling they derive from the attentive service in an elegant restaurant. Still others prefer the intimacy of a neighborhood bar or coffeehouse. Amazingly, Collectors Cafe and owner/artist Thomas Davis has managed to fuse all three environments. We can't imagine anyone who wouldn't be satisfied spending an evening here.

In the dining room, columns and high ceilings exude elegance, and original paintings depict Lowcountry seascapes as well as Parisian cityscapes. Beyond the dining room, a grill room with oversize canvases and hand-tiled, bar-height tables allow you to watch Collectors' chefs chop and sizzle. In the coffeehouse room you can relax and feel a little bohemian while surrounded by more original art that includes not only hanging canvases but artwork on every surface, table, wall, and chair.

Surrounding patrons with all this art, Collectors Cafe serves up a feast for the senses as well as for the appetite. (By the way, most of the art is available to add to your own collection.)

The restaurant bills itself as serving Mediterranean cuisine. Appetizers include a fillet of beef carpaccio with extra virgin olive oil, spicy mustard, balsamic vinegar, and Parmesan cheese. A favorite entree is pan-sautéed crab cakes with crisp, grilled asparagus. The roasted garlic turnip puree is pleasantly different—and delicious. Of course, there are also pasta and salad selections as well as veal and lots of fresh seafood.

After dinner, take time to enjoy the homemade tiramisu, or for that matter any of the desserts; you can walk an extra mile or two on the beach tomorrow.

As a gallery, Collectors Cafe opens at noon, Mon through Sat. The restaurant is open for dinner only, and reservations are highly recommended.

DAGWOOD'S DELI $

400 11th Ave. N., Myrtle Beach
(843) 448-0100
US 17 Business, Surfside Beach
(843) 828-4600
www.dagwoodsdeli.com

Since the 1940s, the term "Dagwood" has referred to a multi-decker sandwich stuffed with anything and everything. That pretty much describes the fare here.

It takes two big hands to handle the monstrous subs at Dagwood's. There's not a lot of ambience—Dagwood's is a frat hangout at its best—but with sandwiches and prices like these, who cares?

Baskets of homemade bread (baked fresh daily) and an authentic deli case greet you at the door—reminiscent of a New York delicatessen. Choose from a variety of hot and cold sandwiches that showcase a mile-high stack of meats and cheeses. You can feast on burgers and Philly cheese steaks, too. At lunchtime local business folk frequent the place, so it's gotta be good.

Dagwoods is open for lunch and dinner. (Suggestion: Come for lunch and eat the other half of your sub for dinner.)

DIRTY DON'S OYSTER BAR & GRILL $$

408 21st Ave. N., Myrtle Beach
(843) 448-4881
www.dirtydonsoysterbar.com

Dirty Don's is small in size but big on character. Serving lunch and dinner, Dirty Don's features oyster shooters, clams on the half shell, a variety of sandwiches, and a tasty seafood chowder. The catfish fingers are fab, especially with a margarita. Bigger appetites are fond of the juicy steaks and king-size shrimp dinners.

Dirty Don's is the perfect place to spend an afternoon out of the sun, noshing on appetizers and drinking tall cool ones.

FIESTA DEL BURRO LOCO $$

960 Jason Blvd. (US 17 Bypass
and 10th Ave. N.), Myrtle Beach
(843) 626-1756
http://centraarchy.com/burroloco.php

Fiesta Del Burro Loco calls itself the Mexican cousin of the California Dreaming/Carolina Roadhouse restaurant chain. The exterior of the building was created to look authentically old and straight from Mexico; its visual appeal alone is a draw.

Once inside, you won't be disappointed. The interior is eclectic and every bit as extraordinary as the exterior. At the door you'll be greeted by a three-sided, 45-foot-tall mural of a bullfight.

Other murals are scattered throughout. A billboard collage covers the ceiling. There's an upside-down velvet Elvis mural above the bar. And the whole place is filled with authentic artifacts—so filled, you'll discover something new each and every time you visit.

And you must visit. Burro Loco manages to assault your senses in a most delightful way. The smell of fajitas sizzling on a mesquite grill will make your mouth water, as will the pizzas cooking in the wood-burning oven. Once you've tasted Burro Loco's handcrafted margaritas (the limes are squeezed by hand) and their made-from-scratch tortillas, your taste buds will be hooked.

Fiesta Del Burro Loco is open for lunch and dinner every day. Reservations are not required, but call-ahead seating is available. Don't miss the fajitas, a house specialty, or the hand-pitted, stuffed jalapeños.

FLAMINGO SEAFOOD GRILL $$$
7100 North Kings Hwy., Myrtle Beach
(843) 449-5388
www.flamingogrill.com

Flamingo Grill's art deco decor—black lacquer accented with pink and blue neon—sets the pace for a trendy evening of dining. Owned by the same folks of Cagney's fame (see this chapter's previous entry), this restaurant has become quite popular.

The menu includes lots of fresh seafood prepared in a variety of ways. The grilled fish with Cajun spices is especially tasty. Other entrees include pasta (the Pasta Flamingo is delish), chicken, prime rib, and steak. As an appetizer, the filet mignon chunks are outstanding. Save room for dessert; the Outrageous Derby Pie is, well, outrageous. A children's menu is also available.

Flamingo Grill serves dinner only. Closed Sundays.

If you ever see a sign that says *Chicken Bog Fundraiser today,* **stop the car and go enjoy! Local organizations usually whip up huge pans of this Lowcountry favorite and sell plates of it as fund-raisers. Chicken bog is chicken, rice, and sausage all cooked together for indescribably good flavor.**

JOE'S CRAB SHACK $$
Broadway at the Beach,
1219 Celebrity Circle, Myrtle Beach
(843) 626-4490
4846 Hwy. 17 S., North Myrtle Beach
(843) 272-5900
www.joescrabshack.com

It's a tacky-looking shack of a restaurant. The interior feels like a Gulf Coast fishing camp, and the menu serves up scads of crabs—cooked in a myriad of ways. As a whole, the Joe's experience is classic, cool, and comfortable. You can pound a few crabs on the patio or slip inside for a newspaper-covered table. Either way, cool beverages enhance the experience. The menu is enormous—not just crabs—and includes plenty of appetizers, sandwiches, salads, steaks, and more.

Obviously, Joe's specialty is crab, and variety is offered year-round. Steamed, barbecued, or garlic style, expect whatever's in season—Alaskan king crab, Dungeness crab, Alaskan snow crab, and blue crab. Joe also offers "Rug Rat" and group menus.

For kick-backed and casual, Joe's can't be beat.

LIBERTY STEAKHOUSE AND BREWERY $$
Broadway at the Beach,
1321 Celebrity Circle, Myrtle Beach
(843) 626-4677
www.libertysteakhouseandbrewery.com

The idea of combining a restaurant and microbrewery is hot these days, and Liberty Steakhouse is doing well sustaining the craze. Here guests enjoy beer that's made fresh every single day. On special holidays, such as Oktoberfest and St. Patrick's Day, seasonal brews are all the rage. Everyone who comes gets the opportunity to observe the working brewery staffed by expert brewmeisters. In itself, the beer-making lesson is worth the stop. The pleasant surprise is that the food is wonderful, too.

The menu includes hearty and delicious standard fare in whopping portions: specialty cuts of beef, original-recipe burgers, and unique appetizers and entrees such as buffalo shrimp.

Liberty is open for lunch and dinner.

THE LIBRARY $$$$
1212 North Kings Hwy., Myrtle Beach
(843) 448-4527
www.thelibraryrestaurantsc.com
The Library is one of the most elegant restaurants in the entire South and is the only restaurant on the Grand Strand to receive both the Mobil Three Star Award as well as the AAA Three Diamond rating. Offering consummate European cuisine and superior service, this restaurant has been quietly collecting fans since 1974. In a *Sun News* survey, locals voted the Library the "most romantic" dining spot on the Strand—with so many restaurants, that's a real coup! The menu includes veal, seafood, duck, beef, and chicken—first class all the way. The name comes from the literary decor, of course; the walls are lined with cases of literature that accentuate the leisurely and almost genteel atmosphere. The tuxedoed staff and table-side service set this place apart.

Open for dinner only.

MAGNOLIA'S AT 26TH $
2605 North Ocean Blvd., Myrtle Beach
(800) 437-7376, (843) 839-3993
www.magnoliasat26th.com
Do you want to experience Southern cooking at its best? This is your place. Magnolia's has been drawing the locals on a regular basis for more than 20 years. Once a part of the old Anderson Inn, Magnolia's expanded in 2004 and is now on its own, complete with a conference center. There are precious few restaurants within Myrtle Beach hotels where the locals book parties on a regular basis as they do here.

Open for all three meals, the restaurant specializes in home-style cooking and is a great place for Southerners to get their "meat and three" (meat and three vegetables). Have some of their amazing fried chicken or even their chicken and dumplings, fried okra, or grits and gravy. At Magnolia's lunch buffet, it's easy to try it all, and you'll be coming back until your buttons pop.

NEW YORK PRIME $$$$
405 28th Ave. N., Myrtle Beach
(843) 448-8081
http://centraarchy.com/newyorkprime.php
New York Prime is one of the area's finest restaurants. This was a dream child of founders Ed Cribb and Jerry Greenbaum, who first envisioned the restaurant when they returned from a trip to New York, where they ate at Peter Luger Steak House, the Palm Restaurant, Sparks Steak House, and Smith & Wollensky. Reminiscing, they wondered if a real New York–style steak house would make it on the Grand Strand. In researching the concept, they traveled around to see what America's best steak houses have in common and discovered that people will pay more for quality, but the food must be truly exemplary.

Concept confirmed, they went to Nebraska, where they established a unique supply chain, purchasing only from two slaughterhouses that ship according to incredibly stringent specifications. Upon receipt, the meat is aged for 28 to 35 days, then trimmed of excess fat.

The cooking completes the technique. No spices and no tenderizers disguise inferior meat. Cuts are extra thick, and ceramic broilers cook at 1,700 degrees.

The same attention to detail in supply and preparation goes into every morsel of food at New York Prime. Expect the freshest fish, giant lobsters shipped direct and kept live (never frozen), fresh Idaho potatoes, sweet Vidalia onions, and tomatoes straight from sunny California. An extensive wine cellar will complement your dining experience.

The prices are steep, but the experience is extraordinary, and the quality entirely justifies the prices. Open for dinner nightly.

NOIZY OYSTER $$

101 South Kings Hwy., Myrtle Beach
(843) 444-6100
www.thenoizyoyster.com

Casual, fun, and consistent, the Noizy Oyster has a broad menu that ranges from alligator bites as appetizers to a broad range of steamed and raw bar offerings. Crabs? Oysters? All fresh and there for the shucking and peeling. And even though seafood is the mainstay, the non-seafood lover in your group may want to try the rotisserie chicken or the ribs; both are worth coming back for.

THE ORIGINAL MR. FISH $$

3401A North Kings Hwy., Myrtle Beach
(843) 839-3474
www.mrfish.com

The name is oh so appropriate. Theodore Hammerman is truly "Mr. Fish." What this man does with fish is pure magic. Hammerman ran the much-celebrated fish shop and lunch counter at Phillips Seafood on the US 17 Bypass and then opened up this small establishment in 2009. It's very small and very local, but very worth it. This is a true Insiders' secret.

Staples include the grouper bites as appetizers and to-die-for she-crab soup. Try the Grouper Mac n' Cheese or the Tilapia B.L.T., but if you're lucky enough to be there the day they have the tuna lasagna, go for it! It sounds a bit odd but is unbelievably tasty. Hammerman loves to get creative. Mr. Fish's, er, Hammerman's daughter Sheina has inherited her dad's talents. Fresh fish is also available for purchase for those who want to try their own hand at cooking.

RIVER CITY CAFE $

404 21st Ave. N., Myrtle Beach
(843) 448-1990
9550 Shore Dr., Myrtle Beach
(843) 497-5299
US 17 Business, Murrells Inlet
(843) 651-1004
208 73rd Ave. N., Myrtle Beach
(843) 449-8877
www.rivercitycafe.com

The River City Cafes are the best hamburger joints on the beach for reasons only a bona fide hamburger connoisseur would appreciate. First, they are the perfect setting: wood-frame buildings that resemble old beach houses. Inside, you'll find worn wooden floors, benches, and chairs. Car tags, bumper stickers, and party paraphernalia adorn the ceiling and walls. River City was described as "one of the best places in the nation to take kids" by *USA Today*.

Although they follow a decorative pattern, each location is distinctive. Outside at the Murrells Inlet location, you'll find a wraparound porch with swings and a sunny deck peppered with big picnic tables. Inside, not a single table or chair matches. Expect a crackling fire to be burning in winter, and the music is great.

At all locations, customers serve themselves from the big bin of dry roasted peanuts and throw the empty shells on the floor—just oozes class, huh? But this all leads to the best part: huge, 100-percent pure-beef burgers topped with a variety of fixins, such as thick slabs of cheese, jalapeños, lettuce, tomatoes, grilled onions, bacon . . . the works!

These burgers require two hands to manage, and although they can be a little messy, they're worth several napkins. Don't forget the homemade jumbo onion rings. River City also serves a variety of other sandwiches and hot dogs. It's been said that only an ice-cold longneck bottle of beer truly complements River City Cafe's burgers. We think Jimmy Buffett's Cheeseburger in Paradise was inspired by this savory spot. Open for lunch and dinner daily.

i There are a few things that true Southern food lovers expect when they sit down to eat. One is "sweet tea," and we do mean sweet. Scoops of sugar accompany the boiled tea before it's ever even slightly diluted and iced down. The other is "a meat and three," meaning your meal consists of a meat and three vegetables. You'll see "a meat and three" listed as an option on many local menus.

ROSSI'S ITALIAN RESTAURANT $$$
9636 North Kings Hwy., Myrtle Beach
(843) 449-0481

Rossi's bills itself as "everything a restaurant ought to be," and we have to agree. A bevy of delights awaits your arrival: overly generous servings of veal, homemade pasta, fresh seafood, and Black Angus beef; fine wines; a cozy dining room featuring weathered brick, stained glass, and chandeliers; a piano bar; live entertainment; and desserts that'll make you do the two-step.

Rossi's is open daily for dinner only.

SEA CAPTAIN'S HOUSE $$$
3002 North Ocean Blvd., Myrtle Beach
(843) 448-8082
www.seacaptains.com

Back around 1930, the Sea Captain's House was a traditional family beach cottage. Converted to an oceanfront restaurant in 1962, it has remained a family-owned and family-operated business to this day.

If you enjoy understated elegance, delicious food, and a panoramic view of the ocean, Sea Captain's House is sure to please. Specials range from grilled salmon fillets with roasted garlic sauce to baked breast of chicken topped with Cajun-spiced shrimp. The kitchen staff is known for its culinary talents, particularly with seafood and Southern recipes.

Visit this lovely Myrtle Beach landmark—another personal favorite—for breakfast, lunch, or dinner.

THOROUGHBREDS $$$$
9706 North Kings Hwy., Myrtle Beach
(843) 497-2636
www.thoroughbredsrestaurant.com

A favorite among locals and tourists, Thoroughbreds's popularity has grown by leaps and bounds since it opened in 1988. When the restaurant became unable to accommodate nightly reservations as well as the community's requests for public and private functions, owner and operator Scott Harrelson made the decision to overhaul. Not someone to do anything in a small way, Harrelson spent in excess of $500,000—and it shows. The new Thoroughbreds, featuring five beautifully appointed dining rooms and a captivating veranda, offers an unparalleled celebration of food, spirits, music, and art.

Arguably, this is the most elegant restaurant on the Strand. The waitstaff is meticulously trained and very professional, harp music often is highlighted, and candlelight abounds. The menu combines gourmet seafood and continental cuisine. Caesar salads are prepared tableside. In our opinion, the certified Angus beef is best, but you'll also enjoy chicken, veal, pork, and even duck.

Thoroughbreds boasts a selection of more than 350 wines and is the recipient of several *Wine Spectator* awards.

Lest you be fooled into thinking Thoroughbreds is too ritzy for your average vacation meal, think again. Yes, it's elegant, and you do need to dress up a bit, but the atmosphere is cozy, the staff is friendly and accommodating, and children are welcome. We think you'll be glad you donned your finery. This is one of our personal favorites.

Only dinner is served, and reservations are suggested.

TONY ROMA'S—A PLACE FOR RIBS $$
Broadway at the Beach,
1317 Celebrity Circle, Myrtle Beach
(843) 448-RIBS
www.tonyromas.com

It's been said that Tony Roma's offers the best ribs in America, and we believe it. The original baby backs are a good choice, but if you're a bit more adventurous, consider one of the other four flavors: Carolina Honeys are basted with a sauce made with real honey and molasses; Blue Ridge Smokies boast a hint of molasses laced with burning wood; Tony Roma's Red Hots feature a nearly electric sauce created from five types of peppers; and Bountiful Beef Ribs are big, juicy, and smoky to the bone.

Tony Roma's also serves sensational salads, grilled specialities, a few seafood selections, chicken, and steak. As for appetizers, don't pass up the fried jalapeños stuffed with cheese. With an ice-cold brew in hand, life doesn't get any better than this. We'd like to point out from personal experience that the staff at Tony Roma's is exceptionally friendly. Obviously, they've realized that service makes the difference in a town filled with dining choices.

VILLA MARE $$
7819 North Kings Hwy. (behind
Bank of America), Myrtle Beach
(843) 449-8654
http://villamarerestaurant.com

This Italian restaurant is an indisputable locals' favorite. Its simple, unassuming location in a strip mall around the corner from a grocery store is deceiving—this place has class. But, for all its class, it's not a bit pretentious. Clothing is casual; "come as you are—just come hungry," says owner Fred Fusco in a lilting Italian accent.

You'll find everything you'd expect on an Italian menu, including calzones and plenty of pastas, and the prices are pleasantly surprising. You can order veal, chicken parmigiana, shrimp piccata, and fettuccine Alfredo and other pasta dishes, all made to order; absolutely everything is good. Plus everyone is friendly, and the atmosphere is light.

We think Villa Mare is a must for anyone who appreciates fine Italian cuisine. Seating is limited, so call ahead for reservations. Villa Mare is open for dinner only Mon through Sat; it's closed Sun.

i **New England has clambakes. The Grand Strand does oyster roasts. The rule of thumb for oyster season is any month that has an "r" in it, but it generally runs from late September until early April. Massive clusters of locally harvested oysters are served in steaming bushel or half-bushel tubs at select restaurants. A dead giveaway that you've found one of those restaurants is that there is a hole in the middle of the table with a trash barrel beneath for you to toss your empty shells.**

SOUTH STRAND

AUSTIN'S CABANA CAFÉ AND
BEACH BAR $$
1 Norris Dr., Pawleys Island
(843) 235-8700
http://austinsatthebeach.com

Located in the Litchfield Inn, this is a twofer. Austin's Cabana Café is an upbeat, island-inspired eatery that offers what few can—an open-air bar with a spectacular view of sea and surf. Toss a shrimp on the bar-b and enjoy the live music! Upstairs is the slightly more formal Austin's Ocean's One, which overlooks the ocean and serves up breathtaking views.

As for the menu, nothing compares to the panko herb-crusted local flounder with roasted tomato and spinach gratin, pancetta potatoes, and shrimp aioli. Also try the blue crab cake with lemon caper and dill sauce and smokey succotash. And there's plenty more to choose from. One of several house specialties is the whole catch of the day—this chef's selection is actually served whole. Call ahead for current details. Cabana Café is generally open Tues through Sun 11:30 a.m. to 9 p.m.—sometimes later, if the bar's hoppin'.

BOVINE'S $$$
3979 US 17 Business (on the waterfront),
Murrells Inlet
(843) 651-2888
www.bovineswoodfired.com

If ever a restaurant was fun, Bovine's is the place: expansive windows overlooking Lowcountry marsh, cozy lighting spilling shadows in every corner, exquisite smells drifting from a wood-burning oven, and the low hum of happy patrons.

Bovine's decor is a tribute to the wonders of the West. Cowhide-covered seats, dark wood, and the mounted head of a gargantuan bull reinforce the theme. The bar scene, separate from the main dining area, spotlights an awesome horseshoe-shaped bar as well as electronic darts, a couple of mounted TVs, and bistro tables scattered about. Comfy booths offer a ringside view of swaying spartina grass and the faraway, blooming lights of Garden City. Feels a little like the summertime hangouts of lost youth—only the patrons are seasoned and a bit more mellow. This is a great place for a beer and an individual-size, gourmet honey-crust pizza from the wood-burning oven. A see-and-be-seen crowd always gathers after work.

As for the food, Bovine's recipe for success features a few ingredients unique to the area. Nearly every selection on the titillating menu boasts a Southwestern slant. A great many choices come from the red-hot, marvelously aromatic, igloo-shaped oven. The variety is quite impressive, including tender char-grilled chicken, melt-in-your-mouth steaks, seafood, and pasta dishes.

Desserts are sinful but worth the mischief. The classic pecan pie is second only to the chocolate walnut brownie.

Bovine's serves dinner only, and reservations are suggested.

ℹ **South Carolina is one of the largest tobacco producing states in the U.S. and as such, laws prohibiting smoking in restaurants have failed to get the support they might need. Still, you will find that many restaurants on the Grand Strand have imposed the ban on their own accord. Surfside Beach has passed a local ordinance prohibiting smoking in any bar or restaurant.**

CAPT. DAVE'S DOCKSIDE $$$
4037 US 17, Murrells Inlet
(843) 651-5850
www.captdavesdocksiderestaurant.com

It's hard to beat the view from Capt. Dave's Dockside. Overlooking the salt marsh, there is a large boardwalk you can stroll if you want to take in the views before dining. Serving food since 1975, Capt. Dave's reopened in 2006 with a brand-new building that includes porches and large, homey rooms. The spacious deck overlooking the water features live music each weekend, and the piano bar in the lounge draws regulars.

Open for lunch and dinner, Capt. Dave's is known for the dishes it has created to cook on its lump charcoal grill, including steak, lobster, and other specialties. The charcoal is actually wood that has been burned into a coal form, which gives the food a unique flavor.

THE CHARLESTON CAFE $$$
815 Surfside Dr., Surfside Beach
(843) 238-2200

Surfside Beach welcomed the Charleston Cafe with appropriate if inauspicious fanfare: Six hours after opening, Hurricane Hugo swept ashore and left the restaurant without power or water for 10 days. In years since, the Charleston Cafe has developed a fine reputation for romantic meals in an intimate setting; attentive, personable service; and creative, attractively presented food. Its popularity prompted the owners to bow to demand in 2009 and serve lunch as well as dinner.

Specializing in certified Angus beef, local seafood, and veal and chicken dishes, the Charleston Cafe also offers a "light eaters" menu with smaller portions of well-liked items. The dessert menu is daunting, and servers parade the choices in front of you. Who can resist?! The Charleston Cafe also features a large list of wines by the glass.

The Charleston Cafe is open for lunch and dinner Mon through Sat, 11 a.m. to 10 p.m. Reservations are accepted and strongly suggested.

CONCH CAFE $$$
1482 North Waccamaw Dr.,
Garden City Beach
(843) 651-6556
www.conchcafe.net

Dining at the Conch Cafe is like inviting 100 or so good friends to your beach house for grilled tuna, baked scallops, conch fritters, tenderloin, teriyaki chicken and shrimp, mussels in garlic butter, and a mess of backfin crab cakes. Throw in a happy hour, and it's not a shabby way to host a party, right?

Did we mention the covered outdoor deck overlooking the ocean? It's great for stargazing and drinking concoctions with tropical-sounding names.

Lunch and dinner are served daily. Come early and stay late.

DRUNKEN JACK'S RESTAURANT & LOUNGE $$$
4031 US 17 Business (on the waterfront), Murrells Inlet
(843) 651-2044
www.drunkenjacks.com

As legend has it, Drunken Jack was a black-hearted pirate who patrolled Murrells Inlet incessantly, seeking treasure until alcohol led him to a watery grave. His namesake, a time-tested restaurant and lounge, is a preferred waterfront dining establishment in the Murrells Inlet area. Take time to have cocktails in the lounge and watch the fishing boats come in. Live musical entertainment is another treat.

Seafood and steaks are the house specialties, including filet mignon, frog's legs (a true Southern delicacy), and Grouper Royale. Lowcountry specialties abound. A children's menu is offered, too.

Drunken Jack's is open for lunch Tuesday through Sunday and dinner each night.

FLO'S PLACE & CAJUN RESTAURANT & RAW BAR $$
3797 US 17 Business, Murrells Inlet
(843) 651-7222
www.flosplace.com

Hats off to owner Flo Triska—literally! For years she and husband Ralph have been running this upbeat Cajun-style restaurant, and people show their gratitude by donating their chapeaus of all shapes and sizes to the area's largest hat display—right in the restaurant. This wood-framed eatery is set on the creek in Murrells Inlet and features Cajun and Creole food that'll make you think you're in steamy New Orleans. In the spirit of Mardi Gras, the clientele has been known to form a conga line through the indoor/outdoor dining room.

An all-time favorite menu item is the Dunkin' Pot, a large cast-iron kettle filled with jumbo spiced shrimp, clams, mussels, oysters, corn on the cob, red potatoes, and crawfish. (If you don't know how to eat crawfish, Flo will come by and demonstrate. It's really elementary: Snap off the tail and suck the head first; then peel the tail shell away, revealing the plump meat, and pop it in your mouth.) Grilled, fried, and sautéed platters include shrimp, oysters, fish fillet, and scallops seasoned with a light lemon, butter, wine, and parsley sauce. All that comes with a bed of seasoned rice, crawfish potatoes, okra and tomatoes, and garlic bread. Other time-tested favorites are the authentic po'boy sandwiches, served on grilled French bread—marvelous!

All the food here is made from scratch. Quench your thirst with a Pitcher of Watermelons, a fruity punch with a kick of rum and vodka. "Good food, great time" says it all.

Flo's Place is open for lunch and dinner seven days a week.

> **i** One of the Strand's smartest secrets is the "early-bird special." Before the dinner rush begins, many restaurants offer reduced dinner and drink prices. This tip is especially helpful for families, who can eat early, eat cheaper, and get back to the beach or hotel pool before turning in for the night.

FRANK'S RESTAURANT & BAR $$$
10434 Ocean Hwy., Pawleys Island
(843) 237-3030
www.franksandoutback.com

Many locals consider Frank's the best restaurant on the entire length of the Grand Strand. It's no wonder. The chef's creations feature an array of different influences, including Southwestern, French, and Asian, including Thai.

Salters McClary opened Frank's Restaurant & Bar, or just plain Frank's as locals call it, in 1988 on the site of the old Marlow's Supermarket in Pawley's Islands. McClary had worked there in high school. Located behind Frank's was the home of Frank Marlow's mother. After Frank's proved to be a huge success, McClary decided to renovate the old house and open another restaurant called Frank's Outback in 1992. Initially, Frank's Outback served only lunch, but demand grew for another good restaurant in the area and the Outback was transformed into a white-tablecloth-and-candlelight restaurant.

The two Frank's menus change weekly, and the selections are guaranteed to tempt the strongest dieter's resolve. A large selection of appetizers is great for combining. The entrees are diverse—classic to cutting edge. Vintage wines and homemade desserts round out a culinary experience worthy of many return visits. Frank's has been featured in *Gourmet, Bon Appetite, Southern Living,* and *National Restaurant Magazine.*

Naturally, fresh seafood is a specialty at Frank's. Selections include a delicious sautéed cornmeal-and-black-pepper-encrusted snapper entree. But seafood is only a beginning. Free-range chicken and veal are featured often, along with crispy duck and roasted lamb.

Frank's and Frank's Outback serve only dinner Mon through Sat from 5 to 10 p.m.

GULFSTREAM CAFE $$$
1536 South Waccamaw Dr.,
Garden City Beach
(843) 651-8808
http://centraarchy.com/gulfstream.php
The two-story Gulfstream Cafe sits high above the marsh and overlooks Murrells Inlet. Sunsets are spectacular and romantic. (Try to talk your host into giving you a table with a view.) Although dress is casual, the menu is upscale, and reservations are recommended.

Appetizers range from lump-meat crab cakes to oysters on the half shell. A popular appetizer is the Gulfstream sampler: stuffed shrimp, bacon-wrapped scallops, oysters Rockefeller, linguine with a delicate clam sauce, and blackened fish. (Hope you're hungry!)

Our No. 1 entree is Gulfstream's Salmon Portobello—perfectly broiled salmon topped with tender sautéed portobello mushrooms.

We've eaten at Gulfstream many times and have never had a bad night. Sounds impossible, but it's true. An early-bird menu, served from 4 to 5 p.m., is a secret well kept by locals. A children's menu is also available. Gulfstream Cafe is open for dinner only.

LEE'S INLET KITCHEN $$$
4460 US 17 Business, Murrells Inlet
(843) 651-2881
www.leesinletkitchen.com
Lee's Kitchen has been serving up fresh seafood in Murrells Inlet since 1948, and what began as a country store with just 10 tables has been enlarged six times over the decades. One of the few Murrells Inlet restaurants still operated by the family of its original owners, Lee's is now owned by the third generation. They treat their customers like family, too, and people return year after year. The menu includes many of the same recipes that Pearl and Eford Lee created when they started the business. Homemade she-crab soup and soft-shell crabs are among the favorites, and you can't beat the homemade pie for dessert!

Lee's is open Mon through Sat starting at 5 p.m. They only accept reservations for parties of 12 or more.

MIYABI KYOTO JAPANESE STEAK HOUSE $$
4201 US 17 Bypass, Murrells Inlet
(843) 651-4616
US 17 N., Myrtle Beach
(843) 449-9294
www.capitaljapan.com/Miyabi.html
Miyabi Kyoto's brings the beloved Japanese tradition of hibachi cooking right to your table. The chef, usually an authentic personality from Asia, wows diners with tricks of his trade—knife juggling and flipping tiny shrimp tails from a spatula to a small bowl high atop his chef's hat. All entrees are served with salad (the gingerroot house dressing is the way to go) and a delicate onion soup.

The main course of chicken, beef, or seafood and a variety of vegetables are diced and cooked right before your eyes. It's so satisfying, you'll literally have to push yourself away from the table.

A trip to either Miyabi location is best enjoyed with a group and is a great way to celebrate a birthday, anniversary, or other special occasion. Try the sushi bar, if you dare, and spring for a glass of sweet plum wine.

Miyabi serves dinner only, and reservations are strongly suggested; the lines can be murderous. But after all, good things are worth waiting for.

OLIVER'S LODGE $$$
4204 US 17 Business, Murrells Inlet
(843) 651-2963
www.oliverslodgerestaurant.com

Oliver's rustic and weathered appearance is a welcoming landmark to everyone who knows and loves Murrells Inlet. Serving fresh, local seafood since 1910 (parts of the house were built in 1860), it's the oldest restaurant in the Myrtle Beach area, and the panoramic view (reason enough for a visit) is breathtaking.

Dinner at Oliver's feels a lot like visiting the home of a much loved family member who happens to be an extraordinary cook. In Southern style, the decor is understated and unpretentious. Don Edwards, Oliver's owner, will likely greet you at the door. Best of all, he's passed on his penchant for fine, friendly service to his staff, so you can expect to feel pampered throughout the evening.

Appetizers include homemade chowders, delicately seasoned crab cakes, crisp-fried calamari, oysters on the half shell, and stuffed mushrooms. Fresh seafood takes center stage and can be served grilled, broiled, fried, or blackened. Steaming oyster and clam pots (in season) and the signature Flounder Roosevelt are ever-popular choices, too. New York strip steaks, chicken Marsala, and at least three other specials are offered nightly. There's also a "sunset special" menu served from 4:30 p.m. to 6 p.m featuring fried shrimp or fish, hamburger steak or grilled chicken, salad, vegetable, and nonalcoholic beverage for $9.99.

Oliver's is open seven days a week for dinner from 4:30 p.m. until the folks stop coming. It is also open for lunch Tues through Sat 11:30 a.m. to 2 p.m.

NIGHTLIFE

Like the song says, "There's no use in sitting alone in your room; come to the cabaret." With the happening nightlife this area has to offer, there is no need to entertain your own company and absolutely no excuse for lamenting that there is nothing to do. When the sun sinks below the horizon, the lights come up around the Grand Strand, alive with the buzz of animated conversation, laughter, and the beat of various musical genres. Locals who can "hang" with the best of them all night long and rested vacationers congregate until the wee hours of the morning in too many nightspots to mention. Besides the places included in this chapter, many restaurants double as late-night spots, and most resort hotels provide lounges with live entertainment. And around almost every corner along the Strand you'll find a little bar or pool hall where the clientele is usually neighborhood locals.

Nightlife really picks up during the spring and summer months, so consult the Friday "kicks!" section of the *Sun News* for the most up-to-date profile on the entertainment scene.

Now let's get into some of the rules and regulations about partying so you can avoid any possible trouble or surprises.

RULES AND REGULATIONS FOR NIGHTLIFE

IDs, If You Please

The legal drinking age in South Carolina is 21, and that is a strict order around here. Some clubs allow underage patrons to enter with a clearly marked hand stamp—they can purchase only soft drinks at the bar. You'll find that Grand Strand club bouncers are fastidious ID checkers, so make sure you have some form of photo identification.

By the Drink

South Carolina lost its claim to serving the nation's strongest drinks in 2004 when the legislature repealed its decades old minibottle law. Since 1973, bartenders in the Palmetto State hadn't had to worry about measuring booze, because every drink was mixed with the premeasured 1.7 ounce minibottle.

Many a patron has almost fainted when they realized their multishot drink meant they had to pay for every minibottle used. The change to free-pour has made some drinks more affordable

and forced a lot of bartenders to change their mixing habits.

It's still up to the bars if they want to stick with the minibottles, but few have chosen to do so.

Drinking and Driving

Local patrol officers show no mercy to drunken motorists, and if you're picked up for driving while impaired, you will spend the night in jail before facing charges. Remember: No excuse is a good excuse where drinking and driving is

i For the uninitiated, the term "shagging" doesn't have the same meaning it does for Brits. Here on the Grand Strand it means a type of dance that resembles a slow jitterbug. Any place where oldies of the region's unique style of beach music is played, you will see couples bopping and moving to the beat. Ocean Drive in North Myrtle Beach is considered "Shag Central" for beach-music lovers, and shag competitions take place regularly.

concerned, so use your head—and stay out of the slammer.

DANCING THE NIGHT AWAY

North Strand

DUCKS & DUCKS TOO
229 Main St., North Myrtle Beach
(843) 249-3858
www.ducksatoceandrive.com

When you come to Myrtle Beach, shagging is a must. Consequently, Ducks & Ducks Too is "a must," as well. If you are shy about trying this quintessentially Strand dance, just drop in to watch—with a cold drink and classic shag tunes, the experience makes for a relaxing end to any day.

Hall of Famers William Greene and Mandy Holt offer professional shag lessons on Wed at 6 p.m. And if you are serious about learning more, Ducks can help arrange regular lessons.

If a shag-inspired special event is being held during the year, odds are good Ducks will be involved. Currently, popular events hosted here include the Dewey Kennedy Mixed Doubles Contest, a popular New Year's Eve Party, "Keepers of the Dance" shag contest, Junior SOS (Society of Shaggers) Contest, the CSA Shag contest, and the Pug Wallace Intergalactic Award.

During summer Ducks is open Wed through Sun. On Sat and Sun, they actually open their doors at 11 a.m. and don't close until 2 a.m. In the slower winter months, you will still find them open Thurs through Sat. If you like shagging, we suggest you call ahead or visit the Web site so you won't miss a sleeper special event.

SPANISH GALLEON
100 Main St., North Myrtle Beach
(843) 249-1047

The Galleon has been a favorite Grand Strand dance club for years. This place houses several dance floors under one roof to appeal to a variety of musical interests, including beach music and high-energy dance music. Live beach music bands entertain Galleon customers throughout the year, and an oceanfront grill keeps everyone from going hungry. Although you can wear T-shirts and shorts, most people tend to turn a night at the Galleon into a fashion show.

Renovated and bigger and better than ever before, Spanish Galleon is traditionally open nightly in the summer and several nights a week in the winter from 8 p.m. 'til . . . Call ahead for specific hours and admission prices.

i A referendum in November 2008 opened the long-awaited doors for the sale of alcohol on Sunday, putting an end to the decades-long "dry Sundays."

Myrtle Beach

BEACH WAGON
906 South Kings Hwy., Myrtle Beach
(843) 448-5918
www.beachwagonnitelife.com

Country music fans have come here for almost 30 years for live concerts and all-night two-steppin'. The club itself is a large, long dance hall with little neon but big rootin'-tootin' fun. Names such as Marty Stuart, John Anderson, Sweethearts of the Rodeo, Aaron Tippin, and McBride & The Ride all played the Beach Wagon just before their careers took off. It just goes to show, the performers you see at this club today might be the country-music stars of tomorrow.

Line-dancing classes are held every Wed and Fri starting at 8:15 p.m. Also on Wed, be ready to take the microphone and try your hand at karaoke.

There is no charge unless there is a performance, and Beach Wagon cardholders can get discounted prices. Concert ticket prices vary.

THE BOWERY
110 Ninth Ave. N., Myrtle Beach
(843) 626-3445
www.thebowery.com

Rocking the beach since 1944, the Bowery epitomizes a true Southern honky-tonk. Still proudly displaying the Stars and Bars, it has made its mark as a favorite among locals and visitors alike. The music group Alabama got its start here, and a plaque at the door proudly proclaims the bar's role in their rise to fame. It's a great place to listen to live country music, and the current house band, the Bounty Hunters, could give Lynyrd Skynyrd a run for its money.

Entrance is free unless a band is playing, and prices vary by performance. The Bowery is open Mon through Fri 11 a.m. to 3 a.m. and Sat and Sun 11 a.m. to 2 a.m.

CLUB BOCA
Celebrity Square
Broadway at the Beach, Myrtle Beach
(843) 444-3500
www.celebrationsnitelife.com
Club Boca could accurately be described as "a party come to life." DJs serve a steamy, steady stream of mainstream, hip-hop, techno, and Latin dance tunes. The result feels like Miami and Vegas colliding in Myrtle Beach.

Dual YAG lasers and a brightly hued kinetic light system make this the place to see and be seen. There is even a special VIP section where tables can be reserved for those who want a retreat within the club. Your $10 cover charge will also allow you entrance to Broadway Louie's, Malibu's Surf Bar, and Froggy Bottomz, all located in Celebrity Square. The drinking age is 21, but 18- to 20-year-olds are allowed in for a higher cover—they just can't drink. Club Boca's doors open at 10 p.m. and the music doesn't stop until 2 a.m. on weekdays and Sat and until 4 a.m. on Fri.

If you're young—or just want to feel like it—make haste to Club Boca.

CLUB KRYPTONITE
2925 Hollywood Dr., Myrtle Beach
(843) 839-9200
www.club-kryptonite.com
The 21,000-square-foot Club Kryptonite has been a force on the Grand Strand nightlife scene since it opened its doors in 2002. A throwback to the days of Studio 54 in New York, the club features its own dancers high above the pulsing dance floor and has a separate cigar and martini bar as well as a champagne lounge.

Boxing fans can take in regular Tough Man bouts, and Club Kryptonite sponsors Teen Nites periodically throughout the year to allow underage dancers to enjoy the club.

Club Kryptonite is open nightly 10 p.m. to 4 a.m., with themes as well as drink specials nightly. General admission is $10.

DEAD DOG SALOON
760 Coastal Grand Circle, Myrtle Beach
(843) 839-3647
4079 US 17 Business, Murrells Inlet
(843) 651-0664
www.deaddogsaloon.com
The Murrells Inlet Dead Dog established itself as a local favorite with what is hailed as the largest outdoor deck—and hence, outdoor bar—on the Grand Strand. The bar sits right on the water, and you can enjoy awesome views while taking in the music.

Dead Dog opened a second location at Coastal Grand Mall in Nov 2006. The huge location has two bars and three bandstands.

Both locations have live music every night of the week, and they take that music outside on the patio during the summer. Dead Dog draws an eclectic crowd ranging from bikers to barristers. Both locations have a better-than-basic menu for seafarers and landlubbers. The atmosphere is fun, and there's no cover charge. Both locations are open for lunch and dinner.

FROGGY BOTTOMZ
Celebrity Square
Broadway at the Beach, Myrtle Beach
(843) 444-3500
www.celebrationsnitelife.com
Here's a one-stop nightclub for diverse live entertainment, current Top 40 tunes, favorite oldies, Latin beats, and plenty that falls somewhere in between. If you can't decide where you want to go and what you want to listen to, count on Froggy Bottomz as a sure bet.

Froggy Bottomz is part of a four-club complex, and one admission will earn you the ability to also party at Club Boca, Malibu's Surf Bar, and Broadway Louie's. If you're age 21 or older, you're golden (18- to 20-year-olds are allowed in for a higher cover—they just can't drink). Froggy Bottomz is open until 4 a.m. on Fri and 2 a.m. on Sat. There are nightly events to look for during the summer months.

MALIBU'S SURF BAR

Celebrity Square

Broadway at the Beach, Myrtle Beach

(843) 444-3500

www.celebrationsnitelife.com

High-energy Top 40 music keeps the crowd gyrating on a dance floor that has a giant shark as its backdrop. This place is usually packed on weekends when tourists and locals wander in from a day at the beach or dinner at Broadway at the Beach.

Call ahead for prices and the frequently changing schedule. Regular admission for patrons is $10, which earns you admission to Club Boca, Broadway Louie's, and Froggy Bottomz as well.

ORIGINAL SHUCKER'S RAW BAR

Celebrity Square

Broadway at the Beach, Myrtle Beach

(843) 626-9535

Happy-hour discounted drink prices make this an excellent end-of-the-day option no matter what mood you are in. The late-night menu rates among the best around. Play pool or cutting-edge video games, watch the establishment's live entertainment, or simply abandon yourself to the simple pleasures of an absolutely excellent outdoor patio. You'll find lots of locals here.

REVOLUTIONS RETRO DANCE CLUB

Celebrity Square

Broadway at the Beach, Myrtle Beach

(843) 444-8032

www.fantasticclubs.com

For sure-fire fun, head to Revolutions. This locals' favorite has been voted Myrtle Beach's No. 1 nightclub numerous times by *Sun News* readers. Featuring songs from the '60s, '70s, and '80s, Revolutions has become a surprising dance-hall hit around here. Music making alternates between DJs and bands, with performers dressed in bell-bottoms, wedgies, and Afro wigs. This is a happening place on weekends. Don't be afraid to don your white jacket and medallions. Get ready to bump the night away to a K.C. and the Sunshine Band tune; say "groovy" all you want. Revolutions is open seven nights a week from 8 p.m., Apr through Oct. It's open only Wed through Sat the rest of the year. A $5 cover charge is always the case on weekends; $7 when a live band is playing. The cover charge also entitles you to admission at Blarney Stones as well as Crocodile Rocks—the home of dueling pianos—across the Square.

STOOL PIGEONS

Celebrity Square

Broadway at the Beach, Myrtle Beach

(843) 272-4123

www.stoolpigeons.biz

Word has it Stool Pigeons pub features the largest selection of draft beers on the entire Grand Strand. While this boast could likely be argued, the deck is undeniably a very cool place to kick back with a beverage—if you can resist the temptation to shoot some pool or toss some darts inside with friends. This is a place well known for excellent live entertainment. In fact, the place is rightfully billed as "the coolest perch on the Strand." Relaxed fun reigns supreme.

STUDEBAKER'S

2000 North Kings Hwy., Myrtle Beach

(843) 448-9747

www.studebakersclub.com

A nonstop dance party unfolds every night at Studebaker's, and at least a couple-decades' worth of patrons would be willing to attest to the fact. This establishment delivers neon and nostalgia—a high-spirited combination that smacks of high-school proms—with all the stuff you loved and nothing you would opt to forget.

Studebaker's is a no-risk option for after-hours fun. From Motown to old school to retro, Studebaker's can be counted on for a party. If you're age 80, zany DJs and shapely Studebopper dancers will make you feel 18.

Studebaker's is open from 8 p.m. until 2 a.m. every night in summer. Hours are abbreviated in the off-season; call ahead. Locals are admitted free year-round, which is a great reason to make this a regular hangout. The cover charge for others ranges from $5 to $10 depending on season and entertainment.

2001 VIP ENTERTAINMENT
920 Lake Arrowhead Rd.,
Myrtle Beach
(877) 662-0016, (843) 449-9434
http://2001nightclub.com

2001 has far outlived the dated name on the marquee. This is an upscale entertainment complex—and one of the longest-running nightlife success stories in a fickle resort community. Three separate nightclubs guarantee a variety of club atmospheres. No matter what your music preference, 2001 is ideal.

VJs spin the greatest hits from the '70s, '80s, and '90s in Funky Town. The sound system is high-tech, and combined with video walls displaying the music videos that accompany the tunes, it will make you feel like dancing even if you didn't expect to. In the very next room, discover Club Touch, which features current dance songs as well as hip-hop and techno.

Bars are interspersed throughout 2001, and professionally trained bartenders can whip up specialty cocktails as well as a few shooters even the seasoned club devotee cannot name. Valet parking adds a touch of class and convenience. With a nod to the area's laid-back resort setting, casual wear passes muster at 2001. Nonetheless, leave your hats in the car and don something besides a tank.

The club is open year-round Mon through Sat from 8 p.m. until well beyond midnight. Last call is at 2 a.m. on Sat. In winter the club often closes on Sun and Mon. Locals are admitted free, but a cover charge applies to all others, and the exact price is contingent upon special nights and the entertainment being featured. Expect to pay an admission that ranges from $6 to $10.

South Strand
CREEK RATZ
4065 US 17 Business, Murrells Inlet
(843) 357-2891
www.creekratz.com

One of Murrells Inlet's newer offerings, owned by the son of a longtime local, Creek Ratz has quickly become a favorite of both locals and tourists. Why? Rustic, nautical appeal. Spectacular views. Good food. Friendly service. Interesting clientele. It also has a reasonably priced menu, a full raw bar, happy hour, live entertainment, and plenty of TVs on which to watch your favorite sporting events. Enjoy shagging—on the edge of one of America's most beautiful creeks—on Sunday afternoon. Happy hour runs from 4 to 7 p.m. Creek Ratz is open 11 a.m. to 11 p.m. and is very family-friendly.

HOT FISH CLUB GAZEBO
4911 US 17 Business, Murrells Inlet
(843) 357-9175
www.hotfishclub.com

The original "Hot and Hot Fish Club" was founded near the end of the 18th century and might have been Murrells Inlet's first dining establishment. Out back behind the restaurant, the Gazebo—overlooking an undeniably spectacular view of the Inlet, offers the South Strand's best view for live nightly entertainment from Wednesday through Sunday. The food is better than average. To start, try the Key West Crabcake and Jack Jennie's Blackened Shrimp. There is also a raw bar and several tempting sandwich selections. Locals patronize this bar, and for many reasons. Discover them for yourself.

BANDS ON THE BEACH

The Myrtle Beach band scene is better than ever. The expanding diversity and increasing number of bands have given the area a wonderful musical texture that includes everything from modern rock and punk to blues, jazz, and Big Band. Renewed attention to "Southern rock," in the wake of the phenomenal success of Hootie and the Blowfish, Edwin McCain, and others, has created an exciting environment for record companies and music promoters to recruit and develop up-and-coming talent. As a result, you will find music to satisfy every taste.

For rock 'n' roll aficionados, the guitar-driven "heavy" sound dominates the scene among several bands playing original music and hoping to take the next big step toward a major label recording deal and regional prominence. Echo 7 continues to be the leader among the heavy rock bands for their outstanding musicianship, smart lyrics, and strong stage presence. Two lead vocalists who complement the hard rock hooks with haunting melodies round out the band's unique sound. Other heavy rock bands regularly heard in local clubs include Red Emotion Riot, Flick It, and Bleen, all of whom put on a great show.

For sophisticated tastes, two bands have filled the niche for "jam" bands quite well. After more than 20 years the Mullets (the fish, not the haircut!) have become local heroes to listeners and club owners. The Mullets pack 'em in every show. A combination of blues and Grateful Dead–type rock 'n' roll, they have established onstage antics that have been known to include tequila shots for everyone in the crowd! The Mullets are truly a Myrtle Beach tradition. Rollo (pronounced Rah-low), the Grand Strand's surfer-dude band, continues to be a favorite with their Southern, soulful approach to rock. The ever-popular Necessary Brothers have now split off to form Matt Necessary and the Necessary Band, known for their funk, soul and rock 'n' roll. The Necessary Band has opened for such acts as the Platters and Jimmy Buffett, and they still rock the house. During the summer, they are almost always playing at Margaritaville. And don't forget to check out the Porch Crickets, whose music has these guys hopping well beyond the Grand Strand.

New, but not so new, is the Rick Strickland Band, headed by local favorite Rick Strickland. After success as a soloist, he pulled together this seven-piece group in 2008. RSB quickly proved to be one of the must-sees for those who enjoy beach music and doo-whop.

If what you crave is the punch and power of bar bands that do their original stuff along with more familiar covers of popular rock, there's Walona and the Tim Clark Band. Both provide straight-on rock 'n' roll from classics to modern fare, with enough original material to keep it interesting.

For eclectic tastes, check out the very theatrical and crunchy punk blast of the Independents. Self-described punk-meets-ska-meets-surf-meets-the-Ramones, with a touch of Elvis, this up-and-coming group is a must-see.

If it's jazz and blues you're after, there are two local Big Bands that keep snowbirds and local retirees glidin' and boppin' across the dance floor. The first is Swingtime, a Myrtle Beach Big Band that showcases well-seasoned musicians and attracts a crowd anywhere and every time they play. Similarly, the popular Andrew Thielan Big Band has established itself as a mainstay at the beach's many festivals and special events. This fantastic ensemble is made up of an all-star cast of musicians and vocalists from across the Carolinas. Its music ranges from the golden era of the Big Bands to the new standards of today. Everything from Glenn Miller to Harry Connick Jr., Disney tunes, Broadway standards, and light rock makes their sound appealing for all ages. Other veteran jazz players in town are the Dan Ramsey Jazz Ensemble, U "N" I, and the longtime duo Jazz Etc.

As for the blues, gritty, down-home, Delta-style blues is always a favorite. Here, an even more popular derivation is the Chicago barrel-house style that has become a local shag dance favorite. Seek out the Smokehouse Brown Blues Band to be shuckin' and jivin' into the wee hours or Southern rockers Mason Dixon Line or Cheyenne, who both have an incredible repertoire of songs. For acoustic Southern rock, check out the highly popular Sawgrass.

For the latest information on bands and schedules, check out the "kicks!" section of the *Sun News* on Friday.

SPORTS BARS

Sometimes you just wanna hang out somewhere, have a brew, watch a game, and play a few rounds of pool or darts. If that's how you're feeling, we have a sports-bar lineup here that should satisfy. While a number of places in town call themselves sports bars (apparently it's quite fashionable to do so), we have come up with some guidelines to ensure the full "sports-bar experience."

By our criteria, a bar was given mention in this section only if it had at least four televisions locked on sporting events and at least two games to play. There's never a cover charge at area sports bars, unless a major boxing event is to be aired. Then you'll have to consult the media to find out which places will be showing the fight and what the admission cost will be.

North Strand

OSCAR'S
4101 US 17 S., North Myrtle Beach
(843) 272-0707
This sports bar is a continuous arena of action, with 100 TVs and an array of games, including trivia, pinball machines, a virtual-reality race car game, and Goldentee.

You're likely to work up an appetite, so it's a good thing Oscar's now offers a full menu until 1 a.m.

Oscar's is open from 11:30 a.m. to 2 a.m. Mon through Sat and noon to 2 a.m. on Sun.

Myrtle Beach

BROADWAY LOUIE'S GRILL
Celebrity Square
Broadway at the Beach, Myrtle Beach
(843) 444-3500, (843) 445-6885
www.celebrationsnitelife.com
Broadway Louie's Grill is great fun for the entire family. The joint boasts 12,000 square feet, including interactive video games, more than four dozen large-screen TVs, the Karaoke Big Show, and extremely comfortable couches in a sports bar that's legendary—if only locally. Enjoy family-friendly competition with the latest and greatest in video arcade and skill games, featuring Star Wars Trilogy, Jurassic Park's Lost World, Rapid Rivers, Daytona 2, and lots more.

Those in the know this is one of the best local places for New York–style pizza. Louie's Grill serves it hand-tossed and fresh from the oven. Extraordinary subs and appetizers round out the menu. Trivia games are available right at your table, and you can also rack 'em up for pool. Doors open at noon every day, and all ages are admitted.

DROOPY'S
5201 North Kings Hwy., Myrtle Beach
(843) 449-2620
Droopy's stays open as late as business dictates Mon through Fri and until 2 a.m. on Sat and Sun. More than 14 TVs are scattered throughout, along with two pool tables, lots of video games, and foosball, too.

Basic appetizers and sandwiches are available from the kitchen, but Droopy's also offers excellent daily specials.

Doors open at 4 p.m. Mon through Fri. Droopy's opens earlier when the NFL season game schedule dictates.

FOSTER'S CAFE & BAR
6307-A North Kings Hwy.,
Myrtle Beach
(843) 449-7945

Foster's offers more than half a dozen televisions, darts, a pool table, and a satisfying menu. While this place is very small, its rough-hewn wood decor exudes a certain coziness, and locals love its off-the-beaten-path allure.

Foster's is open Mon through Fri from 11 a.m. until 4 a.m. and Sat and Sun from 11 a.m. to 2 a.m. The kitchen closes at 2 a.m. on weeknights and at 1 a.m. Sat and Sun.

JIMMAGAN'S PUB SPORTS BAR
6003 North Kings Hwy.,
Myrtle Beach
(843) 497-5450

Jimmagan's Pub, with 35 TVs locked on sporting events, pool tables, and electronic darts, is a small corner location that's cozy and down-home. Jimmagan's guarantees you can see every Sunday NFL game during football season. It is a favorite of motorcycle enthusiasts and has additional locations in Murrells Inlet, south on US 17 Business, and in Little River off US 17 North.

The menu is limited to sandwiches, burgers, and finger foods; wings are always 25 cents. Jimmagan's is open seven days a week—11:30 a.m. to 4 a.m. weekdays; 11 a.m. to 2 a.m. on weekends.

i We know that lines to use restrooms at nightclubs and amusements can be lengthy and, depending on the number of beers you've had, sometimes agonizing. Be forewarned: The only other offense that local police enforce as strongly as drunk driving is urinating in public. If caught, you will be arrested, fined, and taken to jail.

MAGOO'S SPORTS AND SPIRITS
905 Oak St., Myrtle Beach
(843) 946-6683

Magoo's is one of the only dart bars to have sprouted up along the Grand Strand. View one of 12 televisions; head to the back room, chalk up a cue stick, and shoot some pool. Electronic and steel-tip darts are at the front end of the bar.

Under the category of "fine food," Magoo's menu ranges from fabulous burgers to juicy steaks. Their wings have been voted Best on the Beach for several years. Wings for 15 cents and half-price appetizers are the special on Sunday and Monday. Take it from us, it's absolutely delicious!

Magoo's is open Mon through Fri from 4 p.m. until the last sports fan leaves and Sat and Sun until 2 a.m. During football season, the doors open earlier.

MARVIN'S
918 North Ocean Blvd.,
Myrtle Beach
(843) 448-4926

Marvin's has been around since 1975, evolving from a taco stand into a sports bar complete with pool tables. Besides a vast collection of NASCAR memorabilia that owner Marvin McHone has collected over the years, this sports bar is oceanfront, with 80 feet of windows showing off the Atlantic.

The menu is basic bar fare: fried foods and appetizers, chicken wings, pizza, nachos, burgers, dogs, and sandwiches. Marvin's operates from 10 a.m. until at least 2 a.m. seven days a week for most of the year. Hours are 11 a.m. to 1 a.m. daily in Jan and Feb.

MURPHY'S LAW SPORTS BAR
405 South Kings Hwy., Myrtle Beach
(843) 448-6021

Patrons of Murphy's Law, a tried and true sports bar, enjoy two pool tables—positioned in the middle of the tables and chairs—electronic darts, and golf, as well as 25 television sets. Murphy's sells draft beer during happy hour for $1 a glass.

The sandwiches at Murphy's are popular fare and monstrous in their proportions. The "50-yard" steak sandwich will stuff you; the "100-yard" version requires a friend to help you. Raw bar selections include oysters, clams, steamed shrimp, and crab legs. Chicken wings are a hit here, too. Try them.

Murphy's Law is open seven days a week from 11 a.m. to 2 a.m. It is closed for two weeks during the Christmas holiday season.

SHAMROCK'S SPORTS BAR & GRILL
2510 North Kings Hwy., Myrtle Beach
(843) 448-2532

Shamrock's Sports Bar & Grill has 20 beers on tap, and 20-ounce pints guarantee no one goes thirsty. Miller's Highlife comes at the very reasonable price of $6 per pitcher all the time! This club is also noted for a late-night Munchie Special. From 9 p.m. to 1 a.m. from Mon through Fri, everything on the well-loved Munchie Menu is half price. Popular choices include buffalo wings and chili skins, mouthwatering nachos, and other fried favorites. The oysters Rockefeller are some of the best on the Strand. The menu also offers soups, salads, sandwiches, and specialty plates. They have 11 big-screen TVs, satellite, and cable, so you're not likely to miss any sporting event. Shamrock's is open Mon through Wed from 4 p.m. until 2 a.m. and Thurs through Sun from noon until 2 a.m.

South Strand

SUNDOWN RESTAURANT & SPORTS PUB
810 Surfside Dr., Surfside Beach
(843) 238-1240

Sundown offers its patrons eight televisions for viewing games, three pool tables, electronic darts, pinball, and golf machines. A unique and fun feature is the coveted "Liar's Corner" of the bar, where people gather to tell tall tales. There is also a great jukebox.

A full menu is available, but appetizers and sandwiches are the usual order. A free breakfast is served every Saturday morning, whenever the cook gets to fixing the plates. You have to be there when breakfast is ready, or you're out of luck.

It's open all week, 24 hours a day. Sundown is closed on Sun from 2 to 10 a.m.

KARAOKE

We've included karaoke houses in this chapter in case you get an overwhelming urge to put to the test all of those singing lessons your mother made you take. Actually, karaoke has become serious entertainment business. The places we've included feature some tone-deaf singers who can't seem to focus on the words to the song, but you'll be amazed at the majority of everyday Joes and Janes with incredible singing talent.

Karaoke has developed a veritable cult following. Picture this: Someone gets up on stage with the microphone to belt out his or her selected tune and is met with the same audience reaction as if he or she had just blown away a panel of Broadway casting directors at a walk-on audition. The best karaoke performers pick just the right time to perform and, when finished, are met with tears, hugs, and the inimitable Hollywood-style alternate cheek kissing. Hey, it's a lot of fun—and, who knows, there may be an incredible crooner hidden in those vocal chords of yours!

OK, now it's criteria time. There are a number of local clubs and restaurants that offer karaoke at one time or another. But for our purposes, an establishment must offer this form of entertainment at least two nights per week to qualify for mention.

Myrtle Beach

BUMMZ ON THE BEACH
2002 North Ocean Blvd., Myrtle Beach
(843) 916-9111
www.bummz.com

Bummz has been riding high as the only beachfront garden cafe in Myrtle Beach for more than a couple of years. They pride themselves on atmosphere, and rightfully so. From the finely crafted Georgia pine interior to the expansive beach patio, Bummz offers an unforgettable experience for every beach night, regardless of particulars.

Bummz delivers live music on a nightly basis (seasonal) and offers a full menu with excellent specials. Check out karaoke on Wed and Sat evening from 9:30 p.m. until 1 a.m.

HARRY THE HATS
351 Lake Arrowhead Rd, Myrtle Beach
(843) 449-9019

This friendly neighborhood bar and grill is located in the Arcadian Dunes Condo Complex on Lake

Arrowhead Road in the popular Shore Drive area. A sports and beach bar, Harry's has an outdoor deck, a game room, and 20 televisions to watch your favorite game. Karaoke gets rolling at 8 p.m. every Tues, Fri, and Sat night.

UGLY MUG BAR & GRILL
1108 Third Ave. S., Myrtle Beach
(843) 448-3110
http://uglymugbarmb.com
Formerly Warren's Restaurant & Lounge, Ugly Mug Bar & Grill is about as local-yokel as it gets, with karaoke in full swing every night 9 p.m. to 2 a.m. This is a serious singing venue that show-cases a mind-boggling number of terrific singers regularly. Ugly Mug offers burgers, wings, and seafood baskets as well as steaks, ribs, and salads. There are $2 drink specials seven days a week.

i To stretch your vacation dollars, pick up a Myrtle Beach VIP card for $15. It soon pays for itself. The card will get you discounts to most clubs, as well as many restaurants and hotels. It will also garner savings for many attractions, golf courses, minigolf, shops, and transportation. Order through www.myrtlebeachvip.com.

TAKING IN A MOVIE

The Grand Strand strip is sprinkled with class-act movie houses. All are comfortable, clean, climate controlled, and heady with the smell of fresh-made popcorn. What you won't find in this area's cinemas is an assortment of foreign or fine-arts movies. Every once in a while one pops up, but not very often. This is an area where moviegoing audiences eat up blockbuster hits, thrillers, adventures, love stories, and comedies. To find out what's playing where, always consult the Friday edition of the Sun News for its "kicks!" entertainment section. You will find descriptions of current films, what theaters are showing them, box office figures, and a theater-finder map.

As we speak, Grand Strand moviegoers enjoy selection, amenities, and a range of prices. Film buffs have 43 first-run screens to choose from. Viewing times vary from one cinema to the next, so it's best to call ahead for that specific information.

North Strand

CARMIKE BRIARCLIFFE 12
Myrtle Beach Mall, 10177 North Kings Hwy., North Myrtle Beach
(843) 272-6277
www.carmike.com
The Carmike Briarcliffe is one of only two movie houses along the Grand Strand housed in a shop-ping mall. The first show of the day is just $5.50; after that, all matinees before 5:30 p.m. are $6.50 a seat every day. In the evening, adults ages 12 to 59 pay $8.50 to see a show; children ages 3 to 11 pay $6.50 all the time; and seniors 60 years or older pay $5.75 per ticket.

Myrtle Beach

BROADWAY CINEMA 16
Celebrity Circle
Broadway at the Beach, Myrtle Beach
(843) 445-1616
www.carmike.com
Another Carmike Cinema, Broadway is the larg-est cineplex of its kind in South Carolina and sits amid the hustle and bustle of a shopping and entertainment complex. Eight of the "plexes" here are auditoriums that guarantee unsurpassed viewing and sound quality. Matinee seats are sold for $6.50 per person except for the last matinee of the day, which is a bargain $5.50. Regular prices are $8.50 for adults and $6.50 for children ages 11 and younger and those 59 years of age or older.

CINEMARK AT MYRTLE BEACH
2100 Coastal Grand Circle, Myrtle Beach
(843) 839-3221
www.cinemark.com
All nine of the theaters at Cinemark feature stadium seating and digital surround sound. Matinees are considered to be any show before

6 p.m. The first matinee is only $4.50, while the others are $5.75. For regular shows adults pay $8; children under 11 and seniors pay $5.75.

GRAND 14 AT MARKET COMMON
4002 DeVille St., Myrtle Beach
(843) 282-0550

These new high-tech theaters were voted Best of the Beach in 2008. Located in Market Commons, the Grand 14 theaters offer bargains of $4.50 for the first matinee showing and $6 for matinees following. Regular pricing is $8.25 for adults, $5.75 for kids, and $5.50 for seniors. Students and members of the military pay $7.

IMAX DISCOVERY THEATER
Celebrity Square
Broadway at the Beach, Myrtle Beach
(843) 448-IMAX
www.myrtlebeachimax.com

At IMAX you not only watch a movie, you experience it. The screen is an incredible six stories tall, and a six-track digital sound system surrounds you. Located at Broadway at the Beach, the Grand Strand's IMAX thrusts its guests into the action in a way no ordinary movie can. Featuring images that fill peripheral vision and 12,000 watts of sound so intense participants swear they can feel it, IMAX movies are absolutely unmatched at the art of transporting their audience to another place and time.

Join all those gone before and discover the world's greatest theater experience. IMAX features a variety of wholesome, family-friendly movies at the top of every hour. Movies vary seasonally, so there's always something to please everyone. The IMAX Cafe offers a wonderful selection of treats to enjoy during your movie experience. And afterward, do leave time for browsing among unique gifts and educational toys in the gift shop.

Adults pay $13 for a ticket. The cost for children ages 4 to 12 is $11. Children younger than age four are admitted free of charge. Group and school rates are also offered.

South Strand

REGAL INLET SQUARE 12 CINEMAS
Inlet Square Mall, Murrells Inlet
(843) 651-5500
www.inletsquaremall.com/inlet-movieinfo
.html

At Inlet Square you can enjoy 12 screens equipped with Digital Theater Sound (DTS). Admission for adults is $8. Those 60 years of age or older and kids ages 3 to 11 can buy tickets for $6, while the military and students pay $7. All matinees before 6 p.m. are $6 a seat. Combo specials usually apply here, giving a price break on popcorn, drinks, and candy.

CIGAR-FRIENDLY HAUNTS

No amount of official health warnings or nose-holding whining has put a dent in the demand for good cigars. As managing editor of *Cigar Aficionado,* Gordon Mott, said, "A cigar helps create an environment where sociability and relaxation are promoted."

Thousands of golfing enthusiasts who come to play on Grand Strand courses every year feel not fully equipped for the day without stuffing a few fine cigars in with their clubs. As a matter of fact, there's now a cigar on the market called "The 18 Hole Special" that is big enough to last a full round of golf.

It's only fitting that the Grand Strand should have a cigar-friendly atmosphere; this area has always been home to tobacco farming. Whether you want to enjoy a puff after dinner or while sipping on a good single-malt scotch, the following establishments (many of which you can read more about in the Restaurants chapter) invite you to light up to your heart's content.

i Even if the romantic sunrises over the ocean make you impetuous enough to want to tie the knot while you're on vacation, Horry County maintains a 24-hour waiting period before a marriage license will be issued. The county courthouse in Conway takes applications; no blood test is required.

North Strand

DICK'S LAST RESORT

Barefoot Landing, 4700 US 17 S.,
North Myrtle Beach
(843) 272-7794
www.dickslastresort.com

Dick's encourages cigar puffing, albeit preferably in the bar area. In true Dick's style, a spokesperson declared, "There's something wrong with a person who can't enjoy the smell of a good cigar."

Myrtle Beach

BLARNEY STONE'S PUB & CIGAR BAR

Celebrity Square,
Broadway at the Beach, Myrtle Beach
(843) 626-6644
www.fantasticclubs.com

This is Myrtle Beach's only authentic Irish pub. As such, the joint focuses on pint beer and ales from the British Isles. On the mezzanine level, an upscale cigar and martini bar features more than 50 varieties of martinis, nearly three dozen wines and champagnes, and almost as many cigar selections. In season Blarney Stone features nightly entertainment from Thursday through Saturday. As it should be, St. Patrick's Day is celebrated on the 17th of each month. Happy hour runs from 4 until 7 p.m. On weeknights Blarney Stone's is open from 4 p.m. until 1 a.m. On weekend evenings, hours are 4 p.m. until 2 a.m.

COLLECTORS CAFE AND GALLERY

7726 North Kings Hwy.,
Myrtle Beach
(843) 449-9370
www.collectorscafeandgallery.com

Collectors Cafe normally carries more upscale brands, including Davidoff. At Collectors you can savor a cigar in the bar and lounge areas, where they also shake or stir a list of martinis—even chocolate flavored. The art on display is an added benefit.

LIBERTY STEAKHOUSE AND BREWERY

Broadway at the Beach
1321 Celebrity Circle, Myrtle Beach
(843) 626-4677
www.libertysteakhouseandbrewery.com

This establishment has been cigar-friendly since it opened in Nov 1995. Liberty brews its own beer, and a manager there claims that people who tend to drink more flavorful beverages are more likely to enjoy a cigar with drinks.

NEW YORK PRIME

405 28th Ave. N., Myrtle Beach
(843) 448-8081
http://centraarchy.com/newyorkprime.php

New York Prime is as known for its cigar selection as it is for its prime meats and fine wines. The restaurant has the air of a private club, and the staff members are schooled at helping you select just the right stogie from their offerings.

ROSSI'S ITALIAN RESTAURANT

9636 North Kings Hwy.,
Myrtle Beach
(843) 449-0481

Puff away in the lounge and piano bar sections of Rossi's, where cigars start at $4 and range up to a $17 Porlorranaga and $25 Cohiba. Rossi's pours vintage port wines and four single-malt scotches.

THOROUGHBREDS

9706 North Kings Hwy., Myrtle Beach
(843) 497-2636
www.thoroughbredsrestaurant.com

Thoroughbreds Restaurant allows patrons to light up in the outdoor courtyard or in the bar after 11 p.m. It is known for mixing a mean martini and also stocks a good selection of fine cognacs.

South Strand

FRANK'S RESTAURANT & BAR

10435 Ocean Hwy., Pawleys Island
(843) 237-3030
www.franksandoutback.com

Frank's tries to keep about 10 fine cigars on hand for patrons at all times, which can be smoked in the bar or outdoor dining area. A cigar at Frank's will run you $5 to $35.

ADULT ENTERTAINMENT

The Grand Strand region has its fair share of adult entertainment establishments, even though area authorities and courts seem to be constantly debating club locations and what constitutes the appropriate amount of nakedness displayed therein. One court battle determined that bare butts must stay outside of 6 inches from a patron's face to be within the law. However, no details were given as to how this would be enforced or whether or not it posed a health risk.

We won't list the clubs here, because all you have to do is consult the yellow pages or ask almost anyone—after a wink and a nod, you'll be set in the right direction. Besides, isn't half the fun just getting there? Sort of like a fleshy version of a treasure hunt? There is even one club that showcases only male dancers who strut their stuff in cages . . . things that make you go "hmmmm."

SHOPPING

From the warehouse-size to the quaint and oh-so-small, from grab-bag dollar stores to exclusive designer clothiers, the Grand Strand is a resort destination for bargain hunters as well as quality seekers. It is true that many people come here for no other reason than the shopping—seemingly oblivious to sunshine, theaters, golf courses, and the beach.

Belk, JCPenney, Sears, and Dillard's department stores all have multiple locations here. Almost every major clothing, department, and dry-goods store has an outlet here. You'll find some of the largest booth-rental flea markets in the South. Antiques stores appear in every section of the beach. And some of the very best shopping opportunities can be found in the small, privately owned stores and shops.

It goes without saying that this chapter can't even begin to detail every shop, every store, or even every shopping center that is part of this 60-mile-long shopping spree. Even locals are overwhelmed by the variety; thus, we tend to migrate to the geographic part of the Strand where we live.

If you are a seasoned shopper, born to shop, then you already know as many secrets as we do for finding the best stores; at best, we can make a road map for you and highlight some of the more interesting concentrations of shops. Keep your eyes open; 'round every curve in the crowded highway there's yet another clutch of shops to browse and burrow through.

As for the basics, we've already mentioned Belk department store, which can be found at any one of three area malls. Other notable department stores with a presence on the Strand include JCPenney, Sears, and Dillard's. Several discount "chain" stores pepper the Strand, including Wal-Mart, Kmart, and Target.

The larger supermarket chains include Food Lion, BI-LO, Kroger, and Winn-Dixie; most are open 24 hours a day (except Sunday nights). The local favorite is the Piggly Wiggly, a chain that has been in the area for more than 60 years. The food selection is about the same, but it's hard to pass up a chance to buy Mr. Pig T-shirts.

It's impossible to take an overview of shopping without mentioning the plethora of T-shirt and souvenir stores along the Grand Strand. Stores such as Eagles, Pacific, and Wings sparkle with bright lights and seemingly every-other-block locations. They specialize in swimsuits, suntan products, sunshades, beach chairs, rafts, umbrellas, souvenir items, beach toys, T-shirts, and summer sportswear of the most casual sort. And believe it or not, in many of these stores you can actually negotiate with the sales staff for the very best prices.

Although seasonal hours are frequently abbreviated, many places are open seven days a week.

MAJOR MALLS AND OUTLETS

North Strand

BAREFOOT LANDING
US 17 N., North Myrtle Beach
(843) 272-8349
www.bflanding.com

Barefoot Landing bills itself as "the East Coast's most exciting waterfront shopping, dining and entertainment destination center." While the truth of such marketing hype is disputed by other shopping areas, the fact is that Barefoot Landing plays host to an estimated seven million visitors every year. Its restaurants, shops, and attractions have been featured in magazines, newspapers, and television clips throughout the nation. *Southern Living, the Wall Street Journal, USA Today, Barron's Investment, Forbes,* and *Country America* are just a few of the biggest media names that have come to know and love Barefoot Landing.

Built around a 27-acre freshwater lake, fronted by US 17 North, and bordered in back by the Intracoastal Waterway, Barefoot has more than 1,800 feet of floating dock on the waterway as well as miles of rocking-chair-peppered boardwalks and bridges. This development, a rare marriage between commerce and preservation, prides itself on environmental sensitivity. While strolling among the more than 100 specialty and factory-direct shops, 13 waterfront restaurants, and an array of attractions, you can enjoy sea gulls swooping over the lakes, alligators swimming stealthily, and all manner of waterbirds, including swans, geese, blue herons, snowy egrets, ducks, and pelicans; you can even feed the fish (fish-food-filled gum-ball machines abound) from many of the boardwalks.

Barefoot Landing's eclectic villages of shops and restaurants are housed in quaint, cedar-shake buildings with bright green awnings. Specialty stores feature resort wear, jewelry, designer fashions, Western wear and accessories, handmade gifts, and unusual collectibles.

The Boardwalk Shops, Lakeview Courtyard, and Waterway Village are separated by floating bridges and are accessible by walkways that are well worth a stroll even if you don't buy a thing. But don't think there will be no temptation—stores like Anything Joe's, Conley's House of Magic, Earthbound Trading Company, Klig's Kites, Peace Frogs, and Black Market Mineral will mesmerize you with choices of baubles and toys to take home. H2O Plus is your skin-care fitness center. Barefoot General Store, Surf & Sand Beach Shoppe, Pineapple Cove, and the Sunglass Hut make for a lot of bags to carry home. You could even redo your wardrobe at Chico's, the Izod Factory Store, and Birkenstock. There are a dozen factory outlet stores that sell fine apparel and designer merchandise at 20- to 50-percent savings. With this irresistible combination of atmosphere and savings, you could redecorate your life.

This breezy complex is also the home of Alligator Adventure (see the Attractions and Kidstuff chapters), the Alabama Theatre (see the Entertainment chapter), and the House of Blues (see the Restaurants and Entertainment chapters). Throughout the year, Barefoot Landing also hosts such events as car shows and chili and rib cook-offs for charities. Barefoot Landing is also just across the river from the spectacular Barefoot Resort & Golf, which features a yacht club, country club, four golf courses, as well as condominiums and private residences. (See the Golf and Real Estate chapters for more details.)

i It's Christmas year-round in quite a few shops in the area. Fantastic decorations are always available at such stores as Christmas Mouse at Barefoot Landing, Christmas Elegance Village in Myrtle Beach, and St. Nick Nack's in Calabash, North Carolina.

MYRTLE BEACH MALL
10177 North Kings Hwy.,
North Myrtle Beach
(843) 272-4040
www.shopmyrtlebeachmall.com

Formerly the Colonial Mall, Myrtle Beach Mall is a one-level facility. Since opening in 1986, the mall has undergone a major renovation. Now anchored by Belk, JCPenney, and Bass Pro Shops, the Myrtle Beach Mall is also home to stores such as Bath & Body Works, Foot Locker, and American Eagle.

Restaurants at the mall include Islamorada Fish Company as well as Ruby Tuesday. The food court includes Chick-fil-A, Sakura Japanese, and Aunt Annie's Pretzels.

Myrtle Beach

BROADWAY AT THE BEACH

1325 Celebrity Circle at
21st Ave. N., Myrtle Beach
(843) 444-3200
www.broadwayatthebeach.com

Broadway at the Beach is the centerpiece of the Burroughs & Chapin Company's plan for the future of Myrtle Beach. The complex already features more than 100 shops; a live-entertainment theater; a multiscreen IMAX theater; dozens of restaurants, including the Hard Rock Cafe; and a nightclub street named Celebrity Square that features well-known musical acts and signed handprints in cement from more than 30 celebrities, such as Donna Summers, Johnny Mathis, Barry Manilow, and Wayne Newton.

Trying to provide an entertainment venue, a restaurant district, a complex of high-energy nightclubs, and a quaint shopping village (complete with the Disney technique of three-quarter-scale building) seemingly would be an unobtainable mixture of tasks, but Burroughs & Chapin is pulling it off well. And despite the initial failure and closure of 30 or more stores, the crowds keep coming—and new merchants keep opening.

In 2007, Burroughs & Chapin closed down the much beloved Pavilion Amusement Park (some believe to drive more people to Broadway) and relocated some of the favorite attractions to Broadway at the Beach. The Pavilion Nostalgia Park at the corner of 21st Avenue and US 17 Bypass includes most of the longtime favorites, such as the Herschell-Spillman carousel, the tea-cup ride, and the German Baden band organ, built in 1900.

Do more people visit Broadway at the Beach for the shopping and the restaurants, or is it the huge attractions like Ripley's Aquarium (see the Attractions chapter) and activities like the Fourth of July and Halloween parties that the management throws? Fortunately, no one has to choose, and there is enough to draw everyone, from the right jeans at Gap to collectibles from Sports Heroes. The shopping is divided into five districts: Caribbean Village, Charleston Boardwalk, New England Village East, New England Village West, and Heroes Harbor. With a range of stores from Kute Kids to Fresh Produce and Victoria's Secret to Lids, Broadway is a specialty store extravaganza, so be sure to bring your birthday and Christmas present list along.

In addition to the shopping, Broadway at the Beach has a fine selection of restaurants that, in addition to the popular seafood theme, also have specialty themes such as Harley-Davidson motorcycles, sports and rock stars, movie memorabilia, and race cars. These restaurants also have some of the most popular gift shops around. (Check out the Restaurants chapter for details on the food.)

COASTAL GRAND

2000 Coastal Grand Circle, Myrtle Beach
(843) 839-9100
www.coastalgrand.com

The Coastal Grand Mall, just off the US 17 Bypass near US 501, is the largest mall on the Grand Strand. With almost 1 million square feet of retail space, Coastal Grand is home to 130 stores and counting. The anchor stores are Belk, Dillard's, Sears, Dick's Sporting Goods, and Bed Bath & Beyond, but notables such as Victoria's Secret, Rack Room Shoes, and Cache are also there. A host of professional services make their home there, including LensCrafters, Pearl Vision, Visionworks, and MasterCuts.

The mall's food court includes Charley's Steakery, Chick-fil-A, China Express, and Tokyo Japan, but there are also full-service restaurants in the area around the mall. The amusement section of Coastal Grand houses the Cinemark Theaters.

ℹ️ The Myrtle Beach Convention Center is host to a few shopping extravaganzas throughout the year. The Grand Strand Boat Show has been held annually since 1984 and showcases just about anything to do with water sports. Of course, the perennial Gun and Knife Show makes the circuit. Contact the convention center at (843) 918-1225 to find out what events are going on while you're in town.

MARKET COMMON

Howard Parkway,
Myrtle Beach
(843) 839-3900
www.marketcommonmb.com

Built as part of the redevelopment of the old Myrtle Beach Air Force Base, Market Common has quickly caught on as a great place to shop and dine. The 114-acre site features shopping, dining, and entertainment as well as office and residential space. Shops range from the quirky Dixie Divas, Big Tuna, and Lazy Gator to the more refined William-Sonoma, Brooks Brothers Country Club, and Ann Taylor. Food options include Gordon Biersch Brewery, King Street Grille, P. F. Chang's China Bistro, Jugo Juice, and Cold Stone Creamery.

TANGER OUTLETS

4635 Factory Stores Blvd.,
Myrtle Beach
(843) 236-5100
www.tangeroutlet.com

Myrtle Beach's famous Factory Stores outlet on US 501 was bought out by Tanger Outlets in 2003, and it's easy to see why these stores helped launch Myrtle Beach as a shopping destination. One visit will give you a vivid understanding of exactly why "shopping" comes in a strong second—just behind "beaches"—when folks explain why they choose the Myrtle Beach area for their vacations. Best of all, every purchase will net you a savings of 20 to 70 percent off original retail prices!

With nearly half a million square feet, this outlet center is among the top 20 largest outlet projects in the country. This pleasantly designed "village" of shops now boasts more than 123 brand-name outlets. The names are well known: J. Crew, Liz Claiborne, Perry Ellis, Cole Haan, Casual Corner, Brooks Brothers, Nike, Polo/Ralph Lauren, and more.

TANGER OUTLETS

US 17 intersection with Veterans Highway,
10785 Kings Rd., Myrtle Beach
(866) 838-9830, (843) 449-0491
www.tangeroutlet.com

A sister to the Tanger Outlets on US 501, this Tanger offers 114 brand-name stores in a 43-acre complex where US 17 meets Veterans Highway. Specialty stores include Fossil, Coach, Anne Klein, Old Navy, and Kenneth Cole. Visitors enjoy a pedestrian-friendly design that features landscaped courtyards and a diverse food court.

Tanger Outlet Center is a joint venture between Tanger Properties Limited Partnership and Rosen-Warren Myrtle Beach LLC. Rosen Associates Development Inc. has developed retail properties throughout the country and is active in multifamily developments.

Tanger Factory Outlet Centers Inc., based in Greensboro, North Carolina, essentially founded the concept of factory outlet shopping centers nearly three decades ago. Today the company owns 32 outlet parks in 21 states—representing more than 1,100 brand-name outlet stores.

South Strand

THE HAMMOCK SHOPS

US 17, Pawleys Island
(843) 237-8448
www.thehammockshops.com

Once you've been to the Hammock Shops, you'll understand what many of the other outdoor shopping complexes on the Strand are attempting to imitate. Just to see it is an experience; we even considered including it in the Attractions chapter, but its function as a shopping destination cements its place here.

In 1889 John Joshua Ward, a young riverboat captain who shipped supplies up and down the

Waccamaw River from Pawleys Island to Georgetown and Charleston, created the first Pawleys Island hammock. In an attempt to find relief from the scratchy straw mattresses then used on river barges, he first tried working with canvas, then knotted string; but both were as uncomfortable as the straw. What finally evolved was a hammock of soft cotton rope—woven, rather than knotted, and held open by use of a curved "spreader bar." The new design allowed air to circulate, making the hammock far cooler and more comfortable than the scratchy straw beds. And the spreader bar lent a gentle curve, keeping the soft weave from collapsing inward.

This concept behind the famous Pawleys Island hammock spawned a design faithfully retained for more than 100 years. Ward taught the intricacies of the pattern to his brother-in-law, A. H. "Cap't Doc" Lachicotte, and soon the Lachicottes and Wards were busy making hammocks for family members and friends. In the late 1930s "Doc" set up a small shop on US 17 to sell the hammocks to travelers, and that modest business became the nucleus around which today's famed Hammock Shops at Pawleys Island sprang up. The Lachicottes remain one of the most prominent families on the South Strand and head a real-estate conglomerate on Pawleys Island.

Quaint might be an overused adjective, but it is truly appropriate when applied to the Hammock Shops. This clutch of retail establishments is the kind of place you can return to again and again, finding something new and unique each time. Two dozen shops, many offering the work of Carolina artists and craftspeople, are now clustered beneath moss-draped trees on the edge of a beautiful salt marsh. Some occupy historic Lowcountry buildings that include an original post office and schoolhouse. The newer shops are careful not to compromise the mood of the original architecture; they feature old beams, used timber, and ballast brick. Clearly this complex is a welcome respite from the razzle and dazzle of Myrtle Beach.

But this little complex features much more than beautiful nature scenes and great ham-

mocks. You will also find gourmet foods at the Carolina Gourmet, wildlife prints at the Audubon Shopping Gallery, handcrafted jewelry and contemporary clothing at Three Feathers Gallery, toys and gifts for the child in all of us at Hollipops, and a host of other distinctive and unusual items. If you want a genuine taste of local color without the neon, glitter, and paved parking lots with numbered rows, then you must visit the Hammock Shops. Springtime visits offer the extraordinary beauty of blooming azaleas, dogwoods, and tulip trees. Around Christmas the trees sparkle with tiny white lights, and all the stores don holiday finery, making the holiday season a particularly enjoyable time to visit.

INLET SQUARE MALL
10125 US 17 Bypass,
Murrells Inlet
(843) 651-6990
www.inletsquaremall.com
Anchored by Belk, Kmart, Stein Mart, and JCPenney, Inlet Square offers most of what you'd expect from a typical midsize mall: apparel shops, a bookstore, electronics, jewelry, shoes, a cinema, and more. The Body Shop is a familiar name appreciated by tourists and locals.

The food court at Inlet Square offers Chick-fil-A, a fast-food staple of almost every mall in America. Corrado's Pizza and the Flaming Wok are also there.

Whether it's free Saturday-morning movies for kids at the theaters, the most elaborate Christmas centerpiece on the Strand, or live elephants and a real circus, promotions at Inlet Square Mall provide vacationers special diversions that they likely couldn't find at malls back home.

DISTINCTIVE SHOPPING STOPS

North Strand

The Town of Calabash

Calabash is one of those sleepy little towns that is beginning to awake to the alarm of Myrtle Beach's growth. Even though it's in North Carolina, Calabash can't escape progress; it's only 15 minutes across the border from North Myrtle Beach. A series of small shops has sprung up, creating an atmosphere akin to Barefoot Landing or the Hammock Shops (see previous entries), featuring antiques, flowers, fashions, and curiosities. This is also where all the Calabash-style restaurants you see in North Myrtle Beach and Myrtle Beach get their cue from, so you might want to stay and try out the originals, such as the Docksider, Ella's, and Captain Nance's. Most of the restaurants are waterfront with scenic views.

CALLAHAN'S OF CALABASH–NAUTICAL GIFTS
9973 Beach Dr., Calabash, NC
(910) 579-2611
www.callahansgifts.com

Aside from the seashell roadside stands that clustered around the restaurants of Calabash, the nautical gift shop was one of the first stores in the area, and it has been growing every year for the past 30 years. The long arm of this L-shaped store has a fudge counter, a clothing section, weather vanes, and a whole selection of items from a $1 harmonica to $3,500 brass and leather telescopes.

St. Nick Nack's completes the other arm of the L, and it probably has the most, if not the best, selection of Christmas decorations around. The displays of St. Nick Nack's are breathtaking. Glass ornaments from teeny to colossal surround you, oversized reindeer vault down from the ceiling, thick garlands trim everything, and Christmas trees are tucked in every corner. There is also a Halloween and an Easter room.

The Pea Landing Mercantile Country, Home, and Garden section was added, with a plethora of nature-inspired selections from frogs to wind chimes. During the summer, Callahan's is open 9 a.m. to 10 p.m. In the winter months they close at 9 p.m. Sun through Thurs.

VICTORIA'S RAGPATCH ROW
10164 Beach Dr., Calabash, NC
(910) 579-2015

Nestled against a backdrop of live oaks, this row of shops gets its name from Victoria's Ragpatch, a fashion standby for many locals. Victoria's is heavily stocked with everything from casual wear and evening gowns to perfumes. The whole store drips with style and creative displays. The Mole Hole is next door, one of five in this successful chain that is the epitome of a gift store; you will be delighted at every turn.

Just across the way is one of the cutest post offices we've ever seen; the little cottage has scalloped trim and an old-fashioned life-preserver ring for a sign. Across the pathway from the post office is the Art Plus Gallery, featuring quite a few pieces of pottery among all the paintings and prints.

The Town of Little River

Little River looks like the rest of Myrtle Beach as you drive through on US 17. However, its distinction lies in its waterfront: Little River has a working coastline. Instead of children building sand castles, when you see the ocean from Little River, you will find shrimp boats pulling up to dock, happy fishermen back from the Gulf Stream, and well-fed pelicans roosting on the piers. Instead of lifeguards, the fresh seafood restaurants (with inlet views) await you. The waterfront of Little River is canopied by resplendent live oak and Spanish moss, creating a setting that looks as good as the local hush puppies taste. To find the waterfront, and the heart of Little River, turn at Mineola Avenue from US 17.

TOBY'S WORLD GIFTS
1530 US 17, Little River
(843) 249-2174
www.tobysworldgifts.com

Toby's World Gifts is a special store where Southern hospitality and old-world charm collide in positive fashion to deliver a unique shopping experience. Located on US 17 in Little River, this historic circa-1912, two-level building is filled to the brim with gift items, collectibles, home accents, gourmet food, and more. While listening to the genuine old player piano, you can browse through the store and enjoy both the unique inventory and the unusual antiques that are used to display it. The building's historic atmosphere is captivating.

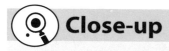
Want to Cook like a Southerner—Instantly?

Biscuits, grits, and pork rinds: the foods that come to mind when someone mentions Southern cooking. And once you've been to Myrtle Beach, Calabash moves up to the top of that list. But there are some other dishes to be explored, delicious items that most visitors haven't heard of or that restaurants won't serve because they're tired of explaining, for example, what a Lowcountry boil is.

Fortunately, quite a few gourmet shops exist along the Grand Strand, and they all rightfully place an emphasis on the down-home, wholesome flavors that abound in this region. Better still, the stores carry instant mixes so you can carry these home to relish your vacation memories for the rest of the year and maybe even share the tidbits with friends.

The **Barefoot General Store,** at Barefoot Landing, of course, emphasizes the good old days with a penny candy counter, a roasted-nut corner, and a soda counter dispensing glass-bottled 6.5 ounce Coca-Colas. Amid all the merchandise, vintage bottles and tins, speckled enamelware, and antique hand tools, the Barefoot General Store also has a few aisles of savory concoctions to take home. The Carolina Kitchen line is there, featuring a luscious Creamy Vidalia Dressing. The Bubba's brand, which you'll see all over, is a whole line of marinades, salsas, and seafood seasonings out of Charleston.

The peanut, also known as the goober pea, is one of the most revered foods of the South and manifests here in many forms, from boiled to buttered. Around the turn of the 20th century, the South's cotton crop was nearly destroyed by the boll weevil. This is when the legendary George Washington Carver saved the day by convincing farmers to plant the legume for its many uses. Today boiled peanuts can be found at every roadside stand, and a few lucky cities have the **Peanut Shop.**

Also in Barefoot Landing, the Peanut Shop successfully re-creates the old-time mercantile. The shop carries its own line of nuts and soup mixes, and it showcases some of the finest delicacies around, all smartly packaged for you to take home. The *New Southern Cookbook* was spotted on their shelves, right along with jars of Carolina Swamp Stuff. These jars are accented with twine and hand-scrawled labels that recollect roadside stands hidden deep in the swamps of this state, where few people make their way. Pine Tar is a spicy salad dressing and marinade; Seaweed Splash is a tasty pesto dressing. A Fiery Sweet Peach Salsa, labeled with the claim that it "tastes like a hot Southern night," is available. Try out the mix for Vidalia Onion Cheese Biscuits, or a few of the blends from Gullah Gourmet: Grandputter's Fried Oysters, Lobster Pasta with Slap Yaself Silly Cream Sauce, Hush Dem Puppies. Mixes like these are even more irresistible because of the packaging; along with the amusing descriptions, the mixes come in cotton bags with vintage illustrations and usually a tie of ribbon or twine. A similar brand, Southern Ease (the name says it all), entices you with shrimp and grits and she-crab soup.

While in the south end, stop by the **Carolina Gourmet** at the Hammock Shops. Carolina Gourmet also carries its own line of canned goods, ranging from peach preserves (from Carolina peaches, of course) and Vidalia Onion Summer Tomato Dressing to muscadine and scuppernong preserves. Benne wafers, which abound in nearly every gourmet shop from here to Savannah, are plentiful. Benne seeds are also known as sesame seeds, but this particular recipe hails from a slave tradition of carrying benne seeds for good luck. The crispy and rich wafers come in a range of flavors from cheese to sweet. Carolina Gourmet's specialty is gift baskets, which they pack with expertise and ship anywhere.

North Myrtle Beach

BOULINEAU'S
212 Sea Mountain Hwy.,
Cherry Grove
(843) 249-3556
www.boulineaus.com

It's pretty much one-stop shopping at Boulineau's. This locally owned store, or stores we should say, has been in operation for over a half a century. Look for the lighthouse and you'll see what we mean. The two-story building has a complete grocery store on the lower level, complete with breads baked fresh daily and an ice-cream store with 24 flavors of hand-dipped ice cream. Upstairs is a department store with all your beach needs as well as apparel and gifts. Next door? A complete hardware store. Like we said—it's one-stop shopping.

MAIN STREET
Ocean Drive section, North Myrtle Beach

Shag clubs and ice-cream shops sum up this small-town-style Main Street. Ocean Drive is quintessential North Myrtle Beach and sets the mold for a summertime, seaside community. The mom-and-pop shops here make for great window shopping and browsing; they also serve to break up the shag clubs that line Main Street. Windows are filled with shag record albums, bathing suits, hand-painted rocking chairs, and historic O.D. (as Ocean Drive is referred to by the locals) memorabilia. If you claim to be a Myrtle Beach fan, you don't want to miss the place where it all started.

Myrtle Beach

CHRISTMAS ELEGANCE
4301 North Kings Hwy., Myrtle Beach
(843) 626-3100

Christmas decorations in the middle of July? No, really. The complex features seven stores in a natural setting. This wonderland has a seemingly endless variety of holiday decorations in addition to items such as music boxes, collector-quality dolls, electric trains—even a cutlery shop. Other stores carry yard ornaments, fine handmade jewelry, candles, and cards. While most of the shops carry lots of Christmas merchandise, you'll find gifts for all occasions.

THE GALLERIA
9600 US 17 and Lake Arrowhead Road,
Myrtle Beach
(843) 449-7576

If you're looking for convenience, the Galleria is a place to keep in mind. Its location in central and visible Restaurant Row makes it easy to find, and the stores there thrive by providing you with the essentials—as well as the conveniences—you might need on your vacation. The Kroger grocery store dominates the highway front and offers everything from produce and a full pharmacy to beach chairs. From Kroger a long line of storefronts ensue: Smoothie King, Athina's ice cream, Honey Baked Hams, and Fudge Nut. You can also drop off your dry cleaning at Sunny Cleaners, get your hair done at McQuaigs, send a fax from Mail Boxes Etc., and pick up breakfast at Manhattan Bagels.

GAY DOLPHIN
916 North Ocean Blvd. at Ninth Avenue N.,
Myrtle Beach
(843) 448-6550
www.gaydolphin.com

No chapter on Grand Strand shopping worth its salt could overlook Gay Dolphin, a world-famous shopping attraction and Myrtle Beach institution for more than five decades. Even if you're not interested in shopping, you'll be wowed by an inventory of more than 60,000 items, ranging from postcards to collectibles. You've got to see this place to believe it.

This gift shop actually has "coves," small shops within the larger store, extending from the Boulevard to the oceanfront. Collector's Cove features Hummel figurines, clowns, gnomes, bells, and more. More than 50 other coves include merchandise such as stuffed animals, souvenirs, golf memorabilia, shark's teeth, nautical items, toys, swimwear, ceramics, and shells.

In operation since 1952, it used to call itself the World's Largest Gift Shop, but it still reigns as the largest on the Grand Strand. Not much has changed in the last few decades, but the shark's-tooth cove alone is worth a visit.

HIDDEN VILLAGE SHOPS
9902 US 17 N., Myrtle Beach
On the east side of US 17, look for this interesting strip of specialty stores. There has been a great deal of changeover in recent years, but the new shops are just as fascinating. Relax a bit at Live Oak Yoga or peruse the new or previously owned musical selections at Sounds Better. Humans and canines alike can get groomed here. The upscale Salon Joey's is for the two-legged; next door you'll find Woofies for the four-legged. If you are looking for specialty jewelry, need a watch repaired, or need to have something appraised, try Trost Jewelers.

KINGS HIGHWAY
Kings Highway at 79th Ave. N., Myrtle Beach
Two impressive shopping centers face each other across Kings Highway (also called US 17), forming a busy intersection. On the inland side is Northwood, where an extensive Stein Mart offers clothes for everyone. A Food Lion grocery store, a GNC (in case you need some protein powder), and the soothing Michael & Company Hair Salon & Spa also occupy Northwood, as does the Atlanta Bread Company, serving a medley of sandwiches on their own fresh-baked breads. A Bank of America and Blockbuster form the out-parcels. Across Kings Highway, at the Professional Plaza, the Jolly

i Jammin' Leather, (843) 903-3936, www.jamminleather.com, has set up shop on US 501, just off Carolina Bays Parkway. If you are vrooming in on your Harley (or just wish you were), stop and check out the merchandise and all the other customers' impressive rides. If you're on the south end of Myrtle Beach, stop at Myrtle Beach Harley Davidson, right on US 17 as you get to Surfside, or call them at (843) 651-5555.

Roger is a time-tested Myrtle Beach favorite and features fine home furnishings. The Wacky Rabbit is a whimsical gift shop featuring bunnies and samples of chocolate fudge. Back at 79th Avenue, a produce stand sets up during the summertime under a big umbrella, offering some of the best local watermelon around.

A few worthwhile shops radiate south on US 17 from these two centers.

One block down at 75th Avenue North, on the same side of US 17, is Joan Crosby's. This women's-wear store has been a Myrtle Beach institution since 1952 and is a particularly nice find for older women seeking traditional clothing styles in sizes that leave Kate Moss out in the cold. Again on your left, 2 blocks south at 73rd Avenue North, is Country Vogue. This elegant shop features scads of popular, high-quality apparel from Lanz, Liz Sport, Liz Claiborne, and J. H. Collectibles. Styles lean toward classic more than trendy, and Country Vogue has a good selection of petite sizes, too. The clothing here is top-quality—the kind of stuff you wear around your country club buddies who recognize designer names.

RAINBOW HARBOR
Kings Highway at 49th Ave. N., Myrtle Beach
(843) 449-7476
This group of retail options is clearly designed for people who cherish the finer things in life.

The Foxy Lady has its largest store on the Beach here. Foxy Lady has been an institution on the Grand Strand since 1972. Paula Benik founded the upscale fashion boutique, which has come a long way since she opened it in the apartment she shared with her husband. Now, her daughter Hailey handles day-to-day operations. From shoes to gowns, Foxy Lady is the place to go if you have to dress to go.

In 1996, the Melting Pot joined Rainbow Harbor as the only fondue restaurant along the Grand Strand. Dining tables are furnished with their own hot plates to keep oil, broth, cheese, or chocolate bubbling as you cook your food on skewers. Other specialty shops include Studio Gifts, Burjac's Big & Tall, and The Men's Store.

South Strand

ANTIQUING IN MURRELLS INLET

US 17 Business and Bypass,
Murrells Inlet

With a deep history, Murrells Inlet is a great find for antiques collectors. Both US 17 Business and Bypass here are peppered with a number of antiques shops. This strip of the Grand Strand is less developed and more relaxed in atmosphere, brimming with history and full of Lowcountry color. The drive itself is pleasant and pretty. Begin at Wachesaw Row Antique Mall, just south of Inlet Square Mall on US 17 Business, where you can pick up a brochure that will list all the antiques shops. Also in Murrells Inlet is Legacy Antique Mall, where you'll find estate jewelry, silver, and paintings.

HARRINGTON ALTMAN LTD.

10729 Ocean Hwy., Pawleys Island
(843) 237-2056
www.harringtonaltman.com

Just north of the Island Shops is Harrington Altman Ltd., an extraordinary gift and interior design shop on the west side of the highway (look for the big digital clock). The inventory here leans toward elegant—with more than a touch of "cozy" tossed in for spice. This shop features a rotating selection of tastefully striking furniture: coffee tables, sideboards, china cabinets, bookshelves, and dining tables. Many items are hand-painted and one of a kind. It also stocks a medley of what your mom might call "knickknacks" or "whatnots"—lovely collectible pieces of tabletop decor that could add a touch of whimsy or an element of class to an existing display. Harrington Altman showcases some art, flower arrangements, fancy pillows, lots of handmade heirlooms, and an impressive collection of upholstery fabrics.

THE ISLAND SHOPS

US 17, Pawleys Island

Just south and across the highway from the Hammock Shops are the Island Shops. Nestled beneath gnarled, weathered oaks, these shops are filled with one-of-a-kind finds. A ribbon of wooden walkways and bridges amid a series of small ponds unites the different shops and boutiques. Be sure to pause and enjoy the antics of the friendly population of ducks. Happily splashing in and out of their Lowcountry "swimming hole," they graciously accept tasty tidbits from shoppers. And if the web-footed friends can't calm your shopping frenzy, cozy benches, oversize rockers, and well-placed hammocks surely will do the trick.

If you're curious about what you'll find, here's a few of the shopping selections: Locals "in-the-know" travel from miles around to visit the Cricket Shop. Featuring fine swimwear from leading designers, this fun shop also boasts sportswear and dresses.

Seaside Cottage is an infinitely intriguing little gift shop that's become a Pawleys Island landmark. There's no telling what delightful trinket you might discover. Your child will be the best dressed on the beach with the creative clothing designs for kids found at Lollypop Junction. Lollypop also carries distinctive items for infants, as well as furniture.

VILLAGE SHOPS

10744 Ocean Hwy., Pawleys Island

The cluster of shops is just south of the Hammock Shops and is easy to spot because of its porches. It's not very big but the cross section of stores is huge. Scrapbookers and even those who are just curious will enjoy peeking in at Silver Lining Scrapbooks. Looking for a swimsuit or resort wear? Try the broad range of suits at Dawn's Swim Wear. Havana Cabana carries one of the largest selections of cigars and fine tobacco products on the beach. You can even smoke one out on the deck next door at the Island Bar and Grill. The Island has a huge deck to sit back and relax and recover from your shopping.

> **i** If you start having sympathy for some toothless shark after seeing so many fossilized teeth for sale—don't. Sharks have anywhere from five to fifteen backup rows of teeth. A tiger shark alone can produce 24,000 teeth in a 10-year period.

BOOKSTORES

North Strand

BOOKENDS
753 Main St., N. Myrtle Beach
(843) 280-2444
www.bookendsonline.com
Locally owned, this is a great place to pick up something to read on the beach. Bookends sells used books, audio books, and a selection of reading glasses should you need them.

Myrtle Beach

BARNES & NOBLE
743 Hemlock Ave., Myrtle Beach
(843) 839-3435
3639 Pampas Dr., Myrtle Beach
(843) 238-8076
www.bn.com
One of America's oldest bookstores, Barnes & Noble's large freestanding building on Seaboard Street can be seen from the US 17 Bypass, just south of Broadway at the Beach. A second location, on the old Myrtle Beach Air Force Base, is not big, but it's equally functional. The stores are more than complete sources of reading materials, including a tremendous selection of newspapers and magazines, as well as software and a Starbucks Cafe. Barnes & Noble also offers the occasional book signing by current authors, so be sure to stop by and pick up their flyer to fill in your idle or rainy-day time.

BOOKS-A-MILLION
800 Coastal Grand Circle, Myrtle Beach
(843) 448-9184
10177 North Kings Hwy., Myrtle Beach
(843) 361-1674
10125 US 17 Bypass, #E5, Murrells Inlet
(843) 651-8793
www.booksamillion.com
Having only been in the Grand Strand area since 2002, Books-A-Million has made its mark, opening three stores along the Strand. The chain is the third-largest book retailer in the United States, with more than 200 stores in 19 states and the District of Columbia. These stores aren't as fancy as some, but the prices sure make them attractive.

BOOK WAREHOUSE
3278 Waccamaw Blvd.,
Myrtle Beach
(843) 236-0800
Book Warehouse offers a tempting selection of literature and pulp at discount prices. Best sellers are 20 percent off, and the rest of the inventory is up to 50 percent less than usual.

ENTERTAINMENT

It all started in 1986 with Calvin Gilmore's Carolina Opry, a family-style opry house in Surfside Beach. Locals clearly remember that the buzz around town was, "It'll never make it. . . . There are not enough people to support it year-round. . . . This Gilmore guy is crazy." But before long, shows were sold out in advance as throngs of residents, bus tours, and visitors vied for tickets to see the countrified, musical/comedy production that was whispered to be "better than anything in Nashville or Branson." If you didn't have your tickets to the Christmas show by June, you were certainly out of luck.

Gilmore was crazy—crazy like a fox, that is. The former time-share salesman opened Carolina Opry only after conducting extensive marketing research that indicated the Myrtle Beach area was fertile ground for such grand entertainment. Regardless of most locals' patronage, estimates showed the opry house could survive on ticket sales from tourists and the ever-growing retirement community. The rest is a history lesson in success.

Gilmore and the Carolina Opry were the forerunners of an entertainment explosion that now includes Dolly Parton's *Dixie Stampede*, Alabama Theatre, Medieval Times, and *Legends in Concert*. And the list of entertainment options doesn't stop there. As you read on, you'll discover the full extent of live performances here. As a rule, the variety shows are wholesome and entertaining for the entire family. Tickets are sold by reservation, so call ahead to secure seats. Keep in mind that prices are subject to change; we've listed what we knew at press time.

Refreshments are sold before each show and during intermission. Few venues serve alcohol.

NORTH STRAND

ALABAMA THEATRE
Barefoot Landing, US 17 N.,
North Myrtle Beach
(800) 342-BAMA, (843) 272-1111
www.alabama-theatre.com

Each year the Alabama Theatre hosts musical productions guaranteed to astonish and delight any Myrtle Beach visitor. Its signature show, called *One—The Show*, changes 50 percent each year. The process apparently works: In 2007 the theater was voted No. 1 on the Strand by Myrtle Beach's visitors. The theater boasts a Celebrity Concert Series that has featured Patty Loveless, Diamond Rio, Kenny Chesney, the Oak Ridge Boys, Lou Rawls, George Jones, Wayne Newton, and, of course, the theater's namesake, Alabama.

Season passes are available. To purchase, you pick a guest artist, and the price associated with it allows you admission to that show, one visit to *One*, plus entrance to the *Christmas in Dixie Show*. After you attend those shows, any further visit to One or the Christmas show will cost you only $6.

Showmanship, eclectic music, lavish costumes, and dazzling special effects . . . Alabama Theatre has it all. You'll wonder why you didn't visit sooner.

HOUSE OF BLUES
Barefoot Landing, 4640 US 17 S.,
North Myrtle Beach
(843) 272-3000
www.hob.com/venues/clubvenues/
myrtlebeach

It was an exciting time for Grand Stranders when the House of Blues officially opened to the public with a gala ceremony that featured the Blues Brothers—Dan Aykroyd and John Goodman—and the Godfather of Soul himself, the late James

Brown. Even South Carolina's then-governor, David Beasley, roared in on a Harley for the event.

The House of Blues now stands as the area's only true music hall, a massive space that can hold 2,200 people at one time. Sellout crowds have come to the House of Blues to see ZZ Top, Steve Winward, Hootie and the Blowfish, K. C. and the Sunshine Band, Gregg Allman, Collective Soul, and the Wallflowers. Acts are booked year-round depending on artist availability. Each performance commands its own ticket price, but it's safe to say you'll pay $20 and up for admission to any of the shows. Except for low seating and scattered bar stools, the music hall is a stand-up, dancing venue.

In its trail-blazing style, the House of Blues also brought Gospel brunches to the Grand Strand, with continuous seating between 9 a.m. and 2 p.m. on Sun.. The House is spiritually inspired by gospel choirs singing praises while the audience dines on a Southern-style all-you-can-eat buffet meal. Gospel show and buffet is $19.95 per adult and $9.95 for those 6 to 12 years of age; children under 6 need not pay.

For more on the House of Blues, which also has a restaurant, see the Close-up in the Restaurants chapter.

MYRTLE BEACH

CAROLINA OPRY
North Kings Hwy. (at US 17 Bypass),
Myrtle Beach
(800) 843-6779, (843) 913-4000
www.thecarolinaopry.com

Since 1986, when Calvin Gilmore opened the Carolina Opry and launched the entertainment industry in Myrtle Beach, the Grand Strand has taken its place among the nation's most popular centers for live entertainment. Taking in at least one show is an absolute must, and the *Carolina Opry*, the area's original show, is one great choice. Need proof? *USA Today* called it "a big hit." The *New York Post* said it was "a hot ticket." The *Saturday Evening Post* wrote, " . . . tourists can't beat the two-hour show at the Carolina Opry." And *Southern Living* magazine delivered this accolade:

"Music, comedy and glitter . . . an entertainment phenomenon." And locally, it's been voted the No. 1 show on the beach 23 years running.

Offering something for everyone, this ultimate variety show is a mix of Nashville, Vegas, and Broadway and showcases stellar performances by world-class singers, musicians, comedians, and dancers. In this 2,200-seat show palace with premier sound and lighting systems and three giant screens, every guest sees every performer "up close and personal."

The *Carolina Opry* has remained the only show that has won every major South Carolina tourism award, including the Governor's Cup and Most Outstanding Attraction. Readers of the Myrtle Beach Knight-Ridder newspaper the *Sun News* have voted this live music and comedy variety show the Best of the Beach year after year. These accolades only reinforce what people who see the show already know: The *Carolina Opry* entertains with America's best-loved music and is widely acclaimed as Myrtle Beach's best show. Visit their Web site for show photos and videos, as well as to purchase tickets online.

Shows begin at 8 p.m. except during Nov and Dec, when the curtain rises at 7 p.m. Tickets range from $34.95 to $49.95 in the regular season. From Nov through Dec prices are $39.95 to $54.95 because of their annual *Carolina Opry Christmas Show*. Discounts are offered for children and for groups.

COMEDY CABANA
9588 North Kings Hwy., Myrtle Beach
(843) 449-HAHA
www.comedycabana.com

If you're in the mood for a good belly laugh, the Comedy Cabana is the only five-star comedy club on the Grand Strand. The cabana features three new professional comedians each week. Such comedy notables as Jay Mohr, Gallagher, James Gregory, Lewis Black, and Jimmy "JJ" Walker have played there.

Comedy Cabana is divided into two rooms. The Good Humor Bar and Grill is open before and after shows for food and drink. A full menu is

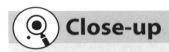 **Close-up**

Calvin Gilmore

You see his name on billboards and marquees and in countless publications—Calvin Gilmore. This is the man who single-handedly turned around entertainment on the Grand Strand by bringing in live music and variety shows with his *Carolina Opry*. It's almost impossible to list all the tourism awards Gilmore has received because of his efforts. Before the *Carolina Opry*, nothing like it existed, and since its creation, countless others have followed in its footsteps.

A Missouri-born farm boy, Gilmore grew up in a musical family and set his sights on being a performer early on. But marriage and two children found him pursuing a career in real estate while putting those dreams on hold. A devoted family man, he couldn't see himself leaving his family behind to go on the road.

His love of music and real estate meshed together in almost cosmic perfection in 1986. Gilmore had begun working with country music star Porter Wagoner to open a musical theater in the Lake of the Ozarks when he decided to make one last call to someone in Myrtle Beach to see if there was any land here for a similar project. While calling information for a telephone number, he told the operator what he was looking for. The operator not only knew of a defunct nightclub for sale but the name of the bank handling it. Call it fate. The deal was struck in days, and the Gilmore family was packed up and moved to the Surfside Beach while dad risked everything.

The deal closed February 2, and by May 2 the Carolina Opry opened its doors. Gilmore harvested talent from North and South Carolina, some of whom—like Kym Shurbutt, Rita Gumm, and Steve Templeton—still perform with the Opry today.

Talk to Gilmore now about it and he just laughs as he recalls how he and his fellow musicians would rehearse on stage behind a plastic sheet while dump trucks, bobcats, and construction crews moved earth and materials around to create the auditorium.

"I'd been to shows like this wherever, and I just knew I could do this ... or even better," Gilmore said, reflecting on those early days.

His gamble has paid off. Shows began selling out immediately, and thousands have spent their evenings being thoroughly entertained at the Opry, which is now housed in a gorgeous 2,200-seat theater on the north end of Myrtle Beach. Gilmore is constantly tweaking the program, moving things around to keep it fresh for those who come back time and time again. But the success has given the Opry a life of its own. And there are plans to build a hotel on the property adjacent to the Opry.

"The Carolina Opry is bigger than just me," he said proudly.

Both his son and daughter are now involved in the family business, something he thought he'd never see but refers to as "sharing the dream." Jeff is an assistant director and Jordan is marketing director. Gilmore no longer performs each night, but far from resting on his laurels, he's also tweaking himself. He still records his own music and has performed numerous times at that other opry, the Grand Ole Opry in Nashville. He's also trying his hand at acting, having recently had parts in a movie about the life of band leader Charles "Buddy" Bolden and another with actors Robert Duvall and Bill Murray.

"I'm never satisfied with the status quo. I can't just coast," Gilmore said.

A sign on the Gilmore Entertainment office door quotes an Emerald City guard from the movie the *Wizard of Oz:* "Nobody gets in to see the wizard. Not no way. Not no how." While not entirely accurate about not getting to see him, it's certainly true that Gilmore has worked magic on the Grand Strand and can definitely be called a wonderful wizard.

offered, including appetizers, sandwiches, pizza, steak, chicken, and pasta. Performances are held in another theater room, where the seating is intimate, cabaret style. Dinner is also served during the show. As is the norm with most comedy clubs, guests must buy at least two items during the evening. The cabana stocks a full bar, plus a good selection of coffee drinks, nonalcoholic elixirs, soft drinks, and sparkling waters. You must be 18 to attend. Teens as young as 16 can come if they are accompanied by a parent.

Doors open at 6:30 p.m. Performances are two hours long and begin at 8 p.m. Tues through Sat during spring and fall, with an additional 10:15 p.m. show on Fri and Sat. During the summer season you can enjoy comedy every night of the week. The cover charge is $15. Reservations are recommended.

CROCODILE ROCKS DUELING PIANOS SALOON
Broadway at the Beach
1320 Celebrity Circle, Myrtle Beach
(843) 444-2096
www.fantasticclubs.com
Crocodile Rocks is a unique show that features nonstop dueling pianos. Two grand pianos face one another on stage, and alternating players ensure high-energy tinkling of the ivories all night.

It's usually packed on weekends, and audiences normally clap and scream with laughter at bawdy renditions of songs. Patrons are brought up on stage during the show to become the brunt of a joke or to participate in enacting the lyrics of a tune. The singer-musicians at Crocodile Rocks are incredibly talented. Requests (with a little cash) for songs are taken throughout the evening.

Use caution if escorting an ultraconservative relative or child; some of the skits could make even your drunken cousin blush. Admission to Crocodile Rocks is $5 per person ($7 on Fri and Sat) and allows you entry into Revolutions Retro Dance Club across the square. Doors open at 7 p.m., and the pianos start at 8 p.m.

i The Grand Strand's own Long Bay Symphony orchestra has made quite a name for itself by offering this area outstanding performances. Visit www.longbaysymphony.com to learn more.

DIXIE STAMPEDE
North Kings Hwy. at US 17
Bypass, Myrtle Beach
(800) 433-4401, (843) 497-9700
www.dixiestampede.com
Dixie Stampede, a Dollywood production that's been in Myrtle Beach since 1987, is a dinner attraction that combines country cookin' with a rodeo-style show for a rompin', stompin', finger-lickin' good time. And we're not just whistling "Dixie" about the finger-lickin' part: Don't expect silverware for your four-course dinner of creamy vegetable soup, whole roasted chicken, hickory-smoked pork, corn on the cob, herb-basted potato, homemade bread, dessert, and beverage. And just in case you're wondering, the soup is served in a drinking cup. Thankfully, you can wash your hands with warm, wet towels provided by the singing waiters and waitresses.

Before dinner everyone is corralled into the Dixie Belle Saloon (no alcohol served) for live musical entertainment, specialty drinks served in boot mugs, popcorn, and peanuts. Then the audience is seated in stadium fashion above the arena where the action is held. Country-music artist and icon Dolly Parton had a hand in developing this $5 million dinner attraction, so expect Southern belles, glitzy costumes that light up in the dark, cowboys who perform trick riding with some 32 trained horses, and audience participation that's downright neighborly. The show's theme is created from the romance of the Old South and the rivalry of the Civil War. Let's face it, a pig race between Ulysses S. Grunt and Robert E. Lean is pushing the cornball, but it sets the pace for a knee-slapping good time.

Dixie Stampede was responsible for bringing ostriches to the Grand Strand to step up the show's North-South conflict. Two riders, one in Union blue, the other in a Confederate uniform, jockey their big birds around the arena. These feathered racers are between three and six years old, already 7 feet tall, and weigh in at about 350 pounds.

Tickets are $46.95 (preferred seating) or $41.95, plus gratuity for adults and teens, and children 4 to 11 are $24.95; kids younger than 4 are admitted free if they sit on their parent's lap. The theater seats about 1,000, but call ahead for reservations. Regular shows are held at 6 p.m. daily from Mar through May. Two shows, at 6 and 8 p.m., are performed nightly from June through Aug. You can catch one show per evening at 6 p.m. during Sept and Oct, and performances are scheduled for every Mon, Wed, Fri, and Sat night at 6 p.m. in Nov and Dec.

The holiday *Christmas at Dixie* show is performed from mid-Nov up until New Year's Eve. The yuletide season finds the trick horse rider dressed as a toy soldier and the sassy girls bantering about who (the North or the South) celebrates Christmas with the most style.

MEDIEVAL TIMES DINNER & TOURNAMENT
2904 Fantasy Way, Myrtle Beach
(800) 436-4386, (843) 236-8080
www.medievaltimes.com
There's nothing on the Grand Strand quite like Medieval Times. This 60-mile stretch of vacation paradise offers plenty of great places to dine, but none features the awe-inspiring thunder of rare Andalusian stallions. There are theaters, more than a few, but not one has a more fantastic (and authentic!) story line. There are world-class performers, but none more committed to excellence. Dinner at Medieval Times is anything but a typical night on the town. Dinner at Medieval Times is a journey into the past . . . a journey into fun . . . and a unique vacation experience.

Medieval Times is family entertainment from the Middle Ages, when the lord of the castle would invite a thousand friends, neighbors, and foes to a feast and royal tournament. Guests should expect to eat without utensils and experience horsemanship, swordplay, falconry, sorcery,

and romance created by the cast of 75 actors and 20 horses.

As a member of the royal audience, you'll boo and cheer as six Knights of the Realm compete to become Champion of the Evening. The champion knight is bestowed the pleasure of choosing his Queen of Love and Beauty from the audience and crowning her as such.

A young relative adamantly swears that Medieval Times is the best place to go out for an evening—that the entertainment and food are second to none!

Tickets are $47.95 plus tax for folks over the age of 12 and $29.95 plus tax for children age 12 and younger. Kids younger than age 3 are admitted free of charge. Prices do not include gratuity.

It's best to call ahead to secure reservations. (See the Kidstuff chapter for more information.)

THE PALACE THEATRE
Broadway at the Beach, 1420 Celebrity
Circle (off US 17 Bypass), Myrtle Beach
(800) 905-4228, (843) 448-9224
www.palacetheatermyrtlebeach.com
The Palace Theatre is located at the hugely popular shopping and entertainment complex known as Broadway at the Beach. Characterized by the style of theaters built in the 1950s, the Palace is easily one of the most elegant venues of its kind. Crowned with a striking cupola dome easily visible for miles, the theater makes a memorable first impression even before guests pass through the doors. In true antebellum style, the luxurious foyer showcases a winding staircase, enormous marble columns, and grandiose chandeliers. The 2,700-seat auditorium is equally impressive. With its magnificent Austrian curtain measuring an awe-inspiring 30 by 75 feet and weighing more than 7,000 pounds, a state-of-the-art lighting and sound system, and a truly elegant seating arrangement, you are sure to enjoy the show—whatever it is. Since 2007 the Palace has been home to Le Grand Cirque, an intoxicating performance that follows the Cirque de Soleil style of acrobatic feats. Prices range from $35 to $45 for adults and $10 for children ages 3 to 12.

Book your tickets for special holiday shows at least six months in advance. By June of any given year, a waiting list for available seats is already being compiled at most of the area's entertainment venues.

SOUTH STRAND

LEGENDS IN CONCERT

301 US 17 Business S., Surfside Beach
(800) 960-7469, (843) 238-7827
www.legendsinconcert.com

Words alone cannot describe the music and magic of *Legends in Concert*. A live, on-stage re-creation of performances from the world's best-loved entertainers, Legends showcases astounding impersonations of stars that include Tom Jones, Dolly Parton, the Blues Brothers, Elton John, Madonna, the inimitable Elvis, and more! *Legends's* stars deliver much more than uncanny resemblances to the stars they portray. Their acts are not lip-synched; this lineup of performers actually sing the memorable tunes you remember. Close your eyes and you'll swear Dolly is on stage. Elvis has mastered "the King's" legendary moves. And if it is at all possible, the Blues Brothers may actually bring even more vim and vigor to their act than the original Brothers did!

In addition to the *Legends'* glittering re-creations, this world-famous show showcases an accomplished lineup of singers and dancers, as well as the smooth sounds of the live Legends Orchestra. State-of-the-art sound, lighting, and multimedia special effects round out a spectacular full-stage production that's anything but ordinary. *Legends in Concert* has been awarded the titles Show of the Year, Entertainers of the Year, and Show of Shows by the International Press Association. The annual Christmas show is a particular delight.

Ticket prices range from $34.95 to $39.95 for adults and $14.95 to $39.95 for children ages 3 to 16.

ATTRACTIONS

The Grand Strand is an attraction in itself, with its beautiful beach and plentiful restaurants, theaters, shopping, and golf. But no visit is complete without taking advantage of what else the area has to offer, including amusement parks, water parks, nature centers, historic gardens, museums, zoos, racetracks, bumper boats, arcades, hundreds of miniature golf courses, driving ranges and par 3 courses (see the Golf chapter for details)—more attractions than you can possibly imagine. If you have kids, or just want to feel like a kid, be sure to peruse the Kidstuff chapter; it's filled with neat stuff we don't list in this chapter. This chapter culminates with a special Historic Churches section featuring some architectural treasures.

Here are a few suggestions to get you started. In many instances prices and hours vary seasonally. We provide peak-season rates and times; call ahead during the off-season.

AMUSEMENT PARKS

North Strand

ALLIGATOR ADVENTURE
Barefoot Landing, US 17 N.,
North Myrtle Beach
(843) 361-0789
www.alligatoradventure.com

Alligator Adventure adjoins Barefoot Landing and is different from any other attraction along the Grand Strand. One of the largest facilities for reptile life in the world, this unique facility's natural 20-acre setting is home to a variety of exotic birds, frogs, snakes, tortoises, and lizards, as well as a huge collection of alligators and crocodiles.

Here are a few examples of the fascinating things you and your family will see: two rare, snow-white albino American alligators; giant Galapagos tortoises; West African dwarf crocodiles (they're often referred to as "ferocity in a 4-foot package"); a serpentarium that holds enormous pythons, boas, and anacondas (the largest species of snake on earth); beautiful but deadly king cobras (some more than 13 feet long); and hundreds of American alligators, from newly hatched to 13-foot-long adults that weigh nearly a half ton. In 2002, Utan, the largest crocodile to ever be exhibited in the United States, made the journey from Thailand to Myrtle Beach to call Alligator Adventure home. Weighing in at more than a ton, he is more than 20 feet long.

Alligator Adventure's 5,000 feet of boardwalk weave in and out of natural surroundings that emulate the beautiful wetland habitats to which these animals are accustomed. Thanks to unusual plants, colorful birds, rare species, giant snakes, and 'gators galore, photo opportunities abound around every bend in the boardwalk. To help visitors understand the wildlife of the wetlands, a rotating collection of exciting and informative exhibits is displayed throughout the park, and demonstrations are scheduled. For example, an on-site amphitheater with 700 seats hosts a "show" of sorts every hour. Often, but not always, these shows feature hands-on interaction with the audience. But don't waste time worrying about safety; Alligator Adventure is supervised by a safety-minded, world-renowned staff dedicated to protecting guests and animals alike.

Alligator Adventure is wheelchair accessible. The park is designed for self-guided tours; guests can wander the entire 20 acres or choose only the exhibits and demonstrations they find interesting.

During the summer, general admission for folks age 12 and older is $14.95; kids ages 4 through 11 get in for $8.95; and little ones age 3 and younger get in free. Senior-citizen price is $12.95. Rates drop slightly during slower seasons.

Alligator Adventure is open year-round. Hours vary from season to season, but generally the park opens at 9 a.m. Closing time depends on the time of year, so please call ahead. Tickets are sold until an hour before closing. For more information on Alligator Adventure, see the Close-up in the Kidstuff chapter.

BAREFOOT LANDING
US 17 N., North Myrtle Beach
(800) 272-2320, (843) 272-8349
www.bflanding.com

Barefoot Landing is a scenic attraction; the wood boutiques blend with the lake setting comfortably (see the Shopping chapter), and the Intracoastal Waterway as a backdrop makes Barefoot unique. Barefoot highlights this with fireworks displays all summer long, plenty of wildlife to ooh and ahh at, and Carousel Courtyard for the kids. Additionally, Barefoot has gathered a superior selection of restaurants (see the Restaurant chapter for more information) that is an attraction in itself.

Myrtle Beach
BROADWAY AT THE BEACH
21st to 29th Avenues S. and US 17 Bypass, Myrtle Beach
(843) 444-3200
www.broadwayatthebeach.com

Broadway at the Beach deserves mention in this chapter because it has gone way past the whole nine yards it takes to lure tourists to its facility. In addition to all the shopping, kidstuff, and restaurants (see the pertinent chapters for more details), Broadway also has some delightful attractions and activities—beyond the simple fact that there is already so much to do in one place. Broadway's attractions can be summed up in one word: spectacular. From Memorial Day to Labor Day, there is a fireworks display every Tuesday. The lake in the center of it all isn't just for the ducks; you can take a water taxi or get yourself around in a paddleboat. There are even a few specially padded spots just for kids, including Carousel Park, so see the Kidstuff chapter for more details.

i Get the most out of a trip to one of our amusement parks: Get an all-day pass, go early, and stay late. Day passes even allow you to leave the park and come back later.

FAMILY KINGDOM
300 South Ocean Blvd., Myrtle Beach
(843) 626-3447
www.family-kingdom.com

Since the demise of the Pavilion, Family Kingdom now lays claim to being Myrtle Beach's only seaside amusement park and is making the most of it. It's a prime destination for families or those just wanting a break from surf and sand.

We remember back in the 1960s when the Swamp Fox roller coaster was being built in a (then) newly paved marsh. It was planned to be the largest old-style wooden roller coaster (with a 62-foot drop) in the South. It wasn't until some years later that the South's largest Ferris wheel—nearly 100 feet in diameter—was added to the complex.

Owned today by the Sea Mist hotel, Family Kingdom is open to one and all. Kids of all ages love the miniature locomotive that tours the perimeter of the park. An antique carousel is also a favorite of those who might not be daring enough for the roller coaster or Ferris wheel. There is even an indoor arcade in the center of the park.

This home of family fun takes a great deal of pride in its reputation as a family-friendly park. Little kids are the focus here; in fact, there's a special separate area called Kiddie Land that's just for toddlers and tots. In Kiddie Land you'll find lots of "small" rides for the small fry, including a miniature Ferris wheel and kid-size roller coaster.

Family Kingdom Water Park is just across the street, and you'd better come prepared to get wet (see the separate listing later in this chapter). The complex has a lazy river for those who feel, well, lazy, and waterslides of varying thrill levels.

If hunger strikes, enjoy pizza, hamburgers, ice cream, and lemonade. There are a number of ticket-pricing plans that vary depending on the time of year and the options taken; it is best to call ahead. Individual tickets for the amusement park are $1, however, and day passes are available. A combo pass for both the amusement park and the water park is $33.00 plus tax for an adult or child. A pass for the park only is $23.50.

Family Kingdom is open from late Mar to late Sept. Hours vary depending on crowd size, but during the height of the season, the amusement park side is generally open from 4 p.m. until midnight, while the water park is open June through Labor Day at 10 a.m. daily and closes between 5 and 6 p.m.

FREESTYLE MUSIC PARK
211 George Bishop Parkway, Myrtle Beach
(843) 236-7625
www.freestylemusicpark.com

Freestyle opened its gates in 2009 amid much fanfare. This music-themed amusement park is spread out over 50 acres and covers almost every genre of music—hence the name "freestyle." Guests are invited to "indulge your inner rock star" while sampling not just rock 'n' roll but country, reggae, beach music, pop, R&B, alternative, Christian, and even disco. Freestyle replaces the short-lived $400 million Hard Rock Park, which barely lasted a season.

Live music is a part of the total experience. Regular concerts are booked at the multipurpose amphitheater, which includes an ultramodern sound system. Freestyle is designed for people to come and stay all day. In addition to the rides and shows, there are restaurants and cafes as well as stores. General admission is $39.95 for adults and $29.95 for children.

NASCAR SPEEDPARK
Broadway at the Beach, US 17 Bypass, Myrtle Beach
(843) 918-8725
www.nascarspeedpark.com

NASCAR SpeedPark is designed to bridge the gap between go-kart family entertainment and the professional NASCAR stock-racing circuit.

The 26-acre park is an authentic replica of the NASCAR experience: 151 downsized NASCAR race cars, 4,000 Goodyear Racing Eagle tires, 17 NASCAR show cars on display, a scoring system measuring the lap speed of each car with a $1/1000$ of a second margin of error.

There are seven tracks to test your driving skills and courage. "The Qualifier" is specially designed for the younger driver; children at least 40 inches tall can take on this 220-foot track. For the "Champions" 725-foot track, add 8 inches to that minimum.

With the "Family 500," things get serious; you must be at least 60 inches tall to compete with 24 other drivers. However, passengers of at least 48 inches are allowed on this 1,200-foot track featuring both a tunnel and a bridge. The "Slidewayz" track is an indoor, tough challenge for anyone more than 54 inches tall.

"The Intimidator" is so tough that it is named for NASCAR champion Dale "Intimidator" Earnhardt and is for drivers at least 54 inches tall. "The Intimidator" features an 800-foot slick track and 12 open-wheeled cars in each race. "The Competitor" is considered high performance, which raises the height minimum to 62 inches. This is a chance to race half-scale NASCAR-style cars side by side on a 36-foot wide, D-shaped oval with high-banked curves.

Finally, "Thunder Road" is the largest rack with the most realistic cars—just what you've been looking for. The 0.5-mile twisting, turning road is also the fastest experience at the Speed-Park. The $5/8$-scale NASCAR Winston Cup–style cars were custom-built for this wind-in-your-face experience. Anyone 16 years or older, with a valid state-issued driver's license and a height of at least 64 inches, can race.

When you get too dizzy from racing around, the SpeedPark also offers the "Speed Dome," a state-of-the-art arcade, a souvenir shop, an indoor/outdoor restaurant, the NASCAR Challenge miniature golf course, and free parking for you and 1,000 competitors. Racers, start your engines!

NASCAR SpeedPark opens year-round at 10 a.m. Closing hours depend on the time of year.

Purchase a 9-ticket package for $20 or 25 tickets for $50. You can get an all-day wristband for $32 or an annual pass for $120. Moms play free when they purchase a ticket for their child.

PAVILION NOSTALGIA PARK
21st Avenue and US 17
at Broadway at the Beach
(843) 913-9400
www.pavilionnostalgiapark.com

Newcomers to Myrtle Beach will still appreciate this tribute to the Pavilion Amusement Park, which was the heart and soul of Myrtle Beach until it was demolished in 2006. The Pavilion Nostalgia Park offers a collection of classic rides from the old park, like the famous Herschell-Spillman Carousel, Wave Swinger, adult and kiddie Pirate Ship rides, and the Caterpillar, Dune Buggie, Boat, and Teacup rides. The historic German Baden Band Organ plays here, too! There is a blast-from-the-past retail shop, five midway skill games, a Pavilion Museum, and much more. Individual rides are $3 but discounts are given with 9 rides for $20 and 25 rides for $50.

South Strand

GARDEN CITY PAVILION ARCADE
103 Atlantic Ave., Garden City Beach
(843) 651-2770

This attraction is one of those classic finds that really sets the Grand Strand apart as a unique vacation spot. In this relatively quiet section of the South Strand known as Garden City Beach, you'll find the incongruously flashy Garden City Pavilion Arcade. Featuring the neon and clamor of more than 200 arcade games, this little gem feels exactly like the Myrtle Beach of 50 years ago. In fact, if you want to know what it was like to visit the Strand in the early 1960s, stop by here; though, we have to admit that the arcade games are a lot more high-tech than we remember from those black-and-white television days.

Within walking distance are lots of carnival-type games and a batting cage, as well as several souvenir shops. In addition, ice-cream, snow-cone, popcorn, and hot dog booths make a showing to appease both your appetite and your sweet tooth. Peak-season hours are 9 a.m. to 2 a.m. daily.

WILD WATER & WHEELS FUN PARK
910 US 17 S., Surfside Beach
(843) 238-3787
www.wild-water.com

Water, waves and wheels: What more could you ask for in an amusement park? Oh yeah, some minigolf thrown in for good measure. Wild Water & Wheels is one-stop shopping for active entertainment and the sort of place one can—and will want to—spend all day. The huge complex has water slides and wave pools of every size imaginable, and the park has been creative in making sure its attractions can suit any age group.

On the race course, kids 10 to 100 zip around in go-karts tricked out as formula racers while the more serious drivers go for the speed racers. The "slick track" course tests a driver's skills in the curves. But don't forget the smaller kids. Children six to nine years old can take a turn at the wheel on the mini Indy track, and the putt-putt course is often labeled as one of the most fun on the Grand Strand.

Slides with names like Free Fall Cliff Dive, the Dark Hole, and Head Rush are not for the faint of heart. Or you can just float along the lazy river. The bumper boat rides allow you to challenge friends and even strangers to race around this huge pool, sidelining your competition along the way. Mini-bumpers allow three- to five-year-olds to experience much of the same.

There are food vendors on-site serving pizza, hot dogs, and other amusement-park fare, so you can refortify yourself before going back in for more fun.

Generally, the park is open 10 a.m. to 5 p.m., but during the summer it stays open until 8 p.m. on Fri. Entrance on Fri between 5 and 8 p.m. is $9.95 plus tax; all-day passes will run you $24.98 plus tax for adults and $16.98 plus tax for seniors as well as children under 48 inches tall. Prices drop after 3 p.m. You can upgrade to get a ride pass for just $10 more. Season passes are also available for $74.98 plus tax.

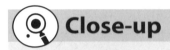 **Close-up**

Old & New

THE PAVILION, 1948–2006

You will often hear the term "The Pavilion" when people refer to the heart of town or amusements along the Beach, but if you go looking for it, you will be disappointed. In 2006, to the consternation of many, Burroughs & Chapin Company closed the almost 60-year-old amusement center and tore it down, moving some of the park's most popular attractions to their shopping/amusement complex Broadway at the Beach.

The Pavilion building was built in 1948 and stood on Ocean Boulevard at Ninth Avenue North. Even before Myrtle Beach truly became a resort town, this was the place to go. The two-story concrete structure was filled with an arcade and food vendors, as well as a dance club up on the second floor. A courtyard and boardwalk allowed a place for people to eat cotton candy or a candied apple, stroll, or just sit and watch the ocean.

An 11-acre amusement park with a roller coaster, carousel, and a host of other rides grew up across the street, and the city of Myrtle Beach literally grew up around this gathering place. While the rides and the arcade games would cost you, being there did not. The Pavilion was a rare free and open space that was a focal point for the city and those who visited there.

The sport of people-watching was an art form at the Pavilion, and you could sit for hours and see every sight imaginable. The benches on the second-story balcony along the Boulevard were prime real estate on which to do it. The Boulevard in that area was a favorite for cruising in cars, and during spring break or at the height of summer, those in the know would park blocks away and just walk, because driving down the Boulevard in that area could take you 30 minutes to go a span of 5 blocks.

This was where the Sun Fun Festival, which launches the Grand Stand's summer season, would kick off and where the parade viewing was held. It also served as the viewing area during air shows. In 2007, for the first year in its 55-year history, there was no Sun Fun Parade.

Burroughs & Chapin announced the Pavilion's closing in March 2006, but as of 2009, it has not revealed plans for the site, which has been cleared of both the building and the rides. B & C has moved the famous Herschell-Spillman carousel and the historic German Baden band organ, as well as many of the other rides over to what has been named Pavilion Nostalgia Park at Broadway at the Beach. The new park has a boardwalk and arcades, but there is no view of the ocean.

FREE STYLE MUSIC PARK, 2009–

It is an ambitious undertaking. Freestyle Music Park opened in May 2009 amid celebration and anticipation after its predecessor, the much ballyhooed Hard Rock Park, lasted only a few months. Hard Rock was a $400-million park and the first major theme park built in the United States in more than a decade. It opened amid a recession and quickly closed. Freestyle took what was left behind and rebuilt it to have a broader appeal. Some of the Hard Rock rides remain, as do the amphitheater and general layout. But Freestyle's music includes everything from rock 'n' roll to reggae, hip-hop, gospel, and even disco.

Rides are grouped according to music theme. Freestyle also includes shows, children's play areas, restaurants, cafes, and retail stores.

It is the sort of place that could take an entire day to even attempt to experience it all. Of course, live music is a part of the total experience. Regular concerts are booked in the multipurpose live-music amphitheater, which includes an ultramodern sound system.

![i] Keep your eyes open for coupons, because they are out there. In almost every lobby or information booth, you will be sure to find something that will save you either $2 or 10 percent.

WATER PARKS

All tourist areas seem to have a water park or parks. But like many things on the Grand Strand, we've outdone them all with a wild-and-wicked collection of water-park rides and slides. Food concessions are available at all parks, as are lockers and clean restrooms. Get ready for some really serious water splashing.

Myrtle Beach

FAMILY KINGDOM WATER PARK
300 South Ocean Blvd., Myrtle Beach
(843) 916-0400
www.family-kingdom.com
Located just across the street from Family Kingdom amusement park, this is the only oceanfront water park in Myrtle Beach. Known for its water flumes and looping speed slides, it also includes slides for those who want to take things a little easier.

For those who feel, well, lazy, the complex includes a 425-foot-long lazy river, so you can spend your day just floating. The park is open daily 10 a.m. to 5 p.m. from June through the beginning of Sept. A day pass is $18.95 for adults and $17.70 for kids, plus tax; there are combination passes for the amusement park available for $33 plus tax.

MYRTLE WAVES
3000 10th Ave. N.
(off US 17 Bypass), Myrtle Beach
(843) 448-1026
www.myrtlewaves.com
This 20-acre park of waterslides and rides is the Strand's largest water park, with more than 30 rides and attractions. It is anchored by a 10-story Turbo Twisters, three completely enclosed dark tubes that send you spiraling through darkness

at 50 feet per second! Myrtle Waves is staffed by certified lifeguards.

The just-for-kids Tad-pool, only 18 inches deep, includes a Little Dipper Slide and the Magic Mushroom water fountain. The lazy river is a leisure soak-and-float pool. Then there are a host of waterslides: Snake Mountain, Arooba Tooba, and Super Chute. Of course, there is a flume ride; in fact, Myrtle Waves has two body flumes. Myrtle Waves even has a wave pool; Ocean In Motion uses wave-making machines to create an effect that many amusement parks in other parts of the country use as their central attraction. Finally, there's Saturation Station with a 256-foot Racin' River that swirls riders around at nearly 10 mph and the Bubble Bay leisure pool with bubbler jets.

Food concessions and a picnic area are available. Footwear, such as aqua booties or sandals, is suggested but not required. Prices vary by day according to planned activities, but a season pass can be purchased for $79.

The park is open weekends from April through May and throughout Sept, and daily from late May through Aug. Operating hours are 10 a.m. to 5 p.m., with extended hours until 6 p.m. during peak season.

NATURE CENTERS

North Strand

T.I.G.E.R.S. PRESERVATION STATION
Barefoot Landing, North Myrtle Beach
(843) 361-4552
www.tigerfriends.com
T.I.G.E.R.S. Preservation Station is an interactive conservation effort that lets you get up close and personal with the rare and endangered golden tabby tiger as well as a host of other animals. The golden tabby became extinct in the wild in 1932. There are just 30 tabbies left in the world, and the Preservation Station has the largest population of them. Open only from 5 to 9 p.m. daily, this free interactive exhibit and museum is aimed at helping save tigers from extinction. For a VIP fee, you can even have your picture taken with tiger cubs sitting on your lap.

At 10 each morning, except Wed and Sun, T.I.G.E.R.S. offers a two-hour Wild Encounter tour of the 50-acre preserve, which is located about 20 minutes away. These tours (which have a fee) must be booked in advance, and children under the age of six are not allowed for safety reasons.

On the tour, visitors can see Siberian tigers, royal white tigers, golden tabbies, "Bubbles" the African elephant, apes, falcons, and even Sinbad, a lion-tiger mixture or liger, the world's largest cat. Because many of the animals have been trained for use in movies and television shows, you can get close to them and have photos taken.

Preservation Station is largely funded through moneys received from the use of its animals as actors.

Myrtle Beach

WACCATEE ZOOLOGICAL FARM
8500 Enterprise Rd, Myrtle Beach
(800) 849-1931, (843) 650-8500
www.waccateezoo.com

For kids and animal lovers, this is a not-to-be-missed opportunity to view myriad unusual animals. This is a real off-the-beaten-path surprise! For more information see the Kidstuff chapter.

South Strand

BROOKGREEN GARDENS
US 17 S., Murrells Inlet
(800) 849-1931, (843) 235-6000
www.brookgreen.org

One of North America's most renowned sculpture gardens is on the Strand. If you see no other natural beauty here, do visit Brookgreen. Less than 20 miles south of Myrtle Beach are more than 550 classics of American sculpture showcased amid botanical wonders in this 9,200-acre Grand Strand secret. In addition to its sculpture and plant collections, Brookgreen is also home to a 50-acre wildlife park that protects the habitats of indigenous animals.

The property that is today Brookgreen Gardens once flourished as four rice plantations. A designated National Historic Landmark, Brookgreen's history is awash in famous faces. "Swamp Fox" Francis Marion, the South's much loved and legendary guerrilla leader, plied its waterways during the American Revolution. Washington Allston, celebrated painter of the Romantic period, was born on Brookgreen Plantation in 1779. In April 1791 George Washington enjoyed an overnight stay at Brookgreen. Theodosia Alston, daughter of Aaron Burr and wife of former South Carolina governor Joseph Alston, made her home at the Oaks Plantation, one of the four aforementioned rice plantations, until her tragic disappearance at sea in 1813. Carolina golden big-grain rice, which played a central role in the Old South's economy, was discovered and cultivated at Brookgreen. And Pulitzer Prize–winning author Julia Peterkin used the plantations as a backdrop for several of her novels published in the 1920s about the descendants of the slaves who worked this land.

It was through the extraordinary vision and generosity of railroad magnate Archer Milton Huntington and his wife, sculptress Anna Hyatt Huntington, that this magnificent site was dedicated to the preservation of nature and art. In 1930, when the Huntingtons purchased the four colonial plantations that make up the Brookgreen property, their plan was to establish a winter home. But the beauty and history of the land quickly transformed their simple vision into something far more grand. In 1931 they organized a nonprofit institution with a dual mission: to preserve habitats for native plants and animals while providing an outdoor showcase for American figurative sculpture.

Under the directorship of only one curator from the day it opened until 1995, Brookgreen became world-famous for its sculpture collection, and it still is for its skillful integration of superb art with the complementary beauty of nature. What began with a small number of artwork from the Huntington's personal collection as well as Anna's own creations has grown into the world's largest and finest outdoor collection of American figurative sculpture. You'll find works from the country's premier contemporary figurative sculptors, such as Marshall Fredericks and Charles Parks, as well as many of the greatest sculptors in American history, including Augustus Saint-Gaudens and Carl Milles. And with each passing year, the sculpture collection continues to grow in size and stature.

Brookgreen's botanical gardens feature more than 2,000 species and subspecies of plants. The collection includes moss-laden oaks, magnolias, and wildflowers as well as numerous naturalized and exotic species, including propagated azaleas and camellias. Beneath the stately oaks and nestled around murmuring fountains, the beautifully orchestrated plant collection provides a breathtaking backdrop for the diverse sculpture. The simple beauty of green foliage against cool, white marble or the visual excitement of brightly colored blooms in contrast with bronze exemplifies the cooperative interplay of the plant and sculpture collections. While each of the gardens has its special emphasis, all mesh into a delightful medley of landscapes and walkways.

Brookgreen is also home to a 50-acre wildlife trail that exhibits indigenous animals in their natural environment. The young and young-at-heart always enjoy the Cypress Aviary, Otter Pond, Alligator Swamp, Fox Glade, Raptor Aviary, and the White-Tailed Deer Savannah.

Free walking tours (included in the admission price) are offered every day at Brookgreen Gardens. For an additional fee tour guides are available. Light refreshments and lunchtime fare are available in the Terrace Cafe, and there are picnic areas. Brookgreen Gardens is completely wheelchair accessible and wheelchairs are provided.

The E. Craig Wall Jr. Lowcountry Center, a newer addition, has allowed Brookgreen to expand programs that seek to teach the distinctive nature and culture of the Lowcountry. The $4 million renovated center, once a maintenance facility and stables, now houses Learning Laboratories, an exhibition hall, auditorium, information desk, Courtyard Cafe, Program Shed, a cultural garden and courtyard with a rice-field trunk replica, and native plants. Wildlife sculpture completes the connection with nature.

Some of the programs hosted at the center include Lowcountry: Change and Continuity, which traces the changes and constants in Low-

country land with unusual artifacts, interesting information, and Tom Blagden's glorious nature photography. Gray Oaks Mystery is a 10-minute film that gives a great historical overview of the gardens and how they have evolved. In Meet the Animals, trained interpreters show several native animals. The Trekker is a custom-made overland vehicle offering an hour of driving the back roads and trails through Brookgreen's vast nature preserve. You will see distinctive environments of the Lowcountry, a beautiful view of the Waccamaw River, and silent reminders of once-thriving rice plantations and the people who lived on them.

One of the most popular tours is the 50-minute exploration of the waterways around Brookgreen Gardens on the 48-foot pontoon boat, The Springfield. View the scenic cypress swamps, remains of irrigation systems, Spanish moss–covered trees, and abandoned rice fields.

Brookgreen Gardens is open daily year-round, 9:30 a.m. to 5 p.m. Hours are slightly abbreviated during winter months (call for details). Admission is $12 for those age 13 and older, $5 for children 6 to 12, and $10 for seniors 65 and older.

HOBCAW BARONY NATURE CENTER
US 17, south of Pawleys Island
(843) 546-4623
www.hobcawbarony.org
The Hobcaw Barony Nature Center is part of Hobcaw Barony, the former home of stockbroker and 1940s power broker Bernard Baruch.

The Hobcaw Barony Nature Center, on 17,500 acres, features displays and audiovisual programs on Hobcaw's history, local wildlife, coastal environments, and the teaching and research programs of the Baruch Institutes. If you want to get a real "feel" for the animals that call our area home, stop by the center and visit the saltwater touch tank and snake displays. Audiovisual programs are also shown daily. There are no walking trails or self-guided tours, and advanced reservations are required for guided tours and special programs.

Hobcaw Barony Nature Center is open year-round, and admission is free. Operating hours are

9 a.m. to 5 p.m. Mon through Fri. Guided tours are $20 per person and are only available Tues through Fri.

MUSEUMS AND EDUCATIONAL ACTIVITIES

North Strand

LA BELLE AMIE VINEYARD
1120 St. Joseph Rd. (corner of Highway 90 and St. Joseph Road), North Myrtle Beach
(843) 399-WINE (9563)
www.labelleamie.com
At La Belle Amie, it's about the wine and the festivals, and they have developed a big reputation for being a great place to experience both.

The name La Belle Amie has dual meaning. First, it is French for "beautiful friend," but it also pays homage to the Bellamy family, who has owned the land on which the vineyard is located since the 1800s. The land was originally a tobacco plantation, but in 1995 sisters June and Vicki hatched a plan to cultivate up to 38 acres for a wine vineyard.

The land had been owned by their Uncle Gifford, who was famous for his homemade wines. The grapes he used for his muscadine wine were from vines more than 100 years old. Uncle Gifford passed away in 1993, leaving the property to his sister Berta, June and Vicki's mother. The girls could think of no better tribute to Gifford than to start the winery.

While La Belle Amie still makes Gifford's Red wine from his old vines, most of the other varieties are from grapes imported from Europe, the Bellamy's ancestral roots. The wines are unique blends and have a flavor that will surprise and delight those who poo-poo the idea that good wine can be cultivated on the Grand Strand.

Almost from the beginning, La Belle Amie began hosting festivals, and the names and themes are always changing. Past events include the Winter Parrot Head Festival, the Blues & Jazz Festival, and the Whole Lotta Shakin' Oldest Music Fest. Check the calendar on their Web site for a constant array of activities.

Tour buses are welcomed, but individuals can have a whole lot of fun here. Self-guided tours of the vineyard are available Mon through Sat from 10 a.m. to 6 p.m. Guided tours hosted by Vicki are conducted Tues, Thurs, and on non-festival Saturdays. Wine tastings are held Mon through Sat from 10 a.m. to 5 p.m. There is a gift shop next to the tasting room that has a host of fun wine-related items.

Myrtle Beach

CAROLINA SAFARI JEEP TOURS
606 65th Ave. N., Myrtle Beach
(843) 497-4330
www.carolinasafari.com
This unique attraction is brought to you by the team of Virgil Graham, photographer and naturalist, and Valerie Graham, nature and history writer, who guide passengers through the history and natural beauty of the Lowcountry. Covered Jeeps take you on a tour, complete with binoculars. Turn to the Kidstuff chapter to get all the details of this safari experience.

THE CHILDREN'S MUSEUM OF SOUTH CAROLINA
2501 North Kings Hwy., Myrtle Beach
(843) 946-9469
www.cmsckids.org
A visit to this museum guarantees a fun-filled day for adults and children of any age, while sneaking in a little education.

Exhibits include Discovery Lab and Bubble Mania, among others; a hospital room was added so kids can experience the fun and science side of a hospital. See the Kidstuff chapter for information about hours and admission fees.

FRANKLIN G. BURROUGHS AND SIMEON B. CHAPIN ART MUSEUM
3100 South Ocean Blvd., Myrtle Beach
(843) 238-2510
www.myrtlebeachartmuseum.org
Open since 1997, the Franklin G. Burroughs and Simeon B. Chapin Art Museum was founded as

a way to highlight artists of the Grand Strand as well as to bring in exhibits from elsewhere. The museum's own collection highlights locals such as Alex Powers, John Gore, Dixie Dugan, and Mack Miller. Located near the Springmaid Beach Pier, the gallery also features a great gift shop where you can purchase a variety of Lowcountry art. There is also a cafe on-site, making this a great place to spend an afternoon.

For more details, as well as information on hours and admission, see the Arts and Culture chapter.

IMAX DISCOVERY THEATER
Broadway at the Beach, Celebrity Square, Myrtle Beach
(843) 448-IMAX
www.myrtlebeachimax.com

With its six-story screen and state-of-the-art sound technology, this John Q. Hammons theater makes you feel involved in every picture. Please refer to the Nightlife and Kidstuff chapters for more information.

RIPLEY'S AQUARIUM
Broadway at the Beach, between 21st and 29th Avenues N., Myrtle Beach
(800) 734-8888, (843) 916-0888
www.ripleysaquarium.com

Ripley's Aquarium is a $40 million, state-of-the-art, 87,000-square-foot aquarium experience. It is one of South Carolina's most visited attractions. Guests are entertained by some of the worlds' most beautiful, fascinating, and dangerous aquatic life. Visitors are surrounded by menacing 10-foot sharks as they travel through Dangerous Reef, a 750,000-gallon tank, on the world's longest (330-foot) moving glide path.

Other spectacular features include Ray Bay, highlighting a variety of rays from multiple viewing levels, and Friendship Flats, where guests touch Atlantic and southern cow-nose rays and bonnet-head sharks. Rainbow Rock offers a stunning view of thousands of brilliantly colored Pacific fish from Hawaii, Australia, and the Indian Ocean through an acrylic window the size of two movie screens.

The freshwater Rio Amazon exhibit showcases piranha and other exotic species unique to the Amazon rain forest. A collection of delicate undersea life such as the Pacific giant octopus, sea anemones, living corals, jellies, weedy sea dragons, sea horses, and pipefish are featured as art in the Living Gallery.

The Schooling Fish Tank, a 10-foot cylindrical exhibit, is home to a unique collection of beautiful lookdowns. Guests experience the thrill of holding horseshoe crabs at the Sea-For-Yourself Discovery Center, an interactive, multimedia playground and educational resource center that fascinates children and adults of all ages. Dive shows and marine-education classes are presented hourly.

Ripley's Aquarium is open daily from 9 a.m. to 10 p.m. Admission for teens and adults age 12 and older is $17.99. Children ages 5 to 11 enjoy the fun for $9.99. Children ages 2 to 4 cost $3.99, and children under 2 years of age are free.

RIPLEY'S BELIEVE IT OR NOT! MUSEUM
915 North Ocean Blvd., Myrtle Beach
(843) 448-2331
www.ripleys.com

Explorer and cartoonist Robert Ripley has put together a bizarre collection of human oddities, amazing artifacts, and displays of the unbelievable, including a two-headed calf, shrunken heads from Ecuador, and a man who could put three golf balls in his mouth and whistle at the same time. Check out the replica of Cleopatra's barge made entirely out of confectioner's sugar—the ship's detailing is incredibly "delicious." Take a self-guided tour of the more than 500 exhibits displayed throughout the two-story museum.

Don't expect a museum in the traditional sense. This is more of an attraction than a museum; most displays are either reproductions or pure fantasy. But that doesn't take away any of the fun.

Tickets cost $12.99 for adults and $7.99 for children ages 6 to 12; children age 5 and younger are admitted free of charge. Ripley's is open year-round. Summer hours are 10 a.m. to 10 p.m.; off-season hours vary, so call ahead for specifics.

SOUTH CAROLINA HALL OF FAME
Myrtle Beach Convention Center
21st Avenue N. and Oak Street,
Myrtle Beach
(843) 626-7444
www.theofficialschalloffame.com
Regional-history buffs will find the South Carolina Hall of Fame provides interesting insight into the growth of the state. Set as a display inside the Myrtle Beach Convention Center, this designated area honors native South Carolinians who achieved fame as well as people who were born elsewhere but made significant contributions to the Palmetto State. Portraits of each inductee are accompanied by a written biography.

Admission is free. The convention center is open 8:30 a.m. to 5 p.m. Mon through Fri year-round.

South Strand
HOPSEWEE PLANTATION
494 Hopsewee Rd.,
12 miles south of Georgetown
(843) 546-7891
www.hopsewee.com
Yes, this is South Carolina, and you can visit a Tara-like mansion here.

The house at Hopsewee Plantation, a National Historic Landmark, is an early Georgian-style mansion—a typical example of a Lowcountry rice plantation dwelling of the early 18th century. Although it was built nearly 40 years before the Revolutionary War, only five families have owned it. Surprisingly, it is not a publicly owned tourist attraction, but rather a privately owned plantation.

Built of black cypress, the history-steeped residence features four rooms opening into a wide central hall on each floor. In particular, note the charming attic rooms as well as the full brick cellar, lovely staircase, hand-carved molding in every room, and beautiful heart pine floors.

Hopsewee was the home of Thomas Lynch Sr. and Thomas Jr. Both men were distinguished political figures, and they were the only father and son who served in the Continental Congress. Unfortunately, the elder Lynch suffered a stroke and could not sign the Declaration of Independence. A space remains on the document where his signature was supposed to appear.

Featuring a beautiful vista of the North Santee River, Hopsewee is open to the public 10 a.m. to 4 p.m. Tues through Fri from early Mar through early Nov. Other times are available by appointment. Frank and Raejean Beattie, the current owners of Hopsewee, will happily serve as tour guides.

Admission is $10 for adults and $5 for children ages 5 through 17.

MANSFIELD PLANTATION
1776 Mansfield Rd., Georgetown
(800) 355-3223, (843) 546-6961
www.mansfieldplantation.com
Mansfield really isn't a museum per se, but it sure is filled with history. To experience this rarity, a reservation is required, as are groups of 15 or more. This authentic antebellum plantation stands as a poignant reminder of the Old South. It was once owned by Dr. Francis and Mrs. Mary Parker; the gentleman was one of the signers of the Ordinance of Secession. Approximately 100 slaves once lived and worked at Mansfield. Today Mansfield is owned by Parker's descendent John Parker and his wife, Sallie, who invite guests to come visit one of the most beautiful Lowcountry plantations around. The 45-minute tour costs $12 per person and takes visitors through the old slave village and chapel, the old rice fields, serene marshlands, and the only winnowing building (where rice chaff was separated from rice kernels) that still stands in these parts.

Because Mansfield is now an exclusive bed-and-breakfast, entrance to the house is limited. Spend the extra money and pay $17.50 for the Tea and Tour, which gives you the opportunity to see the interior of this incredible plantation home filled, with mid-19th-century American paintings and furnishings. You'll also enjoy the residence's special features: double parlors, a grand dining room, beautifully carved woodwork, elaborate mantelpieces, and genuine antique furnishings. The tour is capped off with tea and sweets served in the dining room of the big house. The tea is poured from antique silver teapots, and the homemade sweets are created from 19th-century recipes adapted for 21st-century tastes. (Both the original recipes and the adapted versions are available to visitors.)

RICE MUSEUM
633 Front St., Georgetown
(843) 546-7423
www.ricemuseum.org
The Rice Museum, in the beautifully renovated heart of Georgetown, offers a concise and fascinating overview of the society that flourished around rice cultivation. Old maps, dioramas, artifacts, and a 17-minute-long video give the visitor an intriguing glimpse into the past—into a history that literally changed the face of this country. A changing exhibit gallery provides revolving exhibits—contemporary as well as historic.

The building itself was erected as a two-story structure in 1842 and is known locally as the Town Clock because it has clock faces on all four sides of its bell tower and, presumably, can be seen from all directions. Originally a hardware store, this building has evolved from two to three stories over the past 150 years.

In 1878 a rear addition was added and the facade remodeled. Since then, the museum has undergone two major renovations, the latest of which was completed in 2004. The second floor now houses five exhibits, which range from Plantation Footprints, about two antebellum rice plantations near Georgetown, to a tribute to Joseph Rainey, America's first black congressman. The third floor is home to the Brown's Ferry Vessel exhibit. Built in the early 1700s, the 50-foot-long wooden freighter is the oldest vessel on exhibit in the United States.

Tickets are $7 for adults and $5 for seniors (60 and older). Students ages 6 to 21 are $3, while children under 6 who are accompanied by an adult get in free. Group rates are available. The Rice Museum is open year-round Mon through Sat from 10 a.m. to 4:30 p.m. and is closed on major holidays.

Beyond the Strand
HORRY COUNTY MUSEUM
428 Main St., Conway
(843) 915-5320
www.horrycountymuseum.org
This place is actually off the Strand, just west of Myrtle Beach. The name of the Horry County Museum is a bit misleading in that it showcases not only Horry County history, but also much of the surrounding area's history. You'll find a variety of informative displays, interesting artifacts, old photographs, life-size animal specimens, scale models, and memorabilia galore.

Originally a post office, the building stands on what was formerly the grounds of a historic home. Just outside the museum, the twisted arms of the stately old Wade Hampton oak tree welcome visitors. A plaque on the oak commemorates the day in 1876 when Confederate general Wade Hampton brought his campaign for the governorship to Conway and addressed the residents from beneath the tree. Many years later, when construction of a railroad threatened the historic oak, a spirited local lady named Mary Beaty brandished a loaded shotgun and ordered workers, "Touch not a single bough." Her defiance inspired other residents to actively protect the town's magnificent live oaks.

Start your self-guided museum tour by ambling among display cases filled with wildlife specimens. One fascinating display—a favorite of visitors both young and old—features a black bear family. Papa bear, tipping the scale at 300 pounds, was actually hit by a car on US 501 many years ago. Papa represents an estimated population of 400 black bears that still call the less-developed areas of Horry County home.

Other exhibits feature birds of prey such as owls, hawks, ospreys, and herons, as well as a 400-pound, 11-foot-long alligator.

Resources of the Land, a three-dimensional exhibit, brims with photos and scale models of naval stores produced in the area in the 1700s. Loggers and Locomotives boasts nearly life-size images of loggers, wagons, and other lumber-related subjects. Antiquated logging equipment is also on display. It's truly fascinating to see how much life has changed.

For another surprise, be sure to peruse the Native Americans of the Coastal Plains exhibit. Displays feature tools, arrowheads, and other artifacts, along with models that re-create the intricacies of the original inhabitants' daily existence.

The museum is open from 9 a.m. to 5 p.m. Monday through Saturday year-round. Tickets are $7 for adults and $5 for seniors (60 and older). Students ages 6 to 21 are $3, while children under 6 who are accompanied by an adult get in free. Group rates are available. Special events and exhibitions are hosted throughout the year. Call ahead or check the Web site for details.

HISTORIC CHURCHES

Some fine examples of historic churches are still in operation, if you'd like either a soul-saving or a historic peek. See the Worship chapter for an overview of the Grand Strand's spiritual scene.

South Strand
ALL SAINTS EPISCOPAL CHURCH
3560 Kings River Rd., Pawleys Island
(843) 237-4223
www.allsaintspawleys.org
All Saints, in Pawleys Island, is a not-to-be-missed historic site. The church was established by an act of the Colonial Assembly of South Carolina on May 23, 1767, primarily because it was very difficult for worshipers to get from the Waccamaw Neck area to Georgetown for services at Prince George Winyah. The first chapel was built on land donated by George Pawley II. In 2007 the church celebrated its 240th anniversary.

After the War Between the States, All Saints came close to perishing due to a lack of funds. The church's only income came from the rental of a house built in 1854 as the rector's summer home. By 1876 Rev. William Habersham Barnwell was hired at a salary of $700 a year. From that point All Saints began its journey down the road to recovery.

It is an understatement to say that the original All Saints is a lovely church. It's overhung with enormous oaks, and the historic setting is peaceful and genuinely captivating. The cemetery offers a fascinating history lesson in itself. (Alice Belin Flagg, who is mentioned in the History chapter, is buried here.)

i There are eight churches in Horry and Georgetown Counties that are listed on the National Register of Historic Places. The national registry also recognizes 15 districts in those counties, including the historic district of the fishing village of Murrells Inlet.

PRINCE GEORGE WINYAH EPISCOPAL CHURCH
700 Highmarket St., Georgetown
(843) 546-4358
www.pgwinyah.org
Prince George Winyah is one of the town's most fascinating examples of historic meeting places. Its story begins in the early 18th century.

The Parish of Prince George, formed in 1721, was named for the man who eventually became King George II of England. The first sanctuary was situated in a bend on the Black River, roughly 12 miles north of the current Georgetown location. Due to the area's growth, the parish divided in 1734. Since the original church fell within the boundaries of the newly established Prince Frederick's Parish, commissioners were appointed to build a new sanctuary for the Parish of Prince George. The first rector, sent by the English Society for the Propagation of the Gospel in Foreign Parts, held the initial service in Prince George on August 16, 1747.

The church building was ravaged by enemy troops in both the Revolutionary War and the War

Between the States. In 1809, following the American Revolution, the existing gallery and chancel were added. The steeple that overlooks the shady streets of Georgetown was added in 1824.

The box pews still used today were a customary feature in colonial churches. Heating systems were nonexistent, so pew owners usually brought charcoal burners to their own "boxes" in winter. The design of the box pews helped to retain some of the heat lost to the beautiful building's high ceilings.

The stained-glass window that graces the back of the altar is English stained glass and was originally in St. Mary's Chapel at Hagley Plantation on the Waccamaw River. St. Mary's was a lovely little sanctuary built by Plowden C. J. Weston for his slaves. (Colonial churches did not have stained-glass windows.) The windows on either side of the church were installed early in the 20th century. Four of the original clear windows remain. Prince George is one of South Carolina's few original colonial church buildings still in use.

Beyond the Strand

FIRST UNITED METHODIST CHURCH
1001 Fifth Ave., Conway
(843) 488-4251
Organized in 1828, First United Methodist is on the National Register of Historic Places and on the Register of United Methodist Historic Sites. The original church, now home to the Hut Bible Class, was built in 1844 and was replaced by a Gothic building in 1898. The mission-style church, now a fellowship hall, was built in 1910. The present Georgian-style sanctuary was built in 1961. Of special interest is the cemetery, with graves dating from the 1830s.

KINGSTON PRESBYTERIAN CHURCH
800 Third Ave., Conway
(843) 248-4200
West of Myrtle Beach, the city of Conway boasts its own taste of history. Kingston Presbyterian is on the National Register of Historic Places and is designated as an American Presbyterian and Reformed Historical Site. No one knows exactly when Presbyterians started meeting in Conway, but local historians believe it was before 1754. The church was assigned its first preacher, Rev. William Donaldson, in 1756.

One of the first churches on the site overlooking Kingston Lake was destroyed in 1798 in a storm (probably a hurricane) and wasn't rebuilt until the 1830s. In fact, one local historian, Catherine Lewis, said Conway survived for about 40 years without any churches at all. However, Conwayites didn't neglect their worship during those years; they simply met in private homes and at a campground outside the town. In 1858 the present building was erected. Since then it has been extensively renovated.

The yard of Kingston Presbyterian Church is undoubtedly one of the most serene spots in the Grand Strand area. The lake, huge oaks, dogwoods, camellias, and azaleas add to the sense of history and beauty. A community burial ground that dates from the 1700s makes for a fascinating afternoon excursion.

KIDSTUFF

Kidstuff. It's a trick word. If you cruise the attractions geared toward kids along the Grand Strand, you are going to discover that the word kid has very little to do with age and refers more to fun. While clearly there are scores of Grand Strand adventures that anywhere else in the world would be loved by kids only, here at the beach kidstuff fun overtakes everyone, regardless of age.

But step away from the ocean; the Strand offers outdoor playgrounds, water parks, arcades, adventures, candy makers, amusement parks, racetracks, adventure theaters (not recommended for some so-called adults), skating, splashing, oversize playpens, and even a supervised overnight lockup inside a giant playground/mall. In fact, the only thing lacking here is time; there is just not enough in one vacation to hit all the kidstuff and the beach.

Be sure to scan the Water Sports, Fishing, Attractions, and Parks and Recreation chapters for more stuff we didn't list or detail here because, like we said, it is all kidstuff!

NORTH STRAND

ALLIGATOR ADVENTURE
US 17 N., North Myrtle Beach
(843) 361-0789
www.alligatoradventure.com

Alligator Adventure, an alligator park and reptile research institute that adjoins Barefoot Landing in North Myrtle Beach, is completely different from any attraction along the Grand Strand. It's a must-see for children.

Alligator Adventure is wheelchair accessible. The park is designed for self-guided tours; guests can wander through the 20 acres or choose only the exhibits and demonstrations they find interesting.

Hours and rates are seasonal, so definitely call before you go. At press time, general admission for adults was $15.95. Children ages 4 to 11 get in for $9.95, seniors pay $13.95, and children age 3 and younger are free. Refer to the Attractions chapter for more details. Also see the Close-up in this chapter.

BAREFOOT LANDING
US 17 N., North Myrtle Beach
(843) 272-8349
www.bflanding.com

Despite the more grown-up venues of night-clubs, bars, and boutiques, Barefoot thoughtfully includes distractions for kids. You can start with the above-listed Alligator Adventure, then walk the planks over the lake to check out the enormous fish, take a ride on the carousel in Carousel Court, and, finally, round off the whole afternoon at Johnny Rockets, where the chirpy waitstaff will serve you a sizzling burger and milk shake while singing and dancing to favorite, bouncy '50s tunes. Just don't step on their blue suede shoes. For more on Barefoot Landing, see the Attractions chapter.

> **i** In the open boardwalk area between Mad Boar and the General Store, Barefoot Landing in North Myrtle Beach has a jungle gym for kids.

INLET POINT PLANTATION
5800 Hwy. 236, North Myrtle Beach
(843) 249-2989

Horseback beach and trail rides, carriage rides, and a horse-lover's adventure on a private island all highlight this attraction for kids of all ages.

Ride through hundreds of acres of fields and forests, over high rolling terrain, past salt marshes, and along miles and miles of uninhabited barrier island beaches. This family-fun adventure offers a genuine alternative to the glitter and ping of the high-tech arcades and amusement-park rides.

Reservations are highly recommended because prices and hours vary greatly. One-hour trail rides begin at $50 per person, and you must be age seven or older. Beach riding is two and a half hours for $100.

MYRTLE BEACH

BROADWAY AT THE BEACH
US 17 N. Bypass at 21st Avenue North,
Myrtle Beach
(843) 444-3200
www.broadwayatthebeach.com
Broadway successfully strives to cater to everyone's vacation dreams—and that includes kids. On-site, permanent attractions include the Interactive Fountain, the Carousel Park & Kiddie Rides section, Dragon's Lair Fantasy Golf, and, finally, an activity that will really wear anyone out, pedal boats to get around the whole Broadway lake by your very own leg power. Additionally, Broadway has street performers sparking laughter everywhere and hands-on dinosaur statues. For more on Broadway see the Attractions chapter.

BUILD-A-BEAR WORKSHOP
Broadway at the Beach, Myrtle Beach
(877) 789-2327, (843) 445-7675
www.buildabear.com
"Choose me, stuff me, stitch me, fluff me, name me, dress me, take me home!" The Build-A-Bear Workshop is an activities-oriented, stuffed-animal store where cuddliness abounds. You choose your teddy bear from more than 30 forms: from the classic brown teddy ($18) to a 14-inch-long floppy bear ($10) to the sumptuous white Polar bear ($25). When we visited, a frog, a cow, and a few bunnies were also waiting for homes. The store is set up like a factory, which is where the stuffing and stitching and fluffing and naming

come in. The end of the production line is at a wall full of clothes and accessories for your newfound friend (all at an extra charge). This is definitely the place for kids who like hands-on activities and handmade souvenirs.

CAROLINA SAFARI JEEP TOURS
606 65th Ave. N., Myrtle Beach
(843) 497-4330
www.carolinasafari.com
These tours are the first of their kind in the Lowcountry. Tour directors Virgil and Valerie Graham, who are a magazine photographer-naturalist and a nature and history writer, respectively, have a professional knowledge of the area, so you can look forward to more than a few unique and beautiful sites. Each specially designed tour vehicle seats 14 passengers and a tour guide "safari-style," allowing for an extensive and personalized overview of area history and local ghost lore as well as tons of narrative information.

The itinerary includes natural coastal attractions, historic areas, old plantations, a barrier island, and an unexpected abundance of natural beauty; until you've seen the natural side of the Grand Strand, you're missing something extraordinary. You'll see the lovely old homes of Pawleys Island (including slave cabins and rice and indigo planters from the 1700s and 1800s), the oldest resort area in the United States; a maritime forest; mystery-shrouded marshes; historic grave sites; nesting bald eagles; and more.

Binoculars are provided, and you're welcome to bring cameras; you'll likely encounter lots of photo opportunities for the vacation scrapbook. Don't worry about inclement weather; the tour Jeeps have covers and heat and are winterized. Carolina Safari will even pick you up at most area resorts.

Tours run seven days a week most of the year. Check for the winter schedule. Ask about tours to additional locations. Rates are $40 for adults, $35 each for groups of ten, and $25 for kids 12 and under. Coupons are available. Call for reservations.

ℹ The Myrtle Beach Area Chamber of Commerce prints a monthly calendar of all activities to be held along the Grand Strand and includes times, location, and pricing. The calendar is free and can be picked up the chamber offices. It is also online at www.visitmyrtlebeach.com under "festivals and events."

THE CHILDREN'S MUSEUM OF SOUTH CAROLINA
2501 North Kings Hwy., Myrtle Beach
(843) 946-9469
www.cmsckids.org

Adjacent to Myrtle Square Mall and next door to Office Depot, the Children's Museum features exhibits with good kid names: Circuit Center, Bubble Mania, Fairway Physics, Fossil Hunt, the Magic School Bus, and Starlab. Ideal for children of all ages, this place sneaks a little education into a fun-filled adventure, and the kids are none the wiser (yet all the more informed!). There are always creative events taking place, like meetings with the Easter Bunny or celebrating Dr. Seuss's birthday.

The Children's Museum is open Tues through Sat from 10 a.m. to 4 p.m. Admission is $7 for anyone age one year and older. Group pricing is available.

DIXIE STAMPEDE
North Kings Highway at US 17 Bypass, Myrtle Beach
(800) 433-4401, (843) 497-9700
www.dixiestampede.com

It's always a fun addition to pencil in *Dixie Stampede* (see the Entertainment chapter) on your vacation agenda. Created by a league of talented planners, performers, and all-star dreamers, *Dixie Stampede* is brought to you by the Dollywood Theme Park Association and is the same famous show as the ones in Pigeon Forge, Tennessee, Branson, Missouri, and Orlando, Florida. For one all-inclusive admission, this unique dinner attraction serves up heaps of Southern food,

unlimited beverages, and as much rib-ticklin' horse-filled show as a body can stand. Even if they're too young to understand the context, kids will love the thrilling reenactment of the North/South rivalry, complete with prancing horses, handsome heroes, and fair maidens. The spectacular finale showcases no fewer than 15,000 sparkling lights. Admission is $41.95 or $46.95 (preferred seating), plus gratuity for adults and teens, with discounts for children; prices are subject to change, so please call ahead. Little ones age three and younger can enjoy the fun for free if they sit on an adult's lap and share the grown-up's meal.

You can't just walk in as in a traditional restaurant; there are specific show and dinner times, and generally there is only one sitting (two during peak season). You will need reservations, because the place is always packed. (See the Entertainment chapter for showtimes.)

IMAX DISCOVERY THEATER
Celebrity Circle
Broadway at the Beach, Myrtle Beach
(843) 448-IMAX
www.myrtlebeachimax.com

More than 700 million people have viewed giant-screen productions in more than 150 permanent IMAX theaters around the world. This amazing high-tech filming and projection process puts you in the middle of movie action in a way no ordinary screen presentation can. At this theater you don't just watch a movie; you'll actually feel propelled into the scene as you view six-story-tall images and listen to digital surround sound. With titles such as Sharks, Space Station, and Wild Safari, it should be quite a show.

There are shows every hour of every day, though operating hours vary from month to month. The theater is open 364 days every year (it's closed Thanksgiving Day), and prices are $11 for kids ages 4 through 12, $13 for adults. See the Nightlife and Attractions chapters for more details.

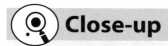 **Close-up**

Alligator Adventure

In the heart of North Myrtle Beach awaits a place inhabited by some of the most spectacular creatures on earth. Alligator Adventure, the world's largest reptile park, occupies more than 20 acres of wetland habitat. In this natural setting, a series of boardwalks connects numerous tastefully designed exhibits that serve as home to an array of nature's most impressive and unusual reptiles. A wide variety of waterfowl and other exotic birds abound in indoor sanctuaries that separate the main attractions.

Alligator Adventure is the proud home to more than 800 alligators ranging in size from 8-inch infants to 13-foot adults that weigh 500 to 600 pounds. In the main alligator exhibit pool, more than 300 large adults wait patiently while skilled lecturers explain the fascinating life history of these ancient creatures. The talks are climaxed with staff members feeding the large reptiles by hand.

Alligator Adventure is also home to dozens of rare and unusual reptiles. "Spot," the giant alligator snapping turtle, lies motionless underwater with jaws agape, wiggling his pink wormlike tongue in hopes of attracting unsuspecting fish. This, the largest of the freshwater turtles, can weigh nearly 200 pounds. The odd mata mata turtle, with its flattened leaf-like head, also resides in the exhibit, as does the rare pig-nosed turtle, with flippers like a sea turtle. Many species of lizards can also be viewed, including the deadly gila monster, one of the world's only two venomous lizards, and the prehistoric-looking rhinoceros iguana. Additionally, many varied and colorful frogs and toads supply their own unique appeal.

And then there are the snakes.

This state-of-the-art facility is fully air-conditioned and houses an impressive assortment of the world's snakes. Species such as the giant green anaconda, the world's largest snake (can grow to more than 37 feet!), and the reticulated python (rivals the anaconda in size and occasionally preys on deer) coil peacefully in spacious and artfully decorated cages. Many poisonous varieties are also on display, including the king cobra, which may reach 18 feet in length and is considered by some to be the most intelligent snake. Rattlesnakes, deadly African and Asian vipers, bizarre tree snakes from Madagascar, and lemon yellow eyelash vipers are but a few of the many specimens to be observed. This exhibit is considered by many to be one of the best reptile houses in any zoological park.

Crocodile Cove is a special area of the park dedicated to a wide variety of the world's crocodiles. More than 13 species are currently on exhibit and range from the fearsome saltwater crocodile, which can attain lengths of 20-plus feet and sometimes preys on humans, to the tiny West African dwarf crocodile, with large brown eyes and a bulldog-like appearance. The Cove's star attraction is Utan, the king of the crocs. Weighing in at more than a ton, he is 20 feet long and is the largest crocodile to ever be exhibited in the United States.

MEDIEVAL TIMES DINNER & TOURNAMENT

2904 Fantasy Way, Myrtle Beach

(800) 436-4386, (843) 236-8080

www.medievaltimes.com

Imagine the year is A.D. 1093, and you are a noble guest of the Spanish kingdom's royal family. The lord of the castle has invited more than 1,000 of his friends, neighbors, and foes to enjoy the sport and splendor of a royal tournament. As you step back in time nearly a millennium, you will feast on a hearty four-course meal. You'll marvel as spirited stallions perform intricate equestrian drills, and you'll gaze in awe as fearless knights compete in daring tournament games, jousting matches, and sword fights. Sound intriguing? You bet it is!

In North America there are currently nine Medieval Times castles in locations from Florida to Ontario to California; all operate within the same program format, and all have been tremendously successful. Produced by a Spanish-owned company, the spectacle is based on an actual event in the family history of one of the company's founders. (You can guess which side is his family after you see the show.)

At Medieval Times (see the Entertainment chapter), the evening of quality family entertainment begins as you cross a drawbridge into the 11th-century castle.

Once inside you are personally greeted by the Count and Countess of Perelada, who invite you to share in a sumptuous banquet while cheering for brave knights on horseback.

Festivities begin as trumpeters herald the guests into the Grand Ceremonial Arena. Gracious serfs and wenches scurry to fill glasses and attend to the count's honored guests, who feast on succulent roasted chicken, tasty spare ribs, and castle pastries. An awe-inspiring thunder of hooves fills the arena as the master of ceremonies leads a talented cast through a truly spectacular array of medieval pageantry. Sitting proudly astride colorfully attired Andalusian horses, the valiant knights of yore face their competitors in breathtaking and authentic tournament games, including the ring pierce, the flag toss, and the javelin throw.

The one-price admission includes the show, dinner, and two rounds of beverages (and adults can order alcohol). Sales tax and gratuity are extra. Adult and teen admission is $47.95. Children age 12 and younger get in for $29.95. Kids younger than age 3 are admitted free of charge. Reservations are suggested.

PAVILION NOSTALGIA PARK
**21st Avenue and US 17 at
Broadway at the Beach
(843) 913-9400
www.pavilionnostalgiapark.com**
Newcomers to Myrtle Beach will still appreciate this tribute to the Pavilion Amusement Park, which was the heart and soul of Myrtle Beach until it was demolished in 2006. The Pavilion Nostalgia Park offers a collection of classic rides from the old park, like the famous Herschell-Spillman Carousel, Wave Swinger, adult and kiddie Pirate Ship rides, and the Caterpillar, Dune Buggie, Boat, and Teacup rides. The historic German Baden Band Organ plays here, too! There is a blast-from-the-past retail shop, five midway skill games, a Pavilion Museum, and much more. Individual rides are $3 but discounts are given with 9 rides for $20 and 25 rides for $50.

THE RIPKEN EXPERIENCE
**3051 Ripken Way, Myrtle Beach
(866) RIPKEN9, (843) 913-5278
www.ripkentournaments.com**
Ripken as in Hall of Famer Cal Ripken. This facility offers kids an experience of a lifetime, but it does require some planning ahead because there is a limit on the number of kids who can take part in the "tournaments." This is a one-of-a-kind youth baseball complex with professional fields, beautiful grounds, easy access to beaches, shopping, dining, and more. The Ripken Experience, Myrtle Beach, is a true destination for baseball players and families. It gives players, coaches, and families a unique opportunity to enjoy tournament baseball while visiting the Grand Strand. It offers summer weeklong tournaments for ages 10 to 16. Spring camps as well as spring and fall tournaments are offered for a variety of age groups.

RIPLEY'S AQUARIUM
**Broadway at the Beach, between 21st and
29th Avenues N., Myrtle Beach
(800) 734-8888, (843) 916-0888
www.ripleysaquarium.com**
This 87,000-square-foot aquarium, right in the middle of Broadway at the Beach, is a stunning fish-behind-glass exhibit.

Expect to tour on a moving pathway; get up-close and personal with sharks, eels, and stingrays; and experience the glorious beauty of a living coral garden.

Five major portions of the aquarium explore different sea habitats. Dangerous Reef is centered around a shipwreck swarming with large sharks, poisonous predators, Caribbean reef fish, and green moray eels. Rainbow Rock re-creates the Pacific Ocean as the home of more than 1,000 fish, which dazzles with a swimming kaleidoscope of colors. To take it all in, the aquarium is viewed through two movie-screen-size windows. The Living Gallery is also a Pacific environment. The inhabitants are unusual, even mythic, and include the Pacific giant octopus, jellyfish, and sea anemones. Rio Amazon highlights the threatening piranha. At the Sea-For-Yourself Discovery Center, the experience is hands-on as you actually get to touch some of these creatures.

Ripley's Aquarium is open 365 days a year from 9 a.m. to 10 p.m. Admission is $18.99 for adults, $9.99 for children ages 5 through 11. Children ages 2 to 4 are $3.99, and those younger than 2 are free.

RIPLEY'S HAUNTED ADVENTURE
917 North Ocean Blvd., Myrtle Beach
(843) 626-0069
www.ripleys.com

Jamming yet another attraction in this building on Ocean Boulevard, Ripley's offers a haunted house to scare the daylights out of you. It's billed as "3 Floors of Fright," and they aren't kidding. The tour is a trip through the Grimsby & Streaper Casket Company, where the two owners disappeared mysteriously in 1891. Perhaps they never left? Live actors combine with high-tech tricks to illicit screams from even the most fearless of visitors.

It's so spooky, in fact, that you may want to be careful just how little your little ones are. Children under the age of six are not admitted.

Hours are 10 a.m. to 10 p.m. seven days a week. Adults are $13.99 plus tax, and children 6 to 11 are $7.99 plus tax.

RIPLEY'S MOVING THEATER
917 North Ocean Blvd.,
Myrtle Beach
(843) 448-2337
www.ripleys.com

Ripley's Moving Theater is located within the Ripley's Believe It or Not! Museum right on Ocean Boulevard, where you will also find Ripley's Haunted Adventures. As implied by its name, the theater literally thrusts participants into film adventures, with seats that move in eight different directions. Seats are motion-synchronized with the giant-screen action for realism that's heart-pounding, nonstop fun. You can be sure this pastime will keep your attention from start to finish. This adventure is really for kids who are able-bodied—management describes the ride as "aggressive" and doesn't want anyone with any type of health condition to take any chances.

The cost is $7.99 plus tax for children and $13.99 plus tax for adults. It's also possible to buy packages to visit the museum as well as the Haunted Adventure, located in the same building. Take note: Your little one must be 43 inches tall to climb aboard.

Hours are 10 a.m. to midnight.

RIPLEY'S SUPER FUN ZONE
901 North Ocean Blvd., Myrtle Beach
(843) 626-0069
www.ripleys.com

Just down the street from the Ripley's Museum, Haunted Adventure, and Motion Theater is a state-of-the-art arcade that will keep your kid and even the adult kids entertained for hours. Leave it to Ripley's to truly mean it when they tack the word super on the front of "Fun Zone." Interactive and high-tech games here represent the latest technology in the arcade industry. After playing, you can redeem your winnings for wonderful prizes.

Hours are 10 a.m. to 10 p.m. seven days a week.

WACCATEE ZOOLOGICAL FARM
8500 Enterprise Rd., Myrtle Beach
(843) 650-8500
www.waccateezoo.com

Kids and animal lovers will love viewing the myriad unusual animals here, including Bengal tigers. Waccatee covers 500 acres that include the Waccamaw River and pasture and woodlands for the zebras, buffalo, and deer. In the zoo itself you can see the traditional lions, tigers, bears, and monkeys—more than 100 species of animals. In the zoo the walk is about a mile and a half long and makes for a casual, relaxed, educational afternoon.

Admission is $8 for those age 13 and older, $4 for kids ages 12 months to 12 years. Kids 11 months and younger are free. Hours are 10 a.m. to 5 p.m. every day, year-round, excluding holidays.

SOUTH STRAND

BROOKGREEN GARDENS
US 17 S., Murrells Inlet
(800) 849-1931, (843) 237-6000
www.brookgreen.org
This Grand Strand landmark melds nature and history in an incomparable way. An absolute must for families with kids (and without), Brookgreen Gardens is an unequalled picnic spot. See the Attractions chapter for full details.

CAPTAIN DICK'S SALTWATER MARSH EXPLORER CRUISES
4123 US 17 Business, Murrells Inlet
(843) 651-3676
www.captdicks.com

Discover the amazing collection of plants, animals, birds, and marine life that makes up the best example in nature of a complete ecosystem. Not an artificial environment like a zoo or aquarium, this is the real thing. The captain's saltwater marsh tour is interactive. Various nets and dredges are employed to retrieve specimens from beneath the water. Specimens go into onboard touch tanks where they can be seen, observed, and, when appropriate, touched and held. All living specimens are returned to the water. There's also a fishing demonstration and a beach walk along a barrier island not accessible by car. Frequently, though not always, this adventure includes up-close encounters with bottle-nosed dolphins. All Explorer vessels are equipped with restrooms and operate from late spring through early fall. The two-and-a-half-hour boat ride is conducted by a marine naturalist. Call Captain Dick's for schedules and reservations. Adults enjoy the trip for $21, while children 12 and under are $15.

ANNUAL EVENTS

With all of the entertainment options available along the Grand Strand, you will probably be amazed at this lineup of annual events, festivals, tournaments, and shows. And you can well believe that even though there are 101 things for you to see and do here, these events are well received and attended. The Myrtle Beach Convention Center hosts a number of annual events, and, although we don't provide the center's address in respective listings, we won't leave you in the dark as to its whereabouts—Oak Street and 21st Avenue North in Myrtle Beach. Since plans can vary at any given time when coordinating such large programs, we cannot guarantee that dates, places, times, and prices won't change. Keep your eyes and ears tuned to the news for current information, or call the number listed to verify details.

Now let's get in the game and join in the fun!

JANUARY

North Strand

GRAND STRAND BOAT SHOW AND SALE
Myrtle Beach Convention Center
(843) 238-0485
www.grandstrandboatshow.com
This mid-January/early-February show attracts up to 10,000 boating enthusiasts and more than 90 exhibitors displaying motor boats, fishing equipment, pontoon boats, sailboats, one-person kayaks, and water-sports gear, including scuba-diving equipment and a host of accessories. Safety instruction is offered, and the U.S. Coast Guard is represented. Past seminars have included Flounder Fishing, Live Bait Fishing, and Speckled Trout and Drum Fishing. The show has gotten so large that auxiliary events are also now held at the Marina at Grand Dunes. Admission is $7 for adults, $3 for children between the ages of 6 and 12, and free for children under 6.

NORTH MYRTLE BEACH WINTER RUN
Throughout North Myrtle Beach
(843) 280-5570
This event includes the 5K and 15K road races for the southeastern region. Sponsored by the North Myrtle Beach Recreation Department, this competition, which takes place each year on the last Saturday in Jan, attracts 400 to 500 entrants. Following the grueling race, an awards ceremony is held to recognize the top five overall runners and the best in each age category—including those older than 60! Registration costs $30 for the 15k and $25 for the 5k. There are discounts if you register a month before the race, and registration is open until the day of the race.

Myrtle Beach

LIFESTYLES EXPO
Myrtle Beach Convention Center
(800) 62-SHOWS, (843) 444-0305
www.babyboomerexpos.com
Dedicated to the "50+ generation," this late-January, two-day expo usually attracts more than 6,000 people each year. Continuous entertainment and speakers fill the agenda.

The two-day extravaganza marked its 23rd consecutive year in 2009. Offerings include cooking demonstrations, blood-pressure screenings, and floral-design displays. Nearly 140 exhibitors are on hand, and the entertainment—which is always commendable—is continuous throughout the two-day show. Previously featured acts have included the famous Dancin' Grannies, lots of Big Band groups, the Myrtle Beach Barbershop Quartet, and many others. The admission fee is $5 per person.

FEBRUARY

Myrtle Beach

HORRY COUNTY MUSEUM QUILT GALA
Ocean Lakes Family Campground
(843) 248-1542, (843) 626-1542
www.horrycountymuseum.org/quilt_gala.asp
The first quilt gala was held in 1994 on the grounds of the Old County Courthouse in Conway and featured 40 beautifully colored quilts flapping in the breeze. The event has grown to a two-day festival of sorts and had to find a larger location. This popular event is now held at the Ocean Lakes Family Campground on the south end of Myrtle Beach, where guests enjoy browsing hundreds of quilting entries from South Carolina and the East Coast in categories that include wall hangings, wearables, bed quilts, and more. Hourly demonstrations on quilting techniques and applications are especially popular. Lots of vendors provide supplies and answer questions. There are also door prizes and raffles. Dates vary. Call ahead for details.

MYRTLE BEACH MARATHON
Various Myrtle Beach locations
(843) 293-7223
www.mbmarathon.com
Founded in 1997, this marathon has become a real event along the beach, encompassing not just the marathon itself but a bike race and a host of other runs that offer something for just about anyone who wants to get out and go. Proceeds benefit local charities, including the Leukemia-Lymphoma Society of South Carolina and the local chapter of the American Red Cross. The main event starts at Grissom Parkway and 21st Avenue North and loops around to end at Coastal Federal Field. Entry fees vary per event; see the Web site for details.

MYRTLE BEACH STAMP SHOW
Holiday Inn West, 101 Outlet Blvd.,
Myrtle Beach
(843) 347-0087
Children receive a free pack of stamps and an album to begin their stamp-collecting careers at this mid-Feb event. Ten dealers participate from the Southeastern region and display goods from beginner status to advanced. The U.S. Postal Service is on hand to sell current stamps, and collections are appraised free of charge. About 600 philatelists and other enthusiasts join the fun every year.

i If there's an annual event that particularly interests you, give the coordinators a call to see how you can be of assistance. Most annual events are put on by community volunteers and need lots of people to help run the project. What better way to gain free admission to your favorite event, get the scoop on the inner workings, and, most likely, meet a whole new group of friends?

SOUTH CAROLINA HALL OF FAME INDUCTION CEREMONY
Myrtle Beach Convention Center
(843) 626-7444
www.theofficialschalloffame.com
Two notable South Carolinians are inducted into this hall of fame each year, representing a gallant procession of statesmen, scientists, artists, soldiers, and teachers. Inductees include President Andrew Jackson, jazz legend Dizzy Gillespie, painter Jasper Johns, Gen. William C. Westmoreland, author Elizabeth Boatwright Coker, and more than 30 others. The South Carolina flag that was taken to the moon by NASA astronaut Charles M. Duke Jr. is also on display.

In 2009 King Hagler, an 18th-century Catawba Indian chief, and Pat Conroy, author of *The Prince of Tides, The Great Santini*, and other novels based in the Lowcountry, were inducted into the Hall of Fame. In 2008 the honorees were Eliza Lucas Pinckney, an 18th-century planter and agriculturalist, and Walter B. Edgar, an author and distinguished professor of history at the University of South Carolina.

Civil rights activist, famed attorney, and judge Matthew Perry was inducted in 2007, along with Revolutionary War hero Peter Horry. Horry County, where Myrtle Beach is located, is named after this brigadier general, who also served in the South Carolina Legislature. Previous recipients include Bobby Richardson, who joined the New York Yankees at the age of 19 and played more than 1,400 games while the Yankees were winning American League pennants. Named the Most Valuable Player in the 1960 World Series (still the only player from a losing team to be so named), Bobby holds numerous World Series records, including runs-batted-in in a game, runs-batted-in in a series, and hits in a series. He also holds the record for having played in 30 consecutive World Series games.

Cardinal Joseph Bernadin was ordained to the priesthood in 1952 and served 14 years in the Diocese of Charleston before being named a papal chamberlain in 1959 and a domestic prelate in 1962 by Pope John XXIII. He was appointed Auxiliary Bishop of Atlanta by Pope Paul VI, which made him the youngest bishop in the country. In 1982 Archbishop Bernadin was appointed by Pope John Paul II as archbishop of Chicago and was elevated to the Sacred College of Cardinals in early 1983. He died in 1996.

In 1980 Charles F. Bolden Jr. was selected as an astronaut candidate by NASA, qualified as a shuttle pilot in 1981, and subsequently flew four missions logging more than 690 hours in space. In 1986 he helped deploy the SARCOM KU satellite; in 1990 he piloted the shuttle Discovery, which launched the Hubble telescope. In 1992 he commanded the shuttle Atlantis on NASA's Mission to Planet Earth; and in 1994 commanded STA-60, the first joint U.S./Russian mission. After leaving NASA he was promoted to major general and assumed duties as Deputy Commander, United States Forces, Japan.

The hall is open from 8:30 a.m. to 5 p.m. daily, and admission is free.

MARCH

North Strand

SAINT PATRICK'S DAY PARADE AND CELEBRATION

Main Street and Ocean Blvd.,
North Myrtle Beach
(843) 385-3180
www.stpatnmb.com

Most of the area's nightclubs and restaurants host themed parties for this much lauded party weekend, and the North Myrtle Beach Parade and town square party has become the biggest thing to hit the North Strand since that shimmy-in-your-shoes state dance known as the shag. The first event was held in 1988, and it's grown each year since.

A Saturday parade kicks off this mid-Mar event (look up St. Patrick's Day on your calendar and plan accordingly). The parade begins at 9:30 a.m. at the Surfwood Shopping Center (look for Lowe's) and continues down Main Street. There are dozens of bands, floats, and beauty queens, as well as Irish musicians, cloggers, and more. Plenty of food and entertainment, kids' activities, and a fine display of arts and crafts make this the ideal family outing. After the parade an all-day "Irish Publick Square" commences. Best of all, admission is free of charge!

Myrtle Beach

ANNUAL CANADIAN-AMERICAN DAYS FESTIVAL

Throughout Horry County
(843) 626-7444, ext. 7239
www.canamdays.com,
www.myrtlebeachinfo.com

The Canadian-American Days Festival is the Myrtle Beach area's premier kickoff to the spring season. It attracts more than 100,000 Canadian and American visitors who come to see the sporting events, concerts, parade, and other special activities. The festival, which began in 1961, has been chosen as one of the region's top 20 March events annually since 1989 by the Southeast Tourism Society.

Can-Am, which happens in the middle of the month, traditionally coincides with Ontario's school holiday, so many families attend.

The festival includes a wide variety of indoor and outdoor activities, with an ever-growing lineup of new events each year. Past highlights of the festival included the National Shag Dance Championships, a deep-sea fishing tournament, an antique car show, celebrity look-alike contests, an International Kitefest, Can-Am Little Olympics, and the Can-Am Cup youth soccer tournament.

During this much-anticipated week, local radio stations feature Canadian news and weather broadcasts. For more information call or visit their Web site.

i Each year, new events are added to the Grand Strand calendar. To make sure you aren't missing out on an activity, check out the chamber of commerce's event site, www.grandstrandevents.com, as well as listings on www.thesunnews.com.

NATIONAL SHAG DANCE CHAMPIONSHIPS
To be announced, Myrtle Beach
(843) 497-7369
www.shagnationals.com
For enthusiasts of the shag, the vintage dance born and bred in the Carolinas, this is nothing short of stupendous!

The National Shag Dance Championships originated in Mar 1984 and has grown steadily ever since. This competition, where shaggers dance for placement in four divisions—juniors, nonprofessional, professional, and masters—is often called the longest-running shag contest in the United States. The Nationals contest has won two Feather Awards as Best Swing Event in the USA. National winners have appeared on *Good Morning America, CBS This Morning, The Crook & Chase Show, The Gatlin Brothers Show,* and *From Nashville to Broadway* in Myrtle Beach. They have also performed exhibitions at the Charlotte Hornets games, the Beach Ball Classic, the PGA annual banquet, the Cammy, and more.

The preliminaries are held in Jan; finals are held in Mar. For more information visit the Web site.

South Strand
DAFFODIL DAYS
Brookgreen Gardens, Murrells Inlet
(843) 235-6000
www.brookgreen.org
More than a quarter of a million daffodil bulbs make their debut in early Mar at the historic Brookgreen Gardens. The 40-acre grounds are awash in a sea of yellow as more than 250,000 bulbs show their finest. In addition to being able to tour the gardens, you can see floral exhibits of daffodils and other spring flowers. (See the Attractions chapter for more details about Brookgreen itself.)

APRIL

North Strand
APRIL MUSIC & WINE FEST
La Belle Amie Vineyard
1120 St. Joseph Rd. (corner of Highway 90 and St. Joseph Road), North Myrtle Beach
(843) 399-WINE (9563)
www.labellamie.com
The music is live and the wine flows at this fun-filled event on the grounds of La Belle Amie Vineyard. From noon to 6 p.m., you can wander the grounds and listen to music from some of the best local bands. Admission is $8 per person (those under 18 and over 80 are free). La Belle Amie sponsors numerous festivals on Saturday throughout the year.

S.O.S. SPRING SAFARI
Throughout North Myrtle Beach
(888) SOS-3113
www.shagdance.com
This is the world's largest spring break for mature adults. More than 15,000 shaggers, members of the Society of Stranders, and lovers of the beach gather in North Myrtle Beach in mid-Apr for an annual rite of spring. Ten full days and nights

of beach music and activities are all part of this riotous ritual. There's even a parade along Main Street in North Myrtle Beach, where shag club members design and build their own floats. Just let your imagination run wild! During one of the annual festivities, 3,000 of the crowd danced in unison, completely unconcerned about traffic. Admission to the dance clubs (Ducks and Ducks Too, 229 Main St.; Fat Harold's Beach Club, 212 Main St.; and Spanish Galleon, 100 Main St.) is free for card-holding S.O.S. members. The S.O.S. card costs $30 and entitles you to numerous benefits including discounts at many beach stores and clubs.

Myrtle Beach

ANNUAL DOLL SHOW & SALE
Myrtle Beach Convention Center
(843) 248-5643
www.knightshows.com

You'll find doll dealers from 15 states and more than 200 tables of goods at this show. Items include antique dolls, collectibles, modern artists' dolls, accessories, doll-making supplies, miniature furniture, replacement parts, and molds. Special exhibits and demonstrations are scheduled, and a raffle is held to raise money for a number of area charities. Tickets for adults are $4. Children ages 6 to 12 can enter for a minimal fee of $1.

ANNUAL SPRING GAMES & KITE FLYING CONTEST
Broadway at the Beach, between 21st and 29th Avenues N., Myrtle Beach
(843) 448-7881

This is a great mid-Apr event for veteran kite flyers and novices alike. Professional flyers will take to the breezes for stunt and single-line flying for a points-only competition. Professor Kite will be on hand to give out free kites to participating children and to give demonstrations and lessons.

Look to the empty fields around Broadway at the Beach for this event, which is usually held on a Saturday and Sunday. Admission is free. A donation can be given that benefits a local charity.

ART IN THE PARK
Chapin Park, Myrtle Beach
(843) 448-7690
www.artsyparksy.com

Since 1973, Art in the Park has been held in Chapin Park in the heart of downtown Myrtle Beach and showcases some of the finest artisans in the Southeast. Organized by the Waccamaw Arts & Crafts Guild, the event features more than 120 exhibitors, whose crafts encompass painting, photography, pottery, jewelry, glass, and stone. The two-day affair is free to the public and is open from 9 a.m. to 5 p.m.

GRAND STRAND FISHING RODEO
Apr 1 through Oct 31
(843) 626-7444
www.visitmyrtlebeach.com

The Grand Strand Fishing Rodeo, sponsored by the Myrtle Beach Area Chamber of Commerce, was created over five decades ago in an effort to enhance recreational fishing along the Grand Strand. It has succeeded admirably. There is no entry fee and the seven-month-long tournament awards more than $7,000 in cash and merchandise to recreational anglers entering qualified catches from Apr 1 to Oct 31.

The event includes four divisions: pier, surf and inlet, deep-sea catches, and tag and release. The tag-and-release program has been instituted to award special certificates for marlin, sailfish, swordfish, and tarpon to anglers submitting documentation of their participation. Entrants receive an official Grand Strand Fishing Rodeo decal. An official shoulder patch is awarded to anglers entering the three heaviest fish of each species in each division for that month. Additionally, Fish-of-the-Month awards consisting of various donated prizes are given to the anglers entering the four heaviest fish out of all eligible entries for the month's designated species.

Entry forms are available at any one of the official weigh stations: Cherry Grove Pier, Apache Pier, Second Avenue Pier, Springmaid Beach Pier, Myrtle Beach State Park, Pier at Garden City, Marlin Quay Marina, Capt. Dick's Marina, and Surfside Pier.

For additional information regarding locations, rules, regulations, and other details, please call the Myrtle Beach Area Chamber of Commerce at the number given above.

South Strand

ANNUAL GEORGETOWN PLANTATION TOURS

Throughout Georgetown
(843) 545-8291
www.georgetown-sc.com
www.pgwinyah.com/PlantationTours.htm

Sponsored by the women of Prince George Winyah Parish, one of the oldest and most beautiful churches in Georgetown, this much loved annual event is more than 50 years old. The tour, usually held in late Mar or early Apr, allows an up-close look at a wide variety of plantations and colonial town houses. Most of the homes are privately owned and are graciously "loaned" to this worthy cause once each year. Many are listed on the National Register of Historic Places. A different selection of homes is featured each day.

A one-day ticket for Friday or Saturday costs $35. A two-day ticket costs $60. Histories and maps are provided with the tickets. Tickets are sold at the Prince George Winyah Parish Hall on Highmarket Street in Georgetown on each day of the event. Visitors must arrange their own transportation. At each location trained hostesses are available to answer questions. Box lunches will be available at the Parish Hall and may be reserved in advance for an extra $5. Call ahead for information on advance purchase of tickets.

MAY

North Strand

BLUE CRAB FESTIVAL

On the waterfront, Little River
(843) 249-6604
www.crabfestival.com

Every year about 30,000 people flock to the waterfront streets of this historic fishing village to attend the Blue Crab Festival. Held late in May, this much loved festival features more than 150 arts-and-crafts booths with everything from paintings to brass and copper sculptures, wearable art, jewelry, wood carvings, and children's goods. Food booths boast yummies including steamed crabs, grilled tenderloin, and pizza. The children's area includes a petting zoo, pony rides, face painting, and puppets. Entertainment promises widespread appeal; enjoy a variety of live musical performances, including jazz, country, bluegrass, and gospel. Admission is $5. Children five years of age and younger enter free.

Myrtle Beach

BLESSING OF THE INLET

US 17 Business, Murrells Inlet
(843) 651-5099
www.blessingoftheinlet.com

Founded in 1996, Murrells Inlet's Blessing of the Inlet Festival continues to grow and receive regional and statewide support and recognition. Held throughout the fishing village that's known for its delectable seafood, the daylong event is full of activities and games for the children, arts and crafts for adults, entertainment galore, and lots of delicious local specialties. There is something for everyone and every age at this family-flavored festival. In years past, children's activities have included mural painting, face painting, a climbing wall, candy art, and the ever-popular "Dunking Tank." There is no admission or parking charge, and the event is held rain or shine.

MYRTLE BEACH MIKE WEEK

(843) 651-5555
www.mbbikeweeks.com

As a Grand Strand Insider, you can always tell when "bike week" is fast approaching. Makeshift trading posts (mostly hawking metal and leather goods) spring up all along US 501, the roads begin to rumble and roar, tattoos cease to seem out of the ordinary, and bar owners are smiling ear to ear as they stock up on beer. Rated as one of the top five motorcycle events in the nation—and the oldest dealer-sponsored motorcycle event in the country—the 2010 rally will mark the 70th year on the Grand Strand.

An estimated 300,000 cyclists roar into town for ten days in mid-May. A race is usually held on the Friday of the event at the Myrtle Beach Speedway.

JUNE

ANNUAL SUN FUN FESTIVAL
Throughout the Grand Strand
(843) 626-7444
www.sunfunfestival.com
Now well into its second 50 years, Myrtle Beach's annual Sun Fun Festival is still considered one of the most popular events on the Beach. It was founded in 1951 by a group of local businessmen to entice visitors to the area, and the tourists still return year after year. This fun-filled five-day festival kicks off the summer season along South Carolina's Grand Strand with a host of events featuring national celebrities and fun for all ages. The largest annual event of its kind in either of the Carolinas, Sun Fun attracts more than 300,000 visitors of all ages and interests. The dazzling sights and sounds of a typical summer vacation combine with dozens and dozens of exciting festival events—from celebrity concerts to the Miss Sun Fun pageant—making Sun Fun a tradition with thousands of teenagers and families alike.

During Sun Fun, visitors participate in such beachfront activities as beauty contests, sand castle–building competitions, watermelon eating and bubblegum blowing contests, beach games, and volleyball games galore.

Extensive event listings are available at all chamber offices and on the Sun Fun Web site.

South Strand

HARBORWALK FESTIVAL
Downtown Georgetown
(843) 546-1511
www.theharborwalk.com
The annual Harborwalk Festival celebrates the historic city of Georgetown—South Carolina's third oldest. Festivities are held every year during the last full weekend in June. This summer street festival offers live music on stages throughout the downtown area, food, games, and arts and crafts. The festival is enhanced by its beautiful downtown location—close to the Harborwalk, the Kaminski Museum, and all sorts of historical sites. It runs from 10 a.m. to midnight.

JULY

North Strand

FOURTH OF JULY FIREWORKS DISPLAY
Various locations
(843) 281-2662
Fireworks let loose on the north end of the Strand at 9 p.m. from just south of the runway at Grand Strand Airport. Since the airport is adjacent to Barefoot Landing, the complex offers some parking at the Alligator Adventure entrance. Besides Barefoot Landing as a vantage point to watch the show, try a spot anywhere along US 17 North from 33rd Avenue South in North Myrtle Beach to Barefoot Landing.

Myrtle Beach

FOURTH OF JULY FIREWORKS DISPLAYS
Various Myrtle Beach locations
(843) 444-3200, (843) 626-8480
The only venue in the Myrtle Beach area that shoots off fireworks on Independence Day every year is Broadway at the Beach.

Broadway at the Beach usually begins its display at 10 p.m. and includes a light and music fountain show.

However, throughout the summer the Second Avenue Pier (the second phone number at the beginning of this listing) holds a 25-minute fireworks display every Wed at 10 p.m., which it calls Beach Bang. It can be seen along the beach and in the downtown area.

JUNIOR S.O.S. SHAG PARTY
Various locations
(888) SOS-3113
www.juniorshaggers.com

The Junior S.O.S. Shag Dance Party is a weekend for young folks under the age of 21. All the fun takes place in the Ocean Drive area of North Myrtle Beach. For one weekend only in mid-July, several of the adult shag clubs open their doors and hearts to the juniors to support them and help create a safe and fun event. Around 400 juniors attend this annual event, with more than 20 free Junior Dance Workshops, a Junior Mixed-Doubles Contest, a Juniors-Only Dance Party, a volleyball tournament, and other beach activities. Call for exact dates and details.

South Strand

FOURTH OF JULY FIREWORKS DISPLAYS
Various South Strand locations
(843) 651-5850
The Murrells Inlet Fireworks Display blasts off at 10 p.m. and can easily be seen from just about anywhere in Murrells Inlet and Garden City Beach. Best viewing points cited are the Belin Memorial United Methodist Church parking lot, Captain Dick's Marina, the Marshwalk, and the public boat landing in Murrells Inlet.

Another south-end display begins at 9 p.m. as the city of Georgetown puts on its firecracker show. The display is visible all along the Harbor-walk in Georgetown on Front Street.

MURRELLS INLET FOURTH OF JULY BOAT PARADE
Murrells Inlet
(843) 651-5675
www.murrellsinletsc.com
Since 1984, more than 100 boats have gussied up for the Fourth of July and entertained the multitudes who watch from and picnic on the shores. From 14-foot fishing boats to 40-foot yachts, participating watercraft start the aquatic caravan at high tide at the jetties of Garden City Beach and proceed to Murrells Inlet. Public points of view to watch the flotilla are Captain Dick's Marina, the Marshwalk, the Belin United Methodist Church, and the Murrells Inlet boat landing, all on US 17 Business in Murrells Inlet. Trophies are awarded

to the "best-dressed" docks and boats. This event keeps growing because it is so much fun.

AUGUST

Myrtle Beach

ANNUAL PGA SUPERSTORE WORLD AMATEUR HANDICAP CHAMPIONSHIP
Various Grand Strand golf courses
(800) 833-8798
www.worldamgolf.com
Generally held at the end of Aug, the PGA Superstore World Amateur Handicap Championship is the world's largest amateur golf tournament, with nearly 5,000 participants, 10 major sponsors, 60-plus exhibitors, and more than $500,000 in prizes. There's nothing amateur about the fun at this eagerly anticipated annual event. It's a week most people never forget, leading many to make the annual trek an opportunity to visit with old friends—and make new ones.

The World Amateur has firmly established itself as the premier and largest amateur golf championship in the world. The competition, which began with 680 golfers in 1984, has attracted more than 70,000 golfers of all ages and abilities. The 2006 event drew nearly 5,000 participants from all 50 states and 32 foreign countries.

Appropriately referred to as the Everyman Open, neither skill level, age, height, weight, nor gender affects an individual's ability to participate in the event. Thanks to the golf handicap system, absolutely anyone and everyone can compete. Over the years players with handicaps ranging from 3 to 35 have been crowned World Champions in this four-day, 72-hole event.

The fun begins on Sunday, when participating golfers pick up registration information and a gift bag at the Myrtle Beach Convention Center. The next four days are filled with spirited competition, score viewing, long-drive contests, putting equipment demos, lots of food and drink, and—if you're lucky—bragging rights, too.

Of course, for many the highlight is the event's nightly party, affectionately known as the "World's Largest 19th Hole." The 19th Hole, which covers the entire Myrtle Beach Convention Center, is catered nightly by Myrtle Beach's best restaurants and provides free top-shelf drinks and live entertainment. The centerpiece of the 19th Hole is the PGA Tour Superstore, a 100,000-square-foot golfer's paradise.

CRAFTSMEN'S SUMMER CLASSIC ARTS & CRAFTS FESTIVAL
Myrtle Beach Convention Center
(336) 274-5550
www.gilmoreshows.com
Collectors and unique-gift-givers alike are surrounded by a smorgasbord of authentic, handcrafted items at this arts and crafts show in early Aug. More than 260 exhibitors from 20 states bring in original designs that include pottery, wood, fine art, toys, jewelry, baskets, stained glass, leather, tin, weaving, sculpture, musical instruments, and furniture.

Prices are $7 for adults and $1 for children 6 to 12 years of age. Please call in advance for specifics on group rates.

SEPTEMBER

North Strand

S.O.S. FALL MIGRATION
Various locations in North Myrtle Beach
(888) SOS-3113
www.shagdance.com
The Society of Stranders calls its thousands of active members to return to North Myrtle Beach in mid-Sept for one last big party before winter sets in. Days and nights are filled with activities, shagging, and sightseeing. Eight clubs around the Ocean Drive section pitch in to make sure that every evening resounds with nonstop beach music.

Myrtle Beach

BEACH BOOGIE & BARBEQUE
Valor Park, Myrtle Beach Air Force Base
(843) 916-7239
www.beachboogiebarbequefestival.com
The first Beach Boogie & Barbeque was held in 2006 and proved to be so popular, it's been put on the calendar as an annual event. Held over Labor Day weekend, the three-day event includes a cook-off, free concerts, a car show, outdoor movies, and more. Beach Boogie & Barbeque is held in Valor Park on the former Myrtle Beach Air Force Base.

HOME SHOW
Myrtle Beach Convention Center
(843) 347-7311
http://hbahorrygeorgetown.com/special Events.php
This annual event, sponsored by the Horry-Georgetown Home Builders Association, is literally 100,000 square feet of displays concerning home building, design, and decorating. Past shows have offered designer furniture, floor covering, wallpaper, window treatments, whirlpool tubs, doors, stained glass, and mirror ideas.

For the yard and garden, plants, flowers, shrubs, trees, pools, spas, and statuary exhibits were on hand. The three-day event featured a list of seminars and workshops that ranged from learning to make garden stepping stones using recycled materials to orchid care to the Plant Doctor Booth, where participants could take a sick plant for care.

A one-day ticket for adults is $5. A three-day ticket can be purchased for $8, and children under the age of 14 are admitted free.

ITALIAN FESTIVAL
Chapin Park, Kings Highway at
16th Avenue N., Myrtle Beach
(843) 650-3466
www.sonsofitalylodge.com
This mid-Sept festival began in 1995 and continues to grow. It's a day of food, music, and arts and

crafts—Italian-style. The Sons of Italy and area restaurants that specialize in Italian cuisine bring in the goodies that range from New York–style pizza to pastas. Musical entertainment usually features the smooth sound of the Big Band era, while strolling accordionists provided a little taste of Italy. The event runs from 10 a.m. to 6 p.m. in the park, and admission is free.

GREEK FESTIVAL
St. John the Baptist Greek Orthodox Church
3301 33rd Ave., North Myrtle Beach
(843) 448-3773
www.stjohn-mb.org
Locals have come to look forward to St. John's Greek Festival each Sept. The four-day event is held in the fellowship hall and on the church grounds on the corner of US 17 Bypass and 33rd Avenue North, starting on Thursday of the last weekend in Sept. Live Greek music, Greek dancers, and vendors are just part of the draw. Feast yourself on mouthwatering Greek foods such as gyros, roasted lamb, Greek salad, spanikopita, and moussaka, as well as a wide assortment of Greek pastries and breads. Soft drinks, beer, and Greek wines are also available. Try a baklava ice-cream sundae! Admission is just $1 for adults, and kids are free.

SOUTH ATLANTIC SHRINE PARADE
Along Ocean Boulevard, Myrtle Beach
(843) 448-5797
http://southatlanticsa.org
This four-hour procession in late Sept features Shrine Temple representatives from six states: West Virginia, Virginia, North and South Carolina, Tennessee, and Kentucky. Expect to see a proliferation of wacky go-karts, clowns, and floats traveling along Ocean Boulevard from Sixth Avenue South to 11th Avenue North in Myrtle Beach. The parade usually starts at 9:30 a.m.

The event usually brings approximately 4,000 Shrine families to the area. The South Atlantic Shrine Association supports 22 Shriners' hospitals and three burn institutes.

SOUTH CAROLINA'S LARGEST GARAGE SALE
Myrtle Beach Pavilion Parking Garage,
Kings Highway and Ninth Avenue N.,
Myrtle Beach
(843) 918-1242
www.cityofmyrtlebeach.com/events.html
For one Saturday in mid-Sept, the Pavilions parking garage is filled with the hubbub of hagglers hawking wares. Hundreds of booths set up on every parking level feature household goods, clothing, toiletries, sporting goods, furniture, toys, food, and just plain junk. The sale runs from 7 a.m. to noon, and admission is free.

South Strand
ANNUAL ATALAYA ARTS AND CRAFTS FESTIVAL
Huntington Beach State Park,
US 17 S., Murrells Inlet
(803) 734-0156, (843) 237-4440
For the Atalaya Arts and Crafts Festival, one of the largest art shows in the Southeast, the food-and-fun-with-a-view formula has proved successful since 1975. Scheduled in mid- to late Sept at Huntington Beach State Park, this festival has earned a reputation for attracting some of the region's—even the nation's—finest artisans. Because the show is juried—meaning participating artisans are screened for merit and appropriateness—you can be assured the maze of artwork is of top-of-the-line quality. It is, in fact, quite an honor to be accepted as an exhibitor. Consequently, the festival has become a not-to-be-missed pilgrimage for knowledgeable art collectors and plain-ol' admirers.

Not only does the Atalaya Arts and Crafts Festival give you an opportunity to peruse the wares of talented artists and craftspeople, it offers you a delicious taste of authentic history. Atalaya (pronounced At-a-lie-a, not At-a-lay-a), after which the festival is named, is a majestic Moorish-inspired structure located in the park. Construction was launched on Atalaya in 1931. Archer and Anna Hyatt Huntington, new owners of a vast tract of land that included four colonial plantations, orchestrated plans for the castle that was to be their winter home. Mr. Huntington was a scholar of Spanish history and culture, so it is not surprising his new home was fashioned after the eighth-century Moorish fortresses along the Mediterranean coast of Spain. Mrs. Huntington was a brilliant sculptress, and her creative influence can also be detected in Atalaya.

The breezy courtyard and rooms of this beautiful old building serve as a breathtaking and mystical backdrop for the eclectic works of more than 100 artists and craftspeople. Included are lots of area food vendors offering delicious Lowcountry cuisine. (With the exception of special tours, Atalaya is typically closed to the public, so just seeing the interior of the old castle is reason enough to attend!)

THE PAWLEYS ISLAND FESTIVAL OF MUSIC AND ART
Various South Strand locations
(843) 237-4774
www.pawleysmusic.org
The hugely successful Pawleys Island Festival of Music and Art usually opens in early Sept and runs for three weeks. Begun in 1991, the festival brings a new theme each season and a veritable plethora of music and art performances at venues throughout the South Strand all the way to the historic port of Georgetown. There are far too many events to list separately, and the schedule changes dramatically from one year to another, but if you are the "artsy" type, rest assured you will not want to miss this. Call ahead for specifics.

i The Pawleys Island Festival of Music and Art takes place in the heart of the town's historic district. Pawleys was one of the first resorts in the United States, and the district dates back to the 1750s. It is listed on the National Register of Historic Places and encompasses 500 acres and 12 buildings.

OCTOBER

North Strand

FARM HERITAGE DAY
Indigo Farms, Little River
(843) 399-6902, (910) 287-6794
http://indigofarmsmarket.com
Farm Heritage Day is on the first or second Saturday in Oct at Indigo Farms in Little River, 4.5 miles off Highway 9, at the North Carolina state line. The event features informational presentations on traditional farming methods and culture, as well as farmer games, history talks, and the popular "NASPIG" races. Lots of event specifics change from one year to another, so do take the time to call ahead to find out about everything on tap for this year.

Indigo Farms also hosts Pumpkin Day on the third Saturday in Oct. Enjoy nighttime hayrides and an on-site bakery, ice-cream parlor, and florist. Additional products and services include school tours of farms and animals in spring and fall with hayrides. Farm-fresh, homegrown fruit and vegetables and pick-your-own strawberries (in season) are reason enough to visit anytime.

SHRIMP AND JAZZ FESTIVAL
Little River
www.shrimpandjazzfest.org
(843) 249-6604, (843) 446-3087
Shrimp and jazz. There are a lot of both at this festival, which has begun to compete with Little River's Blue Crab Festival in popularity polls. Family-oriented, the event features fine arts and crafts, children's activities, and an abundance of good food and good music. The lineup of performers offers a broad spectrum of entertainment.

Little River is one of the oldest communities in South Carolina, dating back to the 1700s. The festival pays tribute to the history while drawing people in to be a part of today's community.

Myrtle Beach

HALLOWEEN BASH

Broadway at the Beach, Myrtle Beach

(843) 444-3200

www.broadwayatthebeach.com

Broadway at the Beach invites kids to come trick-or-treat with them from 5 to 7 p.m. Free bags are given to children at the visitor center, and an adult costume contest is held at 10 p.m.

OKTOBERFEST

Coastal Federal Field, Myrtle Beach

(843) 918-1242

Beer and bratwurst are the favorites at this early-Oct celebration of the harvest season. Authentic oom-pah music is played, and arts and crafts are on display. Visitors show up to consume German brown bread, sauerkraut, and sausages in addition to the usual festival fare of hamburgers, pizza, and funnel cakes. Some hot-selling items that you are likely to find are homemade dolls, clothing, and Christmas and Halloween decorations.

Oktoberfest admission is free.

South Strand

ANNUAL WOODEN BOAT EXHIBIT AND CHALLENGE

Front Street (on the waterfront), Georgetown

(877) 285-3888

www.woodenboatshow.com

Here's an exciting twist to the usual boat shows and races: You make your own boat from scratch before sailing! At the Annual Wooden Boat Exhibit and Challenge, two-person teams are given a four-hour time limit in which to construct a functioning 12-foot rowing dory. Each team starts off with the same raw materials and equipment, marine-quality plywood, nails, and oarlocks.

The overall competition takes into account speed, quality, and the results of a short relay race in the dory to Goat Island and back. After being awed by the pace of building, onlookers usually get a real kick out of watching the rowers trying to steer the rudderless, awkward boats in a straight line.

The event also includes all the trappings of maritime life: displays of handmade oars, intricate models of shrimp boats, pillows decorated with nautical themes, knot-tying demonstrations, and simmering pots of spicy, delicious gumbo.

There is no admission fee to the exhibit; spectators are allowed to watch from outside the working tents of the competing teams.

PAWLEYS ISLAND TOUR OF HOMES

(843) 237-8454

The Pawleys Island Tour of Homes, scheduled for mid-Oct, benefits the Georgetown Chapter of Habitat for Humanity. The tour is composed of a dozen or more Pawleys Island beach homes—ranging from 19th-century summer cottages to contemporary year-round residences. Unusual artifacts, windswept landscaping, and porches perched on the edge of the Atlantic combine to make this house tour uniquely enjoyable. Tickets can be ordered in advance; call for prices and details. Even the locals come, so don't miss this.

SURFSIDE BEACH FAMILY FESTIVAL

One block off Surfside Drive, Surfside Beach

(843) 913-6339

www.surfsidebeach.org

What started out as a little ol' family picnic in 1985 has now grown into a full-fledged festival attended by more than 10,000 people each year. It's a daylong affair in early Oct, with plenty of food and arts and crafts for sale, plus information booths if you need directions. Even during a downpour in 1999, an estimated 9,000 people came out to enjoy homespun crafts, games, and performers under a covered bandstand.

Several bands perform, and more than 90 vendors offer everything from hot dogs to rides on an oversized stuffed panda and tiger. This event always coordinates lots of games for children. There is no admission fee. Open 10 a.m. to 4 p.m.

NOVEMBER

North Strand

INTRACOASTAL CHRISTMAS REGATTA
Little River to North Myrtle Beach
(843) 280-6354
www.christmasregatta.com
On the Saturday after Thanksgiving, dozens of vessels get decked out for the holidays. Beginning at 5 p.m., boats launch from Little River Inlet and travel down the waterway for an estimated 7 p.m. arrival at Dock Holiday's Marina at 13th Avenue North in North Myrtle Beach. Viewing sites encompass the restaurants along the Little River waterfront, the Riverboat Restaurant at North Myrtle Beach Marina, the Blue Marlin Yacht and Fishing Club at Anchor Marina, and Marker 350 at Harbourgate Marina. (See the Boating chapter for extensive information on each of these marinas.)

The regatta benefits local children's charities and spurs an annual toy collection for needy kids. Participating boaters pay a $40 entry fee or donate new, unwrapped toys. The event offers a $1,200 grand prize.

MID-NOVEMBER MUSIC & WINE FEST
La Belle Amie Vineyard
1120 St. Joseph Rd. (corner of Highway 90 and St. Joseph Road), North Myrtle Beach
(843) 399-WINE (9563)
www.labelleamie.com
Just throw down a blanket, set up your candelabra, and drink in the live music and, of course, the wine. The annual festival on the grounds of La Belle Amie Vineyard features some of the area's best local bands and runs from noon to 6 p.m.

Admission is $10 per person (those under 18 and over 80 are free). La Belle Amie sponsors numerous festivals on Saturday throughout the year. Join their Festival Club for $60 for admission to the entire series, plus get a La Belle Amie T-Shirt or bottle of wine and discounts in the gift shop.

TASTE OF THE TOWN
Myrtle Beach Convention Center
(843) 448-5930
If you would like to sample foods from a variety of Grand Strand restaurants, make sure you do not miss this early-Nov event. More than 50 restaurants participate each year, serving up the best they have to offer. Taste of the Town has become so popular that it has taken over three rooms of the convention center. Attendance has risen to more than 7,000 people.

The competitive part of the show is watched closely by residents and other restaurants. While the event is always good-natured, a positive showing can mean an increase in business for the coming year; for smaller restaurants that must close to send their staff to Taste of the Town, winning or placing is everything. In fact, some popular mainstay establishments had to bow out because of the tremendous amount of work involved to participate. To give you an idea of the pace, one restaurant served 2,000 portions of food by 8 p.m.

Awards are bestowed for the best overall food, the best entree, the best dessert, and the People's Choice.

This event is a fund-raising project for St. Andrews Catholic School. Taste of the Town is held from 4 to 9 p.m. Admission is $5 for adults; children age 14 and younger are admitted free with a paying adult. Food tickets cost $1 each, and most food items cost from one to three tickets.

Myrtle Beach

ANNUAL DICKENS CHRISTMAS SHOW & FESTIVAL
Myrtle Beach Convention Center
(843) 448-9483
www.dickenschristmasshow.com
You know that Christmas is just around the corner when the Dickens Show gears up at the convention center in mid-Nov. And what a charming way to get in the holiday spirit! More than 350 period-clad vendors help transform the

Convention Center back to Merry Old England. Grand Stranders spend hours decorating the trees and wreaths on display, and the adornments are a sight to behold. The beautifully trimmed tannenbaums and handsome wreaths are usually auctioned off by the end of the festival, and hundreds of holiday gifts and ornaments are available for show and sale. Money collected from the silent auction of the Festival of Trees, decorated by area businesses, benefits Citizens Against Spouse Abuse. The Myrtle Beach Kiwanis are the charity of choice for the proceeds from the Festival of Wreaths. In 1996 a Festival of Holiday Tables (featuring centerpieces) was added; proceeds were donated to Habitat for Humanity of Horry County.

Admission to the show and festival is $8 for adults, $4 for children ages 2 to 12; a multiple-day pass is $12, and children younger than age 2 are admitted for free.

Enjoy an authentic Victorian tea in an elaborate period setting, where you will dine at tables bedecked in red plaid and gold and white, centered by traditional English topiaries, as waitstaff in Victorian costumes attend to your every need.

ANNUAL SOUTH CAROLINA STATE BLUEGRASS FESTIVAL
Myrtle Beach Convention Center
(706) 864-7203
www.aandabluegrass.com
This festival is touted as "the Palmetto State's oldest, largest, and best bluegrass event."

Drawing fans from throughout the eastern United States and Canada, the late-Nov festival is a "who's who" of traditional bluegrass performers. The festival has played host to such performers as the Grand Ole Opry's Osborne Brothers, the Lewis Family, Doyle Lawson & Quicksilver, Jim & Jesse and the Virginia Boys, IIIrd Tyme Out, Ralph Stanley & the Clinch Mtn. Boys, Raymond Fairchild, the Bass Mountain Boys, Mike Stevens, Chubby Wise, J. D. Crowe and the New South, Country Gentlemen Reunion, Mac Wiseman, the Larry Stephenson Band, the Mayor and Buford, Lou Reid, Terry Baucom and Carolina, Bob Paisley & the Southern

Grass, the Del McCoury Band, the Sand Mountain Boys, and the Lonesome River Band.

This music festival differs from most since jam sessions are prevalent and a good number of audience members join in with the bands at any given time. As bluegrass lovers admit, this music represents a way of life.

In addition to an almost seamless stream of performances, the Bluegrass Festival offers arts and crafts booths, food and beverages, and CDs from all of the scheduled artists for sale before and after their shows.

Tickets are available at the gate and are sold at the convention center box office during the festival. Prices vary from year to year. Tickets range from $35 for general admission to $40 for reserved. Children are $20 for general and $25 reserved. Three-day passes are available. Please call ahead for details.

CAMMY AWARDS
Various locations
(800) 342-2262, (843) 272-1111
www.cammy.org
The celebration of the Cammy Awards (Carolina's Magic Music Years) began in 1995 as an exciting party for performers and fans of Carolina Beach Music. Fourteen bands entertained at the first awards show held in Salisbury, North Carolina. In 1998 the Cammys moved to North Myrtle Beach, and the Cammy Weekend was born.

During this fun-filled weekend in Nov, entertainers perform at various beach clubs on Friday and Saturday nights. A Band Fair is held prior to the awards show on Sunday afternoon, and a VIP party, held after the awards event, has become a beloved tradition. The show honors winners in various categories and honors the memory of the pioneers who originated this music and helped make it great.

"MERRILY MYRTLE," A HOLIDAY CELEBRATION
(843) 626-7444
www.visitmyrtlebeach.com
Enjoy Merrily Myrtle by the sea in the Myrtle Beach area from Nov through Dec. The holiday

season shines as the entire beach comes to life with beautiful, holiday decorations. The inviting sights and sounds of the Myrtle Beach area ensure a warm welcome to visitors. All sorts of special events make up the celebration, from Thanksgiving and Christmas services to concerts, parades, children's events, arts and crafts exhibits, festivals, sporting activities, and a slew of New Year's Eve extravaganzas. There is something on the agenda to dazzle both young and old.

THE JACK MONROE BEACH RIDE
Lakewood Campground, Myrtle Beach
(843) 282-2903
www.americanheart.org

Hundreds of horses trot along the Grand Strand shoreline for this annual event that raises money to fight heart disease and stroke. Nearly 1,300 riders raise in excess of $300,000 in this unique event. The name was changed from simply "Ride-a-Thon" to the "Jack Monroe Beach Ride" to honor a longtime supporter.

Registration fee for adults is $150. Group rates are available for 15 riders or more. After the 20-mile hike on horseback, entrants are treated to a barbecue lunch, awards ceremony, and a raffle. The horses are led along the beach by a police escort, and the public is invited to watch from the sidelines.

DECEMBER

North Strand

CHRISTMAS TOUR OF HOMES
Throughout the North Strand
(843) 249-6449

Like its Georgetown cousin, this Christmas Tour of Homes, sponsored by the North Myrtle Beach Women's Club, gives one the chance to see stately homes dressed up for the Yuletide season. Six abodes are opened to the public for one afternoon in Dec. Proceeds from the event help a mix of charities, such as Children's Hospice, the North Myrtle Beach Rescue Squad, the North Myrtle Beach Animal Shelter, and various scholarship funds.

Myrtle Beach

BEACH BALL CLASSIC
Myrtle Beach Convention Center
(843) 213-0032
www.beachballclassic.com

Sponsored by an impressive variety of local businesses since its inception in 1980, the Beach Ball Classic in late Dec is always an exciting showcase of this country's best high-school basketball talent. Teams are rated and selected to play in this tournament before standing-room-only crowds of cheering fans, basketball enthusiasts, and college scouts. To give you an idea of the kind of talent to expect at the classic, check out this impressive list of former Beach Ball stars that wound up in the NBA: Kenny Anderson, Grant Hill, Jimmy Jackson, Don MacLean, Jerrod Mustaf, Billy Owens, Cherokee Parks, Rasheed Wallace, and Dontonio Wingfield.

Games start each day at 3:30 p.m. and culminate around 10 p.m. An admission fee is announced close to tournament time.

SCADA (NORTH-SOUTH ALL-STAR FOOTBALL GAME)
Doug Shaw Memorial Stadium,
33rd Avenue N. and Oak Street, Myrtle Beach
(864) 573-7627
www.northsouthallstarfootball.com

As the name implies, this mid-Dec game showcases the best young players from the northern and southern portions of South Carolina. The teams battle it out on the field, while college scouts get a good look at potential recruits. In the past, head coaches and representatives from Clemson University, the University of North Carolina, and Wake Forest University were on hand to assess the skills of 88 hopeful high schoolers. Tickets for the event cost $10 in advance and $15 at the gate.

SPRINGMAID BEACH CRAFT SHOW
3200 South Ocean Blvd., Myrtle Beach
(843) 315-7162
www.springmaidbeach.com/calendar-of-events.html

This early-December event includes more than 300 booths, representing craftspeople and artists alike. Some 20,000 showgoers are treated to an incredible array of quilts, jewelry, clothing, woodcrafts, baskets, stained-glass dollhouses, and collectibles, plus wreaths and decorations for the holiday season. The Springmaid Beach Craft Show is open to the public, with booths found both indoors and outdoors. Admission is free.

South Strand

GEORGETOWN COUNTY FESTIVAL OF TREES
Litchfield Exchange Mall
(843) 546-3410

Delight in the true spirit of Christmas by attending the Hospice of Georgetown County's Festival of Trees. Breakfast with Santa kicks off festivities on a Saturday morning in early December, and attractions include a breathtaking display of uniquely decorated Fraser firs and a variety of music and entertainment. The Christmas Shop, Country Kitchen, and Santa's Shop offer lots of opportunities for shortening your shopping list, too. Call for a complete schedule.

NIGHTS OF A THOUSAND CANDLES
Brookgreen Gardens, Murrells Inlet
(843) 235-6025, (843) 235-6016
www.brookgreen.org

Come enjoy three weekends of wonder and beauty as these beautiful gardens are decorated for the holidays in a natural style, complemented by luminaria along the paths and twinkle lights throughout. There are special dramatic and musical performances, a Lowcountry oyster roast, and more, all guaranteed to put you in a festive spirit. The cost is $15 for ages 13 and older, $6 for children 6 to 12. The event has been so successful that sellout crowds are always anticipated, so do take time to call in advance or visit the Web site to reserve tickets for you and your family.

ARTS AND CULTURE

In an area replete with state-of-the-art theaters built to showcase international headline stars, you would think that the Grand Strand's community arts scene would head for the beach to bury its proverbial head in the sand. Instead our native artists seem to have absorbed this main-stage professional energy and talent, launching more ambitious programs than ever before.

The loose Latin translation of the word *amateur* is "for the love of it." Never underestimate the momentum and power created by amateur talent that performs and presents out of pure joy, without pay for the hours invested.

The Grand Strand boasts a nationally recognized symphony orchestra, a row of art galleries, a true cafe society, resident artists whose works are being shown worldwide, legitimate entrance to the museum community, and much more.

Not too surprisingly, when summer has packed the beach with tourists, the Grand Strand's arts and cultural organizations taper or curtail their activities. In fact, most of these organizations' seasons run from September to March or April. Traditionally, tourists have not provided large audiences for cultural offerings, and many of the organizations' volunteers are too busy working at their "real jobs" during the summer months to devote more than minimal time to their favorite artistic endeavors.

ARTS COUNCILS

Myrtle Beach

WACCAMAW ARTS AND CRAFTS GUILD
(843) 238-4628
www.wacg.org
The Waccamaw Arts and Crafts Guild was organized in 1969 and now boasts more than 150 members. It is dedicated to promoting interest and creativity in the visual arts. Approximately 75 percent of the members are artists; most others are patrons or fans. Monthly meetings include demonstrations, slide presentations, social gatherings to exhibit members' recent works, and panel discussions on a variety of topics. The guild hosts a spring and fall show each year. Call the number listed if you are interested in joining the guild.

South Strand

CULTURAL COUNCIL OF GEORGETOWN COUNTY
14329 Ocean Hwy., Pawleys Island,
(843) 237-3035
www.culturalcouncil.info
The Cultural Council of Georgetown County (CCGC) was established in 1997 as an umbrella organization for the area's growing lineup of cultural activities. The organization encompasses the performing, visual, and literary arts, as well as the allied areas in architecture, historic preservation, landscape architecture, industrial design, and production crafts. Its purpose is to provide educational opportunities and space for exhibitions and other art activities, and to encourage existing and fledgling cultural organizations to reach their potential. To that end the Arts Exchange—located in the historic Masonic Lodge—is an art

gallery and cultural center. The CCGC currently has a membership of more than 500 members and 25 artist guilds. They sponsor an outdoor free concert during the month of May in addition to many educational opportunities. Each month more than 1,000 visitors come through the Art Exchange Gallery.

The Cultural Council offerings change and expand frequently, so please call or visit the Web site for up-to-the-minute details.

Beyond the Strand

WHEELWRIGHT COUNCIL FOR THE ARTS
Coastal Carolina University, Conway
(843) 347-3161, (843) 349-2502 (box office)
www.coastal.edu

This organization, composed of community members and Coastal Carolina University faculty and staff, supervises the use of Wheelwright Auditorium. The Wheelwright group coordinates the university's arts program, including a cultural arts series and student plays. The Wheelwright Council's stated function is to bring to the area high-caliber art performances that other groups are unable to secure. The council presents a Passport Series that offers experiences in film, dance, and the performing arts.

Ticket prices vary; call box office for prices.

AUDITORIUMS AND THEATERS

Myrtle Beach

MYRTLE BEACH HIGH SCHOOL MUSIC AND ARTS CENTER
3300 Central Parkway, Myrtle Beach
(843) 448-7149
http://mbh.horrycountyschools.net/
students/fine_arts

The Myrtle Beach High School Auditorium is the area's largest auditorium, seating 2,000 people. The school district had planned to build a 1,000-seat venue, but Myrtle Beach residents convinced them to enlarge it so their city could attract bigger and better productions.

Community-raised funds helped pay for the increased cost of the exceptionally well-equipped if not particularly elegant auditorium.

SOCASTEE HIGH SCHOOL AUDITORIUM
49000 Socastee Blvd., Myrtle Beach
(843) 293-2513

When Socastee High School was renovated in 2004, the district made sure it had an auditorium that can be used for things other than high school assemblies. Up to 900 people can watch performances in the facility, which is home to the Socastee Singers, the high school's award-winning chorus.

The auditorium is used for many community events and performances.

South Strand

STRAND THEATRE
710 Front St., Georgetown
(843) 527-2924
www.swampfoxplayers.com

The Strand Theatre seats 160 people. Home to Georgetown's Swamp Fox Players (see subsequent entry), it's often called the Swamp Fox Theatre.

Beyond the Strand

BURROUGHS SCHOOL AND MCCOWN AUDITORIUM
Corner of Ninth Avenue and Main Street, Conway
(843) 915-5490
www.horrycountymuseum.org

The school itself dates back to 1877, and this old auditorium was defunct for many years until Horry County bought it and transformed the entire building. Seating about 400 people, the auditorium is now operated by the Horry County Museum. It is used for many community functions, including elementary-school plays and county board meetings. The building can be leased and rented for special events.

WHEELWRIGHT AUDITORIUM
Coastal Carolina University,
US 501 E., Conway
(843) 349-2502

Wheelwright Auditorium, on the campus of Coastal Carolina University, roughly 10 miles west of Myrtle Beach off US 501, is an elegant facility that seats about 800 people. It features state-of-the-art lighting and sound systems and has practice rooms that can be utilized by those performing there. In addition to Coastal-related performances, Wheelwright plays host to a variety of concerts and plays, including musicals such as *Into the Woods* and *The Nutcracker* ballet. It also hosts the biannual International Contemporary Bass Competition, drawing hundreds to compete for $10,000 in cash and prizes.

i The *Sun News* publishes a special activities section called "kicks!" in its Friday edition.

MUSIC AND SONG

Church Concert Series

Several churches along the Strand now offer quality concert series. They include North Myrtle Beach's Ocean Drive Presbyterian Church, (843) 249-2312; Myrtle Beach's Trinity Episcopal Church, (843) 448-8426; and First Presbyterian Church, (843) 448-4496. The concert series concept was brought here by Brown Bradley, minister of music at First Presbyterian, who participated in a successful series in New York before relocating to Myrtle Beach.

Trinity Performing Arts Series has been entertaining the Myrtle Beach community for almost two decades. Typical annual programming includes five primary concerts, a pipe organ series, and a kids' matinee. The series has featured artists including the Vienna Choir Boys, Peter Schickele of PDQ Bach fame, and the National Opera Company, as well as chamber music, oratorio, Gilbert and Sullivan productions, and Handel's *Messiah*—all with chamber orchestra accompaniment. Events are hosted by Trinity Episcopal Church, a performance venue that is acoustically ideal, visually elegant, and capable of seating in excess of 500 people. For information on upcoming events and season memberships, call the series director at (843) 448-8426.

At the First Presbyterian Church, ticket holders are treated to a variety of featured vocalists and instrumentalists performing classical, pop, and Broadway selections. A popular past event featured the acclaimed violinist Joshua Bell. Each year sellout performances of *The Best of Broadway* are presented. The FPC Players Drama Troupe spotlights local talent in family-friendly shows and in timeless Broadway hits like *Bells Are Ringing*. Season memberships are encouraged.

Since 1991 the Ocean Drive Presbyterian Church Concert Series has provided programming such as the Wheaton College Men's Choir, the Palmetto Brass, Frederico Hayler, and the Furman Singers.

Myrtle Beach

CAROLINA MASTER CHORALE
(843) 444-5774
www.carolinamasterchorale.com

Anyone who relishes the joy of singing is welcome to join the Carolina Master Chorale. This avid group of harmonizers, about 80 strong, offers concert performances for residents and visitors throughout the year. Since its founding in 1982, the chorale has continued to nurture the choral arts in the community. It offers four concerts during its annual season, including the concert for combined choruses at the Festival-By-The-Sea, a weekend-long choral workshop for invited choruses from the United States and Canada, featuring internationally known choral conductors. Tickets for Carolina Master Chorale concerts are $15 in advance, $20 at the door, and $5 with student ID.

INDIGO CHORAL SOCIETY

(843) 833-4236

www.indigochoral.com

Founded in 1997, the Indigo Choral Society is a community chorus in every sense of the word. Drawing members from throughout George-town County, the 40- to 50-voice chorus has evolved into a singing group that fosters true family spirit.

During the Annual Fourth of July Free Concert on the lawn of the Kaminski House on Front Street in Georgetown, families bring picnics, enjoy the scenery beside the Sampit River, and thrill to the patriotic and folk music.

At the Annual Christmas Concert, usually held in Georgetown's beautiful St. Mary's Catholic Church, holiday sounds fill the air. Accompanied by organ, piano, harp, oboe, and flute, the chorus renders old favorites as well as new pieces. A smaller group of madrigal singers blends voices in splendid historical offerings.

In the spring the chorus showcases a different theme each year. Previous works have ranged from Broadway show tunes to Handel's *Te Deum* to spirituals and Thomas Jefferson's writings set to music.

THE LONG BAY SYMPHONY

Long Bay Youth Orchestra

1551 21st Ave. N., Myrtle Beach

(843) 448-8379

www.longbaysymphony.com

The Long Bay Symphony performs a full season of classical, chamber, and pops concerts, including playing the original scores during a silent film.

Many Long Bay Symphony members have performed with such respected organizations as the Metropolitan Opera in New York and the pop-infused Radio City Music Hall Orchestra. With this array of influences, the Long Bay group melds a variety of musical backgrounds, performing selections from classical to pop, as well as full stage productions. It presents approximately 12 concerts each season.

Musicians range from high-school students to retirees, from points all along the Grand Strand.

For concert information or season memberships, call the number listed.

The Long Bay Symphony promotes its approximately 60-member youth orchestra to spark youngsters' interest in "serious music" and to train older members for the symphony orchestra.

Adults who haven't played in years as well as those who are just learning to play can hone their skills with the youth symphony; the addition of adults has prompted some people to call the group the "Long Bay Orchestra for the Young and Youthful." Members of the youth orchestra also have a chance to be awarded scholarships for private lessons.

Under the direction of Dr. Charles Evans, the youth orchestra performs two or three times a year, once with the symphony. The symphony offers master classes for interested musicians.

PERFORMING ARTS

Myrtle Beach

GHOSTS AND LEGENDS

Barefoot Landing,

US 17 N., North Myrtle Beach

(843) 361-2700

www.ghostshows.com

The ghosts of the Grand Strand come alive each night in the *Ghosts and Legends* show at Barefoot Landing. Historical, factual, and chilling, the show features live actors and storytellers re-creating 13 of the best-known legends of the region. The theater is small and intimate, so reservations are highly recommended. Tickets are $16 for adults and $11 for children ages 4 to 12. The shows are performed every day except Christmas between 10:30 a.m. and 11 p.m.

South Strand

MURRELLS INLET COMMUNITY THEATRE

Intersection of Murrells Inlet Road and

Vaux Hall Avenue, Murrells Inlet

(843) 651-4152

www.mictheatre.com

The Murrells Inlet Community Theatre (MICT), founded in April 1998, has established a strong

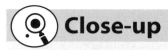 **Close-up**

Jack Thompson

When he was 13 years old, Jack Thompson did what many kids would love to do: He ran away to the beach. Almost 60 years later, he's still there. Thompson is the premier photographer along the Grand Strand and the de facto historian for the region. You can almost judge the importance of an event by whether Thompson shows up with his camera.

The images in his studio on Broadway are a testament to the history he has witnessed and photographed along the Grand Strand. His vintage photographs of celebrities, hurricanes, celebrations, and long-gone beach landmarks such as the Pavilion and the Ocean Forest Hotel show the Grand Strand as it has evolved over the decades.

As luck would have it, his memory is as sharp as his pictures, and if you pull a photograph out of his archives, he can immediately recall when and where it was taken and who is in the picture. And you can be sure you will hear the story of how it all took place.

When you ask him how many pictures he's taken in a lifetime, Thompson replies, "If I could count the stars in the skies, that's how many I've taken."

Thompson spent his early childhood in Greenville, South Carolina, where his father was the editor of the *Greenville News* newspaper. He and some friends heard some older boys talking about "Myrtle," and they decided to hitchhike to this paradise they'd heard described.

It took the kids two days to find it because, back then, the resort town was still so new that few people knew where it was. Their first stop was the Pavilion, and Thompson got no further than the photography booth in the arcade, where he immediately found a job.

The other boys went home, but Thompson did not. His brothers came to join him, and he continued to hone his skills in photography while still going through school.

All of those studio portraits taken of babies? The technique of propping them up and taking a series of shots was perfected by Thompson when he helped JCPenney open their photo studios across the United States. For three years he hopscotched across the country doing his "Pixie Pinups" before he'd had enough.

"I shot a million kids," he laughs. That's almost a literal statement. "I once photographed 14,000 babies in one week alone in Levittown, New York."

His favorite subject, however, has always been the Beach, and the Pavilion in particular. He sighs when asked about the landmark and laments some of the constantly occurring changes. Almost every evolution is captured by his camera.

His gorgeous book of photographs, *Memories of Myrtle Beach,* is a true collector's item and can be found in places throughout the Grand Strand. The best place to get it is right from Thompson himself at his studios, where you can meet him in person and peruse his images. It's prudent to call ahead (843-626-3194) because he is always out exploring the Grand Strand with his camera.

Jack Thompson Studios are located at 915 West Broadway.

presence in the South Strand. The troupe strives to present plays appealing to all ages.

Productions have included romantic comedies, serious dramas, and musicals. The group has performed at the Blessing of the Inlet (see the Annual Events chapter) and for a Readers' Theatre group that entertains at senior centers, schools, and libraries. MICT also offers free seminars on a variety of theatrical topics, including audition preparation, stagecraft, technical instruction in sound and lighting, and a children's acting workshop.

Membership in this dynamic, enthusiastic group is open to anyone with a love for live theater and the desire to take part in the creation and production of stage plays. Dues are $10 annually, which allow members to work on all facets of production. Performance tickets are $8. For ticket information call the number listed above.

SWAMP FOX PLAYERS INC.
710 Front St., Georgetown
(843) 527-2924
www.swampfoxplayers.com
Established in the early 1970s, this amateur theatrical group coordinates at least four productions per year. Since the community seems to be particularly fond of musicals and comedy, many of the Swamp Fox productions are flavored accordingly. Past shows included *A Sanders Family Christmas, Della's Diner,* and *Rainmaker.*

This group calls the Strand Theatre, on Front Street in Georgetown, "home." Tickets range in price. Please call to inquire.

i If you are a student, make sure to travel with your student ID. Many venues offer a student discount when you show your card.

Beyond the Strand
THEATRE OF THE REPUBLIC
331 Main St., Conway
(843) 488-0821
www.theatreoftherepublic.com
Housed within a beautifully renovated historic building on Main Street in downtown Conway, the Theatre of the Republic (TOR) has been entertaining Grand Strand audiences for more than 30 years. TOR is a nonprofit amateur theater group with a history of providing high-quality, affordable theater for the community. In addition to four main season shows, TOR produces musical revues, holiday shows, and children's theater productions and presents classic works through the Theatre of the Republic Repertory Group. Theatre of the Republic was named the Official Theatre of Horry County in 1975. For schedule information please call the Theatre of the Republic office Mon through Fri from 10 a.m. to 6 p.m.

VISUAL ARTS

Myrtle Beach
FRANKLIN G. BURROUGHS AND SIMEON B. CHAPIN ART MUSEUM
3100 South Ocean Blvd., Myrtle Beach
(843) 238-2510
www.myrtlebeachartmuseum.org
The Franklin G. Burroughs and Simeon B. Chapin Art Museum, a former two-story Springmaid beach home donated by Cox Construction Co., is Horry County's first art museum, unveiled in June 1997. The museum features an art gallery, a gift shop, and an art education center.

The art gallery building is housed in the former Springmaid Villa, a 1920s beach house that was saved from demolition. Renovations created 10 galleries with 3,600 square feet of exhibition space, a tearoom, and a large seminar room. Exhibits in the gallery showcase local and regional artists and national art exhibits. The permanent exhibit is the Waccamaw Arts and Craft Guild Purchase Award Collection 1970–1983.

The art education center building, which is attached to the art gallery building, provides ample space for an art library, studio classrooms, a gift shop, and storage space for the museum collection. Past activities have included corporate functions, watercolor classes, and a Christmas ornament–making class.

Admission is free, but docent tours are available for $2 per person. Hours are Tues through Sat 10 a.m. to 4 p.m. and Sun 1 to 4 p.m.

i The Franklin G. Burroughs and Simeon B. Chapin Art Museum features musical performances from time to time. Every month they offer a new feature, so check their Web site, www.myrtlebeachart museum.org, for information.

South Strand

BROOKGREEN GARDENS
US 17 S., Murrells Inlet
(800) 849-1931, (843) 235-6000
www.brookgreen.org

Since opening to the public seven and a half decades ago, Brookgreen Gardens has introduced visitors to an enchanting and compelling showcase of art and nature. The gardens are set on a 300-acre parcel in the heart of a 9,100-acre preserve on the South Carolina coast stretching from the Atlantic Ocean to historic rice fields bordering the Waccamaw River. Ranging from the small and delicate to the truly monumental, the sculptures on display at Brookgreen Gardens represent the works of such prominent American artists as Marshall Fredericks, Daniel Chester French, Gutzon Borglum, Frederic Remington, Carl Milles, and Anna Hyatt Huntington.

Through the Center for American Sculpture, Brookgreen fosters an appreciation of the American figurative sculpture collection; some 900 works by 330 sculptors range from 1819 to the present. Offerings include an outdoor sculpture exhibition of 550 works in landscaped settings, changing thematic gallery exhibitions, interpretive tours, lectures, and publications, and an annual Sculpture Symposium. The Garden Room for Children contains pieces from the Brookgreen sculpture collection that appeal to younger visitors and their families.

Brookgreen Gardens is open from 9:30 a.m. to 5 p.m. daily. Admission is $12 for adults age 13 and older, $10 for seniors age 65 and older, and $5 for children ages 6 to 13.. Children 5 and under are free.

Beyond the Strand

HORRY COUNTY MUSEUM
428 Main St., Conway
(843) 915-5320
www.horrycountymuseum.org

The Horry County Museum offers numerous exhibits on the history, prehistory, and natural history of Horry (pronounced oh-ree) County at the museum's main location, as well as through the presentation of outreach exhibits and programs in various locations throughout the county. The majority of the museum's collections are stored at the Main Street location and include a highly acclaimed photographic collection as well as hundreds of historic artifacts documenting the unique history and culture of Horry County. The museum is open Monday through Saturday from 9 a.m. to 5 p.m. Admission is free.

PARKS AND RECREATION

There is no debate about it: Some of the most abundant natural beauty in all the world is right here along the Grand Strand. And thanks to the Work Projects Administration (WPA) and the Civilian Conservation Corps (CCC)—federal agencies that were created as part of President Franklin Delano Roosevelt's New Deal program, which was enacted during the Great Depression to create employment by establishing and building parks—these natural resources are preserved today in their original splendor.

During the summertime, sunshine is hot and plentiful in the Carolina-blue sky. The water is cool and equally plentiful. Autumn is brilliant—crisp mornings and breezy afternoons are perfect for beach walks and surf fishing. Winter comes in bite-size pieces: a string of brisk, snappy days, with long warm stretches in between. And when spring quickly arrives bearing wisteria, daffodils, and bright-faced college kids, it's hard to believe another year has passed. This deliciously temperate climate enables tourists and residents to enjoy the great outdoors for most of the year.

So head for the parks and take advantage of the enviable climate and incredible store of natural resources. Myrtle Beach State Park and Huntington Beach State Park are known for being among the best locations on the East Coast for bird-watching. Both parks also feature an ever-changing array of programming for the young and the young at heart.

We've also included a Spectator Sports section for those times when you want to sit in the bleachers and root for the home team. Locals are especially proud of the Myrtle Beach Pelicans, our first professional sports team.

PARKS

State Parks

Myrtle Beach
MYRTLE BEACH STATE PARK
4401 South Kings Hwy., Myrtle Beach
(843) 238-5325
www.discoversouthcarolina.com
Situated in the heart of the Grand Strand, Myrtle Beach State Park boasts one of the most popular public beaches along the Carolina coast. This 312-acre oceanfront park is one of the last remaining natural areas along the northern shores of South Carolina. Natural beauty reigns here and gives visitors a glimpse of the way the entire Strand looked long ago before its development as a glittery resort mecca.

Myrtle Beach State Park was developed by the Civilian Conservation Corps. During World War II, the U.S. military took over the park as a coastal defense staging area. In Mar 1945 the park was returned to the citizens of the state. It was the first state park opened to the public in South Carolina, and it also holds the distinction of having the first campground and fishing pier on the Grand Strand.

Park facilities include approximately 350 camping sites. (See the Accommodations chapter.) The park also offers five cabins, two apartments, and picnic areas with shelters. In addition to the 730-foot pier, there's a nature trail and nature center. A park naturalist conducts activities year-round and interprets the natural history of the coast. Surf fishing and pier fishing are allowed. Swimmers can splash about in the ocean or in the park's pool. The park also provides a snack bar and playground equipment.

The park is open daily 6 a.m. to 10 p.m. Mar through Nov and from 6 a.m. to 8 p.m. Dec through Feb. Park office hours are Mon through Fri 8 a.m. to 5 p.m. and Sat and Sun 11 a.m. to 5 p.m. Admission is $4.00 for adults, $2.50 for South Carolina seniors, $1.50 for children ages 6 to 15, and free for children 5 and younger.

i **Myrtle Beach and North Myrtle Beach both have a beach-going wheelchair program to ensure that wheelchair-bound people get to enjoy the ocean, too. There is no charge, but there is a time limit of one hour to ensure that everybody gets a turn. The wheelchairs are sturdy, have large balloon tires that allow the chair to be pushed through the soft sand, and come equipped with umbrellas. Beach-going wheelchairs and handicapped parking are available at the following locations: First Avenue South, North Myrtle Beach, and in Myrtle Beach at 77th Avenue North, 72nd Avenue North, 54th Avenue North, 24th Avenue North, 5th Avenue North, 8th Avenue North, and 8th Avenue South.**

South Strand
HAMPTON PLANTATION STATE HISTORIC SITE
1950 Rutledge Rd., McClellanville
(843) 546-9361
www.discoversouthcarolina.com
Southwest of Georgetown, Hampton Plantation is not technically a part of the stretch of real estate we call the Grand Strand. However, Hampton offers a peek at one of the most impressive restored plantation homes in South Carolina and, therefore, is well worth the short drive.

Adjacent to the Santee River, this 322-acre property was once a coastal rice plantation and last served as the home of Archibald Rutledge, noted writer and South Carolina poet laureate. The state purchased the property from Mr. Rutledge in 1971.

A National Historic Landmark, the Hampton mansion stands as the centerpiece of the park and is a monument to the state's glorious rice empire. The mansion's colossal Adam-style portico is one of the finest and earliest examples of its kind in all of North America, while its interior—purposely unfurnished—highlights the structure's design and construction. Cutaway sections of walls and ceilings exhibit the building's evolution from a simple farmhouse to a grand mansion. Exposed timber framing, hand-carved mantels, and delicately wrought hinges and hardware reveal the 18th-century builder's craft.

The grounds surrounding the mansion offer a unique opportunity to examine the wildlife of the Carolina Lowcountry. Cypress swamps, abandoned rice fields, and pine and hardwood forests are home to a staggering variety of flora and fauna. From the massive live oaks to the wildflowers and shrubs, Hampton Plantation is a naturalist's and photographer's delight in every season.

In addition to the beautiful home, the park includes a picnic area and marked nature trails.

Park hours are 6 a.m. to 6 p.m. daily, year-round. From Labor Day to Memorial Day, mansion hours are 1 to 4 p.m. Thurs through Mon. Admission to the plantation grounds is free; house tours are $4 for ages 16 and older, $3 for children 6 to 15, and free for South Carolina senior citizens and kids age 5 and younger. Guided tours are offered at no extra charge. House tours are held on the hour Thurs through Mon at 1, 2, and 3 p.m.

HUNTINGTON BEACH STATE PARK
US 17 S. (across from Brookgreen Gardens), Murrells Inlet
(843) 237-4440
www.discoversouthcarolina.com
Huntington Beach State Park, worth a visit even if you see nothing else on the Strand, offers the best-preserved beach on the Grand Strand and one of the best we have seen anywhere in the world. Observe the diverse coastal environment at the freshwater lagoon, salt marsh, nature trail, and along the wide, beautiful beach.

The 2,500-acre park is also the site of the imposing Spanish-style castle Atalaya, the former winter home and studio of American sculptress Anna Hyatt Huntington. Mrs. Huntington and her husband, Archer, were the visionary founders of Brookgreen Gardens. Seasonal tours of Atalaya are available.

Park facilities include about 135 camping sites, picnic areas with shelters, a boardwalk, and a general store. Activities such as surf fishing, swimming, and crabbing are encouraged, and the park offers one of the finest bird-watching sites on the East Coast. Nature programs and playground equipment are available for the young and young at heart. Atalaya Arts and Crafts Festival, a prestigious juried arts and crafts show, attracts thousands of visitors to the park every fall (see the Annual Events chapter for details).

Park hours are 6 a.m. to 10 p.m. daily from Apr through Sept and 6 a.m. to 6 p.m. daily from Oct through Mar. Office hours are 9 a.m. to 4:30 p.m. Mon through Fri and 11 a.m. to noon on Sat and Sun year-round. Admission to the park is $5 for adults, $3 for kids age 12 or younger, and free for children younger than age 5.

City Parks

City parks pepper the Strand and are perfect for a little rest and relaxation. Several parks provide playground equipment, basketball courts, and running tracks for your use and enjoyment; others offer serene picnic areas complete with tables and restrooms.

North Strand

For more information about the parks in North Myrtle Beach, call the recreation department at (843) 280-5570. There is no admission fee, and the city parks are open 24 hours a day.

CENTRAL PARK/J. BRYAN FLOYD RECREATION CENTER
1030 Possum Trot Road, North Myrtle Beach
This 20-acre park is a kind of athlete's track and field course. The J. Bryan Floyd Recreation Center/ Central Park Recreation Center features four soccer/baseball/softball fields; four tennis courts; a quarter-mile paved trail; a roller hockey rink; four basketball courts (including one indoor court); and a recreation center with two playgrounds, a concession stand, a press box for games, restrooms, and twelve outdoor picnic tables.

CITY PARK ON THE OCEAN
First Avenue S. and South Ocean Blvd., North Myrtle Beach
This cartoon-colored park serves as a convenient ingress and egress to the beach in the Ocean Drive section of North Myrtle Beach. Matching the pavement of nearby Main Street, the small park is constructed of brightly tinted concrete; the restroom facilities and concession stand are in a modern art deco style suited to the beach, accented with palm trees, of course. The delightful design won national recognition from the National Recreation and Park Society in 1989. Amenities also include beach wheelchairs, boardwalks onto the sand, a parking lot, and an outdoor shower. The concession stand is open only in the summer from 9 a.m. to 5 p.m., and the restrooms are locked for the night at 9 p.m. and "when it gets cold," says city maintenance.

HILL STREET PARK
Hill Street, North Myrtle Beach
The one-acre spread showcases what might be the North Strand's best lighted tennis court and a complex of playground equipment in addition to the standard swings, as well as a picnic area.

MCLEAN PARK
Second Avenue S., North Myrtle Beach
McLean Park is a couple of blocks from the ocean and is sometimes used for outdoor concerts, Easter egg hunts, and small local festivals. In addition to two tennis courts, a roller hockey court, and playground equipment, the park features a picnic area, a small lake, and a softball/baseball field. Restroom facilities are available as well.

VIRGIL YOW PARK
Windy Hill Road, North Myrtle Beach
This quaint neighborhood park features a basketball court, playground, picnic area, restroom facilities, and a charming decorative archway made from branches. The parking lot for this park is hidden; drive around the corner to Eyerly Road, then walk through the archway and trees to get to the playground.

Myrtle Beach
The City of Myrtle Beach has 4 recreation centers, 2 indoor swimming pools, 4 indoor gymnasiums, 2 outdoor basketball courts, 3 weight and fitness rooms, 16 tennis courts, a skateboard park, a roller hockey rink, a golf course, a fitness trail, 8 picnic shelters, 17 playgrounds, and some 45 landscaped parks—not to mention 9.5 miles of beach. Those listed below are just a sampling. For more information call the recreation department at (843) 918-2280. There is no admission fee to the city parks, and they are open 24 hours a day.

CHAPIN PARK
16th Avenue N. and Kings Highway, Myrtle Beach
In the very hub of downtown traffic, this favorite park offers an unbelievably tranquil setting featuring a beautiful arbor area, picnic tables, and garden swings. Local business folk seeking to escape the rat race frequent the calm of Chapin during lunch, especially in the spring and fall. The swings are ideal for reading the paper, eating a homemade sandwich, or simply for taking in the sights that surround you.

Political candidates, outdoor festivals, and a host of city functions favor the atmosphere and location of Chapin Park. Weekends bring a variety of activities, including art shows, outdoor concerts, and small festivals. Also, more than a few couples have exchanged wedding vows in the two-story gazebo that sits in the heart of this pretty green space. The playground, favored by local parents, features wooden equipment and lots of sand.

HURL ROCK PARK
20th Avenue S. and Ocean Blvd., Myrtle Beach
Wooden decks create a lovely trail through Hurl Rock Park, which features a spectacular view of the beach. This park is great for photo opportunities, hand holding, and people watching.

MIDWAY PARK
19th Avenue S. and Kings Highway, Myrtle Beach
Tennis is the name of the game at Midway, with six lighted courts. But that's not all. You'll also find a lighted basketball court here complete with two goals as well as a rest area and bathroom facilities.

South Strand
For more information about the parks in the South Strand, call the recreation department at (843) 650-4131. There is no admission fee, and the city parks are open 24 hours a day.

ALL CHILDREN'S PARK
10th Avenue S. and Hollywood Drive, Surfside Beach
This innovative playground, designed and equipped for both able-bodied and disabled children—hence its name—has set a nationwide example.

All Children's Park features "standard" equipment modified to suit the needs of challenged youngsters—without separating them from their peers. Specially designed equipment includes a slide with tiered ramp along its side, mesh-net swings, and an elevated tic-tac-toe board and sandbox. A landscaped, shaded area with picnic tables and an adult swing adjoins the park.

FULLER PARK
Surfside and Myrtle Drives, Surfside Beach
Fuller Park is an ideal family destination, with two lighted tennis courts, two basketball courts, a playground, and a picnic area with bathroom facilities. The Horry County Memorial Library is immediately adjacent, so make time to stop there, too.

W. O. (BILL) MARTIN PARK
Lakeside Drive and Eighth Avenue S.,
Surfside Beach

A great place for a family reunion, the W. O. (Bill) Martin Park—formerly Lakeside Park—features a large picnic area and the Floral Clubhouse (which can be rented by calling the Town of Surfside Recreation Department at 843-650-4131). A large, open area adjacent to the park is perfect for Frisbee tossing, kite flying, and informal baseball and football games.

Residential Parks

The following parks are public residential facilities maintained by the City of Myrtle Beach. Carefully manicured landscapes and multicolored blooms create a delightful series of green sanctuaries— retreats from the hustle and bustle of resort living. Read a book, take a nap, ponder the mysteries of life. For more information call (843) 918-2280.

Pinner Place Park is at Pinner Place and Pridgen Road.

You'll find Withers Park at Second Avenue South and Myrtle Street.

Loblolly Park is on Loblolly Circle in the prestigious Dunes section.

Gray Park is a pretty little space on 45th Avenue North and Burchap Drive.

Memorial Park, at Porcher Avenue and Haskell Circle, is a gem.

Right around the corner, McMillan Park is on Haskell Circle and Ocean Boulevard.

Another Boulevard park is Cameron Park at 28th Avenue North.

You'll find Springs Park at Springs Avenue and Hampton Circle.

McLeod Park is on 61st Avenue North.

RECREATION

Myrtle Beach offers visitors opportunities to participate in lots of healthy sports, such as bicycling, kayaking, and beach volleyball, as well as "thrill sports" such as parasailing, bungee jumping, and skydiving. Health and fitness clubs abound; recreation centers and leagues provide organized activities for kids and adults alike. Of course, you'll find plenty of tennis and golf opportunities at nearly every turn as well. Golf is so popular, in fact, we've devoted an entire chapter to it in lieu of discussing it in depth here.

Beach Volleyball

Setting and spiking on the inviting sands of the beach is a favored activity during the summer season. The level of competition ranges from that found at family picnics to competitive tournaments with skilled professionals.

In the summertime pickup games abound all along the beach from Surfside to North Myrtle. Public volleyball nets in Myrtle Beach are set up at Downwind Sails, 29th Avenue South (adjacent to Damon's restaurant), and at Kingston Plantation (see the Accommodations chapter), located on the beach near Restaurant Row.

Biking

Bicycle paths in Myrtle Beach are clearly marked along the beach and Ocean Boulevard, and the residential area north of 54th Avenue North features an outdoor fitness trail with exercise equipment along the beach. Bicycles and adult-size, laid-back tricycles can be rented from a variety of locations along the beach, including the following vendors.

North Strand

THE BIKE DOCTOR
315 Sea Mountain Hwy.,
North Myrtle Beach
(843) 249-8152

This shop is a full-service and fully stocked bicycle outlet, just 2 blocks from the beach. Parking is provided, so you can leave your car and ride your new or rented bike. Rentals include beach cruisers, standard two-wheel bikes, three-wheelers, "funcycles," tandems, and four-wheel, four-passenger bikes. Fees start at $4 per hour per bike. Gear, such as helmets and pads, is not included in the rental rate.

The Bike Doctor is open Mon through Sat from 9:30 a.m. to 5 p.m.

Myrtle Beach

BICYCLES-N-GEAR

515 US 501, Myrtle Beach

(843) 626-2453

http://bicycles-n-gear.com

Beach-cruiser bikes can be rented for $10 a day, and although it's not their primary business, you can also rent in-line skates from this store for $20 per day. Both rentals include helmets and protective gear.

This bike outfitter is open every day from 10 a.m. to 7 p.m.

THE BIKE SHOP

715 Broadway St., Myrtle Beach

(843) 448-5335

www.beachbikeshop.com

Open 8 a.m. to 5 p.m. Mon through Sat, the Bike Shop loans customers complimentary helmets, locks, and baskets with every rental. Beach cruisers cost $10 for the whole day, $50 for the week. A whole day of mountain biking is $15, and a week is $75.

Fitness Clubs

Fitness is a thriving industry along the Grand Strand, which probably stands to reason if you take into consideration the premium locally on firm bodies, male and female.

All of the area's gyms and fitness clubs welcome visitors at any time of the year. It's not unusual to see packed aerobic classes during peak tourist times when visitors pop in to get their exercise high while on vacation. That most

i Beginning at around 5524 North Ocean Blvd., you'll find a half-mile workout trail. Erected by the City of Myrtle Beach and community sponsors, the trail stretches along the beach near private cabanas. Each of the 20 stations has instructions regarding a different exercise to get the most out of your workout. The stations include 30 different exercises.

of these clubs are so affordable might pleasantly surprise you. To join an aerobics class for an hour or so, rates usually run $4 to $6. Annual memberships to fitness centers average $35 to $60 per month, although some might charge an up-front initiation fee.

North Strand

LIFEQUEST SWIM & FITNESS CLUB

4390 Spa Dr., Little River

(843) 399-2582

www.lqfitness.com

Lifequest has lined up a variety of programs, from step aerobics to karate. The Next Generation Nautilus machines fill the weight room, along with treadmills, steppers, a Skywalker, Lifecycles, and recumbent bikes. To accommodate the wetter side of a workout, Lifequest has indoor and outdoor pools (aqua-aerobics classes are available), a whirlpool, steam room, and sauna. If your workout leaves your muscles sore, massage therapy is available.

Lifequest is open Mon through Thurs from 5:30 a.m. to 10 p.m., Fri from 5:30 a.m. to 9 p.m., Sat from 8 a.m. to 6 p.m., and Sun from 1 to 5 p.m. The club offers a variety of rates and fees.

Myrtle Beach

AMERICAN ATHLETIC CLUB

Highway 544 and 3901 North Kings

Highway, Myrtle Beach

(843) 916-0077

www.americanathleticclub.com

The popular American Athletic Club in Socastee now has a second location in the heart of Myrtle Beach. Both clubs feature 20,000-plus square feet, and both offer services and equipment to address all your fitness needs. You'll appreciate fully equipped weight rooms, private aerobic studios, dry-heat saunas, and nutrition centers with a juice bar. The Socastee location also has an indoor swimming pool.

American Athletic Club is open Mon through Fri from 5:30 a.m. to 9 p.m., Sat from 7 a.m. to 7 p.m., and Sun from 1 to 5 p.m.

CURVES

7727 North Kings Hwy., Unit 14,
Myrtle Beach
(843) 449-3488
4006 Postal Way, Unit E, Myrtle Beach
(843) 236-7270
3901 Dick Pond Rd., Unit I, Myrtle Beach
(843) 650-9128
804 Inlet Square Dr., Unit 7, Murrells Inlet
(843) 651-3100
www.curves.com

This popular chain of women-only gyms has taken the Grand Strand by storm. Created specifically for women, Curves offers a complete fitness and nutrition solution. The Curves 30-minute workout exercises every major muscle group and burns up to 500 calories through a proven program of strength training, cardio, and stretching. Curves members on vacation at the Strand can use their membership at any gym.

FITNESS ONE-ON-ONE

(843) 449-6486
www.fitnessoneonone.com

Whether you're a neophyte or seasoned in body-building regimes, and no matter what your age, Fitness One-On-One promises to take you to the height of your fitness potential. This is the only one-on-one, personalized-training facility on the Grand Strand. All individually tailored programs combine a personal workout plan with nutrition advice, cardiovascular exercise, and weight training. Owner Herb MacDonald offers clients weight-loss programs, body toning, beginner and advanced bodybuilding, and spot training. Designed specifically to benefit vacationers, Mac-Donald will come to you, or you can choose to meet him at the Sands Health Club at the Ocean Dunes/Sands Resort at 201 75th Ave. N..

GOLD'S GYM

951 Jason Blvd. (10th Avenue N. and
US 17 Bypass), Myrtle Beach
(843) 448-3939
www.goldsgym.com

Probably the longest-standing fitness outlet in the area, Gold's has been locally owned and operated by Ted and Nancy Capp since 1982.

This is a venue for serious workouts, as evidenced by folks Olympic and power lifting in the weight room, where many competitive bodybuilders come to pump up and shape their muscles. Besides free weights, complete Stair-Master and BodyMaster systems are available. Warm up on treadmills, bikes, steppers, or a stair climber. The gym also has a full aerobics schedule and a boxing class. Operating schedules change seasonally, as do rates, but for the most part, Gold's is open Mon through Thurs from 5 a.m. to about 9 p.m., Fri from 6 a.m. to 7 p.m., Sat from 6 a.m. to 7 p.m., and Sun from 1 to 7 p.m.

KINGSTON PLANTATION SPORT & HEALTH CLUB

9760 Kings Hwy., Myrtle Beach
(843) 497-2444
www.kingstonplantation.com

This $4-million facility is perhaps the prettiest club along the Grand Strand, nestled amid the beautiful setting of Kingston Plantation. It has a complete cardiovascular center with Life Fitness Circuit (a computerized system) equipment for strength training. Aerobics and "aquacise" programs are scheduled daily. With 50,000 square feet, it has plenty of room for you to get the workout you need.

On the grounds you'll find clay and hard-surface tennis courts as well as racquetball and volleyball courts. Other features of this club include indoor and outdoor pools, a whirlpool, sauna, tanning beds, and massage therapy. The Sport & Health Club is open from 6:30 a.m. to 10 p.m. Mon through Thurs, 6:30 a.m. to 9 p.m. on Fri, 7:30 a.m. to 9 p.m. on Sat, and 7:30 a.m. to 6 p.m. on Sun.

South Strand

PLANTATION RESORT HEALTH & SWIM CLUB

1250 US 17 N., Surfside Beach
(843) 913-5060
www.plantationresort.com

This fitness club is as comprehensive as it gets—

even offering programs for those who suffer from arthritis. It's no surprise that Plantation Resort has a full aqua aerobics program, as the club sports a 70-foot-long heated pool and giant whirlpool. Amenities include men's and women's saunas and steam rooms, a children's playground, a fully equipped weight room, and an aerobic space with Exerflex floor, where aerobics, yoga, and karate classes are held.

Plantation Resort is open 6 a.m. to 10 p.m. Mon through Fri, 7:30 a.m. to 10 p.m. Sat, and 9:30 a.m. to 10 p.m. Sun. Membership fees vary, based on particular programs or full use of club facilities.

Horseback Riding

Horseback riding is another popular pastime, but not many Grand Strand stables have horses for rent. NOTE: Horses are prohibited from the beach in some areas during the busy summer tourist season. See the Beach Information chapter for details.

BEST VIEW FARM
6129 Best Western Trail, Myrtle Beach
(843) 650-7522
Call and speak to Caroline to discuss boarding facilities or riding lessons. Best View Farm is nestled on 45 densely wooded acres. Full-service boarding is available for $250 a month, and rides are priced individually. Call ahead for details.

HORSEBACK RIDING OF MYRTLE BEACH
(843) 294-1712
When horseback riding is allowed on the beach, from Sept 15 to May 15, Horseback Riding of Myrtle Beach will make arrangements to meet you on the beach for an hour-and-a-half ride. Call for rates. The company also offers trail riding in a forest preserve in Conway, but again, arrangements should be made ahead of time. The trail ride is $50 per horse.

INLET POINT PLANTATION
5800 Hwy. 236, North Myrtle Beach
(843) 249-2989
www.inletpointplantation.com

This plantation offers beach and trail horseback riding, carriage rides, and a horse lover's adventure on a private island for adults and children.

Ride through hundreds of acres of fields and forests, over high rolling terrain, past salt marshes, and along miles and miles of uninhabited barrier island beaches. This family-fun adventure offers a genuine alternative to the glitter and ping of the high-tech arcades and amusement-park rides.

Reservations are highly recommended because prices and hours vary greatly. One-hour trail rides, for those age seven and older, begin at $50 per person. Beach riding is two and a half hours for $100. This is a sister farm to Peachtree Equestrian.

PEACHTREE EQUESTRIAN
810 Hickman Rd.,
NC 57 (just off US 17), Calabash, NC
(910) 287-4790
Peachtree Equestrian is listed as one of the best equestrian centers in the Southeast. One-hour trail rides can be booked for $50 per person. Call Gloria or any of her staff to reserve a horse. (See the Kidstuff chapter for additional information.)

Kayaking

Kayaking has grown in popularity, both along the beach and in local rivers and swamps. The following places (see the Water Sports chapter for details) are worth investigating if you're interested in this up-and-coming sport.

Myrtle Beach
DOWNWIND SAILS
2915 South Ocean Blvd.,
Myrtle Beach
(843) 448-7245
www.downwindsailsmyrtlebeach.com
Downwind Sails rents ocean kayaks for fun and frolic in the surf. This shop is open between Apr and Sept. Rates vary with the time of year and availability of equipment. See the entry in the Water Sports chapter for details.

SAIL & SKI CONNECTION

515 US 501, Myrtle Beach

(843) 626-SAIL

www.sailandskiconnection.com

This outfitter bills its kayak tours as "the adventure of a lifetime." New tours are scheduled weekly, and some are customized to suit group interest. Safety is a top priority: Complete supervision is provided (if desired), and the rules of boating are stressed every step of the way. See the entry in the Water Sports chapter for rates and schedules.

South Strand

BLACK RIVER OUTDOORS CENTER

21 Garden Avenue,

US 701, Georgetown

(843) 546-4840

www.blackriveroutdoors.com

Black River Outdoors Center offers half-, full-, and multiday tours on the area's abundant marshes, rivers, and creeks. Explore the aptly named waters of the Black River, the tidal creeks leading to the secluded beaches of Huntington Beach State Park, and the deserted and mysterious Drunken Jack Island—reputed to hold treasures of the pirate Blackbeard. See the entry in the Water Sports chapter for details.

i **Skateboarding and in-line skating are prohibited in downtown Myrtle Beach, where the prime flat property is full of railings and curbs to hop—but also, unfortunately, lots of people on the sidewalks to avoid. The city has come up with a solution: a skate park. The city built the park for the many enthusiasts the sport is attracting. It's built behind the Pepper Geddings Recreation Center, (843) 918-2280, and has all sorts of demanding obstacles and ramps for skaters and, of course, no pedestrians.**

Miniature Golf

Serious golfers, forget about tee times, golf-cart fees, and buckets of lost balls! By playing any one of dozens of miniature golf courses along the Grand Strand, you can enjoy spirited competition with the kids (your own as well as those you might wander upon) and the joy of sinking a hole in one—without breaking the budget. Actually, miniature golf might be even more challenging than a professional course. After all, how many long-necked llamas, bearded pirates, or spooky caves have you tripped over on a fairway lately?

Several miniature courses are part of amusement parks as complete properties. Most courses are open from 9 a.m. to midnight and have snack bars or cold-drink machines. Admission ranges from $2 to $9 per putter. Special prices are offered for all-day play, which means you can play for a while and then come back later to play some more.

North Strand

HAWAIIAN RUMBLE MINIATURE GOLF

33rd Avenue S., US 17,

North Myrtle Beach

(843) 272-7812

www.prominigolf.com

Ranked by *GOLF Magazine* as the No. 1 miniature golf course in the United States, Hawaiian Rumble offers a challenging variety of shots in a lush and expertly landscaped setting of tropical palms, hibiscus, and other plants. The course circles and climbs up around a rumbling volcano, leis in almost every color are handed out to the players, and gentle Hawaiian music plays in the background. Hawaiian Rumble also sponsors the Masters Putting Championship, with a purse of $20,000—definitely worth a shot!

MAYDAY MINIATURE GOLF

US 17, North Myrtle Beach

(843) 280-3535

www.maydaygolf.com

Two 18-hole courses make up this extravaganza. The centerpiece of the course is an actual plane crash-landed in the jungle. It is your mission to herd your ball around the 18-hole Mayday Mountain Course and then, if you have the fortitude, escape the thundering waterfall and wild animal calls of the Rescue Falls course. The Rescue Falls course features 18 holes, is wheelchair accessible, and uses premium putting carpet that's as fast as a pool table, the owners say. Mayday does have all-day play until 5 p.m. Call ahead for all-day rates and daily specials.

Myrtle Beach
CAPTAIN HOOK'S ADVENTURE GOLF
2205 North Kings Hwy.,
Myrtle Beach
(843) 913-7851
Based on the timeless story of Peter Pan, Captain Hook's offers two imagination-inspiring 18-hole courses. Players can choose the Lost Boys' course or the more challenging Hook's course, which has uphill shots and includes water holes and sand traps.

DRAGON'S LAIR FANTASY GOLF
Broadway at the Beach, 1197 Celebrity
Circle, Myrtle Beach
(843) 444-3215
A favorite attraction at the huge Broadway at the Beach complex is the fire-breathing volcanic mountain for you to putt around, through, and inside. You'll also putt over water, through castle doors, and up hills. This huge multicourse indoor complex is touted by its owners as employing cutting-edge minigolf technology. Whether or not this is true, we can assure you that it is the only miniature complex amid the shopping, theater, and dining action of the Broadway at the Beach complex.

JUNGLE LAGOON
Fifth Avenue S. and Kings Highway,
Myrtle Beach
(843) 626-7894
www.junglelagoon.com
In this tropical jungle setting you might wish you had a machete instead of a putter. You'll have to

contend with lots of uphill shots, fast downhill curves, and angles on both courses (18 holes each). Special rates are offered for children age five and younger. All-day play is available. There is also a 1,000-square-foot covered patio with picnic tables.

JURASSIC GOLF
29th Avenue S. and Kings Highway,
Myrtle Beach
(843) 448-2116
You guessed it—ferocious dinosaurs threaten your score. Choose from two 18-hole courses. Discounts are offered to children age five and younger. All-day play ends at 5 p.m.

MT. ATLANTICUS MINOTAUR GOLF
707 North Kings Hwy.,
Myrtle Beach
(843) 444-1008
Built high atop what was Chapin's Department Store, Mt. Atlanticus gives you golfing challenges and views for miles. First opened in 1988 at a cost of $3 million, it offers two huge courses (the Minotaur and the Conch) in a truly unique setting atop the art deco–style building. The courses twist through Chapin's three floors, up stairs on the side of the building, and up to the roof with views of the beach and roller coasters. The holes themselves are challenging and creative.

PIRATES WATCH
1500 South Kings Hwy.,
Myrtle Beach
(843) 448-8600
Enjoy 36 holes brimming with action-packed waterfalls, daunting pirates, water traps, and lagoons. Oh, and don't forget the smoking skull! All-day play is offered until 5 p.m., 9 p.m. in fall.

RAINBOW FALLS
9850 US 17, Myrtle Beach
(843) 497-2557
Probably one of the oldest putt-putt courses on the beach but still a lot of full. Tricky corners, animal caves, and fairy-tale castles make up 36 holes

of these two courses. One or two uphill holes could throw your game. Special rates are offered to groups and children age four and younger. All-day play is available until 5 p.m.

SPYGLASS GOLF
3800 North Kings Hwy.,
Myrtle Beach
(843) 626-9309
This 18-hole course has a fun degree of difficulty and offers discounts to senior citizens, children, and groups. Waterfalls, uphill holes, and those bloody pirates are the main obstacles. All-day play ends at 6 p.m.

TREASURE ISLAND
48th Avenue N., Myrtle Beach
(843) 449-4754
A hole in one is not easy to come by on this 18-hole course, but the play at Treasure Island is definitely worth the challenge. Discounts are available for senior citizens, children, and groups. All-day play ends at 6 p.m.

South Strand
ADVENTURE FALLS
735 US 17, Surfside Beach
(843) 238-3811
Animals and castles overlook the 36 holes of two courses. Groups and children are offered discounts, and all-day play ends at 5 p.m.

BUCCANEER BAY
6001 US 17 S., Surfside Beach
(843) 238-3811
Two courses filled with pirates and big boats—36 holes between them—will make you ache to walk the plank. Several holes feature difficult angles and tricky obstacles. All-day play ends at 5 p.m.

Parasailing

Parasailing has become a popular activity along the beach. Participants wear a parachute and are pulled by a towrope behind a speedboat. The parachute fills with air and lifts the para-

sailer to heights around 300 feet. Parasailing adventures are offered through the following businesses: Parasail Express, 4091 US 17 Business, Myrtle Beach, (843) 357-7777; Downwind Sail, 2915 Ocean Blvd. (in front of Damon's, at 29th Avenue S.), Myrtle Beach, (843) 448-7245; Ocean Watersports, Fourth Avenue South, Myrtle Beach, (843) 445-7777; Myrtle Beach Water Sports, 5835 Dick Pond Rd., Myrtle Beach, (843) 497-8848; Captain Dick's Marina, 4123 US 17 Business, Murrells Inlet, (843) 651-3676; Express Watersports, Myrtle Beach and Murrells Inlet, (866) 566-9338; and Marlin Quay Parasailing, 1508 South Waccamaw Dr., Garden City Beach, (843) 651-4444.

Recreation Centers/Leagues

The recreation centers we've included in this section offer a smattering of leagues for kids. Call each respective center to find out about sign-up dates; parents often get upset if they miss a registration deadline.

North Strand
NORTH MYRTLE BEACH AQUA & FITNESS CENTER
1100 Second Ave. S., North Myrtle Beach
(843) 289-3737
www.nmb.us/afc/
North Myrtle Beach's new Aqua & Fitness Center is about the nicest public health facility you'll run across. A complete fitness center, AFC has 26 treadmills, 13 elliptical machines, bikes, weights, and countless other machines to help you get in shape. There are numerous classes, including some geared for seniors. The center offers a three-lane warm-water teaching and therapy pool, as well as an eight-lane, 25-yard lap pool. There is also a whirlpool to soak in afterwards. If you think you need a massage, the AFC offers that as well.

The facility is open from 5:30 a.m. to 10 p.m. Mon through Fri, 8 a.m. to 6 p.m. Sat, and noon to 5 p.m. Sun. The pool closes a half hour earlier than the facility each day. Child care is available Mon through Fri 8 a.m. until noon and again from 3:30 p.m. to 7:30 p.m., and on Sat from 9 a.m. until noon. Membership prices vary according to age, whether you are an individual, a couple, or an entire family, so check the Web site for details.

Myrtle Beach

CANAL STREET RECREATION CENTER
901 Canal St., Myrtle Beach
(843) 918-1465
www.cityofmyrtlebeach.com/recreation.html
The City of Myrtle Beach's Canal Street Recreation Center offers a wide variety of recreational opportunities for all ages. The center features a full-size gymnasium, weight room, an indoor swimming pool, banquet hall with mini-kitchen and ice machine, meeting rooms, game room, dressing rooms, an arts and crafts room, and two playgrounds. A wide variety of fitness and instructional classes and activities are available.

Canal Street has annual, monthly, or daily membership options. The center is open Mon through Thurs from 8 a.m. to 8 p.m., Fri from 8 a.m. to 6:30 p.m., and Sat from 10 a.m. to 5 p.m.

GRAND STRAND YMCA
904 65th Ave. N., Myrtle Beach
(843) 449-9622
www.gsfymca.org
The local YMCA actively sponsors community events, many geared toward children. Kids enjoy T-ball, baseball, soccer, swim classes, after-school day care, and day camps. Adults can enjoy coed volleyball, basketball, shag and ballroom dancing, softball, and health-enhancement workshops. The center features a Nautilus and free-weights center, a selection of cardiovascular equipment, and aerobics classes. Fees are competitive, ranging from a $3 one-day fee to $420 per family per year—and numerous levels in between. Call for all the details. Hours are Mon through Thurs 6 a.m. to 9 p.m., Fri 6 a.m. to 8 p.m., Sat 8:30 a.m. to 4 p.m., and Sun 1 to 4 p.m.

PEPPER GEDDINGS RECREATION CENTER
3205 Oak St., Myrtle Beach
(843) 918-2280
www.cityofmyrtlebeach.com/recreation.html
Pepper Geddings is the most complete recreation center in the area. This facility features a 25-yard heated indoor swimming pool that is fully accessible to the physically challenged. Programs include American Red Cross swimming lessons for all ages and abilities, a variety of water-exercise programs, and a swim team, as well as lifeguard-certification and water-safety classes. You can pump up in the weight room with free weights and Nautilus equipment under the supervision of a professional trainer. Instructional classes include arts and crafts; a variety of dances such as ballroom, shag, and tap; and bridge and other card games. The Parks and Recreation Department also offers after-school care and a summer day camp.

City-sponsored aerobics, swimming, and team sports including basketball are coordinated through this center. In addition to meeting rooms and a game room, the complex is surrounded by softball, baseball, and football fields; three lighted tennis courts; and a picnic shelter with a grill and tables.

Fees for most classes are nominal, and annual passes for the weight room and swimming pool are available. The center is open six days a week: Mon through Thurs from 6 a.m. to 9 p.m., Fri from 6 a.m. to 6:30 p.m., and Sat from 10 a.m. to 5 p.m. Fees are reasonable.

South Strand

SURFSIDE BEACH RECREATION DEPARTMENT
H. BLUE HUCKABEE RECREATION COMPLEX,
Spanish Oak Drive and Glenns Bay Road
Surfside Beach
(843) 650-4131

DICK M. JOHNSON CIVIC CENTER
Pine Drive, Surfside Beach
(843) 650-4131
The Surfside Beach Recreation Department provides year-round recreational programs for all ages. Many of the sports activities are held at the H. Blue Huckabee complex, which boasts three ball fields. Instructional courses and seminars, held at the Johnson Civic Center, include arts and crafts, dance, aerobics, and more. Special events

include Easter-egg hunts, Sun Fun volleyball competitions (see the Annual Events chapter), an Old-Fashioned Family Festival in October, a Christmas Tree Lighting Ceremony, and a Santa Hotline.

Tennis

If spirited competition on the courts is what you love, you can slam an ace or volley for fun on any one of numerous tennis courts that span the length of the Grand Strand. We'll start with the freebies, available on a first-come, first-served (pardon the pun) basis. Pay-as-you-play courts require reservations, so call in advance.

North Strand

CENTRAL PARK

1030 Possum Trot Rd.,

North Myrtle Beach

(843) 280-5570

www.northmyrtlebeachchamber.com/parks

Central Park offers four outdoor, lighted asphalt courts. Lights-out is 11 p.m.

HILL STREET PARK

Hill Street (off Sea Mountain Highway),

North Myrtle Beach

(843) 280-5570

www.northmyrtlebeachchamber.com/parks

Be the first to grab the one lighted asphalt court. The lights go out at 11 p.m.

MCLEAN PARK

First Avenue S., North Myrtle Beach

(843) 280-5570

www.northmyrtlebeachchamber.com/parks

McLean offers two outdoor, lighted asphalt courts. Lights-out is 11 p.m.

OCEAN CREEK TENNIS CENTER

US 17, North Myrtle Beach

(843) 272-7724, ext. 1011

www.oceancreek.com

Ocean Creek Tennis Center offers eight courts—three with Har-tru surfaces, two lighted for evening play, and one devoted solely to practice. The hourly rate is $15 for hard courts and $20 for Har-tru courts. Lessons are available from the center's on-site professional.

Myrtle Beach

CITY OF MYRTLE BEACH COMMUNITY TENNIS CENTER

3301 Robert Grissom Parkway, Myrtle Beach

(843) 918-2440

www.myrtlebeachtennis.com

The Myrtle Beach Tennis Center, right in the middle of it all, has 10 courts, including 8 that are lighted for nighttime playing. There are also two sand volleyball/beach tennis courts.

The price is $2 per person per hour, with no court time fees. Lessons are offered, and there is even a match setup service. The facility is open Mon through Fri from 8 a.m. to 1:30 p.m. and again from 3 to 8 p.m. On Sat it's open from 8 a.m. to 1:30 p.m. and again from 2:30 to 6:30 p.m. It is closed Sun.

GRAND DUNES TENNIS CLUB

US 17 Bypass, Myrtle Beach

(843) 449-4486

www.grandedunes.com

Two of the 10 composition courts are lighted. You can practice with the ball machines or at the free backboard area. Full-time tennis professionals offer adult and junior programs year-round. Courts cost $15 per player per hour for singles and $5 per player per hour for doubles. A match setup service and racquet stringing are available. There's also a pro shop.

KINGSTON PLANTATION SPORT & HEALTH CLUB

9760 Kings Hwy., Myrtle Beach

(843) 497-2444

www.kingstonplantation.com

Past host of the GTE Tennis Festival, which featured pro players such as Pete Sampras, Michael Chang, Andre Agassi, and Jimmy Connors, this $4-million health club offers four outdoor clay courts and five Har-tru courts. All courts are lighted, and lessons are available for a minimal fee. Call to schedule an appointment.

MIDWAY PARK
19th Avenue S & US 17
No phone
www.cityofmyrtlebeach.com/recreation.html
Part of the Myrtle Beach recreation system, there are six lighted courts and restroom facilities here.

MYRTLE BEACH PUBLIC COURTS
3200 Oak St., Myrtle Beach
(843) 918-2280
US 17 and 20th Avenue S., Myrtle Beach
No phone
www.cityofmyrtlebeach.com/recreation.html
The two outdoor, asphalt-surfaced courts on Oak Street are next door to the Pepper Geddings Recreation Center. Lights allow you to play all night; however, when the center closes at 9 p.m., so do the restroom facilities.

The 20th Avenue South complex has six lighted courts, along with restrooms and outdoor water fountains. All courts are asphalt-covered.

PRESTWICK HEALTH & TENNIS CLUB
1375 McMaster Dr., Myrtle Beach
(843) 828-1000
www.prestwickcountryclub.com/
Prestwick offers 11 clay courts, 3 lighted courts, and 2 lighted hard-surface courts. Nonmembers pay $15 an hour per court. Private lessons are available for $40 an hour from the head pro. If you're really in top form—or want to get there—you can have a videotape made of your match to see what needs improvement.

South Strand
LITCHFIELD RACQUET CLUB
Hawthorn Drive, Litchfield Beach
(888) 766-4633, (843) 237-3411
www.litchfieldbeach.com
The club maintains 17 Har-tru clay courts, 3 of which are lighted. Instruction is available from two full-time professionals. Ball machines are also available. Litchfield also offers a year-round tennis school.

SURFSIDE BEACH PUBLIC COURTS
Fuller Park
Surfside Drive, Surfside Beach
(843) 650-4131
All three of these outdoor lighted courts are treated with asphalt. Restroom facilities and water fountains are nearby.

SPECTATOR SPORTS

Auto Racing

MYRTLE BEACH SPEEDWAY
4300 US 501, Myrtle Beach
(843) 236-0500
www.myrtlebeachspeedway.com
Amateur and professional drivers thrill racing fans as the roar of engines ricochets off the asphalt of the Myrtle Beach Speedway. With each wave of the checkered flag, this spectator sport draws increasingly larger crowds.

Races are held most Saturday nights and feature five divisions: NASCAR Whelen All-American Series late model stock cars; super trucks; limited late models; street stock; and mini-stock.

The local racing season is highlighted by the Winston Racing Series and also includes the All-Pro, NASCAR Dash, Open Wheel Modified, and Busch Grand National touring series.

The roots of stock-car racing in this area can be traced back more than half a century, when dirt tracks were carved out of remote forests near modern-day downtown. The present speedway facility was built in 1958 and was known as the Racing Association of Myrtle Beach Inc. (RAMBI) Raceway. At that time racing fans were following the budding careers of Richard Petty, Ralph Earnhardt, Ned Jarrett, and David Pearson. After a decade of dirt-track racing, the speedway was paved in 1969.

The popularity of auto racing fell during the 1970s but produced a name to be reckoned with—the late Dale Earnhardt. In 1978 Earnhardt won the late-model sportsman championship at Myrtle Beach Speedway. A year later he joined the Winston Cup roster and won Rookie of the Year honors.

Since the mid-1980s, auto racing has gained momentum. It's not unusual that hot racers at Myrtle Beach Speedway become stars later.

Pit gates open at 1 p.m. and the grandstands open at 4 p.m. Drivers take practice laps before the green flag drops on the first of five heats at 7:30 p.m.

Concession items are available, including beer, soft drinks, and snack food such as hot dogs, chips, and candy. Spectators are permitted to bring small handheld coolers.

Seating is stadium style, so you might want to bring a blanket or a cushioned seat for comfort. Admission varies widely per race.

Baseball

MYRTLE BEACH PELICANS

Coastal Federal Field 1251, 21st Avenue N., Myrtle Beach
(843) 918-6000
www.myrtlebeachpelicans.com

The Pelicans are an Atlanta Braves Class-A affiliate.

The $12 million Coastal Federal Field provides a suitable nest for the Pelicans and brings fans right into the fast-paced action of the game while providing a load of amenities. There are 2,676 box seats and 1,481 reserved seats originally from Fulton County Stadium, former home of the Atlanta Braves. There are lounges, suites, patio boxes, picnic areas with views of the field, and a wheelchair-accessible children's playground. Parking is free. Specials, such as dollar drafts, are often announced, and entertainment such as the Steel In Time steel-drum band plays during halftime. Dinger the Home Run Dog also scores with some impressive maneuvers. Dinger, a sleek, yellow retriever, runs bases, shags fly balls, and retrieves bats. And, of course, hot dogs and popcorn, in addition to a few Myrtle Beach specialties, are available, with plenty of napkins on hand.

The Pelicans are part of the Carolina League, which over the past years has turned out Muscle Shoals, Willie Duke, Woody Fair, Harvey Haddix, Crash Davis, Earl Weaver, Wade Boggs, Rod Carew, Dwight Evans, and Barry Bonds. The current Pelicans team is composed of professional athletes playing hard for the chance to wear the A and the tomahawk of the Atlanta Braves.

The home team has the advantage of a clubhouse designed to assist them in their strenuous struggle to the major leagues. To complement the Braves' modified strength and conditioning program, the workout room has Cybex weight equipment, a training room, whirlpools, and batting cages.

Box seating is $9, reserved seating is $8, and grass seating is $7.

Coastal Carolina University Sports

Sports fans may be interested in checking out events at Coastal Carolina University, about 14 miles west of Myrtle Beach on U.S. Highway 501.

During the academic year, Coastal Carolina University fields 8 men's and 9 women's teams that compete in 17 sporting events, all of which are open to the general public at the campus. As members of the NCAA's Division I Big South Conference, the Chanticleers play soccer, tennis, volleyball, basketball, golf, baseball, and football. For specific details the sports section of the Sun News is a comprehensive resource. For complete schedules contact the athletic department at Coastal Carolina University at (843) 349-2820 or on the Internet at www.goccusports.com.

To give a sense of how far the sports program has come since its start in the 1970s, the Chanticleers took home the Big South Women's All Sports Trophy for 2008–2009 after finishing as runner-up the year before. In 2007, the Chanticleer's men's baseball team had seven players selected for first-round draft picks by Major League Baseball. It could have something to do with the fact that Coastal ranked No. 1 for the season in the NCAA Regionals. The baseball team has won five conference championships and in 2002 won the Big South regular season. The team plays at the Charles L. Watson Baseball Stadium.

Coastal Carolina's men's basketball team won four Big South championships from 1987 to 1991 and advanced to the NCAA tournament in

1991 and 1993. The team plays in Kimbel Arena, 2 blocks east of campus on an unnamed dead-end road between US 501 and Highway 544.

The men's tennis team won conference championships in 1988, 1989, 1993, and 1994.

The men's soccer team won five conference championships from 1986 to 1995, and again in 2001, and has participated in two NCAA tournaments. The soccer season lasts from September to November.

The baseball, tennis, and soccer venues are on the Coastal Carolina campus.

Golf

The Grand Strand has established itself as a veritable golfing mecca.

A number of golf tournaments are played around the Grand Strand, mostly for charity. Myrtle Beach National Golf Course (see the Golf chapter) hosts the Retired Military Golf Classic every May; call (886) 469-7853. The Mark Sloan Memorial Golf Tournament is played in August at Wild Wing Golf Plantation; call the Coastal Carolinas Association of Realtors at (843) 626-3638. And the Charles Tilghman Junior Tournament is set for December at the Surf Club; call (843) 249-1524.

For more information on myriad golfing opportunities—regulation, par 3, and minigolf courses—and tournaments, see the Golf chapter.

GOLF

"Fore! . . . Five. Six. Seven. . . . " The old golf joke gets seriously out of hand on the Grand Strand, especially if you are counting golf courses instead of strokes. At one time, the Grand Strand boasted more than 120 golf courses. The number now stands at 104, but the popularity of chasing that little white ball has helped stretch Myrtle Beach's tradition of summer vacationers into the spring and fall, when the climate in the Carolinas yields the most enjoyable temperatures for golfing.

In 2008 golfers played more than 3.4 million rounds here, making the Myrtle Beach area one of the world's most popular golf destinations. Though no one keeps a central count of how many actual golfers come here every year, it is projected—comparing those more than 3 million rounds with hotel occupancy figures—that approximately 1.3 million golfers come to the Grand Strand every year.

The average golfer comes to the Grand Strand with three other golfers, spends three days here, and is a 39.8-year-old male with a household income of about $52,000. Golf has ranked as the number two generator of tourism revenues here since 1996, pulling in players primarily during spring and fall.

Yes, golf is a big deal here. It's so big, in fact, that golfing legend Gary Player has commented, "If you do not have a high-profile presence in Myrtle Beach, you are not considered a serious player in the golf industry."

OVERVIEW

Most courses market either through hotel package deals or through an advertising co-op association; package deals usually include a welcome gift, breakfast, greens fees, and a cart. Heavy discounts in the off-season (summer for golf) have begun to bleed over into the once-inflated fall fees.

Although the sheer abundance of courses is staggering, perhaps more impressive than the quantity is the quality. This 60-mile stretch of real estate boasts a collection of the country's finest course layouts. Creations of golf-great architects such as Jones, Player, Nicklaus, Fazio, Palmer, Maples, and Dye, these courses offer a lot more than what you might expect—they're everything golf fantasies are made of.

In 2007 *Golf Digest* included 10 Grand Strand courses on its 2007–2008 America's Top 100 Greatest Public Courses list, more than any other golf destination in the country. The highest ranked was the Dunes Golf and Beach Club, coming in at number 28.

Something you might not know about the Grand Strand is that the topography of the countryside is delightfully diverse. If you're a beachgoer, you might know and love the salt-scrubbed beaches, sand castles, sailboats, sea oats, and little else. But wander inland just a bit; you'll discover bountiful secrets in the corners of our counties. You'll find undulating river bluffs and panoramic river vistas, shadowy swamplands, stately old oaks weeping silver moss, sandy pine forests, and seemingly unchanging marshlands. The assortment of ecosystems continues to provide golf-course architects with some of the richest natural resources in the world.

Mother Nature not only has given us an abundance of beautiful real estate but has blessed us with a subtropical climate that makes the outdoors pleasant almost every day of the year.

Crisp days and aqua-blue skies make autumn and spring the favored seasons of many golfers. Still, lots of folks are learning the local secret that outrageous bargains abound during the summer and winter months. Since our weather is governed by cool Gulf Stream breezes when temperatures rise and warm Gulf Stream breezes when temperatures dip, golfing is a year-round delight.

Like everything else in our neck of the woods, golf offerings are eclectic, electric, and just plain fun. Provocative and dazzling new courses flourish, along with the vintage, time-tested tracks graced with history and tradition. Pine Lakes International Country Club, a semiprivate layout designed by Robert White in 1927, launched golf's popularity in this area and today is appropriately known as "the Granddaddy." Myrtle Beach's highly regarded Dunes Golf and Beach Club, designed in 1948 by Robert Trent Jones, carried on the tradition. In decades following, a parade of splendid designs have come to maturation along the Strand. As the number of courses spirals past 100, the area's reputation blossoms accordingly.

With so many courses, the Grand Strand is naturally host to many tournaments for any and every kind of golfer. One of the oldest and biggest golfing events along South Carolina's Grand Strand is the PGA Superstore World Amateur Handicap Championship, billed as the world's largest on-site championship. *Golf Digest* dubbed the August event the "Everyman Open," and *Golf World* crowned it the "mother of all golf tournaments." Little wonder. For more than 20 years, roughly 70,000 golfers from all over the world have participated in the four-day, matched-handicap competition. For information regarding participation, call (800) 833-8798.

The WorldAm tournament is held at various courses, as are other tournaments hosted by Myrtle Beach Golf Holiday: the International Summer Family Golf Tournaments, the Veteran's Golf Classic, and the National Police Golf Championship.

Myrtle Beach Golf Holiday, founded in 1967, is a nonprofit association of accommodations and golf courses along "the Carolinas' Golden Golf Coast," from Georgetown, South Carolina, to Southport, North Carolina. The organization's mission is to increase consumer awareness of the advantages of a Myrtle Beach–area golf vacation and make it as easy as possible for a golfer to reserve accommodations of a preferred level of luxury or economy. Devised as a tax-exempt advertising co-op program and originally put together by the head of a local ad agency, the organization has allowed hotels and golf courses to advertise at rates and in media that they could never initially afford; it is a brilliant promotional tool for Myrtle Beach golf.

Prospective vacationing golfers and travel agents can call (800) 845-4653 or visit www.golfholiday.com to receive a free vacation planner complete with information on 82 resorts and 96 golf courses, as well as travel tips and information on how to directly book a golf vacation with a member accommodation. There are also toll-free numbers to call from the United Kingdom, Finland, France, Germany, Ireland, Japan, the Netherlands, Norway, Sweden, and Switzerland.

The Classics of Myrtle Beach is an umbrella organization that represents 13 of the Grand Strand's top courses and 10 of its best resorts. Their collection demands strict standards of quality and offers deluxe amenities that include fine restaurants, exercise and relaxation facilities, and entertainment options. They have truly mastered the small details that ensure your golf vacation is first class. Booking a Classic package couldn't be easier. Just select a resort and the courses and tee times you want; they will take care of everything else. Visit www.myrtlebeachclassics.com for additional information.

Service-oriented Myrtle Beach caters to a golfer's every need; there are also more than a dozen golf schools in town, many with PGA instructors, great student-teacher ratios, and programs keyed to all levels of play.

For the inside scoop regarding golf on the Strand, refer to *SCORE* magazine. You'll discover scads of interesting editorial, dining, and entertainment tips; a directory of courses; maps; and much more. The magazine is available free at most golf stores throughout the Grand Strand.

TOURNAMENTS

With so many courses, the Grand Strand naturally hosts many tournaments—local, national, and international—for any and every kind of golfer, not just the pros. For instance, one of the oldest and biggest golfing events along South Carolina's Grand Strand, the PGA Superstore World Amateur Handicap Championship (see subsequent entry), is billed as the world's largest on-site championship. Call (800) 845-4653 for information about MBGH-hosted events.

Of course, many tournaments carry large cash purses, including sizable sums awarded to the winners. Spectators also win, as they are treated to some of the best golf played by some of the best golfers on the planet. But the real winners of all PGA (and Nike) tour events are charitable organizations. In 1997 the United Way of Horry County, Disabled American Veterans, Make-A-Wish Foundation, Mobile Meals in Myrtle Beach, Hook-A-Kid-On-Golf, and the Elizabeth Chapin Patterson Community Assistance Center shared $200,000. In 1999 the SENIOR PGA TOUR tournaments combined raised a record $11,050,000 in charitable donations. In 2002 Myrtle Beach Golf Holiday hosted a 9/11 Memorial Golf Ball Tournament. Firefighters from across the country came to Myrtle Beach to raise money for the Thomas Elsasser Fund, a charity backed by the United Firefighters Association (UFA) and designed to benefit families of fallen firefighters. The tournament provided an opportunity for firefighters, many of whom assisted in the recovery efforts at Ground Zero, to gather in the Golf Capital of the World. Even the South Carolina–based band Hootie and the Blowfish have gotten involved, sponsoring their annual Monday After the Masters Pro-Am. From 1995 to 2009, the tournament has donated more than $4 million to the Hootie & the Blowfish Foundation, which supports the educational needs of South Carolina and the South Carolina Junior Golf Foundation.

GEORGE HOLLIDAY MEMORIAL JUNIOR TOURNAMENT
(800) 882-2614
www.georgeholliday.com

Played every year over Thanksgiving weekend, this exciting junior tournament is one of the largest, most popular events at the Beach. More than 10,000 juniors have enjoyed this tournament over the years. The golf tournament was established to honor a successful junior and collegiate golfer, George Holliday, who was tragically killed in 1967 in an automobile accident at the age of 22. His family founded the tournament to give other young golfers an opportunity to excel. The 2009 version of the tournament included three championship rounds and was limited to the first 420 golfers. Call Michael Burnside at (800) 882-2614 for information.

PGA SUPERSTORE WORLD AMATEUR HANDICAP CHAMPIONSHIP
(800) 833-8798
www.worldamgolf.com

The venerable PGA Superstore World Amateur Handicap Championship, one of the oldest and biggest golfing events on the Strand, is billed as the world's largest on-site championship. *Golf Digest* magazine dubbed the August event the "Everyman Open," and *Golf World* magazine crowned it the "mother of all golf tournaments." Little wonder. During the past 25 years, well more than 70,000 golfers from all over the world have participated in the four-day, matched-handicap competition.

GRAND STRAND GOLF COURSES

With 105 courses on the Grand Strand, there are far and away too many for us to tell you about more than a fraction. Nonetheless, here's a representative assortment featuring different styles, prices, and locales. You should also take into account that, for the full picture of Grand Strand golfing, we extend the Grand Strand beyond the state line to include the southern tip of North Carolina, as it touches the traditional Grand Strand. This "extension" of the Strand applies only to our look at golfing, and we do so because those North Carolina courses really are part of the local golfing community.

Area golf courses reserve the right to alter greens fees at any given time. It's almost a sure bet that rates will be higher from March 1 to May 1 and during September and October; these times of year feature prime golfing weather and golf-course conditions. Morning greens fees are usually highest, with rates dropping beginning around noon and continuing to fall as the day gets warmer. To give you a proper perspective on greens fees on Grand Strand courses, we include the highest greens fees (including a cart unless otherwise noted) during peak season (March to May) for each entry. We also state each course's policy on walking.

Yardage from the men's white tees and par are provided in the course description. Remember, although there are oodles of courses to choose from, tee times are precious, especially during prime seasons. Call well in advance—three months or more—to book reservations.

North Strand

BAREFOOT RESORT & GOLF
4980 Barefoot Resort Bridge Rd.,
North Myrtle Beach
(843) 390-3200
www.barefootgolf.com

One of the Grand Strand's newest golf resorts, Barefoot is also one of the most spectacular. It offers four distinctive championship courses, all unique, visually striking, and fun to play. The venue was designed by the top golf course designers in the world, Greg Norman, Davis Love III, Tom Fazio, and Pete Dye. The courses can be played by average golfers as well as those with a low handicap.

The Dye Course is the only one that is semi-private, and some would argue that it is the best of the four. The layout of this 7,343-yard par 72 is beautiful and treacherous.

The Fazio Course has been strategically designed to incorporate tree cover and lakes into the landscaping. Water can be seen on 15 of the holes, yet they are in out-of-play areas. Tee and fairways consist of GN-1, a hybrid turf developed by Greg Norman. The approach is Tifsport Bermuda, while the greens are an A-1 bent grass. The par 71 is 6,834 yards long.

Embracing a tradition of Lowcountry character, the Love Course has wide-open fairways and generous land areas. The course is par 72 and plays over 7,000 yards. The Norman Course is par 72 as well and plays 7,200 yards. Seven holes of the Norman Course are along the Intracoastal Waterway, and with its open green complexes and fairways running up to the sand, the course presents a real challenge for any golfer.

All of the courses allow walking. Rates are subject to change so check with the course when you book. They range from $105 to $185 for 18-hole walk-ons.

> **i** Barefoot Resort & Golf boasts a "folio system," which implements bar codes and bypasses the obligatory check-in prior to tee time.

BRUNSWICK PLANTATION AND GOLF RESORT
US 17, Calabash, NC
(800) 835-4533, (910) 845-6928
www.brunswickplantation.com

Brunswick Plantation inhabits a convenient, central point between Myrtle Beach, South Carolina, and Wilmington, North Carolina (which is an hour north of Myrtle Beach) and lies just minutes from beautiful Carolina beaches.

The 27 holes of this par 72 course measure 6,200 yards, and the natural beauty of the terrain is emphasized by integrating quick bentgrass greens and beautiful lush fairways with wooded Carolina pines.

The first nine holes of the Magnolia Course draw from the historic links of Scotland. The extensive mounds and large sand and grass bunkers present the challenge of this nine. The second nine, the Azalea Course, is carved from thick Carolina woodlands. Water is the dominant theme on many of the holes, demanding thought and strategy on every shot. The fourth hole is an island green accessible by bridge and surrounded by beautiful oyster shells. The Dogwood Course, which composes the final nine, meanders along the historic Caw Caw Run among the dense hardwood trees. The No. 6 hole will provide you with another challenging island green, and you can look forward to the No. 7 hole, where you'll discover a 300-year-old cypress tree that's more than 10 feet in diameter!

Greens fees range from $25.95 to $69.95, depending on the course and the time of year. There is no walking and carts are extra.

CROW CREEK GOLF CLUB
US 17, Calabash, NC
(877) 730-3600, (910) 287-3081
www.crowcreek.com

Just 2 miles north of the state line, Crow Creek has become one of the top destinations for golfers in the Grand Strand area. Created by Rick Robbins, it has an imaginative layout, L-93 bentgrass greens, and manicured Tifsport Bermuda fairways.

Built on developer Jerry McLamb's 500-acre family homestead, this track combines two styles of design. You'll find a windswept links-style front nine with mounding and bunkers rolling through what had been tobacco and vegetable gardens, and an old-style fishing shack on No. 8. The back nine cuts through an old forest and features tree-lined fairways and rolling contours for a decidedly wilder environment. Opening in 2000, this course quickly became one of the best new courses in the Myrtle Beach area.

The par 72 course is 7,100 yards. Rates vary per time of year from $59 to $89; no walking.

GLEN DORNOCH WATERWAY GOLF LINKS
US 17 N., Little River
(800) 717-8784, (843) 249-2541
www.glendornoch.com

This 270-acre site along the Intracoastal Waterway was created as a tribute to Dornoch, Scotland, the birthplace of golf legend Donald Ross. The 18-hole, 6,035-yard, par 72 Clyde Johnston design, which opened in Sept 1996, is set amid pines, oaks, lakes, a river, marsh, and the Intracoastal. It's consistently listed by *Golf World* and Zagat's as one of the top courses in South Carolina. At least four holes flank the waterway, and dramatic elevation changes—you'll find some 35-foot drops to the water—are nothing short of spectacular. Bring your most accurate game—there are no wide-open fairways here.

Greens fees range from $64 to $108 depending on tee times and the time of year; no walking. Glen Dornoch includes a self-contained resort with a hotel, condominiums, and an array of related facilities.

i Before you call your favorite courses to schedule tee times, check with the folks in charge at your hotel or rental management firm. Odds are good they will be able to score deep discounts on greens fees on your behalf.

HEATHER GLEN
4650 Heather Glen Way, North Myrtle Beach
(800) 868-4536, (843) 249-9000
www.heatherglen.com

Timeless oaks and stately pines stud the 400-acre historic setting of Heather Glen, a course reminiscent of the best Scotland has to offer. Designed by Willard Byrd and Clyde Johnston, this course was pegged a masterpiece as quickly as it opened for play. *Golf Digest* named it 1987's Best New Public Course in America and one of the 50 Best Public Courses in America in 1990. It consistently garners accolades and in 2008 was listed by *Gold World* as one of the top 22 courses in South Carolina.

Heather Glen made a great thing even better when it expanded from 18 to 27 holes. This allows golfers to personally design their rounds by picking two of three stellar sets of nine holes from among the Red (3,127 yards), White (3,198 yards), and Blue (3,183 yards) Courses, all par 72. Greens fees start at $52; no walking.

Back at the 18th-century-style clubhouse, cap off your round in an authentic-style pub serving Bass Ale and grilled sandwiches.

THE BIG CATS OF OCEAN RIDGE
Ocean Ridge Plantation
351 Ocean Ridge Parkway SW
Sunset Beach, NC
(800) 233-1801, (910) 287-1717
www.big-cats.com

Ocean Ridge is now home to four spectacular courses, all with daunting names of jungle predators. Since opening in 1991, the untamed Lion's Paw has often been described as Willard Byrd's finest work. Given Byrd's résumé, that description heartily endorses Lion's Paw as a course worth considering. This masterful layout is simultaneously wild and peaceful. Perhaps the most striking feature of Lion's Paw is the contrast between the front nine holes and the back nine. The front nine feature a traditional layout, with natural elevation changes and features such as Carolina pine trees. The back nine, however, is links-style after the great courses of Great Britain, with low-lying, mounded farmland and no trees.

No. 3 is a par 3 requiring a carry over water. Oyster shells flank each side of the fairway. No. 18 has a water hazard in the second-shot landing area, and the green is a peninsula surrounded by water. In all, this par 72 course measures 6,457 yards.

Panther's Run came next. Designed by Tom Cate, this 7,086-yard course features a beautiful woodland setting with deer, osprey, and owls. You'd be hard-pressed to find a more incredible variety of elevation in one location. Add twisting fairways and the classic beauty of a nature preserve and marshlands, and you've got a course that's as memorable for its scenery as for its challenge. The 13th hole is a monster par 4, and with its lake winding in front of the tees, it is also one of the loveliest holes on the course. Avid golfers swear this is one of the finest driving holes to play.

Wildlife abounds here, so you might want to bring your binoculars. Panther's Run golf shop was rated in the top 100 in 1997 by *Golf Digest,* so bring your wallet, too.

Cate also designed Tiger's Eye, which has been lauded by many as one of the best courses in the U.S. Each of its 18 holes has its own unique style. Tiger's Eye measures 7,010 yards from the championship tees.

The breathtaking Leopard's Chase is the newest of the Big Cats. Traversing more than 220 acres of natural landscape, the par 72 course stretches a formidable 7,155 yards and carries a slope of 140. The scenery is breathtaking, and your game will be memorable. Green fees vary so check when you reserve your time; no walking.

THE LONG BAY CLUB
Highway 9, North Myrtle Beach
(800) 344-5590, (843) 399-2222

The fact that the Long Bay Club is a Jack Nicklaus "signature course" is reason enough to pen it in on your golfing schedule. Open since 1988, the course continually has ranked among the top courses in the country.

A typical Nicklaus design, the 6,565-yard, par 72 layout showcases deep pot bunkers and vast waste areas; challenges abound. If the definition of a great layout is "a course with holes that become etched in memory," then Long Bay is indisputably great. In fact, the 10th hole, which features a scalloped, horseshoe-shaped sand trap, is one of the most recognizable holes in the entire golf world.

Greens fees are from $48; no walking.

MARSH HARBOUR
Marsh Harbour Road, Calabash, NC
(800) 523-2631, (910) 759-7300

This Dan Maples course has an interesting claim to fame—some holes are in South Carolina and some are in North Carolina. Marsh Harbour covers wetland along an inlet and the Intracoastal Waterway, making the course every bit as enjoyable to look at as it is to play. The combination of manicured turf and sparkling water creates a green and blue backdrop that's nothing shy of spectacular. Upon opening in 1980, the 6,000-yard, par 71 Marsh Harbour was rated among *Golf Digest*'s Top 25 Public Courses in America.

The course's signature hole is the 570-yard 17th. Marvelously terrifying, this par 5 has three landing areas, two of which sport water on three sides. No one leaves Marsh Harbour without talking about No. 17.

Greens fees are $68 (summer); no walking.

MEADOWLANDS
350 Calabash Rd., Calabash, NC
(888) 287-7529, (910) 287-7529
www.meadowlandsgolf.com

Meadowlands threw open the barn doors in Sept 1997 and has been befriending golfers ever since. The grounds that once were farmland have been carefully and patiently sculpted by Willard Byrd and have been compared to Dan Maples's Man O' War Course (see subsequent entry). Meadowlands is wide open for your grazing pleasure, cultivates tidewater greens, and welcomes you with a 6,000-square-foot, two-story clubhouse in a turn-of-the-20th-century-style farmhouse setting. Meadowlands has a few memorable spots, from the alligator sanctuary located behind the 17th green to the 5-foot vertical drop lurking beyond the 13th. Metal spikes are not permitted, nor is walking. This 6,000-yard, par 72 course ranges from $39 to $84 to play.

OYSTER BAY
Lakeshore Drive, Sunset Beach, NC
(800) 697-8372
www.legendsgolf.com

Yet another Dan Maples design, Oyster Bay really does have it all—6,305 yards set amid pretty lakes, sweeping marshes, and the Intracoastal Waterway, teeming with wildlife. Expect to see all sorts of shorebirds, and don't be surprised if you glimpse an alligator basking in the Carolina sunshine. This par 70 course was rated the Best New Resort Course in America in 1983 by *Golf Digest*. In 1990 the magazine sang its praises again, rating it one of the 50 Best Public Courses in America.

A lake flanks the entire right side of the 13th fairway, and the green is guarded by a cavernous bunker. The 15th and 17th holes are par 3s with island greens, the latter of which is built on a mountain of oyster shells.

Greens fees vary; no walking.

THE PEARL GOLF LINKS
1300 Pearl Blvd. SW,
Sunset Beach, NC
(888) 947-3275, (910) 579-8132
www.thepearlgolf.com

The omnipresent and magnificent Dan Maples strikes again with the Pearl's two courses. Both the East and West Courses easily qualify as some of the finest in all the nation. Both are ranked among the top courses in the Carolinas and have been nominated Best New Public Courses in America by *Golf Digest*.

The par 72 East Course, encompassing 6,543 yards, is the more traditional of the two. Carved from pristine maritime forest, it boasts a dramatic finishing hole along the Calabash River—a mid-length par 4, uphill off the tee and downhill to the green, with the river and salt marsh on the left.

The Pearl's 6,738-yard, par 72 West Course is links-style; lots of wide-open stretches complemented by thick displays of pampas grass. The 18th hole alone is worth the greens fee; it features a finishing hole—in 1997, it was voted best finishing hole by *GOLF Magazine*—along bluffs that overlook the blue ribbon of Intracoastal Waterway. Attention to detail and meticulous grooming characterize this course, which has hosted a number of major tournaments.

Greens fees vary; no walking.

POSSUM TROT GOLF CLUB
US 17 N., North Myrtle Beach
(800) 626-8768, (843) 272-5341
www.possumtrot.com

Open since 1968, Possum Trot bills itself as "the friendliest course down South, where the guest is number one." In 2007 the Myrtle Beach *Sun News* rated it the best course for the money. Noted among locals and returning tourists for consistently excellent playing conditions, this 6,388-yard, par 72 course features wide fairways that make for a low-maintenance round whether you're an average golfer or a low handicapper.

Possum Trot also offers a unique 16-acre practice facility; a driving range complete with chipping, pitching, and putting greens; and a practice bunker. Greens fees start at $42 and walking is allowed at times; call ahead.

RIVER HILLS GOLF & COUNTRY CLUB
US 17 N., Little River
(800) 264-3810, (843) 399-2100
www.riverhillsgolf.com
Just one year after opening, River Hills was nominated by *Golf Digest* as its Best New Course for 1989. Also in 1989, *Golfweek* named the course one of the Southeast's Top 50.

A public resort facility in an impressive country-club setting, River Hills remains an outstanding course that offers a pleasing blend of old and new design features, frequent elevation changes (more than any course in the area), and championship conditioning. This 6,285-yard, par 72 course is definitely worth adding to your playing schedule. Greens fees start at $46; no walking.

ST. JAMES PLANTATION
US 211, Southport, NC
(800) 247-4806, (910) 253-3008
www.stjamesplantation.com
Managed by industry leader Troon Golf, St. James features four fabulous courses that are a cut above. The members-only clubs are in a gorgeous natural setting of marsh, maritime woodlands, lakes, and the ever-beautiful Intracoastal Waterway. Opened in 2008, the award-winning Nicklaus-designed Reserve Club is the newest course. The par 72, 7,100-yard layout emphasizes strategy and shot making amid a rolling terrain. The Founder's Club is a 7,016-yard par 72 that showcases hazards, marshes, and pot bunkers amid undulating greens. It is considered one of P. B. Dye's finest and most challenging courses. Three-time U.S. Open winner Hale Irwin designed

the 27-hole Members Club. A par 72 layout offers 6,687 yards of exciting design with multiple tee boxes and lines of play. North Carolina native Tim Cate is responsible for the 18-hole Players Club. With its 6,940 yards, the par 72 layout is designed with narrow fairways to force accuracy off the tees. Greens fees range from $55; no walking.

SANDPIPER BAY
800 Sandpiper Bay Dr.,
Sunset Beach, NC
(800) 356-5827, (910) 579-9120
www.sandpiperbaygolf.com
With some of the best bent-grass greens on the Strand, Sandpiper Bay, a Dan Maples design, has been a locals' favorite for more than a decade. Players consistently find this 27-hole, 6,020-yard, par 71 course in great shape. With six par 3s and five par 5s, it's a challenge for players of all skill levels. A magnificent clubhouse, set among wind-whispering pines and glassy lakes, reflects Sandpiper Bay's commitment to quality and exceptional service.

Greens fees start at $61; no walking.

SEA TRAIL PLANTATION
211 Clubhouse Rd., Sunset Beach, NC
(888) 229-5747, (910) 287-1157
www.seatrail.com
Sea Trail Plantation has three courses, designed by notable architects Dan Maples, Rees Jones, and Willard Byrd. (With those names, how could you go wrong?) Each course is manageable—not too easy, not too tough—the kind you'll remember fondly once you've returned home. Even so, the traditional design of the Rees Jones course stands out to golf aficionados. Wide fairways, elevated greens, large mounds, swales, pot bunkers, and freshwater lakes add to its aesthetic beauty. But, rest assured, its good looks haven't softened its challenge. In 2005 it was named one of the Top 50 Courses in Myrtle Beach, and *Golf Digest* put it among the Top 100 Courses in North Carolina.

All three courses are par 72. The 6,251-yard Byrd Course costs $85 to play, the 6,334-yard Jones Course is $100, and the 6,332-yard Maples Course is $85. Walking is not permitted, and golfers must wear spikeless shoes on all three courses.

SURF CLUB
1701 Springland Lane, North Myrtle Beach
(800) 765-SURF, (843) 249-1524
www.surfgolf.com

This club opened in 1960 and has been a popular golfing destination for four decades. All the greens were rebuilt to enhance this George Cobb classic. Those who knew and loved the Surf before the renovation will appreciate the way architect John LaFoy retained the course's classic appeal while adding new challenges for golfers of all abilities. One avid local golfer described the Surf simply: "Traditional design without gimmicks. Strong par 4s merit playing." The Surf Club plays host to the Carolina Open.

The 6,360-yard, par 72 Surf Club course costs $93 to play; no walking.

THISTLE GOLF CLUB
8840 Old Georgetown Rd. SW,
Sunset Beach, NC
(800) 571-6710, (910) 575-8700
www.thistlegolf.com

In a relatively short time, Thistle Golf Club has established itself among the best courses the Strand has to offer. Since opening in 1999, the 27-hole Tim Cates Scottish-links design has been ranked among the Top 100 Fairways in America by *Golf For Women magazine*. The course also earned four stars from *Golf Digest*'s "Places to Play." An engaging layout and complimentary range balls, yardage book, and bag tags make this an enviable golf experience. The 6,997-yard, par 72 course boasts generous fairways, large bent-grass greens, five sets of tees, and 12-minute tee times. Golfers of all abilities will enjoy a day at Thistle. Greens fees start at $95; walking is permitted.

TIDEWATER GOLF CLUB & PLANTATION
4901 Little River Neck Rd.,
North Myrtle Beach
(800) 446-5363, (843) 249-3829
http://tidewatergolf.com

If scenic vistas showcasing water suit your taste, you'll fall in love with Tidewater in a hurry. Truly incredible views of the Intracoastal Waterway, saltwater marshes, and the Atlantic Ocean abound. At least one hole plays alongside Hogg Inlet (a popular fishing area for Cherry Grove residents), so you can watch anglers reel in a few as you plan your next shot. This fabulous course was named one of the best new public courses by both *Golf Digest* and *GOLF Magazine* in 1990. Recently it was named by *GOLF Magazine* as number 39 on its Top 100 You Can Play list.

Situated on 560 acres of seaside peninsula, Tidewater gives you plenty of elbow room and privacy. The only hole you can see at any given time is the one you're playing, which creates the feeling of absolute solitude. The course has five sets of tees, so golfers can select those that best suit their games. Depending on tee selection, you can stretch this par 72 course from 4,765 to 7,020 yards.

Tidewater is one of the Grand Strand's most expensive golf courses (greens fees are $145), but when you see it, you'll understand why. Hale Irwin, three-time U.S. Open champion, called Tidewater "one of the finest and most spectacular courses on the East Coast." This course is definitely not to be missed. Walking is permitted.

> **i** Rain policies vary from one course to another. In most cases some form of rain check is available. Contact the individual course for specifics.

Myrtle Beach
ARCADIAN SHORES GOLF CLUB
(at Hilton Myrtle Beach Resort)
701 Hilton Rd., Myrtle Beach
(843) 449-5217
www.kingstonplantation.com

Rees Jones designed this course, which opened in 1974. It features standard Bermuda-grass fairways and lush bent-grass greens. Surrounding the greens and sprinkled along the fairways are no fewer than 64 sand bunkers amid this 6,446-yard, par 72 track—just so you'll remember you're at the beach! A variety of picturesque natural lakes adds to the challenge. In 1993 the course was listed among *Golf Digest*'s Top 50 Resort Courses. *GOLF Magazine,* too, has noted Arcadian Shores's outstanding design.

Greens fees start at $64; no walking.

ARROWHEAD COUNTRY CLUB
1201 Burcale Rd., Myrtle Beach
(800) 236-3243, (843) 236-3243
www.arrowheadcc.com

This Raymond Floyd–designed course continually garners rave reviews. Twenty-seven holes currently are open for play; each nine-hole course has its own name. The appropriately named Lakes Course meanders 3,119 yards through a pristine pine forest and features striking undulations in the fairways, numerous white-sand bunkers, and abundant lakes. The 3,123-yard Cypress Course, in contrast, is set amid a beautiful stand of hardwoods, unique to the Myrtle Beach area. The Waterway Course, which opened in November 1995, stretches 3,060 yards through hardwoods to the Intracoastal Waterway and includes a liberal mix of mounds and lakes. The feel is similar to the Lakes and Cypress Courses but is enhanced by the waterway view. All three courses are par 72.

Arrowhead's design, masterminded in collaboration with Tom Jackson, offers the feeling of playing golf in the Carolina foothills. A beautiful clubhouse, large practice facility, and a well-stocked pro shop add to the quality of this course. Greens fees range from $54 to $122; no walking.

THE DUNES GOLF AND BEACH CLUB
9000 North Ocean Blvd.,
Myrtle Beach
(843) 449-5914
www.thedunesclub.net

The Dunes Club is one of the area's oldest and best-loved courses. A par 72 Robert Trent Jones design, Dunes was only the second course built in Myrtle Beach—back in 1948. Renovations make it one of a handful of courses with PennLink bent-grass greens.

Through the years, the 6,174-yard course has achieved worldwide renown. The 13th hole, rated one of the best 18 holes in America by *Sports Illustrated,* is particularly popular. *GOLF Magazine* included the 13th hole in its 100 Best Holes in America, and *Southern Living* named it one of the 18 Ultimate Golf Holes of the South, proclaiming:

> *If a single golf hole can be given credit for popularizing Myrtle Beach golf, this is it. Its crescent-shaped fairway winds around the former Singleton Swash, now a lake. A monstrous drive is advised, to be followed by a monstrous 3-wood, and you're still a strong iron from a round green. It's a par 6 for most of us.*

So few people have reached the 13th green in two shots that those who have are noted in the Dunes Club's history. The hole is known as Waterloo; don't let it be yours.

The rest of the course is fairly traditional, with wide-open fairways, deep bunkers, and elevated greens. The course's beauty is anything but ordinary. The Atlantic Ocean is the backdrop for several holes, while others wind around and through the marsh. Understandably, this course has a maturity that other Grand Strand courses envy.

Rest assured, when you wrap up at No. 18, you will have used every club in your bag. And you may be hungry. If so, drop by the grill for a quick bite or the elegant dining room for a formal dinner with a panoramic view of the beach.

The Dunes remains one of the Strand's most exclusive private clubs and is available to the guests of a few select member hotels: the Breakers, the Caravelle, the Caribbean, the Driftwood, the Dunes Village, and the South Wind. Tee times are scheduled through the hotels; greens fees are $160 if booked that way.

ℹ️ The highly respected Dunes Golf and Beach Club course was the site of a salt mill in the 1800s. The buildings were burned during the Civil War by Union soldiers. It is believed that the main building stood at the site of what is currently the 18th hole.

GRANDE DUNES GOLF RESORT
1000 Grande Dunes Blvd.
Myrtle Beach
(877) 347-2633
www.grandedunes.com

Grande Dunes has been called "one of the great golf resorts of the world" by *PGA Magazine* and one of the Top 10 You Can Play courses by *GOLF Magazine*. While there are no "dunes" at this golf haven, it does sit high on a magnificent bank overlooking the Intracoastal Waterway.

There are two courses. The par 71 Resort Course is an 18-hole masterpiece measuring 7,618 yards from the back tees. The Myrtle Beach Golf Association classifies No. 11, 14, and 18 as very good and follows up by saying, "the 9th and 10th hole are, in a word, great." The 7,048-yard Members Course was codesigned by Nick Price and Craig Schreiner and takes advantage of this outstanding site's natural beauty and challenging environment. Created for a select number of golfers, the par 71 offers some special shot-making challenges.

The greens fees are $94 to $186; no walking.

THE LEGENDS COMPLEX
US 501, Myrtle Beach
(800) 299-6187, (843) 236-9318
www.legendsgolf.com

Since 1990 the Legends Complex has offered three distinctive courses along the Grand Strand: Parkland, Heathland, and Moorland. The newest, and arguably the best, of the three is Parkland. When members of the Carolinas PGA held a championship here, the pros pointed out similarities to New Jersey's highly acclaimed Pine Valley Course. Parkland requires the ability to draw or fade the ball, and accuracy is an absolute must. This complex is not a place for beginners. Don't try this par 72, 6,425-yard course unless you're up to the challenge; you'll only get frustrated and slow down play.

Heathland is one of the most unusual courses along the Grand Strand. It would seem more at home in the Scottish landscape, given its lack of trees, menacing winds, and rolling fairways. Pot bunkers appear more ominous than they are, so don't be intimidated. One of the more interesting holes requires golfers playing from the men's tees to drive straight over a grove of trees; the ladies' tees are positioned on the other side to bypass the grove. Upon opening, this Tom Doak design was immediately selected as one of *GOLF Magazine*'s Top 10 New Courses. Par 72 Heathland measures 6,190 yards.

Rounding out the Legends Complex is Moorland, which features some of the most feared holes in Myrtle Beach; you'll either love or hate this 6,125-yard, par 72 P. B. Dye course. When Legends's owner Larry Young hired the renowned Dye to design the course, his instruction was simple: "Make it as hard as you can." And Dye did! It can be downright difficult in places, especially the short par 4 called Hell's Half-Acre, although when the tees are placed forward, it isn't an impossible challenge even for average golfers. Ironically, the higher a player's handicap, the more the individual seems to enjoy Moorland.

The Legends has one of the most impressive clubhouses we've ever seen. It climbs skyward from the undulating green terrain like a Scottish castle. Inside, the tradition of elegance continues with an upscale pro shop, comfortable pub, and dining room. There is also a state-of-the-art driving range with greens and flags as targets, instead of the usual wide-open space with distance markers.

Greens fees are $59 (summer); no walking. You can also book tee times at the Heritage and Oyster Bay by calling the listed telephone numbers.

MAN O' WAR
US 501, Myrtle Beach
(843) 236-8000
www.manowargolfcourse.com
World-famous architect Dan Maples definitely won the battle with this legendary layout, created from the depths of—believe it or not—a 100-acre lake. This long-awaited 6,402-yard, par 72 course, which opened in Jan 1996, features a pair of back-to-back island greens (remember when one island green was impressive?) plus an awesome island ninth hole that's surrounded by water from tee to green. Distinctive wide fairways, bent-grass greens, a practice range, and a unique marina clubhouse add intrigue to an already marvelous course. Greens fees are $91; no walking.

MYRTLE BEACH NATIONAL GOLF COURSE
US 501, Myrtle Beach
(800) 882-3420, (843) 448-2308
www.mbn.com
You'll find an outstanding trio of impeccably conditioned courses at Myrtle Beach National, each bearing Arnold Palmer's special touch. (All three par 72 courses were designed by Frank Duane with input from the master himself.)

If you can take your pick, choose the North Course. One of the oldest and most requested on the beach, this course reopened in Dec 1995 following extensive renovations.

Enhancements to the 6,413-yard layout include reshaped and enlarged greens sodded with hybrid Crenshaw bent grass. Trees have been removed to open the course. Several of the Bermuda-grass fairways feature increased undulation, and bunkers and lakes have been dramatically reshaped. The famous par 3 No. 12, which includes sand traps shaped like the letters *SC*, has bulkheads and a footbridge. This is one of the most recognizable holes on the Strand. Kings North's holes No. 14, 16, 18, and 36 are listed by the *Sun News* as among the 100 Best Holes on the Grand Strand.

If you can't get on the Kings North Course, don't despair; you'll enjoy playing the South Creek (6,089 yards) or West (6,113 yards) Courses, too. West is probably the easiest of the trio. All three offer gently rolling fairways, towering pines, and a few perilous lakes. Myrtle Beach National serves up the perfect opportunity for a multi-round day. Walking is not allowed on any of the three courses here.

PINE LAKES INTERNATIONAL COUNTRY CLUB
Woodside Drive, Myrtle Beach
(800) 446-6817, (843) 449-6459
www.pinelakes.com
Affectionately hailed as "the Granddaddy," this is quite literally where Myrtle Beach golf began. This course, the oldest in the area, was constructed in 1927 and was originally called the Ocean Forest Golf Club. Course architect Robert White, first PGA president and a native of St. Andrews, Scotland, endowed the 6,176-yard, par 71 layout with a unique Scottish flair.

There is promise the Scottish tradition will remain. The Miles family, which owned the course since 1927, sold it to Burroughs & Chapin in 2002. They restructured the course to add condominiums, and the redesigned course reopened in the fall of 2008. The back nine reflects White's original design, and the front nine was renovated to enhance the elegant experience golfers from around the world associate with Pine Lakes Country Club. The course is currently on the National Register of Historic Places.

The first golf course on the Grand Strand, Pine Lakes International Country Club is legendary for many things, not the least of which is that *Sports Illustrated* magazine got its beginnings here in 1954.

PRESTWICK COUNTRY CLUB
1001 Links Rd., Myrtle Beach
(843) 293-4100, (888) 250-1767
www.prestwickcountryclub.com
Prestwick, a semiprivate course, is another jewel designed by Pete and P. B. Dye. A 20-acre lake

created for the course separates the 9th and 18th holes in dramatic fashion and highlights the natural beauty of this masterful 6,347-yard, par 72 layout. An assortment of winding streams and ponds bring water directly into play on 8 of the course's 18 holes. Each hole has six different sets of tees to challenge any skill level. Dye-inspired features abound: undulating greens, seemingly bottomless pot bunkers, and railroad ties galore.

Greens fees vary. Only members can walk this course during late afternoon.

RIVER OAKS GOLF PLANTATION
831 River Oaks Dr., Myrtle Beach
(800) 762-8813, (843) 236-2222
www.riveroaksgolfplantation.com

Rated in the Top 5 on the Grand Strand by Golf Course Rankings of America, this course has something for everyone. You can't help but enjoy the 27 holes of undulating greens, mounded fairways, large lakes, and finger-shaped bunkers among the Bear (6,314 yards), Fox (6,345), and Otter (6,425) Courses, each of which is par 72. Greens fees are $55 (summer); no walking.

In addition, the natural beauty and abundance of wildlife make every golf experience a mini-adventure. A professional staff, excellent practice areas, and beautifully manicured fairways, greens, and tees have made River Oaks a popular choice. River Oaks offers the American Golf Academy to help you improve your game. The course's convenient location across from Fantasy Harbor is also appealing.

WATERWAY HILLS
US 17 N., Myrtle Beach
(800) 344-5590, (843) 449-6488
www.mbn.com

Robert Trent Jones, sometimes called the "dean of golf architecture" (Donald Ross fans likely would argue that distinction), designed this gem of a course.

When you emerge from the enclosed tram that ferries you across the Intracoastal Waterway, you'll find 27 superbly maintained holes set amid woodland seclusion, with more than a few lakes for spice.

Traditional in design, Waterway Hills offers rolling terrain and a variety of strategically placed bunkers. The three beautiful courses—Oaks (3,080 yards), Lakes (3,001 yards), and Ravine (2,927 yards), which are all par 72 in pairs—are characterized by landscape challenges that make each course suitably named. The Oaks's 27 holes wind through trees, and its fairways are lined with large oaks. The Lakes features four holes with water hazards and meanders around five substantial bodies of water. And No. 3 at the Ravine is a par 5 with a harrowing hazard: a 60-foot chasm.

Greens fees start at $42 for any 18-hole combination; walking is permitted in the afternoon.

WILD WING PLANTATION
1000 Wild Wing Blvd., off US 501,
Myrtle Beach
(800) 736-WING, (843) 347-9464
www.wildwing.com

Wild Wing Plantation is a highly acclaimed facility that delivers world-class golf in a world-class setting. Once the home of four championship courses, Wild Wing was sold to a group of developers, and now only one course, Avocet, remains. That said, Avocet was always considered the best of the group.

A special distinction at Wild Wing is computerized golf carts. These computers give exact yardages from the ball, wherever it lies, to the center of the green. The computers also offer helpful hints like "bunker on left" and "green slopes to the right." (Sounds a little like cheating, but you have to live with your conscience.)

On the Avocet's opening, the *Sun News* named it Best New Course in Myrtle Beach. Designed as a signature course by Jeff Brauer and two-time PGA Champion Larry Nelson, the Avocet will keep you seeing double; creative contouring presents a host of elevated tees and greens, double fairways, grass bunkers—even a double green. The par 72 course covers 6,614 yards. *Golf Digest* named the course a four-star winner in 2001.

Greens fees are $61 to $72; no walking.

Don't miss WishBones, Wild Wing's restaurant, in the 33,000-square-foot clubhouse. ("Wows" are in order.) It's a favorite hangout for golfing and nongolfing locals alike. A 45,000-square-foot putting green, a practice green with a 138-yard practice hole, and a huge pro shop round out the amenities. Wild Wing is also host to the Glen Davis Golf School. Davis has taught in the Grand Strand for more than two decades and is a highly respected teaching professional. For more information visit the Web site www.myrtlebeach golfschool.net.

THE WIZARD
4601 Leeshire Blvd., Myrtle Beach
(843) 236-9393
www.wizardgolfcourse.com
This Dan Maples design replicates an old-world Scottish course, complete with a Celtic castle-like clubhouse that actually looks worn from age and battle.

Maples moved an astounding 800,000 cubic yards of earth to bring the flavor of mountain golf (complete with rock bridges) to the seaside paradise of Myrtle Beach. This miraculous transformation of landscape has delivered the Grand Strand a premier Scottish-links course. Players always comment on No. 13; its rolling hills on both sides of the fairway give the impression of the Scottish countryside. The par 71 Wizard measures 6,206 yards of old-world charm and challenge.

Greens fees at the Wizard are $50.55 to $63.50; walking is not permitted.

South Strand

BLACKMOOR
Highway 707, Murrells Inlet
(866) 952-5555
www.blackmoor.com
Trite as it sounds, Blackmoor golf club at Longwood Plantation is unique. This beautiful design is Gary Player's first in the Myrtle Beach area. And what a debut! Player's experience as the world's most traveled golfer is evident in every hole.

Flanking the tea-colored waters of the Waccamaw River, Blackmoor's design takes full advantage of the naturally lovely terrain. No. 14 is a dogleg right with water on one side and sand

traps lurking on either side of the fairway; gamblers go for the green, which is 285 yards from the tee. The eighth hole sports a split fairway, and thickets of trees flank both sides. If you play from the left, you'll need a 347-yard drive; from the right side it's a straightaway (if you miss the trees!) 270 yards.

Golf for Women magazine rated this course in the top 100 women-friendly courses in America. At 6,533 yards and par 72, Blackmoor is a challenge for everyone.

Greens fees are $54; no walking. This course is one of our favorites.

CALEDONIA GOLF & FISH CLUB
King's River Road, Pawleys Island
(800) 483-6800, (843) 237-3675
www.fishclub.com
Caledonia, constructed on the site of a former rice plantation along the black ribbon of the Waccamaw River, is dazzling. The oak-lined drive to the antebellum-style clubhouse sets the tone for the experience. It won't take you long to realize that no expense has been spared here. Even the bridges that connect one hole to another feature old Charleston brick.

Designed by award-winning architect Mike Strantz, this course is highlighted by huge oaks, shimmering natural lakes, broad expanses of long-abandoned rice fields, and more than an occasional glimpse of the area's rich wildlife. Caledonia Golf & Fish Club has been named one of the Top 100 You Can Play by *GOLF Magazine,* Top 25 Courses in South Carolina by *Golf Digest,* Top 100 Modern Courses by *Golfweek,* and Top 100 Best Courses for Women by *Golf for Women.*

Caledonia measures 6,104 yards and plays par 72. The picturesque 18th hole borders the plantation's old rice field, and it requires a precise tee shot that sets up a difficult second shot: a forced carry onto a green that is watched closely by the beautiful antebellum-style clubhouse.

Greens fees are $104.50; walking is permitted. When you've finished your round, take some time to hang around the clubhouse, a replica of an 18th-century colonial plantation home. With its rocking-chair-studded wraparound porch, old brick fireplace, soaring ceilings, and delicious food, it's a great place to reflect on your game and watch the sun set. Don't miss this one.

THE HERITAGE CLUB
King's River Road, Pawleys Island
(800) 552-2660, (843) 237-3424
www.legendsgolf.com

The Heritage Club's 6,565-yard, par 71 course, designed by Dan Maples, is built on the site of not one but two historic rice plantations. Here, overlooking the Waccamaw River, you'll feel a little like you've stepped onto the set of *Gone with the Wind*. The majestic tree-lined approach to the plantation-style clubhouse sets the stage. This grand avenue of 300-year-old oaks would impress even Rhett and Scarlett. In contrast to the historic atmosphere of the course, the Heritage also has a technological angle: A computerized yardage system accompanies all carts.

While you play, enjoy not only the captivating hole designs but also the breathtaking views of the scenic Waccamaw River, endless marshes, freshwater lakes, and towering oaks and magnolias. But take heed: The Heritage demands accuracy off the tee.

Greens fees are $72; no walking.

The pro shop, bar, and dining room are exquisitely appointed with rich wood paneling. Before your round, loosen up at the driving range or the practice putting green. Lessons are available.

LITCHFIELD COUNTRY CLUB
US 17 S., Pawleys Island
(888) 766-4633, (843) 237-3411
www.litchfieldbeach.com

Litchfield, sculpted by Willard Byrd from yet another former rice plantation, was one of the first dozen courses built along the Grand Strand. Time has given the course a seldom-found maturity. Litchfield meanders lazily around an upscale neighborhood and, though technically private, the club allows a limited number of visiting golfers. The signature hole is No. 14, a straightaway par 4 with a stream to the right. Add two large traps and a preponderant tree to the left, and you have a murderously narrow hole.

For the most part, however, the 6,342-yard, par 72 course isn't noted for its difficulty, so your round here should provide a pleasant memory. Greens fees start at $54; no walking.

The antebellum-style clubhouse, the tree-and-flower-lined approach—the entire ambience of the club, in fact—will make you feel like you're "walking in high cotton." Actually, you are. So why not continue the self-indulgence after your round? Stay for "supper" and sample the fare that locals love.

PAWLEYS PLANTATION
70 Tanglewood Dr., Pawleys Island
(800) 367-9959, (843) 237-6200
www.pawleysplantation.com

Pawleys Plantation is an upscale residential community of one- to three-bedroom villas surrounding a lush par 72 golf course, 6,127 yards set among coastal tidal plains, golden rice fields, and moss-draped oaks. It was the exquisite setting that ultimately drew Jack Nicklaus to Pawleys Plantation. "I have a particular fondness for the Lowcountry," says Nicklaus. "We used what's there without forcing or changing what Mother Nature provided."

A few of the course highlights include the par 3 third hole, requiring a forced carry over water from tee to green; the par 5 14th hole, where you must negotiate the marsh off the tee shot to a split fairway just before the green; or the tremendous par 4 18th hole, which permits only a well-placed drive down a narrow fairway bordered by marsh, sprawling oaks, and pines. There's an elegant clubhouse with a grill room that's ideal for a little 19th-hole relaxation. *Golf Digest* gives Pawleys Plantation four stars.

Greens fees are $111; no walking.

TPC MYRTLE BEACH
US 17 Bypass, Murrells Inlet
(843) 357-3399
www.tpc.com

The opening of this course in the fall of 1998 had significant impact in the world of Myrtle Beach and golf everywhere. The course was number

100 for the Grand Strand, strengthening its position as the Golf Capital of the World. Additionally, the course is a Tournament Players Club (TPC) endeavor, which means it was designed with PGA players in mind. The design incorporates easy spectator movement and stadium-style seating at key holes.

Included as one of the 100 Top Golf Shops in America by *Golf World Business,* the TPC continues to set the standard for customer service, inventive retailing, and business performance in the Myrtle Beach area. Also recognized by Golfweek magazine as among the Top 10 Courses in South Carolina, the TPC of Myrtle Beach has quickly become one of the most celebrated courses in the TPC Network, the PGA Tour's golf-course management division.

TPC is a 7,014 yard, par 72, 18-hole course. Tom Fazio and Tom Marzolf, of Fazio Golf Designers, created the course, complete with a grand clubhouse, nine lakes (one on the driving range), and L-39 bent-grass greens (some as large as 6,500 feet). The culmination of all their work is softly sculpted ridges that create unobtrusive promontories. Peripheral areas around the greens have been "feathered up" to blend in the spectator locations. The finishing hole is a par 5 with a winding "Wadkin's Creek" and a large lake, culminating at a two-tiered green near the 20,000-square-foot clubhouse. The course has five sets of tees with yardages ranging from just under 7,000 to around 5,100.

On days when the pros aren't playing, the greens fees are $104.50 excluding cart, and metal spike alternatives are encouraged.

THE TRADITION CLUB
US 17 S., Pawleys Island
(877) 599-0888, (843) 237-5041
www.traditiongolfclub.com
The Tradition Club opened to accolades in fall 1995. Adjacent to the upscale Willbrook community, the Tradition Club boasts a legendary, time-tested course (6,508 yards, par 72) with the requisite classic features: large tees, wide fairways, and huge, well-placed greens. Five sets of tees serve golfers of all skill levels.

Course architect Ron Garl has designed courses that have hosted PGA Tour events and have been honored by *Golf Digest* and *GOLF Magazine* as tops in their class. More of Garl's courses have been named to Florida's top-50 list than any other architect's. In addition, the Tradition is rated in the top 75 women-friendly courses by *Golf for Women*. Every indication is that the Tradition lives up to—even surpasses—Garl's own standard of excellence.

Greens fees start at $43; no walking.

The Tradition features the most elaborate practice area anywhere along the Strand. It includes a 43,000-square-foot, clover-shaped putting green with four practice locations. The 18th green is guarded by an 8,000-square-foot clubhouse decorated with Italian marble, leather upholstery, imported designer furniture, and original European artwork. The Tradition is a must-see—certainly among the area's finest courses.

TRUE BLUE GOLF CLUB
King's River Road, Pawleys Island
(888) 483-6801, (843) 235-0900
www.fishclub.com
True Blue is Caledonia's sister course, strategically located across the street. Built on the acreage of a 19th-century indigo and rice plantation by the same name, this course features bent-grass greens and an 18-acre practice facility with a learning center.

All the appeal of True Blue comes from the preservation of the abundant nature in the Lowcountry: native grasses such as field rye, natural elevations, and sandy areas including waste bunkers. On the 14th hole, the tee box is nearly 50 feet above the green.

Greens fees are $89 for True Blue's 6,958 yards at a par 72. Walking is permitted.

WACHESAW PLANTATION EAST
US 17 Bypass, Murrells Inlet
(888) 922-0027, (843) 357-2090
www.wachesawplantationeast.com
This former rice plantation has taken off as one of the centers of golfing on the Strand and was in fact named Grand Strand Golf Course of the

Year in 2007. It is directly adjacent to the PGA TPC course that opened in November 1998.

Architect Clyde Johnston accented the course's traditional 18-hole Scottish-links design with wetlands and lakes amid rolling woods. This 6,933-yard, par 72 course features five sets of tees for golfers of all abilities.

Greens fees start at $57; no walking.

WEDGEFIELD PLANTATION
129 Clubhouse Lane, Georgetown
(843) 546-8587
www.wedgefield.com

Another once-upon-a-time rice plantation, this beautiful course is on the very southern tip of the Grand Strand in historic Georgetown. Cited by *Golf Week* magazine as one of the top 50 golf courses in South Carolina, this course features fairways winding through live oaks and patches of wild-flowers; keep an eye out for the abundant wildlife. Practice up for the 14th hole, where two precise shots are required to carry the lakes. Wedgefield's course measures 6,325 yards (par 72).

Greens fees are $55; no walking. This is a South Carolina golfing experience that you really should take in on your southern leg of Strand play.

WICKED STICK
US 17 Bypass, Surfside Beach
(800) 79-STICK, (843) 215-2500
www.wickedstick.com

With his first-ever signature course in the area, John Daly has brought his "grip it, rip it" style to the Grand Strand. Along with architect Clyde Johnston, Daly has created a stunning links-style course patterned after famed Scottish designs. Wide-open spaces feature expansive "dune fields," large sand waste areas with gorse-like vegetation, deep (read bottomless) pot bunkers, and strategically placed water hazards. This par 72 course measures 6,080 yards (more than 7,000 yards from the championship tees!).

"Our main goal was to design and build a course that is fun for the average golfer to play," said Gary Schaal, former PGA president and a member of the partnership that owns the course. "Together, John and Clyde have mapped out a course that looks intimidating but encourages golfers to 'grip it and rip it.'"

Greens fees are $50.50. Golfers can walk in late afternoon if the course isn't too busy.

WILLBROOK PLANTATION GOLF CLUB
US 17 S., Pawleys Island
(866) 442-8477, (843) 237-4900
www.mbn.com

Dan Maples carved Willbrook Plantation from the fertile forests and wetlands of two historic rice plantations. He calls the course "one of my best"—quite a statement considering his résumé. The course's scenery, design, and inherent challenge are as captivating as its history. In fact, flora and fauna are so abundant here, the course is registered with the Audubon Society to preserve its wetlands and wildlife.

The ruins of an old plantation home are visible from No. 5, and historic markers along the course signify a slave cemetery near the eighth hole as well as an old slave settlement near the fourth green. You don't have to play great to score well; Willbrook is easy in some spots and tough in others, making it an ideal 6,124-yard, par 72 course for golfers of mixed abilities.

Greens fees are $48 $70; no walking.

Beyond the Strand

THE WITCH
1900 Hwy. 544, East Conway
(843) 448-1300, (843) 347-2706
www.witchgolf.com

Just off the Strand, outside Myrtle Beach, the Witch serves up a spectacular 6,011-yard, 18-hole course that seems to rise from the earth like some kind of inexplicable magic; it's nothing short of beautiful. Dan Maples molded this par 71 course—complete with nearly 4,000 feet of bridges—from woodlands and mystery-shrouded wetlands without disturbing the enchanted nature of the setting.

Playing the Witch is like taking a nature walk through swamps, marshes, and forests, with pine, cypress, and live oak trees, as well as deer, fox, and osprey. The par 4 No. 15 requires an uphill drive followed by a placement shot to a landing area surrounded by wetlands. The ninth green is an island surrounded by wetlands.

Deceptively beautiful, the hundreds of acres of wetlands are Mother Nature's perfect hazards. Challenge lurks around every bend of this unforgettable course. Greens fees start at $50.50; walking is not permitted.

MINIATURE GOLF

Driving to and from the more "serious" courses in the Grand Strand, you'll be sure to notice the abundance of colorful, special-effect-filled miniature golf courses. Although most of them are better suited to children, spring breakers, and those who haven't developed their power drive yet, there is one that is worth the traditional golf enthusiast's attention, either to test your skill or to give you another shot at the elusive purse. For more choices refer back to the Miniature Golf section in the Parks and Recreation chapter.

North Strand

HAWAIIAN RUMBLE MINIATURE GOLF
33rd Avenue S., US 17,
North Myrtle Beach
(843) 272-7812
www.prominigolf.com
Ranked by *GOLF Magazine* as the No. 1 miniature golf course in the United States, Hawaiian Rumble offers a challenging variety of shots in a lush and expertly landscaped setting of tropical palms, hibiscus, and other plants. The course circles and climbs up around a rumbling volcano, leis in almost every color are handed out to the players, and gentle Hawaiian music plays in the background. Hawaiian Rumble also sponsors the Masters Putting Championship, with a purse of $20,000—definitely worth a shot!

GOLF DRIVING RANGES

North Strand

HARBOUR VIEW GOLF COMPLEX
901 US 17 N., Little River
(843) 249-9117
www.harbourviewgolf.com
The Harbour View Golf Complex offers great golf for the whole family. The entire facility is open year-round, and it's lighted for evening enjoyment. The driving range includes mat and turf hitting areas, target greens, sand bunkers, chipping areas, and putting green. Small, medium, and large buckets are sold for $4, $6, and $8.

Myrtle Beach

CANE PATCH
72nd Avenue N., Myrtle Beach
(843) 315-0303
Practice your swing year-round starting at 8 a.m. The range is lighted for nighttime practice during summer. All you need is a club and putter, both of which are furnished. Buckets are $7.25 for 45 golf balls, $9.50 for 75, and $13.50 for 120.

South Strand

TUPELO BAY GOLF CENTER
1800 US 17 S., Garden City
(800) 657-2680, (843) 215-7888
www.tupelobay.com
The driving range at Tupelo Bay has a large turf hitting area, great for practicing real course conditions. Tupelo also offers an extensive mat hitting area that is both covered and open. It also features practice target greens to assist in determining your individual club distance. A large practice putting green is also available to help you feel more comfortable with that "magic putter" in your hand. The range is lighted for evening practice so go for it, day or night! A small bucket of 30 balls is $6, medium bucket of 50 is $8, and a large of 120 is $11.

PAR 3 COURSES

Par 3 courses generally only have nine par 3 holes. Considered a good choice for beginners, these courses are often played by skilled golfers with time constraints or who want to work on their short game.

Myrtle Beach

CANE PATCH
72nd Avenue N., Myrtle Beach
(843) 315-0303
From March through Labor Day, 9 holes cost $13.50 and 18 holes, $19.50. Those prices fall off-season. The yardages at the three nine-hole courses are 698, 672, and 653. Locals are always privy to discount passes at Cane Patch. This course also organizes leagues that play members of other par 3 courses in town.

MIDWAY PAR 3
3030 South Ocean Blvd., Myrtle Beach
(843) 913-5335
Midway was the Beach's first par 3 course that offered a "situation golf" experience, designed to test and nurture a player's entire range of golf skills by offering a different built-in challenge at each hole. The challenges, such as pine straw, a fairway bunker, or a side-hill lie, allow the golfer to practice the full range of golf skills while enjoying three well-manicured nine-hole courses.

This course was voted as one of the Top 10 Short Courses in the U.S. Revamped and expanded, Midway, at South Beach Resort, has 27 holes and is open from 8 a.m. until midnight. Nine-hole play is $13.50, and 18-hole play is $18.50. Pull carts are available for $4 for nine holes and $5 for 18. Clubs are available for no charge.

South Strand

TUPELO BAY GOLF CENTER
1800 US 17 S., Garden City
(800) 657-2680, (843) 215-7888
www.tupelobay.com
If you're looking for a family-flavored golf course in the Surfside/Garden City area, Tupelo Bay Golf Center is the place for you. In addition to the nine-hole par 3 golf course, Tupelo Bay offers an 18-hole Executive Golf Course, an award-winning driving range, golf lessons, golf-club rentals, and golf packages. The par 3 course is great fun for the entire family. It also provides a great short-game workout with holes ranging from 73 to 105 yards, and the course is lighted for evening play.

Club rental (four clubs and bag) is available for $1, and a pull cart is available for $2. The adult rate for nine holes is $13. Eighteen holes is $16. Kids age 12 and younger can play 9 holes for $9 and 18 holes for $12. Tupelo Bay is open from 7 a.m. to 11 p.m.

FISHING

With the Grand Strand's 60 miles of beachfront for surf fishing, eight piers, deep-sea fishing charters, and even freshwater fishing, just how is an angler to choose? And for that matter, you could know nothing about fishing. What better opportunity to learn?

The waters off the coast of South Carolina and the Grand Strand are teeming with everything from sport fish to fish that simply make for some darned good eating. The Gulf Stream pulls the flow of water along the coast from the tropics and keeps the waters pretty warm. In fact, during the summer months, the ocean can have the feel of bathwater. That same flow brings a variety of migrations of fish, and it would be a mistake to think all fish are created equal, or that they can be caught in the same manner. This chapter will answer the who, what, where, when, and, often, the why questions about fishing along the Grand Strand. If you don't find the answers to your questions here, the South Carolina Department of Natural Resources, Marine Resources Division, in Charleston, is a wonderful resource; call (843) 953-9000 or visit them online at www.dnr.state.sc.us.

They can also help with licensing. According to South Carolina state law, people (age 16 and older) harvesting oysters or clams, fishing for marine finfish from privately owned boats, or transporting catch in privately owned boats must purchase an annual or temporary Saltwater Recreational Fisheries License. Fishing piers and chartered vessels charging a fee for fishing and those offering fishing boats for rent must purchase a Marine Recreational Fisheries License annually. Nonresidents can get an annual license for $35 and 14-day license for $11. No license is needed for those under 16.

SURF FISHING

Surf fishing is the most "friendly" form of the sport since you only need to bring a rod and reel to the edge of the Atlantic Ocean. Common catches from the surf—which can be plentiful—include bluefish, flounder, whiting, spot, pompano, and channel bass. With a simple tackle rig and a bucket for bait and catch in hand, surf anglers can be spotted along the coastline at just about any time of the year. But if you're serious about snagging dinner for the family, the less humid fall months are best for this type of fishing, especially when the sea is relatively calm.

Experienced surf casters suggest using fresh shrimp, minnows, or whiting (not more than 3 inches long) as bait. For best results consult tide tables and hit the beach at low tide. Look along the shoreline for washed-out areas that resemble creek beds in the sand leading out to the ocean's breakers. If you can discern a slough, pool, or drop-off, cast into that area; it's often 2 feet or more deeper than the surrounding water. Now comes the fun part. . . . Just sit back, watch, and wait for the big bite.

Surf Casting for Pompano and Whiting

The delicate, fine-tasting pompano is relatively abundant during late summer. But to catch them you must be accurate in your fishing technique. Pompano frequent the surf zone, right where the waves break in "suds" on the beach. There they feast on tiny mole crabs before the crustaceans have time to burrow into the sand. Pompano anglers use a small #1 or #2 hook tied directly to the line (8-pound test is recommended)—no leader necessary. Flip the baited hook into the breakwater and allow it to drift with the current. A split shot $^1/_{16}$- or $^1/_{32}$-ounce) attached about 12 to 18 inches above the hook will keep it slightly down in the water column as it drifts.

Whiting, which feed on small worms, crabs, and shrimp, can be caught from the surf during the summer. Fish the areas around groins, sloughs, and cuts along open beaches. A two-leader rig with #1 or 1/0 hooks, baited with cut shrimp and fished on the incoming tide, frequently yields good results.

Both pompano and whiting generally weigh less than a pound and don't put up much of a fight, but they are certainly excellent table fare.

INSHORE FISHING

Nothing will acquaint you as graciously with the pulse, sounds, and smells of Lowcountry life along the Grand Strand as fishing its coastal waters, estuaries, and salt marshes. The slow-moving, dark, acrid waters offer up sweet mysteries of lively marine life for the avid angler. At the mercy of tidal change, inland waters can cover everything at high tide, then unmask an incredibly bustling sea-life community at low ebb.

Fishing inland waters provides an opportunity to snag crevalle jack, Florida pompano, sheepshead, Southern flounder, black drum, spotted sea trout, king mackerel, Spanish mackerel, red drum, and whiting. Inshore-fishing action usually slows with the heat and mosquitoes of summer—especially compared with spring and fall. But if you're so inclined, summer fishing can be thrilling, too, as coastal waters teem with bait fish and shrimp—favorite meals for game fish.

Making the Most of Inshore Fishing

If spotted sea trout is your catch of choice, look in lower parts of estuaries during the summer and around oyster bars, rocks, and pilings in spring and fall, when tidal currents are running strong. Cooler periods of the year will be your best bet, though, as the fish form larger schools. When luring the sea trout around areas with a structure, fish your bait either on the bottom, with a

slip sinker placed above a 20-pound-test monofilament leader attached to a 1/0 or 2/0 hook, or from a float rig. The recreational size limit for the sea trout is 13 inches, and only 10 can be kept per day in aggregate.

During July juvenile red drum leave shallow creeks and form schools in the main estuaries. They're easy to catch en masse at this time of year but are often smaller than the allowable minimum size in South Carolina—14 inches. Late summer is the time to catch adult drum (often between 20 and 30 pounds) around jetties and at the mouths of bays and sounds. Their favorite bait seems to be live menhaden and finger mullet bottom-fished with fish-finder rigs. Use a smaller (4/0) hook for live bait so it can swim more naturally in the current. Five red drum a day is the legal keeper limit.

South Carolina fishing laws dictate that gigging red drum or spotted sea trout is prohibited from December through February. However, on a calm, hot summer's eve, while estuary waters are clear on an early incoming tide, flounder gigging can yield a hearty harvest. Shallow-draft boats are the best for this type of flounder hunting; one person poles the boat while another stands on the bow and spears any flounder seen on the bottom.

Summer trolling for flounder around inlets is a favorite Grand Strand sport. Troll live bait, such as mud minnows, slowly along the bottom or adjacent to rock jetties. Flounder must be at least 12 inches long to keep, and 20 per day is an angler's limit.

Sheepshead like to hang out around jetties, piers, and bridge pilings during summer months. They're very fussy eaters and usually will not bite anything other than the favored fiddler crab or live shrimp. Successful sheepshead anglers suggest a $^1/_4$- or $^3/_8$-ounce split shot crimped to a 20-pound-test monofilament leader. Appropriate hook sizes for sheepshead are #1, 1/0, or 2/0.

Black drum are the bottom-feeding cousins of the red drum; they do not consume other fish and prefer to be around rocks, pilings, and piers. Whether 5 pounds or 40, the black drum cannot resist a large piece of blue crab. A tried-and-true method of luring this fish is to pull the top shell from the crab and cut the meat into quarters. Thread a large piece onto a 5/0 to 9/0 hook tied onto a swivel with a 50-pound-test monofilament leader. Above the leader, which should be 18 to 24 inches long, attach a two- to three-ounce slip sinker to get the bait to the bottom. Black drum connoisseurs insist that a fish heavier than 15 pounds will have coarse flesh and be less tasty.

Although they don't make spectacular runs like a king mackerel or perform graceful jumps like the tarpon, the crevalle jack is considered one of the toughest fish you'll encounter around these parts. At night or at dusk, jacks lurk around rips during ebb tide, feeding on their favorite fish. Experienced anglers use a 20-pound-test line on a large-capacity reel and a moderately stout rod. Best baits for jacks are surface-popping plugs, such as the Striper Swiper, or swimming plugs by Redfin, Rebel, or Rapala. Sought after mostly for sport, jacks are not good eating and should be released.

OFFSHORE FISHING

From sea bass hugging underwater reefs to blue marlin racing through the Gulf Stream, the Grand Strand is a point of departure for a variety of offshore fishing opportunities.

During the summer, sometimes following four or five consecutive days of flat, calm conditions, many of the area's blue-water fish move to within 15 miles of the coast. Of course, in early spring you'll have to travel by boat about 50 miles offshore to catch the same fish.

Offshore marine fishes in these waters include the blue marlin, yellowfin tuna, great barracuda, crevalle jack, wahoo, dolphin (the fish, not "Flipper"), king mackerel, little tunny, Spanish mackerel, white marlin, amberjack, and sailfish. Downriggers and planers are key elements to a successful offshore trip during the summer, especially during the steamy days of July and August. Summer heat polarizes much of the feeding activity of these fish into early morning and late afternoon, as they keep to deeper, cooler waters.

Avid offshore anglers continually argue the question of what bait is best for these fish. Natural baits offer real food—so if the fish strikes short, it will more than likely return for another nibble. On the other hand, artificial lures can be trolled faster, allowing more area to be fished, and don't require extra time to rig the bait.

Making the Most of Offshore Fishing

Blue- and white-marlin fishing is most productive in ocean depths of 300 to 1,200 feet during summer months and around 80 feet in cooler weather. Successful fishing for marlin usually calls for large bait—mullet, ballyhoo, ladyfish, and Spanish mackerel—rigged to skip across the surface or to swim. The bait often is dressed with brightly colored plastic skirts or attached to artificial lures.

Many blue marlin in local waters are in the 125- to 200-pound range—typically below the 99-inch minimum fork length for this species.

Sailfish reach peak abundance during July and August and may be caught only 10 miles off the beach, but many are below the legal minimum 63-inch fork length. Weed lines, current rips, and natural reefs in 120 to 300 feet of water are the best areas for these prized game fish. Averaging 35 to 45 pounds, sails prefer smaller baits than their larger marlin cousins. Effective trolling for sails requires small- to medium-size ballyhoo and mullet with a small artificial lure or colored skirt placed ahead of the bait. Sails have even been caught on spoons and plugs intended for king mackerel.

As summer progresses, the size of both dolphin and wahoo gradually declines. Dolphin start summer at 10 to 20 pounds and drop to about 8 pounds, while wahoo start at 35 to 50 pounds and weigh in around 20 pounds by season's end. The best concentrations of these species can be found at 180- to 600-foot depths.

The same typically holds true for the yellowfin tuna, though, unlike the dolphin and wahoo, tuna increase in size during the summer to an average of 45 pounds.

Effective live bait for dolphin, wahoo, or tuna includes ballyhoo or mullet rigged with a small- to medium-size artificial lure or colored skirt. Although all baits are usually fished on the surface from outriggers, it is wise to run at least one line 60 to 70 feet deep via a downrigger.

For an action-packed day of offshore fishing, try trolling for amberjack and barracuda along artificial reefs and coastal shipwrecks. Tenacious fighters, these fish go out of their way to test an angler's equipment and skills.

Most anglers fish for amberjack with a 50-pound-class outfit, but for the ultimate experience, challenge the 'jack with 20- or 30-pound-test line. Wire leader is mandatory for barracuda (whose teeth are razor sharp), while heavy, 100- to 150-pound-test monofilament works well for the 'jacks. Large live baits, such as mullet up to 14 inches and menhaden, floated or free-lined down current, often are successful. Depending on the test line you use, a 5/0 to 8/0 extra-strength hook is recommended—stainless steel, please, since most of these fish are released, not eaten. Artificial lures have also proven effective: The 'jack and 'cuda are partial to surgical rubber tubing colored dark green, chartreuse, and hot pink. They have also been known to get excited enough to strike at noisy surface lures.

Artificial and natural reefs are focal points for schools of king mackerel. These fish are very unpredictable and finicky during the summer months and frustrate anglers into wild goose chases with every bait and lure known. The only agreed-upon technique for summer king mackerel fishing is to pull in the rod and reel by 10 a.m., when macks seem to disappear. The larger female mackerel prefers nearshore waters just outside bays and sounds, while the males frequent depths of 60 to 120 feet.

Considered great game fish, but not esteemed as food fish, little tunny (locally known as bonito), crevalle jack, and Spanish mackerel are abundant in summer 15 miles from shore. One to 5 miles outside bays and sounds and around artificial reefs are prime areas for schooling fish. To determine prime casting areas, just locate

the wheeling and diving terns feeding on the bait fish pushed to the surface by these voracious feeders. Small silver or gold spoons such as Hopkins, Clark, Captain Action, and Tony Accetta are the most productive; try fishing them on a 20-inch, 60-pound-test wire leader to prevent cutoffs. These fish are extremely fast, so you must retrieve your lure as quickly as possible or troll at a rapid pace.

i If you're going to be fishing without a local captain or guide, check on current regulations before embarking on your fishing trip. Fines for illegal fish can be substantial.

THE LOWCOUNTRY TRADITION OF SHELLFISHING

Oysters and Clams

Harvesting oysters and clams has been part of the Lowcountry culture for generations. From Hogg Inlet behind Cherry Grove Beach to the salt marshes of Murrells Inlet and Pawleys Creek, many Lowcountry families fed themselves with the natural bounty of shellfish. That all came to an end in 1987 when nearly all the marshes were closed to the public due to pollution from a bacteria linked to human and animal waste.

Today portions of Murrells Inlet and North Inlet are open in Georgetown County, and only one location, on the north end of Huntington Beach State Park (US 17), is accessible without a boat. Oyster and clam gathering is limited to South Carolina residents who have a bona fide saltwater fishing license.

South Carolinians can harvest only two U.S. bushels of oysters and/or a half U.S. bushel of clams per day. Clams must be at least 1 inch thick. No person may gather more than one personal limit of shellfish on more than two calendar days per any seven-day period. There is a maximum of three personal limits per boat or vehicle, or boat and vehicle combination. In authorized harvesting areas, no one can disturb oyster or clam beds between May 15 and September 1 of any year. A license for harvesting costs $10 annually.

For specific questions and current shellfish bed closings, the local Department of Health and Environmental Control is a great resource; call (843) 915-8804.

Shrimping

If you like working with nets, you can try your hand at snaring shrimp, America's most popular seafood. The coastal marsh creeks are home to two penaeid shrimp species, brown shrimp (*Penaeus aztecus*) and white shrimp (*Penaeus setiferus*). As shrimp become larger, they leave the brackish waters and move gradually toward the higher salinity of the ocean. Once they've reached about 4 inches in length, they inhabit coastal rivers and spend some time maturing, then move into the lower reaches of sounds, bays, and river mouths.

Recreational harvest of brown shrimp by cast nets and seines usually starts in early June in the tidal creeks. White shrimp initially are caught in these same creeks in late July or early August but disappear completely by late October. Harvesting by drop nets from docks and seawalls is most popular during the fall when larger white shrimp are moving seaward.

Seines for shrimping cannot exceed 40 feet in length, and webbing must be a 1/2-inch-square mesh or larger for nylon nets. Law also prohibits the blockage of more than one-half the width of any slough, creek, or other waterway on any tidal stage. Seines must be pulled by hand, not by any engine-powered boat or staked to poles. The most effective way to pull a seine is with the falling tide and along banks or sandbars, which provide areas to haul nets ashore and remove the shrimp. Less expensive and cumbersome than seines, cast nets are used more often for shrimping. Cast nets are also devoid of restrictions on lengths or mesh sizes. Casting is popular in creeks with a mud bottom during low tide. Deeper areas of 3 or 4 feet or more often produce larger shrimp during the day since the shrimp avoid light. A

cast net can be used from a boat, creek bank, pier, or even while wading in the water. The lawful harvest of shrimp by cast net is limited to 60 days between September 1 and November 15.

Drop nets can be fished from bridges, docks, or seawalls and are almost exclusively used at night. Unlike the other meshed methods, drop nets require bait, and the best, we're told, is smoked herring. Drop netting typically doesn't yield large quantities of shrimp, but it sure is enjoyable and relaxing.

The legal daily limit for shrimp is 48 quarts (heads on) or 29 quarts (heads off) per boat or seining party. A shrimping license costs $11.

Crabbing

Despite its fearsome appearance and aggressive nature, the blue crab is greatly cherished in the Lowcountry. Many gourmets prefer the blue crab's sweet meat to all other locally caught seafood.

Males of the species can be distinguished from females by the shape of the abdomen. The male has a T-shape abdomen, held tightly against the body until maturity, when it loosens. The immature female has a triangle-shaped abdomen that is sealed against the body, becoming rounded and loose after the final molt. Large males (often called "Jimmies") usually have brilliant blue claws and legs. Mature females, or "sooks," show off the bright orange tips on their claws.

South Carolina law allows individuals to fish two crab pots without a license if they are properly marked with floats bearing the owner's name. Be careful not to leave the pot in an area that exposes it and crabs at low tide, and check pots twice a day for the best yield. However, you must return a crab to the water if its point-to-point width is less than 5 inches or it is a female carrying an egg mass (sponge). Drop nets and collapsible traps (usually baited with herring) can be fished from docks and bridges. Or you can give "dipping" a try. Dipping involves a long-handled dip net, several yards of string, and a chicken neck or fish head for bait. Tie the bait to the string and throw out into the water. Once you feel a tug, pull the bait and crab close enough to quickly dip the crustacean from the water into a waiting bucket. Always keep crabs alive, cool, and dry prior to cooking. A refrigerator or cooler with a small amount of ice is the best storage method. Never put crabs in a container of water; they will die quickly from lack of oxygen.

Crabs become inactive in winter when water temperatures fall below 50 to 55 degrees. The best time of the year to harvest large, heavy crabs is usually from October through December. Mature females are typically found near the ocean, while large males are most common in rivers and creeks.

FISHING CHARTERS

When casting into the world of deep-sea fishing, we feel the need to give you fair warning. If you have never been on an offshore fishing trip, the night before you leave take medication to relieve seasickness. Even some experienced sailors have been found writhing around the deck, begging for a quick and merciful death. Once a deep-sea fishing vessel is out on an excursion, it will not turn back to shore early for the sake of one or two heaving passengers. Most local pharmacies carry motion-sickness pills—available over the counter—as well as patches that affix behind the ear.

Also, make sure you book your charter well in advance during the summer months. Plenty of people plan their whole trip to the Grand Strand around fishing, so charters get booked up quickly. That said, get ready for some exhilarating fishing opportunities, both inshore and in the Gulf Stream. The following charters are good bets.

i It's customary to tip a guide or charter mate about the same as you would tip a server in a restaurant—between 15 and 20 percent of your total bill.

North Strand

BLACKFISH CHARTER BOAT
Waterfront Drive, Little River
(843) 249-1379

With more than 40 years of experience fishing local waters, Capt. Larry Long will take a party of six people on fishing excursions from spring through fall, specifically Apr through mid-Nov. Half- and full-day trips can be arranged, including shark fishing and trolling the Gulf Stream. As is typical for fishing charters, bait and tackle are included; food and drink are not. Trips on the *Blackfish* cost $600 for a half day and $900 for the whole day. A Gulf Stream adventure is $1,500 for approximately 12 hours. Bottom fishing, trolling, or shark fishing is available on each trip. Shrimping is also available.

Ten-year-old Stephen Manser Jr. from Lake Norman, North Carolina, had the fishing trip of a lifetime aboard Long's *Blackfish* in July 1997. The "tug" on young Stephen's line turned out to be a 12-foot-long, 1,200-pound gray tiger shark that took everyone on the boat three hours to reel in. If no fish are caught, there is no charge, according to Captain Larry.

HURRICANE FISHING FLEET
Hurricane Marina, The Waterfront at Calabash, Calabash, NC
(800) 373-2004, (910) 579-3660
www.hurricanefleet.com
Trips depart daily, Mar through Dec, from Calabash waters. Hurricane's armada includes the 90-foot *Hurricane II,* the 77-foot *Westwind,* the 45-foot *Cyclone,* and the 40-foot *Party Time.*

Bottom-fishing trips range from half day to full day in the Gulf Stream and include excursions specifically for snapper. Trolling and other sportfishing trips of $4^{1}/_{2}$ to 12 hours can be arranged, as well as nighttime shark fishing. Public and private charters are available. Half days are $40 per person for adults and $35 for children; full days run $85 for adults and $75 for children. Reservations are recommended. Rod, reel, bait, and tackle are provided.

LITTLE RIVER FISHING FLEET
4495 Minneola Ave., Little River
(800) 249-9388, (843) 361-3323
www.littleriverfleet.com
The Little River Fishing Fleet delivers fishing at

its finest, and it recently combined forces with Coastal Scuba to also offer diving trips. Capt. Buddy Dennis operates the fishing end of the business, and he has established a reputation for safe fishing trips and providing customers with the finest fishing expertise available for any type of fishing. Captain Dennis's knowledge of the ocean and the best fishing grounds is impressive.

Pride of the Carolina is a 90-foot aluminum all-purpose fishing boat with an air-conditioned cabin, state-of-the-art fish-finding equipment, a full galley, clean restrooms, and first-class mates. Half-day fishing and night fishing trips are $40 for adults and $35 for children ages 12 and younger. For Gulf Stream fishing the cost is $135 for adults and $125 for children. Personal coolers are not permitted, but food, soft drinks, and beer are available on the boat.

The *Sundancer,* a 40-foot fiberglass boat, and the *Safari IV,* a 45-foot vessel, are both fully equipped with state-of-the-art fish-finding electronics. These boats carry 15 to 20 people for bottom fishing and are also available for private full- and half-day charters—all the way to the Gulf Stream, if you like. Prices vary depending on season and number of people on board. Call ahead to ask questions.

Bait and tackle (rod and reel) are supplied on all trips, and all necessary licenses are held by the Little River Fleet. Schedules may vary due to private charters, weather, or season, so be sure to call ahead.

LONGWAY CHARTER FISHING
The Waterfront, 1898 North Twisted Oaks Dr., Little River
(843) 249-7813
www.longwaycharters.com
Captain Chris Carter can accommodate parties of up to six people on *Longway,* his 38-foot fishing boat. Longway accepts both individual and group reservations. A five-hour trip costs $500; an eight-hour trip, $850; and a 12-hour Gulf Stream excursion, $1,400. All prices include everything you need for fishing. Bring your own food and drinks. Charters run year-round.

SHALLOW MINDED
4048 Sand Trap Ave., Little River
(843) 280-7099, (843) 458-3055
www.fishmyrtlebeach.com
In operation since 1999, Shallow Minded says more about the type of fishing than the state of mind of Capt. Mark Dickerson. A lifelong resident of North Myrtle Beach, Dickerson's inshore excursions provide a unique light-tackle experience and a side of the Grand Strand few get to see. The boats fish the backcountry and tidal creeks around Little River Inlet in some of the most beautiful scenery you'll come across.

It's also the sort of fishing that works for those who may not be sure if their stomachs can stand the large open waters. You won't get the big game fish here, but you do get decent-size flounder, redfish, sea trout, Spanish mackerel, striped bass, and bluefish.

The charters are small, for one to four people only. A half day is $350 for one to three anglers, and a full day is $550. One additional person can be added for $100. Sight casting for redfish in the winter runs about $225 for two anglers for a half day.

South Strand

CAPTAIN DICK'S MARINA
4123 US 17 Business, Murrells Inlet
(866) 557-3474, (843) 651-3676
www.captdicks.com
Enjoy deep-sea bottom fishing aboard the *New Capt. Bill, Capt. Bill III,* and *New Inlet Princess.* Trips range from 4 1/2 to 25 hours. Rods, manual reels, bait, and tackle are provided on the shorter trips; electric reels are available only for the much longer deep-sea voyages. Fishing licenses are provided for all anglers who charter from here. Air-conditioned cabins and full food service are featured on all of Captain Dick's vessels. Fishing excursions cost anywhere from $44 to $259 per adult. Special sportfishing junkets can be booked by individuals or groups of six for a half day, three-quarter day, or full day in Gulf Stream waters. Prices range from $599 to $1,399. Captain

Dick's also runs Dolphin Watch tours daily for $29 for adults and $19 for children.

i Don't forget sunscreen while out on the water. The rays of the sun reflect back off the water, and you can easily get sunburned—even if you are wearing a hat. Wind also plays a factor in magnifying the intensity of the rays.

THE EXTREME FISHERMAN
Pawleys Island
(843) 344-0974
www.extremefisherman.com
Extreme Fisherman captain Pete Mercuro offers inshore, flats, surf, and near-shore fishing charters in and around the Myrtle Beach area. Whether light tackle or fly-fishing, you can ride the wild edge where the big fish are found. Murrells Inlet, Litchfield Beach, Pawleys Island, and North Inlet and Winyah Bay in Georgetown are all favored destinations. Captain Mercuro generally accommodates parties of one to four people. Call ahead for pricing and to ask about larger parties.

GEORGETOWN COASTAL ADVENTURES
(843) 546-3543
www.captaintommy.com
Capt. Tommy Scarborough is a self-proclaimed Old-Fashioned Fishing Character. Operating out of Georgetown, his boats travel from Charleston to North Myrtle Beach for charters.

Georgetown Coastal Adventures includes both offshore and near-shore fishing, including inshore and backwater. Offshore trips are on their 31-foot *Contender*, the *Pipe Dream*. They go about 30 miles out into the Gulf Stream and cost $1,400 for four people. Near shore is through Winyah Bay, where there are many wrecks, artificial reefs, and live bottom to choose from. In these fishing grounds, you can try everything from trolling to fly-fishing and even drifting. Prices here are $1,100 for a full day for four people and $850 for a half day.

There are even five-hour catfishing tours through the Santee Lakes and Cypress swamps for the truly adventurous. That runs $400 for four people and $60 for each additional person.

Captain Tommy offers onboard fishing seminars for $450 for one day and $800 for two days. Group and club seminar pricing is available.

FISHING PIERS

Believe it or not, fishing piers are a major business undertaking. A few years ago, it was reported that a developer interested in adding a pier to North Myrtle Beach would spend between $3 million and $3.5 million just for construction. That's why a fishing pier is never merely a structure reaching into the sea from whence you cast a line. All piers on the Grand Strand offer a mixture of shops, arcades, restaurants, and water-sports outlets. There's enough to do to keep you occupied for a few hours or an entire day.

Make the most of your fall pier-fishing excursion by casting your line from the northernmost piers, from the north side. Southward migration occurs at this time as fish of all shapes and sizes respond to shorter days and lower sunlight intensity. They reach these northern piers on the north side first. September usually yields anglers a bountiful catch of king and Spanish mackerel, mullet, menhaden, pompano, spot, and bluefish.

North Strand
CHERRY GROVE PIER
3500 North Ocean Blvd.,
North Myrtle Beach
(843) 249-1625
www.cherrygrovepier.com
Daily admission is $6 for each rod. Seasonal rates are available. Holiday House Motel guests are admitted free. Pier walkers are charged $1.50.

This pier is 985 feet long and is lighted for night fishing. You'll find a full line of pier tackle, plus a gift shop and restaurant. Cherry Grove is open year-round. Hours are 6 a.m. to 12 a.m. from Mar 1 through the Sun following Thanksgiving.

Myrtle Beach

APACHE PIER

Apache Family Campground,
9700 Kings Rd.,
Myrtle Beach
(843) 497-6486
www.apachefamilycampground.com

Welcome to the longest pier anywhere along the East Coast—measuring 1,220 feet in length. Accents include a bait-and-tackle shop, arcade, restaurant, and aquariums filled with indigenous fish. Nightly entertainment is also part of the fun from May 30 through Labor Day weekend.

It will cost you $7.50 a day to fish from the pier or $1.00 to partake in the action as a spectator. That price goes up to $2.00 after 7 p.m. because of the entertainment, although that price is subject to change. Campers staying at Apache Campground (see the Accommodations chapter) pay only $6.50. Hours are 6 a.m. to 11 p.m. from spring through fall and 8 a.m. to 6 p.m. all winter.

MYRTLE BEACH STATE PARK

4401 South Kings Hwy.,
Myrtle Beach
(843) 238-5326
www.discoversouthcarolina.com

Regular admission is $4.00 for adults, $2.50 for South Carolina Seniors, $1.50 for children ages 6 to 15, and free for children 5 and younger. Season passes are available. Fishing rods can be rented for $4 each. The pier is open to the public whenever the park is—daily 6 a.m. to 10 p.m. Mar through Nov and 6 a.m. to 8 p.m. Dec through Feb. Tackle, bait, ice, and a gift shop are on the premises.

PIER 14 RESTAURANT, LOUNGE & FISHING PIER

1306 North Ocean Blvd., Myrtle Beach
(843) 448-6500
www.pier14.com

More popular for the fine dining at the restaurant than for the fishing allure, Pier 14 does its rod-and-reel business from the gift and tackle shop situated right next door. There is a $6 charge for fishing, but anyone can walk the pier or watch the angling free of charge, although there is a donation box for those who are inclined to contribute. For an additional $12 (plus a $20 refundable deposit), you can rent poles from them. An arcade and an outdoor patio are also open to the public. Pier 14 is in full swing from 7 a.m. to midnight all summer long, continuing through the end of Nov. This pier is closed during the winter months, from Thanksgiving until Feb 1.

SECOND AVENUE PIER & RESTAURANT

200 North Ocean Blvd.,
Myrtle Beach
(843) 626-8480
www.secondavenuepier.com

Admission is $8 for a daily pass to fish, $1 for spectators; inquire about season passes. You'll find a full line of bait, tackle, rods, and reels here, plus a gift shop, arcade, and full-service restaurant.

This lighted pier with T-shape end is 905 feet long. Hours are 7 a.m. to 11 p.m. daily from Mar 1 through the end of Sept or early Oct. During the summer months, the pier features fireworks every Wed at 10 p.m.

SPRINGMAID PIER

3200 South Ocean Blvd.,
Myrtle Beach
(843) 315-7100
www.springmaidbeach.com

Bait and ice are sold here, and tackle is available for rent or purchase. Admission price is $9 per angler (spectators are $1), with special weekly and year-round rates offered. Springmaid is open seven days a week year-round from 6 a.m. to midnight; the tackle shop closes at 11:30 p.m. during summer.

South Strand

THE PIER AT GARDEN CITY

110 South Waccamaw Dr.,
Garden City Beach
(843) 651-9700
www.pieratgardencity.com

The Pier at Garden City is generally open seven days a week, 24 hours a day from Mar through Dec. Daily hours may vary, so it is best to call ahead. Daily admission to fish is $9, and spectators are admitted free. Season passes can be purchased for $150 for the first person and $100 for each additional angler. Bait and rental gear are available from the tackle shop.

Stop by the arcade and oceanfront deck of the Pier Cafe for before or after fishing. The cafe itself usually closes from Christmas through Apr 1.

SURFSIDE PIER
11 South Ocean Blvd.,
Surfside Beach
(843) 238-0121
www.surfsidepier.com
Admission to this 810-foot-long pier is $12.50 per angler. Spectators pay $1.00. Weekly and season passes are available. You'll find tackle, bait, and rod-and-reel rentals on the pier along with a gift shop. The biggest tarpon ever caught from a South Carolina pier (142 pounds) was landed here in Sept 1995. The tackle shop and pier are open 6 a.m. to 11 p.m. from Mar 1 through Dec 15.

BAIT AND TACKLE SHOPS

Like any sport, you need the right equipment to complement technique. All Grand Strand piers and fishing venues offer a smattering of outlets where you can get your hands on a rod and reel and bait. But for the serious angler, the following bait and tackle venues offer years of experience, local tips, and top-quality gear.

i **When buying waders or boots, always buy them one and one-half size larger than your shoe size. The larger size will enable you to slip them off in the event that you fall overboard. Boots or waders filled with water will make you sink like a stone.**

North Strand

BOULINEAU'S
212 Sea Mountain Hwy., Cherry Grove
(843) 249-3556
www.boulineausiga.com
Since 1948 Boulineau's has served as one of the area's most popular suppliers of fishing equipment, hardware, cut bait—and lots and lots of free advice. The shop is open year-round from 6 a.m. to 11 p.m. (until midnight on Fri and Sat).

JOHNNY'S BAIT & TACKLE
4377 Sea Mountain Hwy. (Highway 9),
Little River
(843) 249-1288
Cornell Williamson is proud of his decades-old business and is about as experienced an angler as you'll ever meet. He swears by his mud minnows to catch flounder and recommends ballyhoo and rig mullet to troll for king mackerel. Both offshore and freshwater tackle are available. Johnny's is open every day of the year from 6 a.m. to 5 p.m.

Myrtle Beach

CITY BAIT & TACKLE
713 Eighth Ave. N. and Alder Street,
Myrtle Beach
(843) 448-2543
This business, in operation since 1972, is a favorite among fishing enthusiasts. Owner Bill Jackson bought the business a few years back, but he continues to operate it with the dedication to fishing that its founder did. He'll tell you in a heartbeat that the only advertising worth believing in is good customer service and word of mouth.

City Bait & Tackle keeps a steady supply of mullet, shrimp, and squid as preferred bait, as well as a wide range of tackle. Bill is always willing to inform customers where to cast their line for the catch of the day. The store is open from 9 a.m. to 7 p.m. Mon through Sat and is closed Sun.

South Strand

PERRY'S BAIT AND TACKLE
US 17 Business S., Murrells Inlet
(843) 651-2895

This family-run business was originally started in 1954 by Winston Perry and is now run by his son Eric. The store carries a full array of live bait, including shrimp, mullet, mud minnows, bloodworms, sand fleas, and sand crabs. Fishing rods are available for rental. Perry's is open from 6 a.m. until dark Mon through Fri and from 5 a.m. until dark on weekends during the summer.

FISHING TOURNAMENTS

If you reckon yourself an astute angler and want to put your skills to the ultimate test, you've come to the right place. We've listed a handful of area tournaments that are open to all interested participants.

Boating tournaments, usually of the offshore variety, are relatively costly to enter, but prize purses are lucrative, typically totaling thousands of dollars. The pier-fishing contests tend to be cumulative events, lasting several months; awards are less extravagant and often involve goods rather than cold, hard cash.

Regardless of the form or nature of the brass ring, the following tournaments are competitive as well as a great excuse to ply the waters along the Grand Strand.

Boat Fishing

DIXIE CHICKEN FISHING TOURNAMENT
Harbourgate Marina, North Myrtle Beach
(843) 249-1637
www.dixiechickenfishingfunament.com

An inshore/offshore "Funament," the Dixie Chicken has been held each year since 2000 to raise funds to build and increase the size of an artificial reef 2^1/$_2$ miles off Little River Inlet named the Jim Caudle Reef after an avid fisherman. The tournament was started by Jim Caudle's friend Ron McManus and gets its name from Caudle's boat, the *Dixie Chicken*. Caudle's philosophy was

"if it ain't fun, why do it?" and that's the motto of this $50,000 event. McManus says they are the only fund-raiser that pours everything they make back into the ocean.

Held over Memorial Day weekend, the Funament has three divisions. Entry to the inshore division is $100 and includes flounder, trout, and Spanish mackerel. Offshore costs $200 for wahoo, tuna, king mackerel, cobia, and dolphin. At the same time, the North Myrtle Beach Chamber of Commerce sponsors a Flounder Frenzy that costs $35 to enter, and prizes go to the largest flounder caught by any method possible, with a grand prize of $250.

Grand prize in 2009 for the offshore was $2,500, second place received $2,000, and third received $1,000. A prize of $1,000 is awarded to the person who catches the largest of each of the species included. Inshore grand prize is $2,000, second $1,000, third $500, with $500 for each of the largest in that group of fish.

Since 2000, 250,000 cubic feet of reef has been added to the Caudle Reef.

SOUTH CAROLINA GOVERNOR'S CUP BILLFISHING SERIES
(843) 953-9365
http://govcup.dnr.sc.gov

The South Carolina Governor's Cup Billfishing Series, in its 22nd season in 2010, is an umbrella event encompassing billfishing tournaments along the state's coast. The series promotes coastal tourism and encourages tag-or-release angling, as well as conservation of South Carolina's marine resources. It has been recognized internationally for its efforts to conserve billfish and other species through tag or release.

This Governor's Cup tournament involves marinas from Murrells Inlet to Edisto Island. Participants garner points during six fishing events for the biggest billfish caught; points also are awarded for the tag or release of blue and white marlin and sailfish. There are separate awards for tuna, dolphin, and wahoo. Each event sets its own price for entry. The average first-place purse for this event is $12,000. Participating marinas usually include Georgetown Landing Marina in Georgetown, Bohicket in John's Island, Charleston Harbor Marina Resort in Charleston, Charleston City Marina in Charleston, and Edisto Marina in Edisto Beach. (See the Boating chapter for details about Grand Strand marinas.)

Besides receiving a cash prize, winners are invited to the governor's mansion for a celebratory dinner.

TAILWALKERS OFFSHORE CHALLENGE
(843) 527-2495
www.tailwalkermarine.com
Held the second weekend in June, this fishing competition is also a multi-inlet event, with boats departing from Georgetown. First place is $20,000 no matter how many boats participate, but second is based largely on having up to 175 boats participating. The rest of the prize money is divided among anglers with the next 20-largest fish. The event started in 1994 and originally involved only king mackerel, but it was charged in 2003 to include blue-water fish. This tournament costs $350 per boat to enter, but organizers promise that almost every contestant floats away a winner.

Pier Fishing

GRAND STRAND FISHING RODEO
(843) 916-7213
www.grandstrandfishingrodeo.com
If you prefer to cast from one of the Grand Strand's piers, this annual tournament is for you. More than $7,000 in cash and prizes is awarded from Apr through Oct for the biggest "fish of the month." There's no fee to enter the tournament.

PIER KING MACKEREL TOURNAMENTS
(843) 626-7444
These mid-June and Sept pier tournaments are much like the Fishing Rodeo. Pay the $35-per-person entry fee and cast from any pier along the Grand Strand to tempt the tenacious "kings." The total cash purse is based upon the collected entry fees and is allotted proportionally among the first- through fifth-place winners.

Official Weigh Stations

If you're a participant in one of these tournaments and want to throw your day's catch into the hat for competition, the following locations serve as official weigh stations. **On the North Strand:** Cherry Grove Pier, North Ocean Boulevard. **In Myrtle Beach:** Apache Pier, 9700 Kings Rd.; Second Avenue Pier, 200 North Ocean Blvd.; Myrtle Beach State Park, 4401 South Kings Hwy.; and Springmaid Beach Pier, 3200 South Ocean Blvd. **On the South Strand:** Surfside Pier, 11 South Ocean Blvd.; Marlin Quay Marina, 1398 South Waccamaw Dr.; the Pier at Garden City, 110 South Waccamaw Dr.; and Captain Dick's Marina, 4123 US 17 Business.

BOATING

Boating the Grand Strand's waters is a bewitching alternative means of travel through this part of the country, forgone by most. What often gets missed in the wink-of-an-eye speeds of faster modes of transportation stretches out before you in a peaceful panorama when navigating rivers, marshes, and waterways. Like the persona of area natives, the Grand Strand's seaways seem slower-moving, easier . . . belying the churning eddy of activity just below the surface.

In this coastal area, water routes once were the main arteries for the lifeblood and growth of this region and today are steeped in the history of its people. When the marshy inlets of Calabash, Cherry Grove, Murrells Inlet, and Pawleys Island were fair game for anyone, their bulging beds of oysters and clams fed generations of families. There was a time when nets, pots, and traps were seen dangling from almost any dock or even a tree, containing the daily catch of blue crabs and shrimp. The deep, drifting Waccamaw River made rice planters some of the wealthiest people in the world during the 1850s, as its waters fed massive rice paddies along its banks. During summers in the mid-1800s, the river was alive with barges carrying whole families and their favorite furnishings from their inland plantation homes to seasonal abodes on Pawleys Island—a cooler clime and a safe haven from "summer fever" (malaria transmitted from mosquitoes).

The historical development of Grand Strand boating routes seems as murky as the water itself. All that we know for sure is that it was a generations-long process, most likely motivated by economic need or inspired by the discoveries of maverick explorers.

THE INTRACOASTAL WATERWAY

Sometimes referred to as the Inland Waterway, Intercoastal Waterway, or even Watery Route 1, the Intracoastal Waterway stretches from 23 miles north of Boston to the Florida Keys. The ICW is the domain of pleasure craft, small fishing vessels, and, at times, barges. It is a master of quick change: at one moment a narrow, banked channel; at the next turn a broad, hazy inland sea bounded by gold, green, and brown marsh grasses. Dredged to a 12-foot depth from Norfolk, Virginia, southward to Miami, the Intracoastal is famous for hidden sandbars along its path—the main reason smaller craft are recommended.

Because some of its northern sections are closed, mile 0 officially begins at Norfolk. The waterway's history is sketchy at best, but evidence shows it was used by Native Americans to travel the length of the coast. Around 1643 some Massachusetts colonists dug a half-mile-long canal linking the Anniquam River and Gloucester Harbor. President George Washington was responsible for surveying the Great Dismal Swamp, a 200,000-acre wilderness spanning parts of southeastern Virginia and northeastern North Carolina, in 1763. Thirty years later work finally began in the swamp to connect rivers in Virginia and North Carolina. The final portion was completed in 1936 when the federal government became involved and tied in the area between Little River and Winyah Bay in South Carolina.

Today when it comes to boating, the Grand Strand offers practically every imaginable type of waterway, including tea-colored rivers stained by the tannins of cypress roots, briny marshes, and the open waters of the Atlantic Ocean and aqua Gulf Stream.

RULES OF THE WATERWAY

Even though we know you wouldn't launch a boat without knowledge of safety methods and rules, we thought it important to outline your legal responsibilities as a boater.

Accident Reports

The operator of any vessel is required by law to file with local authorities a formal, written report of any accident. This can be accomplished simply by calling the U.S. Coast Guard Boating Safety Hotline, (800) 368-5647, to make a verbal report and acquire a form.

It is necessary to report damage to a vessel or its equipment, injury or loss of life, or any missing passenger. You must also file a report in the case of grounding, capsizing, someone falling overboard, colliding, sinking, striking a boat or propeller, swamping, flooding, fire, an explosion, or the disappearance of a craft. Injury to or the death or disappearance of an individual must be reported within 48 hours, while damage to a vessel or property must be disclosed within 10 days of the incident.

Approaching Vessels and Right-of-Way

When approaching another boat in open waters, each party must move to the right after a short (one-second) horn signal, answered by the other vessel. If crossing paths, the boat to your right from dead ahead to two points abaft your beam has the right-of-way. You should sound one short blast ("I'm altering course to starboard"), two short blasts (". . . to port"), or three short blasts (". . . to stern").

In all situations, the boat being overtaken has the right-of-way, even if the overtaking ship enters your danger zone. The overtaking boat is required to sound two long and one short blasts if it intends to pass on the right; two long, two short blasts if on the left. If you are being overtaken, respond with one long, one short, one long, and one short signal if you understand and agree.

Casting Off

Leaving a slip or dock dictates that you have no right-of-way until you are completely clear of the dock. It is every operator's responsibility to leave port without danger to other boats, and it's a good idea to sound one long blast as you are about to depart. All sailboats under sail alone (no motorized power) and fishing boats have the right-of-way and should be given wide berth. The only exception to this rule is when the sailboat is overtaking a motorboat, in which case the motorized craft maintains the right-of-way.

Common sense guides most boating regulations: Allow large ships with restricted maneuverability the right-of-way; stay away from docks, piers, and swimming areas; and take responsibility for damage caused by your wake.

Life Jackets

In boats less than 16 feet in length, a wearable life vest must be accessible for each person aboard. If the boat is more than 16 feet in length, wearable life vests must be accessible, in addition to a ring buoy or other safety device that can be thrown. All children younger than age 13 aboard any vessel are required to wear life jackets.

The Pilot

Anyone age 16 or older can legally pilot a boat. Those younger than age 16 can run a vessel only after taking a boater education course and passing a test and if they are accompanied by an adult. Courses are offered through the U.S. Coast Guard Auxiliary, U.S. Power Squadron, and the Department of Motor Vehicles. The DMV issues educational handbooks for study prior to testing.

Safety First

If the wind suddenly shifts, or if lightning and choppy water are evident, there's a good chance a storm is brewing; in that case, boating is not a good idea for the time being.

Before casting off into any waters, check your vessel for the following items: a portable radio to check weather reports, a flashlight, extra batteries, matches, a navigation map of the area, sunscreen, a first-aid kit, sunglasses, a raincoat, and an extra length of tie line. It's always best to tell someone where you're going, who is accompanying you, and how long you plan to be away. Before starting the engine, open hatches, run the blower, and, most importantly, sniff for gasoline fumes in the fuel and engine areas. Make sure all fishing and hunting gear is well packed—there's nothing like a loose fishhook to ruin a potentially great outing.

While cruising, change seats carefully, especially if the craft is a small one. The rule is to stay low and near the centerline. Use caution when passing a powerboat, and anchor from the bow with a line that is at least five times as long as the water's depth.

PUBLIC BOAT RAMPS

The following sites (listed geographically by county) are provided by Horry and Georgetown Counties to allow boaters access to waterways.

Horry County:

- County boat ramp: 53rd Avenue, Cherry Grove Beach, on Hogg Inlet and Cherry Grove Creek.
- County boat ramp: Under US 17 bridge, Nixon Cross Roads, on the Intracoastal Waterway.
- North Myrtle Beach landing: Second Avenue S., on the Intracoastal Waterway.
- Garden City boat ramp: End of Highway 816, on Main Creek.

Georgetown County:

- Wacca-Wache landing: End of Highway 62, off US 17, on Waccamaw River and Intracoastal Waterway.
- Murrells Inlet boat landing: US 17 Business, on Murrells Inlet.
- Pawleys Island (north) landing: Pritchard Street W., Highway 46, on Main Creek.
- Pawleys Island (middle) landing: Third Street W., Highway 266, on Main Creek.
- Pawleys Island (south) landing: Shell Road W., Highway 104, on Pawleys Creek.
- Hagley landing. Hagley Plantation Road, on the Waccamaw River.

- East Bay Street (ballpark) landing: East Bay Park, on Sampit River, Georgetown.
- South Island Ferry boat landing: End of County Road 18, on Winyah Bay.
- Pole Yard boat landing: US 17 at North Santee River.

PUBLIC-ACCESS MARINAS

If you're lucky enough to own a powerboat or sailing vessel, we think you'll find the following comprehensive list of area marinas useful in getting around the Strand by watercraft. It's always best to contact the marinas in advance, especially if you'll be arriving late at night or if your boat is experiencing mechanical trouble. Marina personnel usually will make sure someone is there to meet you and that the right equipment is available for repairs. All of the Grand Strand's public marinas listed here are open year-round, even if hours of operation vary from season to season.

North Strand

ANCHOR MARINA
2200 Little River Neck Rd., Little River
(843) 249-7899

"Do it yourself is always welcome" is the motto of Anchor Marina, where sailors are encouraged to pull in for repairs and supplies. A 35-ton travel lift is available, and mechanics are on call 24 hours a day to fix anything from a blister to a broken propeller shaft. Anchor's staff also offer bottom painting, fiberglass work, and power washing.

This 85-slip marina provides wet and dry storage, showers, bathrooms, a ship's store, restaurant, and lounge. General hours for the marina and store are 8 a.m. to 5 p.m. seven days a week; the restaurant and lounge are open from 11 a.m. until the wee hours of the morning.

B.W.'S MARINA
4495 Mineola Ave., Little River
(843) 249-8294
www.bwsmarina.com

B.W.'s is the first stop if you're headed through the Little River Inlet into the Intracoastal Waterway and claims to have the cleanest and cheapest fuel and gas on the ICW. Managed by Michelle Coffey, it has been a part of the Little River community for more than 30 years. Transient boats are allowed to tie up at the 121-foot floating face deck, and 10 slips are available for monthly rental. Water, 110- and 220-amp electrical hookups, and gasoline and diesel fuels are also available. This marina is open from 7 a.m. to 6 p.m. with extended hours during the summer. They also offer Wi-Fi.

COQUINA HARBOUR INC.
4208 Coquina Harbor Dr., Little River
ICW Mile Marker 346
(866) 249-9333, (843) 249-9333
www.coquinayachtclub.com

Russell Edwards manages this 113-slip marina that offers a bathhouse and self-service laundry facilities. Monthly and yearly slip leases can be negotiated. The marina is open year-round.

Coquina can take vessels up to 80 feet in length and has a dedicated cat slip. It's the smallest of the three main marinas in the Yacht Basin, which—with a total of six marinas and 500 slips between them—is the largest enclosed harbor on the East Coast. Shower and laundry facilities are available.

CRICKET COVE MARINA
4495 North Baker St., Little River
ICW Mile Marker 345, Green Marker 11
(843) 249-7169
www.cricketcovemarina.com

Cricket Cove opened in July 1997 and is the last such venture that will be permitted on saltwater marsh because the wetlands are a protected natural habitat. Concrete floating docks offer transient boat storage, and 75-plus wet slips are available for boats from 40 to 55 feet in length. There is 250 feet of face dock on the T of A dock and 200 feet on B, so they do get a lot of large boats. Dry storage can accommodate 340 vessels as long as 35 feet. Two fueling depots, inside and outside, offer gas and diesel fuel pumps. Hookups include water, cable TV, telephone, and

30-, 50-, and 100-amp electricity. Cricket Cove serves guests with showers, bathrooms, and laundry facilities. The Upper Deck, (843) 280-3189, opened in Feb 1998 and serves lunch and dinner. The Upper Deck opens daily at 11:30 a.m. Marina hours are 8 a.m. to sunset seven days a week.

HARBOURGATE MARINA
2120 Sea Mountain Hwy. (Highway 9),
North Myrtle Beach
(843) 249-8888
www.harbourgatemarina.com

This marina, under the Little River Swing Bridge, offers a full range of services, including repairs. You'll find cable TV, laundry facilities, and showers on-site. Harbourgate also boasts a well-stocked ship's store on the premises. Harbourgate Marina is the location of a 100-room Hampton Inn, (843) 249-1997. Guests of the Hampton Inn receive special privileges at the marina and a free continental breakfast every morning during their stay.

MARINA AT DOCK HOLIDAYS
Vereen's Marina
1525 13th Ave. N., North Myrtle Beach
(843) 280-6354

Dock Holidays has a reputation of being a party marina due to the five bars and restaurants located around its harbor. There are 92 privately owned slips in the marina next to Dock Holidays, and Dock is allowed to rent them out with the owners' permission. Otherwise, the marina's space includes six 50-foot slips, 95 feet on an angle dock, a 75-foot face dock, and 350 feet along the waterway itself. Cable TV and phone hookups are available, as is a pump-out station. Thirty- and 50-amp shore power also is accessible. The shower, head, and laundry are located near the club Dynamites!

It's recommended that you call ahead for reservations because the popular marina fills up quickly, and it generally is full every night during transient season. Hours of operation range from 8 a.m. to 8 p.m., depending on the season.

MYRTLE BEACH YACHT CLUB AT COQUINA HARBOUR

714 US 17 N., Little River
ICW Mile Marker 346
(843) 249-5376
www.myrtlebeachyachtclub.com

First built in 1983, Myrtle Beach Yacht Club is the oldest and the largest of the three main marinas in the Yacht Basin, which includes Coquina Harbour. Many of this club's 153 slips are designated for transient use, and boaters can enjoy convenient access to both 30- and 50-amp power. There is a swimming pool, a pool bar and restaurant, as well as showers, bathrooms, laundry facilities, and water and cable TV hookups. The club offers diesel and gasoline fuels as well as a pump-out station. You'll find an on-site ship's store offering beer, wine, and ice, and a number of first-class restaurants are within walking distance. The black-and-white lighthouse at the mouth of Coquina Harbor marks the nautical route to the club. Hours of operation are always 8 a.m. to 6:30 p.m.

NORTH MYRTLE BEACH MARINA

4430 Belle Marina Rd., Little River
(843) 249-1000

This full-service marina offers dry storage and crane service that can accommodate any motorized watercraft or sailboat up to 65 feet in length. North Myrtle Beach Marina specializes in service and repairs. The ship's store at this marina stocks an extensive array of boat supplies and fishing tackle. Hours of operation are 8 a.m. to 6 p.m. daily.

Myrtle Beach

HAGUE MARINA

1 Hague Dr., off Highway 707, at the Intracoastal Waterway, Myrtle Beach
(843) 293-2141

George Russ manages this site. Hague offers yacht service and supplies and storage—wet or dry, covered or uncovered. Located in a wooded half-moon channel just off Mile Marker 368 of the Intracoastal, the marina specializes in boat repairs. Transient dockage is available for $1 per foot per night. Water and electric hookups plus a ship's store are available. Hague is open 8 a.m. to 6 p.m. daily spring through fall, until 5:30 p.m. during the winter months.

OSPREY MARINA

8400 Osprey Rd., Myrtle Beach
ICW Mile Marker 373
(843) 215-5353
www.ospreymarina.com

Osprey is one of the best-kept marinas you'll find. It was named Marina of the Year for all of the United States in 2001. All of Osprey's 96 slips are rented by the year only. It operates at 90 percent capacity year-round. Dry storage is available, as are cable TV, phone, water, and 30- and 50-amp electric hookups. This marina provides a pump-out station as well as gasoline and diesel fuels. Amenities include showers, laundry facilities, Internet connections, and an on-site convenience store and restaurant. Hours run 8 a.m. to 6 p.m.

South Strand

BELLE ISLE MARINA

1228 Belle Isle Rd., Georgetown
(843) 546-8491
www.belleislemarinasc.com

Sporting both floating and fixed docks, Belle Isle provides 120 slips, dry storage, laundry facilities, showers, and bathrooms and also offers diesel fuel or gasoline. Transportation into town is available at no charge. The marina also has a fully stocked ship's store. Belle Isle also has the Grill, a bar and grill open 11 a.m. to 9 p.m. Thurs through Sat and 9 a.m. to 2 p.m. Sun.

In season the marina and store are open seven days a week from 8 a.m. to 7 p.m. When the weather gets cooler and things slow down, they operate from 9 a.m. to 5 p.m.

GEORGETOWN LANDING MARINA

432 Marina Dr. and US 17, Georgetown
(843) 546-1776
www.georgetownlandingmarina.com

This 150-slip deep-water marina has both floating and fixed docks, as well as a floating linear transient dock. Gas and diesel fuels are available. The property is home to the Lands End Restaurant, popular for years with locals who come to sample the daily seafood specials. Georgetown Landing is open 8 a.m. to 7 p.m. Sun through Thurs and 8 a.m. to 8 p.m. on Fri and Sat throughout summer. In the winter, hours are 8 a.m. until dark. A 98-room Hampton Inn, (843) 545-5000, services this marina.

MARLIN QUAY MARINA
1398 South Waccamaw Dr.,
Garden City Beach
(843) 651-4444
www.marlinquay.com
Besides running an array of charters from this marina, the owner offers boat dockage for long-term lease. Bathrooms, showers, laundry facilities, 30- and 50-amp power hookups, and a ship's store are available, as are gasoline and diesel fuel pumps. There is an on-site Grill Restaurant that is open in the summer months. The marina does not allow "live aboards" (where people live on the boat year-round) or Jet Skis. It is open year-round—6 a.m. to 8 p.m. in the summer months and 8 a.m. to 5 p.m. during the winter after Daylight Savings Time ends.

WACCA-WACHE MARINA
1950 Wachesaw Rd., Murrells Inlet
ICW Mile Marker 383
(843) 651-2994
www.waccawachemarina.com
Wacca-Wache maintains 109 floating slips, 15 of which are available for transient vessels. This marina also offers 120 dry-storage slips and a choice of 30-, 50-, or 100-amp electrical hookups. Additional services include cable TV hookups, a pump-out station, gasoline and diesel fuel, a ship's store, laundry facilities, and showers. A courtesy car is available to transient boaters for an hour at a time to boaters docked at the marina. Wacca-Wache is open from 8 a.m. to 8 p.m. during peak boating season, generally June through Sept.

BOATING TOURS AND EXCURSIONS

If you don't have your own vessel and want to explore the Grand Strand from a watery point of view, check out one or more of the following trips. There is something for everybody, no matter what your age or particular interest.

North Strand
GREAT AMERICAN RIVERBOATS
Waccatee 200, Enterprise Rd., Socastee
(800) 685-6601, (843) 650-6600
www.mbriverboat.com
Operating out of Waccatee Zoo in the Socastee area, the Great American Riverboats company offers boat trips on the colorful *Jungle Princess* riverboat. The tropical-themed vessel allows you to spend a few hours or the whole day cruising the Intracoastal Waterway and the Waccamaw River. The vessel includes outdoor decks as well as enclosed, climate-controlled decks with a snack bar, elegant dining area, and comfortable seating. The daytime excursion lasts one and a half hours and costs $16 for adults and $8 for kids ages 3 to 12; it's free for children 2 and younger. The sunset cruise lasts two hours; admission is $17 for adults, $9 for children ages 3 to 12, and free for kids 2 and younger. The two-and-a-half-hour dinner cruise, with a buffet-style meal, costs $36 for adults (tax and gratuity included) and $26 for children.

i **If you're left treading water on a boating excursion, fight hypothermia by keeping on all clothing to trap heat. Avoid moving as much as possible and draw your knees up while floating on your back in your life jacket. If you have a treading companion, huddle together to stay warm.**

HURRICANE FISHING FLEET
Hurricane Marina, The Waterfront
at Calabash, Calabash, NC
(800) 373-2004, (910) 579-3660
www.hurricanefleet.com

"If you haven't experienced the charm of Myrtle Beach from the deck of one of our cruises, you haven't experienced Myrtle Beach," is the motto referring to the Hurricane's roster of sea tours.

Hurricane's Adventure Cruises encourage passengers to join the crew for an afternoon, setting a course for the Atlantic Ocean, where you'll meet up with a shrimp-boat fleet and watch them ply their trade. Shrimping and watching active marine life is the theme of this jaunt, which costs $22 per person age 12 and older and $19 per child age 11 and younger.

Call the number listed for reservations and schedules, because hours and types of cruises change periodically.

South Strand

BLACK RIVER OUTDOORS CENTER

21 Garden Ave., US 701, Georgetown
(843) 546-4840
www.blackriveroutdoors.com

Unlike white water, the waterways along the Tideland Coast are "meandering, gentle, flowing," says naturalist and ecotourism enthusiast Bill Unger, owner of Black River Outdoors Center. Year-round, Unger and his professionally trained guides offer kayak tours upon the area's black-water rivers, cypress-tupelo swamps, salt marshes, and rice plantation canals and creeks. A sampling of the guided explorations, designed for the adventurous types who love exploring, include the wildlife swamp preserves of the Black River; Waccamaw National Wildlife Refuge and Sandy Island; the creeks and canals of Chicora Wood Plantation; and the saltwater marshes of Murrells Inlet and Huntington Beach State Park.

The uninitiated are often surprised to learn that participation requires only a moderate level of physical fitness. Even first-timers have no trouble paddling the gentle waterways of the area. Reservations are required, and guided day tours of three and a half to four hours are priced at a very reasonable $60 (when accompanied by parents, children younger than age 13 are $40). Group rates are available.

If you are hungry for a bit of solitude, you can also rent kayaks and canoes to launch your own self-guided adventure. Life jackets, paddles, cartop carriers, and safety instruction are included.

Touring kayaks are available for the more experienced. Or you can rent a surf kayak to keep at your beach house for a day or a week!

Black River Outdoors Center also offers an impressive stock of kayaks, canoes, small-boat trailers, and paddling accessories at its retail store, generally open Mon through Sat from 9 a.m. until 5:30 p.m., but sometimes earlier, sometimes later, and sometimes on Sunday.

BROOKGREEN GARDENS

US 17 S., Murrells Inlet
(800) 849-1931, (843) 235-6000
www.brookgreen.org

Some of Brookgreen Gardens' most unspoiled vistas can be enjoyed aboard the *Springfield,* a 48-foot pontoon boat that offers an up-close look at some of the Lowcountry's native flora and fauna. Several times each day as the boat winds its way through the scenic waterways, a Brookgreen naturalist tells the story of the long-abandoned rice fields that once thrived in Georgetown County from the mid-18th century until the Civil War. These tours combine the marvels of nature, the thrill of discovery, and the intrigue of history. Wilderness lovers, birdwatchers, botanical enthusiasts, and history buffs will long remember this trip. The price is $7 in addition to admission to Brookgreen Gardens.

CAP'N ROD'S LOWCOUNTRY PLANTATION TOURS

Harborwalk, Georgetown
(843) 477-0287
www.lowcountrytours.com

For a delightful change of pace, Captain Rod offers a selection of relaxing, enjoyable, and educational tours. Comfortably seated aboard the canvas-covered, outboard-powered pontoon boat, you'll explore pockets of solitude in and around Winyah Bay, as well as in five surrounding rivers. Captain Rod, a longtime native and marvelous storyteller, delivers entertaining narrative that includes local lore, natural and American history tidbits, environmental issues, and a hearty helping of good old Southern humor and hospitality.

Daily plantation tours allow participants to cruise peaceful, slow-moving rivers past plantation mansions, long-abandoned rice fields, majestic old oaks, and a plethora of wildlife. Loved by history buffs and nature lovers, these three-hour tours are perennial favorites and attract lots of return clientele.

Lighthouse tours cruise to a remote barrier island—past Hobcaw Barony and over the sunken remains of the USS *Harvest Moon*—where Winyah Bay meets the wide, blue Atlantic. Explore a place where the sea spills its secrets and deposits an ever-changing array of shelling opportunities.

Plenty of snacks and beverages are available onboard, so bring a buck or two—but you need not bring anything more. There are clean restrooms, too.

CAPTAIN BILL'S FLEET
Captain Dick's Marina,
4123 US 17 Business, Murrells Inlet
(866) 557-3474, (843) 651-3676
www.captdicks.com
Discover Murrells Inlet and the Atlantic Ocean from Captain Dick's, located on the waterfront in Murrells Inlet. Make fishing memories and experience the real thrill of catching those big ones. Longer trips travel farther offshore to deeper water and produce a wider variety, greater quantity, and larger fish! From the half-day Sea Bass Fishing Adventure to the all-day Gulf Stream Adventure to the overnight Gulf Stream Excursion, choices abound and range in price from $37 to $142 per person depending on age and which fishing adventure you choose.

i South Carolina ranks third in the nation when it comes to boats per capita. That means there is a boat registered here for one in every ten South Carolinians.

Captain Dick's Saltwater Marsh Explorer Adventure has long remained one of their most popular tours. Discover the area's own marine wonderland in a two-and-a-half-hour boat journey guided by a marine biologist. Experience the vital, living habitat that is home to hundreds of fascinating and mysterious marine creatures. Not an artificial environment like a zoo or aquarium, this interactive tour delivers a glimpse of the real thing. Various nets and dredges are employed to retrieve specimens from beneath the water. Specimens go into onboard touch tanks where they can be seen, observed, and, when appropriate, touched and held. There is also a fishing demonstration and a beach walk along a barrier island that is not accessible by car. Participants occasionally encounter bottle-nosed dolphins—an added delight! All Explorer vessels are restroom equipped.

"Cruisin' The Beach," an ocean sightseeing cruise, is a memorable excursion suitable for the entire family. This cruise departs from the historic inlet, passes through the tranquil natural beauty of the marsh, and ends up on the majestic Atlantic. Cruising the shoreline of the Grand Strand, the Myrtle Beach skyline is newly captivating. Call ahead for scheduling information. Rates are $21 per adult and $15 for children under the age of 12.

Captain Dick's offers more than we have room to tell you about. Dozens of tours include ecology outings, fishing and sightseeing excursions, and pirate adventures. The captain also offers boat rentals, Jet Ski rentals, parasailing, and nearly anything else you can think of. Give the captain a call at the number listed or visit the Web site.

ROVER TOURS
End of Broad Street, Downtown Boardwalk,
Georgetown
(800) 705-9063, (843) 546-8822
www.rovertours.com
Rover Tours is located on the Harborwalk downtown in historic Georgetown. The company operates two boats. The *Jolly Rover* is a tall-ship

schooner, the same kind of vessel once used by shifty-eyed pirates to ply our Lowcountry waterways. This ship, a 79-foot, two-masted, gaff-rigged topsail schooner that can hold 49 passengers, is a carefully and lovingly crafted replica with modern features for which Blackbeard would have yearned: a steel hull, aluminum masts and nylon sails, modern restroom facilities, an inboard engine, and safety lines around the deck to keep little pirates from falling overboard.

Throughout spring and summer, the *Jolly Rover* will feature three tours per day, Mon through Sat. Two-hour "Pirate Adventures" at 10 a.m. and 1 p.m. feature folklore and stories told by a "real" pirate in period clothing. The young and young at heart will enjoy tales of plank walking and buried treasure. Enjoy the fine salt air on deck or relax "down below" as you sail around an uninhabited island and catch glimpses of bald eagles, seabirds, and maybe even a 'gator lurking on shore. At 6 p.m., also Mon through Sat, a two-and-a-half-hour "Romantic Evening Sail" gives lucky guests an opportunity to experience the romance and magic of daylight disappearing over darkening waters. This tour certainly makes for a memorable end to any day!

The *Jolly Rover* is operated by an experienced captain and crew. There's an onboard ship's store with light snacks, beverages, and Jolly Rover souvenirs.

The *Carolina Rover*, a 49-passenger pontoon boat, offers a different kind of tour. Mon through Sat, three-hour daily tours—at 9 a.m., 1 p.m., and 5 p.m.—focus on the Georgetown Lighthouse, shelling excursions, and the lush natural environment of the Carolina Lowcountry.

The ever-popular three-hour Adventure Cruise transports its guests a dozen miles or so over smooth inland waters into the mouth of Winyah Bay, where an uninhabited and wildlife-rich barrier island sports a historic lighthouse—and more shells than most of you have ever seen. Participants are allowed to step right off the boat onto the sun-bleached shoreline to sun, stroll, and pick up shells. Plenty of time is allotted for the beach, so expect to spend roughly three hours blissfully removed from civilization.

The *Carolina Rover* features plenty of shade, snacks, beverages, and clean restroom facilities. An onboard naturalist's informative commentary is an added delight. Consult the Rover Web site or call for prices and other details.

BOAT RENTALS

If you have a penchant to captain your own vessel or are looking to take a leisurely cruise on a pontoon boat, the following is a comprehensive listing of established, year-round outlets that offer this equipment. During the summer you can contact any of the public-access marinas listed earlier in this chapter. Many rent watercraft during the busy season but discontinue rentals right after Labor Day. If you are on the lookout for great kayaking and canoeing opportunities, please refer to the Water Sports chapter.

i Drop into the Original Benjamin's seafood restaurant on Restaurant Row to see fine replicas of famous vessels. Local museum curator and shipwright Jimmy Frost displays his 35-foot-long, 7-foot-tall model of the *Queen Elizabeth* cruise ship that sailed decades ago, as well as a 45-foot replica of the *Mayflower*. Frost showcases his work in the lobby of the restaurant.

Myrtle Beach

DOWNWIND SAILS
2915 South Ocean Blvd., Myrtle Beach
(843) 448-7245
www.downwindsailsmyrtlebeach.com
Right on the beach, Downwind Sails rents 14- or 16-foot sailboats and Hobie Cats from Apr 1 through Oct 25. The general price is $40 per hour for the 14-footer and $65 for the 16-footer, but discounts often apply after Labor Day when business slows down. Lessons are highly recommended for novices and run $65 per hour, which includes ½-hour boat rental after the lesson. Downwind is open all summer long from 8 a.m. to 8 p.m. Downwind Sails is closed during the off-season.

HARBOURGATE WATERCRAFT

2120 Sea Mountain Hwy.,
North Myrtle Beach
(843) 249-1144
www.harbourgatewatercraft.com

Located at Harbourgate Resort & Marina, Harbourgate Watercraft features a fleet of Sea-Doo GTIs, which are available for hourly, half-day, or full-day rental. Rates are $80 per hour or $100 for 90 minutes. They have special discounts on group rentals and longer or all-day rentals, and they are willing to match or beat any competitor's prices. Open daily 8 a.m. to 8 p.m. from Apr 14 to Sept 16.

MYRTLE BEACH WATERSPORTS

5835 Dick Pond Rd., Myrtle Beach
(866) RENT-ATV, (843) 497-8848

LITTLE RIVER WATERFRONT

(866) 4-SEA-DOO, (843) 280-7777
www.myrtlebeachwatersports.com

These two locations rent pontoon boats, Jet Skis, and jet boats and also offer parasailing, island tours, and dolphin watches. Both locations are open seasonally, 10 a.m. until 4 p.m. daily.

SAIL & SKI CONNECTION

515 US 501, Myrtle Beach
(843) 626-SAIL
www.sailandskiconnection.com

The Sail & Ski Connection offers kayak rentals and tours. You'll pay $30 for a single kayak with life jacket and paddle and $35 for a tandem. If need be, Sail & Ski will deliver your kayak to you. Call for delivery information and pricing. Visit the store to browse a wide variety of boating gear.

South Strand

CAPTAIN DICK'S MARINA

4123 US 17 Business, Murrells Inlet
(866) 557-3474, (843) 651-3676
www.captdicks.com

For cruising or fishing the inlet only, Captain Dick's rents 15-foot fiberglass johnboats with 15-hp outboard motors. Each boat accommodates up to four people and rents for $99 for four hours, $149 for eight hours. Pontoon boats for up to 16 people are available for $269 for eight hours and $189 for four hours. Life jackets, fuel, safety equipment, and licenses are included in the rental package. For an additional charge, you can also rent a rod and reel for the trip. Kayaks are offered for $25 for a half day and $45 for a full day. Boat rentals are offered Easter through Thanksgiving. Parasailing trips are an option, too.

GAMBLING BOATS

At the present time there are two gambling boats offering a "cruise to nowhere" for those who love a game of chance. Steeped in controversy and always under threat of a legislative ban, the boats can be good fun for those who don't want to venture all the way to Las Vegas to gamble. Gambling is illegal in the state of South Carolina, and twice a day both vessels leave their docks in Little River and cruise a few miles off the coast to international waters, outside U.S. jurisdiction, where it is legal to gamble. A ruling in June 2007 gave the boats a five-year time frame in which to leave Horry County, but the casino owners are hopeful a compromise will be worked out.

North Strand

BIG M CASINO, THE

4491 Waterfront Ave., Little River
(877) 250-LUCK, (843) 249-9811
www.bigmcasino.com

The *Big M* gambling vessel offers games of craps, blackjack, roulette, and three-card poker, as well as slot machines and video poker. Boarding time is one hour before departure, and the trips are held from 11 a.m. to 4 p.m. Mon through Fri and noon to 5 p.m. Sat and Sun. Evening cruises are 7 p.m. to midnight Sun through Thurs and 7 p.m. until 1 a.m. Fri and Sat.

The *Big M* provides round-trip shuttle service for patrons of any Myrtle Beach–area hotel.

SUNCRUZ
4495 Mineola Ave., Little River
(800) 474-DICE, (843) 280-2933
www.suncruzcasino.com

The 207-foot *SunCruz VIII* departs Little River twice daily to take gamblers out to sea to try their luck at a different sort of fishing—fishing for winnings. The ship features games of blackjack, poker, and Texas Hold 'Em, as well as roulette. There are 22 gaming tables and 380 slot machines aboard, and gamblers drink free. Hot lunches and dinners are available.

The cruises leave from 11 a.m. to 4:15 p.m. Mon through Fri and noon until 5:15 p.m. on weekends and holidays. An evening cruise departs at 7 p.m. and returns at 12:15 a.m. Sun through Thurs and 7 p.m. until 1:15 a.m. Fri and Sat.

There are buses for those who don't want to make the drive, and they will pick you up from more than 40 sites along the Grand Strand. (Check the Web site or call for details and reservations.)

BEACH INFORMATION

With an average annual temperature in the mid-70s and 215 days of Carolina-blue skies and bright sunshine each year, the Grand Strand's mild, subtropical climate is a mecca for sun worshipers and beachcombers alike. Even when the summer temperatures and humidity chase the majority of people into air-conditioned shelter, the beach will always carry a soft, welcoming breeze that defies the heat. The wide ribbon of sandy coast stretches for 60 miles, and the Atlantic Ocean is usually less turbulent than its West Coast cousin, the Pacific Ocean. As hundreds of thousands of locals and visitors will attest, there's nothing like a glorious day at the beach!

A FRIENDLY REMINDER ABOUT SUN EXPOSURE . . .

There are few things in life easier to acquire and more painful to live with than a bad sunburn, and around here you can turn a good stinging shade of pink in just 30 minutes to an hour. Longer doses of sun can send sunbathers to the hospital with blisters, nausea, and excruciating pain.

Don't be fooled by clouds or cool air: You can get a bad burn even on a day when you can't see the sun. Before you hit the Strand, pick up some good sunscreen with a high sun protection factor (SPF). We suggest an SPF of at least 15. Apply it an hour before you start swimming, walking, or bicycling and remember to reapply it after swimming or if you're perspiring—even if it's waterproof. Most experts recommend avoiding the sun during the hottest part of the day: between noon and 4 p.m. Even under the shade the sun can reflect off the water and sand, so you can still get a burn.

When it comes to SPFs and protecting your skin, there's safety in numbers. Ranging from 2 to more than 45, the SPF on a particular sunscreen tells you how many times longer (not how many hours longer) the lotion protects you from a sunburn, compared to the time it would take if you wore no sunscreen at all. So, if your skin normally reddens after 20 unprotected minutes in the sun, slathering on an SPF 15 will let you endure the rays for five hours (20 x 15 = 300 minutes). You can also make an educated SPF decision by keeping tabs on news reports of daily ultraviolet (UV) index numbers. These numbers range from 0 to 10+, depending on the season, cloud cover, and other atmospheric conditions. On a day with a moderate UV reading of 5, wear an SPF 15 lotion and a hat; if the reading is 10 or higher, aim for an SPF of 30 and cover up.

Be sure to wear something on your head. A visor is good to protect your face, but to shield your head and hair, a full hat with a brim that's at least 3 inches wide is best. Good sunglasses that filter out ultraviolet rays should also be part of your standard beach attire. If you've got young children or a baby with you, be sure to take extra care to protect their tender skin. Make them wear hats and reapply sunscreen every few minutes. If kids are determined to stay in the ocean for hours, put T-shirts on them. Some rafts and Boogie boards will cause mild rashes on unprotected stomachs anyway, so the T-shirts will serve two purposes.

If you want to dress to beat the heat, get wise to fabric and weaves. Unbleached cotton, satiny polyesters, and silk either absorb or reflect UV rays, while crepe, viscose, and bleached cottons allow UV rays to pass through, making a direct hit to your skin. Look for tightly woven materials, like cotton twill, that don't allow light to pass through, enhancing its sun protection power. And, while white and pastel shades of clothing may make you feel cooler, dark tones actually absorb UV rays better. For the truly sun sensitive, there are also several brands of clothing that can protect you from UV rays. Many of these clothing lines are sold in beach shops along the Grand Strand.

OCEAN SWIMMING SAFETY

There is nothing quite so seductive as the gently rolling waves of the Atlantic Ocean. It beckons you to walk in and float amid its briny, undulating waters. And, all at once, you're in perfect commune with nature itself. We know how easily common sense can be forgotten while riding the folds of the ocean, but you must always remember that the forces of nature are not only majestic but also unpredictable—and, at times, downright dangerous. That's why swimming is not permitted beyond 50 yards from the beach or over shoulder depth.

Lucky for us all, Grand Strand beaches are prime tourist attractions overseen by trained lifeguards. As a visitor to the area or local resident, it is always a good idea to plant your beach chair near a lifeguard stand. Before you even get one toe into the surf, these watchdogs of the shoreline will let you know the current swimming conditions by posting colored flags: yellow means use extra caution; red means NO SWIMMING! Scoping out a lifeguard-protected area of the beach gives you the peace of mind that comes from knowing you're not swimming alone, your children have an extra pair of eyes locked on them, and, if anything untoward should happen, someone well trained in rescue and CPR is on hand.

Undertow

That incredible force of water that pulls you oceanward when waves recede is an undertow. Depending on weather conditions, it can be very strong. If you find yourself caught in one, don't panic or try to fight it. Stay calm. Float with the waves and you will eventually be brought back to shore. If waves are bigger than usual, it's a good bet that the undertow will be stronger, and it's best to stay in shallower waters.

Riptides

When you combine high waves, a full moon, and hurricanes or tropical storms brewing in the Atlantic Ocean, conditions are rife for dangerous riptides, or rip currents. "Rips" occur when two opposing currents meet, causing a swirling action that can carry swimmers from safer waters. These currents represent an overflow of water coming into shore that travels back into the ocean in a narrow current with considerable force and speed. Telltale signs of riptides are rough, choppy water that appears deeper and darker than normal, with swirling debris, kelp, or sand. Since 80 percent of ocean rescues are a result of swimmers finding themselves caught in a rip current, it's wise to know how to get out of such a force. As with a strong undertow, try to relax. It's useless to fight a rip current. Go along with it and then angle yourself to swim or float parallel to the shoreline. Waves at either side of the rip current will take you back to shore.

BEACH RULES

Alcohol

All Grand Strand beaches forbid alcohol consumption and possession. All open containers with alcohol are forbidden. This rule applies to all public-access areas as well.

Attracting Sharks

No one is permitted to bait, fish for, or otherwise attract sharks to an area within a half mile of the beach.

Cars on the Beach

Driving on the beach is no longer allowed on any portion of the Grand Strand beaches.

Distribution of Literature/Solicitation

You might have wondered why the only advertising along the beach is by airplane banner or a lighted boat. Well, it's because other forms are against the law here. No one can distribute any-thing in the genre of pamphlets, advertisements, handbills, or circulars. It is also a "no-no" to con-duct business of any kind on the beach, includ-ing promotional devices such as free samples or admission passes.

Fireworks

Unincorporated areas of Horry County are the only places where fireworks are permitted (they're not allowed within any city limits). Use is restricted to private property between the hours of 10 a.m. and 10 p.m.

Glass Containers

It is unlawful to take any glass bottle, drinking glass, or other glass containers to the beach with you.

Horses

Horses are not allowed on the Strand in North Myrtle Beach. Riders in Myrtle Beach are only allowed after the third Saturday in November until the last day of February, with access from Myrtle Beach State Park. In Surfside, horses are banned from the beach April 1 through Novem-ber 1, and in Horry County, horses are banned from beaches March 1 through October 31.

Littering

Although you would never believe it, consider-ing the mountains of trash collected along the Strand every fall during Beach Sweep, littering on the beach or in the water is against the law. This includes any glass, bottles, cans, paper, garbage, waste, or refuse.

Motorized Watercraft

In North Myrtle Beach motorized watercraft can-not be launched from the beach between 9 a.m. and 5 p.m. from May 15 through September 15. Vehicles must be kept at least 50 yards from swimmers. In Myrtle Beach, all motorized craft must be at least 50 yards beyond bathers; Jet Skis must be at least 100 yards away. No motorized boats are allowed at Surfside Beach.

All boats must be registered with a permit secured from a lifeguard. Boats must not be left unattended between 8 p.m. and 8 a.m. In Horry County boaters cannot endanger swimmers and must be at least 400 feet from the shore and 500 feet from any fishing pier.

Animal Laws

In North Myrtle Beach, Myrtle Beach, and Surfside Beach, dogs in public must be kept on a leash at all times. From May 15 through September 15, no dogs are allowed on the beach between 9 a.m. and 5 p.m. In Myrtle Beach between 21st Avenue North and 13th Avenue South, no animals are allowed on the beach or on Ocean Boulevard at any time of year.

Rafts and Floats

In Myrtle Beach and in Horry County areas, rafts must be covered with fabric and have ropes attached to their entire perimeters.

Sand Dunes, Sea Oats, and Beach Grass

It is illegal to walk on sand dunes and to pick or otherwise damage sea oats, beach grass, or sand fencing.

Sleeping on the Beach

Myrtle Beach, North Myrtle Beach, and Horry County forbid sleeping on the beach between 9 p.m. and sunrise. In Surfside Beach people must not sleep in or around automobiles or motor vehicles on the street, in an alleyway, or at public accesses.

Swimming

Swimming in the ocean isn't the same as swim-ming in a lake, river, or pool, so don't expect it to be. Veteran ocean swimmers don't fear the ocean, its waves, or currents, but they have a healthy respect for it. Caution and common sense are the keys.

One of the most important things to remem-ber is that the lifeguard, young and good-looking

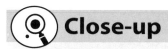 **Close-up**

The Grand Strand Beach Renourishment Project

Few would argue the fact that the Grand Strand's 60 miles of shoreline is the foundation of the area's status as a tourism mecca. Hundreds of thousands of people visit South Carolina's coast each year. In fact, during the summer months the population of Horry County swells to 10 times its winter population.

Unfortunately, many beaches are threatened with the persistent problem of land loss. Population growth and increased development have created a situation in which beach erosion can have severe economic consequences. Estimates reveal that approximately $3 trillion of the nation's coastal development is vulnerable to erosion. It is also estimated that 70 percent of the world's beaches are undergoing erosion, with percentages approaching 90 percent along the Atlantic coastal plain.

There are two general categories of erosion control on sand beaches. The first type is hard stabilization, or armoring, where structures such as seawalls, groins, revetments, and offshore breakwaters are built to help protect development along shorelines. But these structures can be destructive to recreational beaches. Accordingly, South Carolina adopted the Beachfront Management Act in 1988; state legislation now prevents further armoring of the Palmetto State's beaches.

Beach nourishment is a popular option for maintaining recreational beaches.

Beach nourishment, renourishment, and replenishment are interchangeable terms for the process of placing sand on an eroding shore in order to restore and/or maintain recreational beaches. More than 200 beaches in the United States have experienced some renourishment effort. At least nine beaches in South Carolina have been replenished at some point in their history. The state's earliest renourishment project occurred in 1954 on Edisto Island.

Beach renourishment along the Grand Strand is a never-ending process. In November 2007, the Grand Strand began its third major renourishment effort in 20 years. The yearlong, $30-million project stretching from Little River Inlet to Georgetown County was in response to a 2005–2006 State of the Beach Report that declared the whole Grand Strand at risk. Seventy-five percent of the funding came through the U.S. Army Corps of Engineers.

The price tag is actually small considering the last renourishment in 1996 cost $54 million to replenish 25 miles of strand in North Myrtle Beach alone. At that time, offshore sand barges served as sediment sources and hydraulically pumped sand directly to the beach itself, where it was spread by bulldozers.

The first major nourishment undertaking took place in the mid 1980s along the whole stretch of the Grand Strand. At that time, 59,539 dump-truck loads of sand were brought in during a 24-hour-a-day, seven-day-a-week operation. That effort was partially undone in 1989 when Hurricane Hugo roared ashore and emergency nourishment work was needed.

As late as the summer of 2009, the Army Corps of Engineers was reporting that Garden City Beach/Surfside Beach had received 750,000 cubic yards of sand over 7.7 miles. Myrtle Beach was to receive 1.5 million cubic yards of sand over 9 miles and North Myrtle Beach 750,000 cubic yards over 8.6 miles. The sand was dredged from sites about 3 miles offshore.

though he or she might be, has trained rigorously for this job. Listen to the lifeguard.

All Grand Strand beaches set shoulder-deep and 50-yards-offshore limits for swimmers, but the lifeguard has the authority to keep you in closer if he or she believes conditions warrant it. Disobeying the lifeguard can result in arrest and charges; fines can run from $25 to $200.

Thong Bathing Suits/ Nudity

It is illegal to wear a thong bathing suit in North Myrtle Beach, Myrtle Beach, or Surfside Beach. Skinny-dippers and nudists, take note: You can be arrested for public nudity on the beach or at any beach-access point.

Noise

It is a violation to play any radio or similar device loud enough to disturb persons in dwellings, hotels, or residences. This ordinance also includes vehicles and motorcycles with loud exhaust pipes.

BEACH WHEELCHAIRS

Beach wheelchairs are available for free to disabled persons in the Myrtle Beach area. The chairs are designed with oversize rubber wheels that make rolling on a sandy surface easy.

In Myrtle Beach, beach wheelchairs are available at the following lifeguard stands, which also offer handicap parking. For details call (843) 918-1000.

- 77th Avenue N.
- 72nd Avenue N.
- 54th Avenue N.
- 24th Avenue N.
- Eighth Avenue N.
- Fifth Avenue N.
- Eighth Avenue S.
- 20th Avenue S.

In North Myrtle Beach, wheelchairs are available Monday through Friday at the Recreation Center on Possum Trot Road. Call (843) 280-5584 to reserve one. Handicap beach accesses are at the following locations:

- Main Street
- Sea Mountain Highway
- Fourth Avenue N.
- Sixth Avenue S.
- Ninth Avenue S.
- 15th Avenue S.
- 17th Avenue S.
- 21st Avenue S.

- 27th Avenue S.
- 39th Avenue S.
- 46th Avenue S.

In Surfside Beach, wheelchairs are available by calling (843) 913-6368. Handicap beach accesses are at the following locations:

- Third Avenue N.
- Surfside Drive (at Surfside Pier)
- Melody Lane

In the off-season, call the police department for assistance. Although there is no fee for using the wheelchair, a one-hour limit is requested, unless no one else wishes to use it. Beachgoing wheelchairs must be pushed by a second party.

JELLYFISH

Jellyfish visits are predictable when southeastern winds blow the live gooey masses into warm, shallow waters. Some are perfectly harmless, but the stinging variety will produce a swelling welt similar to a wound caused by the lash of a whip. And don't be fooled! They can sting even after they wash up on shore. Common symptoms from the venom of a Portuguese man-of-war, for instance, can include nausea, vomiting, and muscle cramps. The man-of-war type is actually a colony of jellyfish contained below a 10-inch-long purple and blue float. Tentacles have been known to reach 20 feet and are described by experts as "self-contained, spring-loaded venom glands" that zap a swimmer or anything else that gets in the way. If you're frolicking in the ocean late in the summer and see a blue, football-shape mass floating around, get out of the way.

The sea nettle form of the medusa family is the least toxic, unless you're highly allergic to its formula of venom. Sea nettles are umbrella-shaped, usually spanning 6 inches in diameter and showing a red pigment. Their tentacles are 5 to 7 feet long, and even when beached, they can attack if their stinging cells are still wet.

Cabbage head, or cannonball, jellyfish is the only generally harmless variety that descends upon Grand Strand shores. Clear on top with red sides, they get their name from the fact that they resemble a head of cabbage.

Since the water-based toxins of jellyfish react to proteins, meat tenderizer is the most effective way to treat stings, and it should be the first line of treatment. If meat tenderizer is not on hand, some people use vinegar. All area lifeguards carry a specially formulated ointment (cortisone, meat tenderizer, and Vaseline) for jellyfish stings and will be more than happy to share it with you. Most often, tentacles or nettles are left on the victim's skin and need to be removed. Always use tweezers or run the edge of a credit card along the area to remove nettles. Rinse the area with alcohol, then apply ointment or meat tenderizer.

SHELL COLLECTING

Seashells are considered by many to be timeless art treasures. But unlike most objets d'art, they are created by Mother Nature, given to us by the sea, and the price is right—they're free. Since the beginning of recorded time, mankind has been fascinated by seashells. They are found in excavated ancient temples, graves, and sacred statues. Native Americans used scallop shells as dishes and made weapons from the sharp lips of others. Shell cups and ornaments were used in religious and war ceremonies as well as to top burial mounds.

How We Get Seashells

It is important to note that a shell is actually the splendidly built home of a living mollusk, fashioned from lime taken from the seawater. If you collect a shell that is empty, you are justifiably taking a discarded house. But if you snatch one from the beach that still holds a living organism, you are killing that mollusk. A mollusk's internal organs are covered by a sac of skin called a mantle, and this organ manufactures the shell by secreting a substance that mixes with lime taken from food. The richer the food source, the thicker and more colorful the shell. Shell homes are built, bit by bit, in layers. Color comes from a rhythm of

pigments fed to the shell at particular times in its development. Sunlight and heat also influence color, which is why shells of the same species might vary greatly in pigment.

Collection Tips

Whenever there is turbulence in the sea from tropical storms or hurricanes, you can bet that shorelines will be stocked with shells. After Hurricane Fran thundered by the Grand Strand in September 1996, Huntington Beach State Park reported its jetties were knee-deep in whelks and horse conchs.

The Grand Strand beach has also kicked up 60-million-year-old fossils. It's true! In April 1997 a retired high-school teacher identified a strange object, found by the hundreds on a North Myrtle Beach section of beach, as 60-million-year-old casts of clam shells. They were mistaken by many as fossilized turtle heads. Richard E. Petit, a research associate with the Smithsonian Institute, checked them out and confirmed that the molds were formed inside Cucullaea, a mollusk that became extinct in this part of the world a little less than 60 million years ago. Petit explained that they look like miniature stone turtle heads due to the employ shell filling with fine silt that hardened over the millennia.

Normally, the best time to search out shells is during a new or full moon and always at low tide. You'll discover the most abundant selection around jetties in Garden City Beach, Murrells Inlet, and Huntington Beach State Park. If you're a serious collector, a field trip to one of the barrier islands, such as Shell Island, will reveal a treasure trove of seashells, since these keys are uninhabited, virgin territory.

To take full advantage of your seashell-collecting experience along the Strand, we suggest contacting Steve Roth at Huntington Beach State Park, (843) 235-8755; the Grand Strand Shell Club, (843) 397-4890 (or e-mail gsshellclub@ aol.com); or Ken Moran, of the South Carolina Shell and Marine Life Club, at carolinash@aol .com. Beachcombing and shell-collecting romps are offered several times each week year-round and are free with paid admission to Huntington Beach State Park (refer to the Parks and Recreation chapter for details on the park).

The Grand Strand Shell Club has been in existence for more than 15 years, with the express purpose of educating the public and preserving shell species. If you would like to join the 150 members of this shelling club, an annual membership costs a mere $5 for an individual and $8 for your whole family. The group coordinates numerous field trips every year, a Seashell Auction (the main fund-raising event), and exhibitions at area malls. In conjunction with the city of Myrtle Beach, the Shell Club has created an extensive and fascinating shell display that is housed at the Myrtle Beach Convention Center. More than 500 shells are showcased, representing more than 150 species.

For a real treat, feast your eyes on a personal collection of more than 7,000 shells and fossils at the nature center established at Ocean Lakes Campground, 6001 US 17 South in Myrtle Beach. Retired minister Leonard Raker displays the result of his half-century obsession with the sea's bounty.

Actually, it's a love story. When Raker was dating his wife, he found a beautiful and rare shell and gave it to her. She lost it. The young man has been combing beaches from Prince Edward Island, Canada, to Honolulu ever since for a replacement. To this day, he hasn't found that particular shell anywhere, but he has amassed an impressive collection that includes microscopic species.

Leonard Raker receives no salary but shares his shells and fossils with the world and holds educational programs at the center. If you are not a guest at the campground, please call Mr. Raker at (843) 238-4908 to make an appointment to view his fascinating collection.

Species along the Strand

You're in shell-collecting heaven, with more than 700 species washing up regularly on Grand Strand shores, including a host of rare, sought-after varieties. The most common classes of shells to be found are pelecypods (bivalves)—two shells that have a hinge-like closing—and gastropods (univalves), which are one-shelled creatures. Here you'll also find an abundance of sand dollars (echinoderms), relatives of the starfish. Because Gulf Stream currents come to us from Florida, you might be lucky enough to snap up a Florida horse conch, the largest known univalve, which grows up to 24 inches. Another shelling jackpot that can be found along the Grand Strand is the left-handed lightning whelk, considered a prize since it grows counterclockwise and can reach up to 18 inches in size. Bivalves from the cockle family that regularly visit our shores are the lemon, prickly, and giant Atlantic shells. The notated clam, with its zigzag scrawling, is a fairly common find. Keep an eye out for South Carolina's state shell, the lettered olive. It's known for its glossy appearance caused by its owner embracing it before he or she leaves home. And our neighbor North Carolina consistently releases its state shell to us—the very beautiful Scotch bonnet.

HURRICANES: DON'T GET CAUGHT BLOWIN' IN THE WIND

Hurricanes, tornadoes, and gusty tropical storms are no strangers to Grand Stranders. Nearly every year the area is threatened to be directly hit by hurricanes. Each hurricane brings its own brand of wrath, whipping residences and businesses with high winds and teeming rains that raise roof shingles, blow away outdoor signs, and bend palm trees to the ground. With every one of these storms, thousands of residents are left without power for days at a time, and flooding sends riverfront homeowners to higher ground. State officials and locals alike take fast and strong measures to protect life and property when alerted to each impending hurricane, recalling the devastation wrought when Hurricane Hugo hit the Strand in 1989. While many considered the mandatory evacuation order an extreme measure at the time, Hugo reminded folks why

Hurricane Hazel claimed 95 lives in 1954, before advanced mass communication.

The September day Hugo arrived was not unlike any other beautiful fall day along the Grand Strand, with blue Carolina skies, warm but not humid. Light swirls of wind blew around pieces of loose paper by late afternoon, but nothing noticeable foretold of the coming onslaught. Having worked in weather forecasting for years, I (Janice) was more than slightly concerned as I watched the storm growing. At that time, I was working at CNN headquarters in Atlanta, and after talking to our weather guys, my sisters and I ganged up on my mother in a conference call and convinced her to flee the home my grandparents built in the 1930s. Having lived through the horrors of Hazel and seen its aftermath, she agreed, taping up the windows, packing up my grandmother and family photographs, and evacuating to my sister's home in Charlotte.

We remained in touch with terrified neighbors who stayed until they lost their phone lines, and then relived the terror a few hours later as Hugo kept moving inland and slammed into Charlotte, bringing rain and tornadoes. Those whirling dervishes were responsible for tossing around mobile homes, selectively demolishing beach houses, and snapping Carolina pines from the top, leaving behind nothing but seawater-burnt needles.

Be advised, the advent of a hurricane is nothing to fool around with. This special section has been included to give you all necessary information to keep yourself and your family as safe as possible in the face of such a natural disaster.

Hurricanes, Tropical Storms, and Tornadoes

Tropical storms and hurricanes that hit the eastern United States usually begin off the coast of Africa during late summer, when seas near the equator are unusually warm. A tropical depression is the first step in creating a full-fledged hurricane. Winds begin to rotate in a pattern, increasing to about 31 miles per hour as pressure drops near the center. Narrow bands of rainfall form, some resulting in heavy downpours. Tropical depressions are defined as organized, sustained winds of less than 40 mph.

A definite circular wind pattern has developed by the time a tropical storm is upon us. Warm, moist air is pumped into the weather system by wind speeds of up to 74 mph, causing heavy rainfall and a pattern of squall lines. Tropical storms carry winds from 40 to 74 mph.

Hurricanes are huge atmospheric heat pumps that pull in moist air from the ocean's surface to gain power. The air converges in the center and spirals upward. As it rises the air cools and thunderstorms form. The ocean surface under the spiral acts as a low-pressure area. Cool, dry air is cycled downward, where it is warmed by the sea and rises to continue the swirling cycle.

A hurricane's strength depends largely on the degree to which air is allowed to flow unhindered into and out of the central column, or eye. Hurricanes gain their classification when winds roar above 74 mph.

Tornadoes are funnel clouds. Scientists cannot agree on exactly what causes such a phenomenon. Some claim the origin to be vigorous updrafts in a thundercloud; others think the cause is falling hail. In any case, a spinning funnel cloud has been known to lift cars and rip apart buildings as its vacuum action sucks in air from the ground and carries it upward. The weakest type of tornado blows out from a thunderstorm, usually lasting less than five minutes with winds rarely exceeding 150 mph. Large tornadoes can stir up enough wind to travel as fast as 300 mph. In rare instances, twisters have lasted for hours, measured a half-mile wide, and traveled more than 200 miles.

Advance Preparation: Surviving a Hurricane

When you live in a coastal area, you need to have an advance plan for hurricanes, just as you would for a house fire. Since inland motels fill up quickly with the warning of a hurricane, formulate some idea of where you will go if evacuation is necessary. Gather basic supplies required for securing your home and valuables now. Keep them stored in the garage or some other accessible room.

Items to keep on hand: plywood for boarding the outside of windows, tape, rain gear, batteries, rope, bottled water, canned foods (don't forget the can opener), flashlights, a battery-operated radio, candles, and first-aid supplies. All of these items sell out in a hurry when a storm is coming, so it's smart to always keep them in supply.

If both parents in a household work, and if you have children who work, develop a plan of communication in the event of a hurricane warning or evacuation order. Determine where you will meet and who is responsible for what facets of your preparedness plan. Think through how you will assist an invalid or disabled member of your family.

Evacuation shelters offer only the bare necessities. Store your valuables and irreplaceable keepsakes in empty appliances and put plastic bags over household goods such as televisions, lamps, and computers. Before you evacuate, let a friend or relative outside the area know of your intended destination.

What to Do During a Hurricane Watch

A hurricane watch is issued when there is a threat of such conditions in your area within 24 to 36 hours. Begin to monitor storm reports on various radio and television stations. Rely only on facts presented by the media and emergency officials. This is the time to refill any necessary prescriptions (we suggest two weeks' worth) and fill up your vehicle's gas tank. You could lose precious time waiting in line at the gas pump, and if electricity goes out, pumps won't operate. If you will need cash for travel, get it during the "watch" time frame. ATMs also will have waiting lines and do not work without electricity.

Specifically, have these items stocked in your home: canned food and juices; dried fruit; bread; cookies; crackers; peanut butter and jelly; coffee and tea; enough bottled water for a gallon per person per day for two weeks; ice to cool food

and charcoal (for a hibachi or grill) to cook it; a water-purification kit; disposable plates, cups, and utensils; infant-care items; a battery-operated radio, TV, and clock; mosquito repellent; ice chest; plastic trash bags; chlorinated bleach; fire extinguisher; cleanup supplies; toilet paper, paper towels, and premoistened towelettes.

Check mobile-home tie-downs and secure lawn furniture or other loose outdoor items. Moor small watercraft or move boats to safety. Tape, board, or shutter windows to help prevent glass from shattering and wedge sliding-glass doors to prevent them from lifting off their tracks. What will you do with the pets? Now is the time to determine whether you will leave them in the house or take them to a kennel. Evacuation shelters do not allow pets of any kind. For your pet's sake have the following necessities on hand: proper identification collar and rabies tag; carrier or cage; leash; water and food bowls; any medications; newspapers or cat litter; and proof of vaccinations.

i Myrtle Beach has instituted an Emergency Operations Center (EOC) to address hurricanes or other disasters as they're approaching and after their impact. The general phone number for the EOC is (843) 918-1400, but it is activated only when emergency services are being used.

What to Do during a Hurricane Warning

Hurricane warnings are issued when conditions are expected in your area within 24 hours or less. Stay tuned to radio or television for official bulletins and make sure everything is boarded and taped. If you decide to stay in your home during a hurricane, understand that emergency vehicles and personnel are taken off the roads when winds reach 55 mph or more. If any member of your family has special needs, make sure your local EMS has that information.

Stay on the downside of the house away from windows, skylights, and glass doors. Clean appropriate containers and your bathtub for storing water. Use the telephone only in an emergency. If you lose power, turn off major appliances to reduce damage and curtail a power surge when electricity is resumed. A hard-and-fast rule is never to stay in a mobile home or an area within a flood zone under any condition during a hurricane. Before you evacuate, shut off water and electricity at main stations and securely lock up.

Hurricane Shelters

When evacuation is imminent, keep an ear cocked to local radio and television for updated shelter locations. Locations may change or become full during the course of a storm. As of this writing, the American Red Cross reports that the following two shelters will be opened within four hours after each school closes following a voluntary evacuation request from the state's governor: South Conway Elementary School at 3001 Fourth Ave. in Conway and Loris Elementary at 901 East Hwy. 9 in Loris.

In the event of a mandatory evacuation, the following shelters will open as soon as possible: Aynor Elementary School, 516 Jordanville Rd. in Aynor; Aynor High School, 201 Jordanville Hwy. in Aynor; Conway Elementary School, 1101 Snowhill Dr. in Conway; Conway High School, 2301 Church St. in Conway; Pee Dee Elementary School, 6555 Hwy. 134 in Conway; Whitmore Park Middle School, 1808 Rhue St. in Conway; and, in Georgetown County, Pleasant Hill High School, Schoolhouse Drive in Hemingway; and Andrews Elementary School, 13072 County Line Rd. (Highway 41) in Andrews.

Be prepared for shelter accommodations: You will be sleeping on the floor or a cot, food might not be available, there are no provisions for medical services, and pets are not allowed. Bring pillows, blankets, sleeping bags or air mattresses, extra clothing, shoes, eyeglasses, lightweight folding chairs and cots, and personal hygiene items. Have important papers and identification with you. You may want to put these items in plastic bags to protect against moisture.

Contact the local Red Cross chapter at (843) 477-0020 for further information on disaster preparedness for your business and family.

WATER SPORTS

Worldwide, there are more exciting waters to explore, but for the sheer pleasure of participating in water sports, the Grand Strand has its fair share of fans. In fact, our sun-kissed
area is a perfect place to learn and practice the rudiments of a particular water sport. The
Intracoastal Waterway and Black River offer calmer waters to test out waterskiing, there are
plenty of scuba-diving courses available and some interesting underwater ledges and wrecks
to explore, and the relatively less powerful breakers of the Atlantic Ocean have never discour-
aged a novice surfer.

Whether you're adept at a water sport or want to try one out, this chapter should send you
in the right direction.

SURFING

South Carolina waters are not especially good
for surfing except when a hurricane or other
storm is approaching. Unlike the West Coast, our
East Coast has a continental shelf more than 60
miles off the shore that forms a gradual upgrade
toward the beach. By Mother Nature's design,
wave swells start breaking when they hit the
shelf, diminishing the seawater rollers as they
travel inland.

Still the Grand Strand has its share of avid
surfers. On just about any day, you'll see people
waxing their boards and rushing to the water to
ride the wall or hit the lip.

An active and proud community of surfers—
an interesting mix of clergy, business owners,
restaurant workers, and high-school and college
students—is alive and well along the Strand. The
well-established Northern South Carolina Chapter
of the Eastern Surfing Association now hails more
than 200-plus members, ranging in age from 4
to 52 years old. The association holds competitions throughout the year along the Strand; local
amateur surfers hoping to turn professional vie
for points to help them get into meets around
the country. For information call Denny Green at
(843) 997-9184 or e-mail him at nsc@surfesa.org,
or visit www.nscsurfing.com.

Grand Strand surfing enthusiasts all have
slightly different reasons for their love of the
sport: Some refer to surfing as a way of life; others cite the sport as a natural, addictive high; and
some even wax spiritual that surfing is God's way
of teaching love and respect for the ocean.

Whatever the motivation to engage in wave
riding, the smaller, calmer swells along the Grand
Strand give beginners a wonderful chance to
learn the sport while developing the strength,
flexibility, endurance, and balance needed to do
it well.

Rules of Surfing

Surfing is restricted to certain areas and times on
all Grand Strand beaches. All surfers are required
to wear leashes. In Horry County surfers must not
endanger swimmers and must not surf within
300 feet of a fishing pier.

In North Myrtle Beach surfing and skim
boarding are forbidden between 9 a.m. and 4
p.m. from May 15 through September 15, except
in the following areas: near Cherry Grove Pier and
at 13th Avenue South, 28th Avenue South, 38th
Avenue South, and 6th Avenue North.

Surfboards are not allowed in Myrtle Beach
between 10 a.m. and 5 p.m. from April 30 through
September 15, except in four locations: 29th
Avenue South, 37th Avenue North through 47th
Avenue North, 82nd Avenue North to the city
limits, and from the south side of Eighth Avenue

North to the north end of the public boardwalk. (Last location open only from Oct 1 to Apr 15.)

In Surfside Beach surfing is not allowed from 10 a.m. to 5 p.m. except in the area between 14th Avenue North and 16th Avenue North and between 12th Avenue South and Melody Lane. There is no surfing within 300 yards or the pier. For more information on regulations, call (843) 650-4131.

There are a number of shops along the Grand Strand that cater exclusively to the sport of surfing. All of these outlets carry a full line of accessories and apparel, including wet suits, booties, gloves, hoods, and, of course, swimwear.

North Strand

BERT'S SURF SHOP
806 21st Ave. S., North Myrtle Beach
(888) 425-6284, (843) 272-7458
www.bertsurfshop.com
Bert's can set you up with boards from Bic as well as epoxy long boards. You can rent surfboards for 5 to 10 hours at a cost between $20 and $30. Bert's offers a full line of men's and ladies' clothing. The shop is generally open from 10 a.m. until 10 p.m., but seasonal schedules sometimes apply. Call ahead if you need to.

NORTH SHORE SURF SHOP
110 US 17 S., North Myrtle Beach
(843) 280-5071
www.stabilityskateboard.com
North Shore carries Wave Riding vehicles, as well as Action, Liar, and Lost boards. Kayaks, surfboards, and skim boards can be rented for $20 a day. North Shore also offers surfing lessons for $25 an hour.

SURF CITY
3300 US 17 S., North Myrtle Beach
(843) 272-1090
www.surfcitysurfshop.com
Surf City stocks new and used surfboards, skim boards, body boards, skateboards, and other related equipment. Rental rates range anywhere from $10 to $25 per day.

Myrtle Beach

SURF CITY
3001 North Kings Hwy.,
Myrtle Beach
(843) 626-7919
www.surfcitysurfshop.com
In operation since 1978, Surf City sells and rents surfboards, body boards, skateboards, and related equipment.

South Strand

SURF THE EARTH
47 Da Gullah Way, Pawleys Island
(800) 864-6752, (843) 235-3500
www.surf-the-earth.com
Surf the Earth is Pawleys Island's only complete surf shop, offering surfboards, skates and skateboards, surfboats, kayaks of all shapes and sizes, and a full range of clothing. Kayaks and surfboards are available for rental. Surf and kayak lessons, kayak tours, and free local delivery on rentals are also available. The shop is open Mon through Sat from 10 a.m. to 6 p.m., and on Sun from 10 a.m. to 4 p.m. They also offer private surf lessons for $50 and run a weeklong summer surf camp for kids for $250 per child.

VILLAGE SURF SHOP
500 Atlantic Ave., Garden City Beach
(843) 651-6396
2016 North Kings Hwy., Myrtle Beach
(843) 651-8176
www.villagesurf.com
Established in 1969, Village Surf Shop is the oldest hard-core surf shop around. If your passion dictates a custom-made surfboard, and your wallet is willing, this is the one and only place to visit along the Strand. Besides fashioning custom boards, this store carries Perfection, Rusty, Spyder, JC Hawaii, Kechele, RipCurl, Sharp Eye, and Lost name brands.

Owner Kelly Richards is usually found next door to this shop, covered in Styrofoam dust with rock music blaring as he shapes one of his masterpieces, called Perfection Surfboards. For more than two decades, Richards has made boards that are better suited to surfing the East Coast, having a wider surface and heavier weight that allows for a longer ride on smaller waves. The Village also rents surfboards for $20 a day, $30 for two days.

i The Grand Strand Chapter of the Surfrider Foundation is actively involved in efforts to keep beaches clean and safe, educate the public, and protect beach access. The Surfrider Foundation itself is an international, grassroots, nonprofit environmental organization with more than 30,000 members in the United States alone. For more information call (800) 743-SURF.

WATERSKIING

Especially along the Intracoastal Waterway on warm Sunday afternoons, the chugging and screeching of motors from powerboats is a familiar sound. This is when locals launch their vessels to socialize with friends, sunbathe, and partake in the exciting and fun sport of waterskiing.

The Black River in Georgetown is another popular waterskiing venue.

In South Carolina waterskiing is prohibited between sunset and sunrise. It is considered a three-person operation:

- The boat operator ensures the safe navigation of the vessel and skiers. He or she monitors the boat's speed, adjusting it to the abilities or desires of the skier.
- The observer, who must be at least 12 years old, takes responsibility for the skier's safety by keeping a constant eye on the person skimming across the water, the towrope, and the wakes. An alternative to an observer is a wide-angle rearview mirror adjusted so the operator can see the person in tow.
- The skier is responsible for not exceeding his or her abilities, helping to ensure the safe operation of the boat, and communicating with the operator of the vessel. A ski belt or PFD (personal flotation device) must be worn

unless the skier has a first-class or higher rating with the American Water Ski Association. But even if the skier is not wearing such an apparatus, an extra PFD must be aboard.

- For all waterskiing equipment and wet suits, visit the Sail & Ski Connection at 515 US 501 in Myrtle Beach; or give them a call at (843) 626-SAIL or (800) 868-7245.

SCUBA DIVING

Exploring the ocean and discovering its treasures is an unquestionably exciting experience. However, this sport, as much as any other, is inherently fraught with danger. Therefore, we urge you to educate yourself well about the rules, regulations, and risks associated with scuba diving and receive proper training from a certified instructor before strapping on a tank and plunging into the ocean's depths.

No diving is allowed in any waters within the city limits of Myrtle Beach or near piers. The sport can be legally practiced in Surfside Beach, but only if the diver is equipped with a flag to mark his/her underwater location. In all cases you aren't allowed to scuba dive unless you are certified, and every body of water has restrictions on underwater hunting.

Wrecks

Along with artificial reefs—mostly created by intentionally sunken vessels—and live bottom ledges, the Grand Strand offers some fascinating dive sites. Many are historically significant. In 1942 the *Hebe,* a Dutch merchant ship, and the *St. Cathan,* a British submarine chaser, collided and sank; at the time the vessels crossed paths, the *St. Cathan* was under blackout conditions to avoid a U-boat. These two wrecks now rest a quarter mile apart on the ocean floor, as they have for more than 60 years, providing refuge to myriad marine life. Experienced divers say it's a wonderful site to mingle with game fish and tropicals, search for historic artifacts, and take underwater photographs. Two unnamed wrecks occurred in Grand Strand waters in the 1800s, one of which is a copper-clad paddle-wheel steamer. Apparently, the scattered wreckage from each is replete with historic artifacts.

In 1964 while under tow to the Virgin Islands to become a floating hotel and casino, the *Richmond*—a 261-foot, five-deck passenger ship—sank off the coast of Georgetown during a storm. Most of the steel decks and the hull had remained intact since the accident until Hurricane Hugo hit in 1989, collapsing what remained of the hull. The wreckage is scattered but is still home to a wealth of fish species, including angels, butterflies, damsels, grouper, jacks, and spades.

Artificial Reefs

Since the briny waters of the Grand Strand area are underlaid by a sandy ocean floor that by nature offers little "live bottom" to attract sea life, the Grand Strand Saltwater Anglers Association, in conjunction with state and local fishing clubs, developed a program to create artificial reefs. These reefs have cultivated underwater forests where deserts formerly stood on the ocean's floor and turned salvage into ecological treasures. In short, artificial reefs provide abundant fishing and diving sites that are easily accessible to small craft.

One such reef, the Bill Perry—named in memory of a local young fisherman who died in a car accident—was built in 1992, 25 miles offshore. Sunken vessels at this spot include a shrimp boat, a tug boat, and two 115-foot military landing craft containing Polaris missiles, igniters, and control pads. In one year plant growth went wild. The site, a favorite for divers, resembles a thick, underwater forest with such dense fish activity that it is now sometimes difficult to pinpoint the reef. Large ivory coral is the most abundant around Bill Perry Reef.

Creating an artificial reef is not as easy as just sinking a large piece of machinery or broken-down vessel. Whatever is sunk must meet guidelines set forth by the South Carolina Department of Natural Resources. It must be cleaned, environmentally safe, and stripped of all floatable material, plastic, or oils. Then it must be hauled out to sea by barge and tug boat. Objects such as a

cement mixer fall to the ocean floor on their own, but ships must have holes blasted in them to sink as well as to provide the new reef with ventilation and water flow. The Department of Defense is the biggest contributor of materials for artificial reefs; it costs anywhere from $1,000 to a whopping $50,000 to properly prepare and sink them.

Other artificial sites that attract hundreds of divers each year include:
- the 10-mile Barge, where a 200-foot barge was sunk in 1972 in about 30 to 40 feet of water just off the Murrells Inlet coastline;
- the 11-mile Tug and Airplane, created using a 90-foot tugboat and, later, a Navy training plane;
- the BP-25, named after the 160-foot tanker *Bernard Perkins* that's sunk at the spot;
- the 468-foot-long WW II Amphibious Assault Troop Transport the USS *Vermilion,* which was sunk in 1988. The *Vermilion* was originally dropped in 107 feet of water, but the 1989 assault of Hurricane Hugo moved the wreck a quarter mile into 130 feet of water.

The latest, greatest dive site to hit the Grand Strand is called Barracuda Alley. In cooperation with the South Carolina Department of Natural Resources, this 150-foot barge—outfitted with structures of various shapes and designs that attract fish—was sunk in 63 feet of water early in 2000 alongside a group of 20 armored personnel carriers. With much of the structure rising 10 to 20 feet off the bottom, and with more than 100 feet of swim-throughs and a training platform, this is an excellent dive for everyone. Come and visit this site, about 10 miles from Little River Inlet, so you can see how it grows and changes throughout the years.

For further information on South Carolina's Artificial Reef Program, write to Artificial Reefs, P.O. Box 12559, Charleston, SC 29422–2559; call Bob Martore at (843) 953-9303; or visit www.dnr.state.sc.us.

Dive Shops

We suggest you contact or stop by the following dive shops to check out a good selection of scuba gear for sale or rent, to receive instruction and certification, or to book daily diving charters. All of the following shops offer PADI certification, and professional staff members can likely answer any questions you might have.

North Strand

COASTAL SCUBA

1901 US 17 S., North Myrtle Beach
(800) 249-9388, (800) 249-9388
www.coastalscuba.com

Coastal Scuba brings together many years of experience from its captains, instructors, and dive masters to make your diving experience the very best it can be. Every diver—from the newly certified to the seasoned veteran—will find a dive charter through Coastal Scuba; there are more than a half dozen to choose from, and they range in price from $75 to $125. A variety of classes—from minicourses to accelerated "executive-style" classes to full PADI certification and advanced instruction—are also offered.

The *Safari IV*, Coastal Scuba's dive vessel, is a 45-foot customized dive boat sleek enough to get to dive sites quickly and sturdy enough to offer stability against an occasionally unpredictable Atlantic. The boat is spacious and comfortable, complete with a full-size head (bathroom), two ice coolers for snacks, and a professional crew. She carries all Coast Guard–required equipment, including a first-aid kit and oxygen.

i The Myrtle Beach "Beach Patrol" is a vital unit within the city's police department. Every day of the year, 24 hours a day, they blanket the beach with services that include law enforcement, drowning prevention, rescue of distressed swimmers, and immediate at-the-scene care for the ill and/or injured. All Beach Patrol officers are certified ocean lifeguards with appropriate certifications in CPR, First Aid, and Ocean Rescue. For additional information call (843) 918- 1334 or visit www.cityofmyrtlebeach.com/police/beach.html.

Demand for diving is high, especially during the summer and on weekends, so please book early. Visit the Web site for lots of additional information.

Myrtle Beach

NU HORIZONS DIVE AND TRAVEL

515 US 501, Suite A, Myrtle Beach
(843) 839-1932
www.southcarolinadive.com

Nu Horizons is the largest and most complete full-service scuba-diving facility in Myrtle Beach and the only shop to offer dive charters from both the North and South Strand areas. Whether you are taking scuba-diving lessons to learn to dive or you are a seasoned scuba diver, Nu Horizons Dive and Travel offers something for everyone. Train in their indoor 17-foot heated dive tank or take part in open-water classes. Just bring your bathing suit and towel, and equipment for any class is available.

As part of Scuba Schools International, they offer accelerated beginning programs: Try Scuba or the Passport Diver Program. If you're ready to become a certified diver, then the Open Water Diver Program is for you. Those who need to update their skills may try SSI's Scuba Skills Update. The Snorkeling program is full of fun tips and advice to help make snorkeling easier and more enjoyable.

For those who are avid divers, feel free to join Nu Horizons's dive club, "Club Aquarius." There are also scuba-based-activities clubs for children 8 to 15 years old. They also plan regular diving trips to locations both within and outside the United States.

South Strand

EXPRESS WATERSPORTS

US 17 Business, Murrells Inlet
(866) 566-9338, (843) 357-3337
www.expresswatersports.com

Express Watersports is a year-round dive shop that features scuba rental as well as scuba training and dive trips. They rent state-of-the-art dive equipment from Sherwood, Mares, Cressi Sub, TUSA, and Zeagle. Their trips explore the many local wrecks and reefs along the South Carolina coast, with beginner, intermediate, and advanced dives.

The Express marina is directly behind its retail shop, making dive charter services quick and easy. Lessons range from $50 for the Discover Scuba course to $650 to become a dive master. Rates during the winter vary, so please call ahead. Courses are offered to those eight years and older. Dives range from basic open water to wreck diving and even night diving. Scuba Express has a custom-built, 46-foot Newton dive boat that is the top of the line as far as dive boats go. PADI Discover Scuba Diving lessons let you experience the thrill of diving without having to go into open water, as the lessons take place in the on-site pool under the supervision of Express Watersports professional instructors and dive masters. During your adventure, you will master some basic concepts and scuba skills. Express Watersports also arranges dive trips to other resort destinations, such as Hawaii and the Bahamas, from time to time.

WATER-SPORTS OUTLETS

Whether or not you're nautically inclined, you shouldn't miss experiencing the incredible feeling of gliding across the waves on a Windsurfer or WaveRunner; paddling the back bays and estuaries of coastal inland waters in a sea kayak; or soaring, suspended in air, as you parasail above the salty ocean spray.

We include a few establishments that provide the equipment you'll need to participate in these exhilarating activities. Kayaking seems to be the water sport of choice along the Grand Strand, following an impressive emergence of ecologically inclined tours. Kayaking is feasible for folks of almost any fitness and skill level, as it allows paddlers to explore waters and the surrounding landscape at a leisurely pace. If you're combing the area for equipment rentals during summer, you most likely will find more outlets than we've included here. That's because a number of independent businesspeople set up rental stands at local marinas until the end of the summer. If there's a marina close by, call ahead to see if it rents your favorite type of water buggy. (Refer to the Boating chapter for a listing of local marinas.) We mention only those venues that can be contacted year-round and have an established location.

Kayaking

Myrtle Beach
SAIL & SKI CONNECTION
515 US 501, Myrtle Beach
(800) 868-7245, (843) 626-SAIL
www.sailandskiconnection.com
Weather permitting, Sail & Ski runs weekly, supervised kayak tours along the salt marshes of Murrells Inlet. If a group has a special interest, this outfitter will do everything it can to make that interest a reality. They offer two- to four-hour salt marsh tours that range from $45 to $75 per person, depending on your group size. If you want to head out on your own, a one-day rental is $30.

South Strand
BLACK RIVER OUTDOORS CENTER
21 Garden Ave., US 701, Georgetown
(843) 546-4840
www.blackriveroutdoors.com
By canoe or kayak, Black River Outdoors Center takes watery advantage of the tidelands of Georgetown, one of the largest estuarine systems on the East Coast. Hundreds of miles of waterways offer something new and exciting at every turn: the Black River's cypress swamps; saltwater tidal creeks of Pawleys Island and Huntington Marsh; rice plantation canals of the Great Pee Dee and Waccamaw Rivers; the Cape Romain National Wildlife Refuge; the Francis Marion National Forest. All tours are guided and include all necessary equipment, safety instruction, and transportation. The waters are known to be slow moving. Mar through Oct, daily morning excursions last about four hours; evening paddle cruises—Tuesday, Wednesday, and Thursday from Apr until Labor Day—last around one and a half hours. During the winter months, morning trips are offered Wednesday and Saturday.

Kayaking tours of tidal saltwater creeks start out at Huntington Beach State Park and proceed through cordgrass marshes and along sandy beaches of Murrells Inlet to the causeway. This same trip is offered at night around periods of the full moon for the same price as the daytime treks; bring along your own food, drinks, and a flashlight if going at night.

Kayak and canoe tours of the Black River follow the ancient watery route of commerce that served rice and indigo plantations from the 1700s. These treks explore the untouched black-water cypress swamps, alive with ducks, wild turkeys, herons, alligators, and the swamp canary. Prices are the same as the previously mentioned saltwater creek trips.

Departing from East Bay Park Landing on the Sampit River in Georgetown, the Historic Harbor Paddle Cruise passes the Harborwalk, scores of fishing vessels, private yachts, the tall ship *Jolly Rover*, and the Kaminski House and Clock Tower. This tour is offered on summer nights at a cost of $35 per person; children younger than age seven go for free.

If the history of rice planting intrigues you, the Chicora Wood Plantation "Creeks and Canals" trip will take you to the remains of antebellum dikes and trunk gates once used to flood rice paddies. Creeks and hand-dug canals interlace the Great Pee Dee and Waccamaw Rivers and showcase vast plantations that sustained an aristocratic society who made millions growing "Waccamaw Gold."

The daytime version of this trip includes a peek from the water at one of the plantation homes. Half-day excursions cost $55 for adults and teens, $35 for ages 12 and younger. For a complete listing of tours and schedules, visit the Web site.

Jet Skiing, Parasailing, Wave Running, and More

In this section we include personal watercraft rentals where you are at the helm of fast and slick vessels. If it's a pontoon or sailboat you're specifically looking for, please refer to the Boating chapter for related information.

North Strand

MYRTLE BEACH WATER SPORTS OF LITTLE RIVER
Waterfront, Little River
(866) SEA-DOO, (843) 280-7777
www.myrtlebeachwatersports.com
Enjoy beautiful scenic views of Bird Island from your lofty parasail perch. Reservations are required. This water-sport resource also offers pontoons and Jet Skis. Open daily from 8 a.m. to 6 p.m., Mar through Oct.

Myrtle Beach

DOWNWIND SAILS
2915 South Ocean Blvd., Myrtle Beach
(843) 448-7245
www.downwindsailsmyrtlebeach.com
Rentals, rides, and lessons for bananas, Jet Skis, and parasails are available here. Prices vary depending on what equipment you want, the time of year, and what's in stock. It's a good bet, though, that you'll enjoy significant discounts after late August, when heavy tourist traffic dies down. Downwind Sails is open Apr to mid-Oct and is right on the beach. This is a great spot to hang out during the summer, with all of the boating action plus regular beach volleyball tournaments.

MYRTLE BEACH WATERSPORTS
5835 Dick Pond Rd., Myrtle Beach
(866) RENT-ATV, (843) 497-8848
www.myrtlebeachwatersports.com
This water-sports store rents Jet Skis, pontoons, and jetboats by the hour. Specials on rentals and tours are offered throughout the year, so be sure to inquire about any discounts you might be entitled to. This outlet is open seasonally 10 a.m. to 4 p.m. daily.

Personal watercraft have proven to be dangerous water-sports equipment in the hands of an inexperienced or impaired operator. Every year the Grand Strand mourns deaths caused by too young, too reckless, or too drunk personal watercraft drivers involved in boating accidents.

South Strand

CAPTAIN DICK'S MARINA

4123 US 17 Business, Murrells Inlet
(866) 577-3474, (843) 651-3676
www.captdicks.com

Parasailing flights are booked from this marina year-round, weather permitting. Bookings slow down considerably beginning in Oct and continuing throughout winter when winds are friskier and waters choppier. For about $55 you can enjoy a nearly two-hour boat trip and 12 to 15 minutes of soaring 200 to 300 feet above the ocean. Captain Dick's also rents genuine Yamaha WaveRunners. Cost is $75 for 45 minutes of riding inlet channels out into the ocean. You must be at least 16 years old to drive the Jet Ski or have an adult 18 or older on the same Jet Ski. There is no minimum age to ride, but all riders must be large enough to be secure in a life jacket.

MARLIN QUAY PARASAILING

Marlin Quay Marina, 1398 South Waccamaw Dr., Garden City Beach
(877) 670-3474, (843) 651-4444
www.marlinquay.com

This high-flying experience includes a one-and-a-half to two-hour boat ride in the Atlantic Ocean plus a 15-minute flight at more than 200 feet in the air. There must be six people per boat to make the excursion. Parasailing is offered Memorial Day through Labor Day. Call for pricing.

DAY TRIPS

Once upon a time there were lulls of "what can we do today" for Grand Strand visitors. These were usually rainy days when the beach was less than pleasant, long days during too-long vacations that needed a break in the monotony, and those disastrous days when the sun had turned the skin too lobster to handle another burning. But with the more recent growth along the Grand Strand, it is nearly impossible to find a day without some suitable activity, no matter what your particular interest.

This chapter offers suggestions for day trips. Any one of them will give you an up-close look at Southern culture, a taste of the extraordinary beauty and history of the Carolinas' coastal region, and generally something to do if you wonder what is just beyond the Strand's offerings. Zip to Conway or Charleston in South Carolina, or Wilmington, just across the state line in North Carolina, to spend a day enjoying the sights and return; you'll be cozy in your bed before the lines shorten on Restaurant Row.

CHARLESTON

Charleston. The very name of this beautiful city conjures up images of sprawling plantations, honey-dipped Southern belles, and the sweet bouquet of magnolia floating on the ocean breeze. Charleston, a synergy of charm and cosmopolitan flair, is steeped in a history that parallels the South itself—indeed, the little city is a microcosm of the whole South. More distinctive than any other Southern city, Charleston has found its way into operas, novels, movies, television dramas, and even soap operas. Simply put, there's no place like it in all the world, and you don't dare get as close as Myrtle Beach and miss out on the enchantment.

It will come as no surprise that Charleston boasts far too many enticements to mention even a respectable fraction in this chapter. If you want to know more, pick up a copy of Insiders' Guide to Charleston. Cover to cover, it's packed with the particulars you'll need to know to enjoy this fascinating city to its fullest extent.

Anytime is a great time to visit the area, but spring, as a whole, is remarkable, with warm days, crisp nights, and flowers galore. In May the **Spoleto** international arts festival exacts a welcome grip on the city. Consistently a huge success, Spoleto is a celebration of opera, jazz, theater, dance, and visual arts sometimes categorized as classical and sometimes modern enough to cause controversy. People from all over the globe return year after year, and the numbers keep growing. For more information about the festival, write P.O. Box 157, Charleston, SC 29402; call (843) 579-3100; or visit www.spoletousa.org.

In September the **Charleston Preservation Society** opens many of the city's privately owned homes and gardens during its annual candlelight tour series. This is the second of our two favorite times to visit. Many of the tours include chamber music and champagne receptions, and all are imbued with an authentic sense of yesteryear. Learn more by calling (843) 722-4630, or visit them online at www.preservationsociety.org.

Many of Charleston's legendary plantations are open to the public. All of the gardens are memorable; some are outright unforgettable. The most popular and well-known of the lineup: **Drayton Hall,** (843) 769-2600, www.draytonhall .org; Middleton Place, (800) 782-3608, www.mid dletonplace.org; **Magnolia Plantation and Gardens,** (800) 367-3517, www.magnoliaplantation .com; **Cypress Gardens,** (843) 553-0515, www

.cypressgardens.org, which was once part of Dean Hall Plantation; and **Boone Hall,** (843) 884-4371, www.boonehallplantation.com. Admission to the plantations vary but ranges from $6.00 to $17.50. Each plantation offers senior citizen discounts.

Charles Towne Landing, 1500 Old Towne Rd., (843) 852-4200, a South Carolina state park, is also a former plantation. Today the park is dedicated to re-creating and interpreting the first permanent English settlement in the Carolinas, on this site in 1670. There's a film about the history of the Lowcountry, an animal forest, a reproduction of a 17th-century trading vessel, and a colonial area where visitors can observe candle making, open-fire cooking, woodworking, and the colony's first printing press. Bicycles, the best way to get around, are available for rent. Hours are 8:30 a.m. to 5 p.m. Admission is $5.00 for adults, $3.25 for in-state seniors, and $3.00 for children ages 6 through 15. Children 5 and younger are admitted free. Learn more at www.charlestowne.org.

Nearly every schoolchild in South Carolina has been to the **Fort Sumter National Monument** in Charleston Harbor at least once. Many know the story by heart. In 1861 Confederate soldiers fired upon Union forces stationed at the fort, and the Civil War began. You can get to Fort Sumter by boat only, but that's a big part of the fun. Catch the tour at Liberty Square at 340 Concord St. or at Patriots Point in Mount Pleasant. Call (843) 722-1691 for more information or visit www.nps.gov/fosu.

Charleston is home to **The Citadel,** 171 Moultrie St., (843) 225-3294, once an all-male state-supported military college that a few years ago was the center of much controversy over the court-

ordered admittance of women. If you're headed to Charleston, plan your trip to include a Friday when school is in session so you can watch the weekly dress parade; it starts at 3:45 p.m. on most days. Visit the Citadel online at www.citadel.edu.

Charleston is chock-full of museums and carefully preserved historic homes, many of which are open to the public. The Charleston Visitor's Center, 375 Meeting St., (843) 724-7420, is a good place to start your visit. You can buy tickets here to most area attractions, and the staff will offer lots of friendly tourist advice. The center is open Monday through Saturday from 10 a.m. to 5 p.m., and Sunday from 2 to 5 p.m.

If you're looking for excellent shopping alternatives, Charleston sports a fine array. So if your day trip isn't full to overflowing, at least check out King Street and the Old Market area. The selections are overwhelming: old shops, new shops, food shops, open-air shops. It's something you'll have to experience to understand.

Charleston is a scenic two-hour trip from Myrtle Beach. Take US 17 South. Even the trip down to Charleston is a great experience. Driving through **Frances Marion National Park** shows you some of the finest coastal natural beauty in America—and, alas, some of the greatest devastation to forest and wildlife areas by a hurricane (the centuries-old trees will never recover from the damage wrought by Hurricane Hugo, and the area shows the loss).

The historic antebellum village of **McClellanville** (also devastated by Hugo, but well recovered) is about halfway along the route and offers some of the finest white oak–lined streets and hanging moss in South Carolina. Just before you get to Charleston, the little village of Mt. Pleasant will amaze you with roadside huts set up to sell baskets, bowls, and other carriers woven from South Carolina sweetgrass—an art developed by slaves and handed down through the generations to just a handful of old women who still remember the method. These beautiful objects are also among the most utilitarian pieces you can find. Museums pay fortunes for them; here and here alone you can find them on the roadside for what'll seem like a steal.

> **i** If you decide to explore Charleston, be sure to leave plenty of time to stop along the way. If you are staying in Myrtle Beach, the two-hour drive south to Charleston is filled with diversions: a detour into Murrells Inlet or Pawleys Island, a tour of Hampton Plantation, roadside produce stands, historical markers. Watch for the signs!

ℹ️ Though you can find sweetgrass baskets in many shops and markets around the Grand Strand, wait until you get to Charleston for the biggest selection of shapes and styles and so you can meet the craftspeople. In Mt. Pleasant, a suburb north of Charleston that you will drive through, the women who spend their days weaving the reeds set up roadside stands along US 17. Stands with baskets are also in the historic section of Charleston, convenient to the favorite walking paths of tourists and locals alike.

CONWAY

Conway is one of the prettiest little towns you'll ever stumble upon if you seek a typical Southern small town; it's filled with friendly folks who can demonstrate the very essence of Southern hospitality. A mere 14 miles from Myrtle Beach, most people are introduced to Conway as they drive through it en route to Myrtle Beach. Most people don't realize that a few blocks east of the congestion on US 501 Bypass, just beyond the choke of auto exhaust, is Conway's historic section. In addition to its rich history, thanks to the extensive planting and protection of trees, Conway has been designated a Tree City, USA. However, the newest trees aren't the ones that impress visitors most; the enormous age-old oaks are what Conwayites and tourists love best. Local residents have gone to great lengths to preserve and protect their oaks. In some cases they have even constructed roads around the majestic trees! The reward is a cool canopy of shade unfurling across streets where lovely homes date from a century ago and more.

One of the first and finest oaks you'll see as you drive down Conway's Main Street is **the Wade Hampton Oak** in front of the Horry County Museum. A plaque on the oak commemorates the day in 1876 when Confederate general Wade Hampton brought his campaign for the governorship to Conway and addressed a crowd from beneath the tree. Many years later,

when construction of a railroad threatened the historic hardwood, a spirited local lady, Mary Beaty, brandished a loaded shotgun and ordered workers, "Touch not a single bough."

Just across the street from the Horry County Museum, another stately oak spills shade in the yard of the First Methodist Church. Its gnarled branches stretch over the historic graves in the cemetery. Don't miss the oak on Elm Street at Fifth Avenue around which motorists have to maneuver their cars. On Sixth Avenue, near Elm Street, the road literally splits in half to go around another tree. A monument at the foot of this tree was erected in honor of soldiers who died defending the Confederacy. The blacktop makes way for another oak at the intersection of Seventh Avenue and Beaty Street. If time permits, allow yourself the leisure to mosey along nearby streets; you'll enjoy a veritable parade of the beautiful old trees that typify the South at its finest. The Conway Chamber of Commerce publishes *A Guide to Conway's Fine Oaks,* an illustrated booklet with facts, poems dedicated to the trees, and a self-guided tour.

But before you take off for a lazy amble beneath the trees, stop for an enlightening tour at the **Horry County Museum,** 428 Main St., (843) 915-5320. The museum is open 9 a.m. to 5 p.m. Monday through Saturday, and one of its most popular exhibits includes a variety of Lowcountry animals. Sadly, burgeoning development in the area has endangered many species. Those on display were accidentally killed (that's right, there is a "roadkill" display in the museum). In addition to birds, alligators, and more, you can see everybody's favorite: an enormous 300-pound black bear that was hit by a car on US 501 many years ago. The central theme underlying all of the exhibits is the wide range of environmental conditions found in Horry County and how its inhabitants, from prehistoric times to the present, have adapted to these local conditions. Find out more at www.horrycountymuseum.org.

If yours is a spring vacation, Conway is a not-to-be-missed excursion. Flowers begin blooming as early as March and usually flourish throughout most of April. Tulip trees and Japanese magnolias are particular favorites. They're complemented by quince, daffodils, narcissus, goldenrod, white and purple wisteria, crape myrtle, flowering cherry trees, Bradford pear trees, pink and white dogwoods, and thousands of azaleas in vivid, delicious colors.

Conway is the county seat of Horry County. Plans for the town, originally known as Kingston Township, were drafted around 1734. The first settlers arrived a few years later. (It wasn't until the early 1900s that Conway residents began to build vacation cottages at New Town, the summer retreat now known as Myrtle Beach.) As the area's primary transportation route, the Waccamaw River was absolutely vital to early life in Conway. For many, many years the town's economy centered on by-products gleaned from the thick pine forests that surrounded the city. Many businessmen found wealth selling lumber, tar, pitch, and turpentine.

Your best bet is to enter Conway over the Main Street Bridge. (The bridge has been restored to look like it did when it was first erected.) **The Conway Chamber of Commerce,** 203 Main Street, will be the first building on the left. Do yourself a favor and take a few minutes to stop and ask questions. And be sure to get a copy of the *Conway's Historic Tour* brochure so you won't miss a single one of the city's beautiful and significant buildings, many of which are on the National Register of Historic Places. The self-guided tour also features a number of distinctive homes, including Snow Hill, at the corner of Kingston Lake and Lakeside Drives, and the Arthur Burroughs home just across the street.

Conway City Hall, on the left at the foot of the bridge, was designed by Robert Mills, who also masterminded the Washington Monument and several other public buildings in our nation's capital. Constructed in 1824 or 1825, the building was the area's first courthouse. The city clock, which has become a Conway trademark, was added more than a century later in 1939. In recent years, since the city became part of the Main Street USA program, Conway's once-sleepy downtown has been transformed by a host of extensive renovations. Buildings, most of which were built in the early 1900s, have been restored to their original appearances. Numerous businesses have opened and flourished since the restoration began more than a decade ago. A host of department stores, specialty shops, and antiques markets now line the historic streets.

For a town of modest size, Conway has a surprising number of excellent restaurants. A popular spot with locals is the **Trestle,** 308 Main St., (843) 248-9896. Fresh pastries are featured every morning. A doughnut or a cinnamon twist with a cup of coffee will start your historic tour off right. Lunchtime fare includes stuffed potatoes, chicken salad, and a delectable club sandwich made extraordinary by fresh-baked sourdough bread. **Wayne's Restaurant,** 1127 Third Ave., (843) 248-2951, a longtime local favorite, will serve up a sampling of the South's finest: Southern fried chicken, chicken bog (also known as chicken pilau, pronounced "per-low"), corn bread, Southern-style vegetables, collards, and creamy banana pudding.

Conway initiated development of its riverfront area several years ago, and the improvement has been phenomenal. For a change of pace, check out the boats at the city-owned **Conway Marina** at the end of Elm Street. Take a stroll along the scenic river on the updated 850-foot boardwalk. For an especially tranquil day, rent a canoe or pontoon boat at the marina and disappear down the river or into the swamp off **Kingston Lake.** Canoes and pontoons can be rented for a half day or full day. If you can, talk marina operator Dick Davis into serving as your guide. He also rents fishing boats and might be willing to show you where to catch "the big one."

For a more personal look at nature and history, you may want to spend a few hours on a **River Memories** tour. Captain Jim, a Conway native, takes you on a history and nature adventure on a Durry Electric 10-passenger boat. The tour is a must for those who want to learn about Conway's history from the time when Native Americans inhabited the area through the present day. The trip goes along the Waccamaw riverfront and into a swamp dominated by bald cypress trees, moss-draped live oaks, and an abundance of native wildlife including the king of the river—the American alligator. Call River Memories at (843) 246-1495 or visit its Web site at www.rivermemories.org.

Conway boasts several popular annual events. The **Rivertown Jazz Festival,** sponsored by the Conway Main Street program, draws thousands to the riverfront beneath Main Street Bridge. Usually scheduled for May, this event showcases plenty of outrageously delicious food, jazzy toe-tapping tunes, entertainment for kids, and pretty river scenery to boot. Best of all, the festival is free and appropriate for all ages, so bring lawn chairs or a big blanket, stretch out comfortably, and relegate your cares to some other day.

Riverfest is another much-anticipated annual event. Best wear your swimsuit; to truly enjoy this festival, you have to get wet. Events include Waccamaw raft races for all ages, crafts, concerts, lunch, and scads of children's games. The day's most unusual event is undoubtedly the Jell-O Jump. Adventuresome kids actually leap into a chilled vat of Jell-O to recover marked golf balls. Ball markings determine the prizes to be won, including items such as soft drinks and free passes to area attractions. But the grand-prize winner gets cold, hard cash. Riverfest is typically held on the Saturday that falls closest to the Fourth of July and features an explosive fireworks finale.

On the first weekend in December, the riverfront is the focus of another colorful event—the **Christmas Boat Parade.** In 1992 Conway had its first nighttime boat parade. The aquatic procession features boats of all sizes—bedecked in Christmas regalia. The 1992 occasion was an immediate hit, and it has become a much loved annual event.

The Conway Area Chamber of Commerce offers popular bus tours of Conway's historical areas each year in conjunction with **Canadian-American Days Festival** in March (see the Annual Events chapter for details). Call (843) 248-2273 for more information. Another favorite Canadian-American event is the **Taste of Conway.** Not surprisingly, it's held along the riverfront and always draws eager crowds to sample the fine cuisine of Conway's restaurant owners and chefs. Delectable samples of appetizers, entrees, and desserts range from about $1.00 to $3.50.

To get to Conway, take US 501 from Myrtle Beach, Highway 90 from North Myrtle Beach, and Highway 544 (or US 17 Bypass to Highway 544) from the South Strand. (See the Getting Here, Getting Around chapter for more information.)

For a wealth of information about Conway, the following Web sites are helpful: www.conwayscchamber.com and www.cityofconway.com.

INDIGO FARMS, NC

A day trip to Indigo Farms is a simple jaunt into the farm country that surrounds Myrtle Beach. The farm actually straddles the border between the Carolinas and gets its name from the blue crop that originally made this region famous. It's just a quick left and then a right out of North Myrtle Beach; take Highway 9 to Loris and turn right onto Highway 57 (Indigo Farms billboards will be around), then drive straight until you see the farm on the side of the road. Be sure to call (843) 399-6902 first for hours, which vary, and in-season crops, which vary, too.

For locals Indigo Farms is a gardening (especially for their large and priced-right ferns) and produce resource. Everything is grown on the actual farmhouse grounds or in the surrounding fields. The complex has an extensive greenhouse with a few permanent, beautiful specimens of palms growing against the roof (unfortunately, not for sale) among the lush geraniums, lantana, mandavilla, and everything else that's in season. The palms look like they've been around almost as long as the Bellamy family, who runs Indigo Farms, has worked this land. The storefront extends to include an eat-in bakery and cafe with pies galore, some locally made crafts that are on display, and the produce market, where the merchandise is meant to be squeezed and admired.

Indigo Farms is still owned and operated by the latest generation of Bellamys (the exact count is in dispute by family members). The Bellamys seem to want to share the best way to view a farm, which is from the middle of a field. At Indigo they grow quite a few pick-it-yourself crops, from strawberries and blueberries to tomatoes and peaches. Besides being a twist on the usual shopping experience, picking your own fruits and veggies brings out more flavor to enjoy.

As you would expect, fall harvest is a busy time at Indigo Farms. In addition to the usual farm activities, Indigo hosts two fests: **Farm Heritage Day** and **Pumpkin Day,** both in October. Both festivals turn the hardworking farm into something of a handmade amusement park that even the cows can enjoy.

Farm Heritage Day explores the area's original economic and domestic roots. Admission is free to events; children and adults alike can pet all the usual farm animals and some not-so-usual farm animals such as emus. Members of the Bellamy family and their friends provide demonstrations of crafts, usually something the demonstrator specializes in or just needs to get done: candle making or wool dyeing with indigo, which is actually another color before it hits the air and turns blue. There's a lot to learn. Traditional activities include apple bobbing, hayrides, scarecrow making, potbelly-pig races, and tours of the farm facilities. Cornstalks are turned into mazes and tepees for the kids. Pumpkin Day is in preparation for Halloween, of course, and children are invited to draw on their pumpkins.

Throughout the year Indigo Farms is also available for school tours, picnics, open-air parties, and oyster roasts. The Bellamys occasionally plan Christmas events, so keep an eye peeled for their changing, seasonal schedule.

WILMINGTON, NC

Wilmington is a beautiful and historic seaport that affords residents and visitors the very finest opportunities for shopping, dining, culture, and art. Truth is, there's far too much to see and do in a single day, but if you choose carefully and plan your trip before leaving the Grand Strand, you can cover a lot of interesting territory in a short period of time. For a complete guide to this intriguing Southern city, buy yourself a copy of *Insiders' Guide to Wilmington and North Carolina's Southern Coast.* Additionally, you might give the folks at the **Cape Fear Coast Convention and Visitors Bureau** a ring, (877) 406-2356; they're well equipped to answer any of your questions. Their Web site is helpful as well: www.cape-fear.nc.us.

Wilmington boasts the largest urban registered historic district in the entire state of North Carolina. Indeed, it boasts one of the largest districts listed on the National Register of Historic Places, with homes dating from as early as the mid-1700s. Meticulously restored Victorian, Georgian, Italianate, and antebellum homes—from grand mansions to cottages—attest to the perseverance of Wilmingtonians. The area considered historically significant covers 200 city blocks, but much of the fun and captivating charm of Wilmington is concentrated on and near the riverfront. An architecturally unique historic district highlights the downtown area, with a scenic riverfront park overlooking the USS *North Carolina* battleship.

Follow US 17 North from the Grand Strand to Wilmington. Guide signs are posted to point you downtown, where a deep harbor, restaurants, shops, and impressive homes await. The harbor itself offers surprises. With a little luck, a Coast Guard ship or other vessels will be docked there, allowing visitors to board and browse.

As in many historic Southern cities, a good way to begin your Wilmington adventure is with a horse-drawn carriage tour along the riverfront past stately mansions and beautifully restored homes. Various tours, including walking and boat tours, are available at the foot of Market Street by the river. They are well worth the reasonable prices as they provide lively narratives of the area's history and point out attractions you might want to return to on your own. Two popular boat tours on the Cape Fear River are aboard the *Captain J. M. Maffitt* and the *Henrietta III*. The *Henrietta III* bills itself as North Carolina's only true stern-wheel paddleboat. Sightseeing cruises offer opportunities to view real plantations. The *Maffitt* also offers sightseeing cruises on the Cape Fear River. Special fall cruises are a real treat.

During the summer months the *Maffitt*

serves as a river taxi to ferry people to the battleship *North Carolina*. Once the most powerful battleship in the world, the *North Carolina* now rests majestically in the harbor and is easily seen from Water Street; but to drive to it, you have to go to US 17 South and circle the city. (If you save the battleship for your last stop before heading back to the Grand Strand, it will be right on the way home.) If you want to stay downtown for shopping and supper, take the *Maffitt* instead of driving. For more information call (800) 676-0162 or visit www.cfrboats.com.

Battleship *North Carolina,* a 15-story battleship that is 2 city blocks long, is Wilmington's most popular attraction. Dedicated to the 10,000 North Carolinians who sacrificed their lives during World War II, the battleship *North Carolina* participated in every major naval offensive in the Pacific Ocean. But here's a word of warning: If you have a physical handicap, claustrophobia, or any ailment that remotely resembles vertigo, tuck your greenbacks back in your pocket and move on. Only the main deck is wheelchair accessible. One staircase after another requires careful maneuvering, and there are 5- to 6-inch ledges to finesse at every door. There are more than a few tight spots. Granted, you don't have to climb into the turrets, but if you tour the lower deck, you're already into the tight spots before you realize you need to turn back. The brave souls who decide to go ahead will enjoy a wonderful history lesson.

The adventure begins with an orientation film about the battleship and its escapades during World War II. After orientation, choose from two self-guided tours. One tour can take as long as two hours. Winding through the ship's bowels, you'll see the cobbler shop, sailors' quarters, officers' quarters, galley, bakeshop, dining areas, engine room, laundry, print shop, darkroom, a doctor's office and dispensary, an operating room, an isolation area, a financial section, a supply office, and more. It's awesome! A second tour eliminates much of the climbing and takes in fewer decks; it takes approximately an hour.

The ship is open daily from 8 a.m. until 8 p.m. May 6 through September 15 and until 5 p.m. for the rest of the year. Admission costs $12 for adults and $6 for children ages 6 to 11; kids younger than age 6 get in free. For more information call (910) 251-5797 or visit www .battleshipnc.com.

Let's head back downtown for some shopping. In most cases downtown stores are independent specialty stores that brim with surprises from upscale to whimsical. One of Wilmington's brightest stars is the revived **City Market.** (You can enter on South Front Street or Water Street.) The market has fresh fruit and vegetables, a variety of tempting home-baked treats, jellies, honey, and plenty of handmade crafts. On the northern end of the riverfront, the **Cotton Exchange,** (910) 343-9896; www.shopcottonexchange.com, is another not-to-be-missed shopping stop. It's at the corner of Water and Grace Streets. (You can also enter at 321 North Front.) An old cotton warehouse that's been converted into a mall of sorts, the Cotton Exchange houses more than 30 businesses on three levels. Even if you don't like to shop, it's worth the stop to see the displays of cotton bales, weighing equipment, and photographs that recount the building's evolution. At last count there were three restaurants at the **Cotton Exchange,** so don't worry when hunger assails you. **Chandler's Wharf,** an equally charming but smaller shopping complex, is on the extreme southern end of the riverfront. It, too, definitely merits a stop.

If there's any time left in your day, other attractions include **Louise Wells Cameron Art Museum,** 3201 South 17th St., (910) 395-5999, www.cameronartmuseum.com, a 42,000-square-foot facility featuring a permanent collection of North Carolina and American art from the 18th century to the present; **Orton Plantation,** off North Carolina Highway 133 at Winnabow, (910) 371-6851, www.ortongardens.com, an old rice plantation where the gardens are open to the public; and the **Wilmington Railroad Museum,** 501 Nutt St., (910) 763-2634, www.wilmington railroadmuseum.org, a kind of fun house for folks fascinated by trains and train culture.

Wilmington's biggest shindig of the year is

the **Azalea Festival.** It's held in April and includes a parade, street fair, and home and garden tours. For more information about the festival, call the North Carolina Azalea Festival offices at (910) 794-4650 or visit www.ncazaleafestival.org.

And, one last note: You might want to call ahead to see if **Thalian Hall Center for the Performing Arts,** 310 Chestnut St., has a performance scheduled during your visit. Full-scale musicals, light opera, and internationally renowned dance companies are part of Thalian's consistently high-quality programming. Thalian Hall is the only surviving theater designed by John Montague Trumble, one of America's foremost 19th-century theater designers. Historic

tours are offered. Call (800) 523-2820 or (910) 343-3664 in advance for reservations and exact tour schedules. The Web site, www.thalianhall.com, is also helpful.

Because of the large international film industry headquartered in Wilmington (Dino DeLaurentis's studio is there, and several major films have come from Wilmington, including *The Crow, Blue Velvet, Cape Fear, King Kong,* and others), there is a large artsy avant-garde community. Walk along cobblestone Front Street any night to sip espresso at the coffeehouses, listen to live music in the bars, or enjoy New Age cuisine in one of the cozy little restaurants. Oh, and don't forget to smile and say hello to any of the visiting movie stars who might be there on location.

REAL ESTATE

If you choose to visit the Grand Strand in the early spring, you'll probably be surprised at how early the flowers blossom—and by how much construction is going on. For spring fix-up (as opposed to spring cleaning), Grand Stranders get out their hammers and wrenches, nail guns and compressors, bulldozers and cranes to prepare for the busy summer months ahead. Burgeoning growth is evidenced by a wealth of new construction, too. In fact, the 2001 Census put Horry County as the 13th-fastest growing area in the nation.

The Strand's permanent population has tripled in the last 30 years. Horry County is one of the nation's fastest-growing retirement communities. In fact, nearly 20 percent of the population in both Horry and Georgetown Counties is older than 65. That figure can be compared to only 9 percent in 1980.

With a relatively low cost of living (despite regressive state sales tax on food, clothing, and housing), the Myrtle Beach area appeals to active retirees, singles, and new families. Residential opportunities abound: golf-course villas, country clubs, sprawling residences with amenities, smaller single-family neighborhoods, friendly mobile-home communities, and condominium villages.

As is the case in many resort areas, real estate scams have posed problems in Myrtle Beach. Federal consumer watchdogs have done pretty well in helping to close down many real estate shams in the past several years.

Do be careful before you sign on the dotted line, but don't fret; with a little research and homework, you should do fine. Take time to analyze your real estate purchases carefully, whether for investment or permanent occupancy. You should consider the long-term potential of the property. Is high tide already lapping at the back deck? Is insurance a manageable expense? Is an oceanfront view worth it, or should you consider a purchase off the beach . . . on a lake, the Waccamaw River, or a golf course? Do zoning ordinances protect the long-term integrity of your investment? And don't forget to inquire about homeowner-association fees; these are not included in your mortgage but are assessed monthly or annually—and can increase rather considerably, and unexpectedly, as well.

Myrtle Beach boasts many reputable and well-established communities. Historically, these areas tended to be concentrated on the North Strand. That is changing, albeit slowly. Enduring communities such as the Dunes, Pine Lakes, and anything on Ocean Boulevard from 30th to 80th Avenues North will certainly prove a strong purchase. In these areas, zoning laws are already in place to protect the value of your purchase. As a result, such properties come with a hefty price tag. But there are plenty of newer developments all over the Strand that are well worth considering. One of the most exclusive addresses in America, with past residents including Amy Vanderbilt and professional football player Michael Fox of the Carolina Panthers, is the South Strand neighborhood of DeBordieu (locally pronounced "debby-doo"). Remember, these days a place "at the beach" doesn't necessarily mean "on the beach."

The subsequently listed developments represent a few of our favorite communities. These are followed by a sampling of the dozens of real estate agencies with strong reputations.

RESIDENTIAL DEVELOPMENTS

North Strand

BAREFOOT RESORT & GOLF
4980 Barefoot Resort Bridge Rd.,
North Myrtle Beach
(888) 237-3767, (843) 390-3200
www.barefootgolfresort.com

Barefoot Resort has united the experience and talent of four of golf's most recognized names—Greg Norman, Davis Love III, Tom Fazio, and Pete Dye—to create incredible golf surroundings. In addition to golf, Barefoot Resort includes a selection of residential communities that features more than 1,000 homes and 2,600 multifamily units for primary, retirement, or second-home living.

At the heart of the resort is a town center planned to be reminiscent of Savannah's Riverfront and Charleston's Market, where residents and visitors stroll brick sidewalks past open-air cafes, retail stores, and service establishments. Amenities include a 174-slip marina, full-service resort accommodations, access to a private beach club, and specialty retail shops.

Within Barefoot, single-family communities have floor plans ranging from 1,000-square-foot patio homes to 3,500-square-foot estate homes. Homes with homesites are priced roughly from $150,000 to $500,000. Multifamily communities feature all shapes, sizes, and price ranges of condominium villas from $200,000 to around $500,000.

HILLSBOROUGH
Highway 90 between US 501 and
Highway 22, Conway
(843) 272-8700
www.chicora.com/newhouse

Hillsborough is located in a part of the Grand Strand that is developing quickly because of the easier access newer roads are providing. This quiet country setting is convenient to both Myrtle Beach and Conway and is scarcely 10 minutes from the beach itself. This community offers three- and four-bedroom homes with two-car garages and spacious floor plans. Hillsborough also features a four-acre amenity center with a clubhouse, pool, recreation area, and walking and bike paths. Situated in a highly regarded school district, Hillsborough is an ideal community for families. Perhaps best of all, this community is extremely affordable, with prices starting in the upper $190,000s.

LIGHTKEEPER'S VILLAGE
US 17, Little River
Inquire through local Realtors

Overlooking the Intracoastal Waterway and adjacent to Coquina Harbor, this 35-acre community offers three types of properties: Lighthouse Pointe, Watchmen's Cottages, and Yacht Club Villas.

Lighthouse Pointe, priced from $250,000, includes waterway villas. Three-bedroom floor plans prominently feature natural light. The neighborhood boasts a waterfront pool with spacious sundecks and a waterfront clubhouse with a bar, sitting areas, and a fitness room. For more information visit http://lighthousepointe.us.

Watchmen's Cottages, priced from $275,000, feature elegant and finely detailed two- and three-bedroom homes. The single-level design was created specifically with retirees in mind.

The two-bedroom, two-bath Yacht Club Villas are priced from $160,000. Residents enjoy the tennis court, putting green, three pools, sundecks, two clubhouses, and waterway and harborside boardwalks. Boat slips also are available.

TIDEWATER GOLF CLUB & PLANTATION
4901 Little River Neck Rd.,
North Myrtle Beach
Inquire through local Realtors

Like more than a few residential communities in this area, Tidewater is probably best known for its golf course. This community offers homes on-course or off-course.

Developers at Tidewater carefully planned this community to preserve and protect the area's dense maritime forest and to offer homeowners spectacular views of saltwater marshes, freshwater ponds, and the Atlantic Ocean. You'll find luxurious condominium villas, custom-finished homes, and spacious courtyard houses. Each of the residential districts at Tidewater features its own distinct architectural style and landscaping. Villas range from $145,000 to $195,000, and homes with lots start at approximately $225,000 and range to more than $950,000.

Tidewater sports its own swim and racquet club with a junior Olympic-size pool, a kiddie pool, and tennis courts.

THE WATERFRONT AT BRIARCLIFFE COMMONS
US 17, Briarcliffe
Inquire through local Realtors
Briarcliffe is a pleasant stretch of tall pines between North Myrtle Beach and Restaurant Row that can be easily overlooked as you zoom by in your car on US 17. Residents like their community that way; green and relatively undisturbed.

The Waterfront at Briarcliffe Commons makes the most of this enticing location by offering 188 condominiums between US 17 and the Intracoastal Waterway. Buildings overlooking the waterway are five stories, and the lake-and-lagoon-view buildings have three levels. The development also includes a pool and hot-tub complex overlooking the waterway, two levels of terraced walkways, bridges, gazebos, fishing pier, and a secure entrance.

The floor plans offer three bedrooms (one as an alternate den/office), 9-foot or vaulted ceilings, walk-in closets, and large screened verandas. Prices start at $149,900 and extend to $250,000 for the prime waterway view.

The allure of this location is compounded by a highway-front commercial center containing a California Dreaming restaurant, a Fuddruckers, and a Marriott Courtyard hotel. Not only is this center convenient for residents, but it also serves as a buffer to the gates of one of the North Strand's most enticing condominium communities.

Myrtle Beach

THE DUNES GOLF AND BEACH CLUB
9000 North Ocean Blvd.,
Myrtle Beach
Inquire through local Realtors
If living among the local ruling class and the old

money is important to you, this is the place to choose: There are not many nouveau riche here. The homes, sold through various Realtors, are quite beautiful—though many are older than you might expect. Appropriately, the upscale Dunes Golf Club anchors this community. Many homes feature golf vistas; a precious few feature ocean views.

Buying a home here doesn't qualify you to enjoy the many amenities; memberships are additional, and the dues are steep. Home prices at Dunes start around $400,000 and climb upwards of $1,500,000.

KINGSTON PLANTATION
9770 Kings Rd., Myrtle Beach
(800) 382-3332, (843) 449-6400
www.kingstonplantationrealestate.com
Kingston Plantation is 145 heavily forested, park-like acres with freshwater lakes and a half mile of secluded beach. Expect to see wildlife, including black swans, egrets, mallard ducks, and sea turtles.

A $4.5 million health club features an indoor pool, three squash and racquetball courts, an aerobics studio, weight-training and cardiovascular equipment, a sauna, a whirlpool, and locker-room facilities. There's even a professional masseuse on staff. Outdoors you'll find a junior Olympic-size pool and exceptional tennis facilities. (See the Parks and Recreation chapter for related information.) In addition, each of Kingston's different communities typically features unique amenities.

From luxury oceanfront residences to clusters of lakeside villas and townhomes, Kingston has a home to suit virtually any taste, with 90 different floor plans in all. Prices vary dramatically—from roughly $150,000 to $650,000.

PLANTATION POINT
3800 US 17 Bypass, Myrtle Beach
Inquire through local Realtors
Plantation Point is well known as one of the more expensive communities in the Myrtle Beach area. Just off the bypass in Myrtle Beach, it's right in the heart of the action. The Myrtlewood Golf Club wraps around the development. Some lots and homes flank the Intracoastal Waterway.

ℹ While the economic downturn has affected real estate sales on the beach, buying on the Grand Strand is still a great investment. The average cost of a new home in 2009 was $237,000.

There are many different residential options at Plantation Point, and what you choose determines what amenities you may access. Charleston Place is the newest offering, with single-family brick homes fronting the course. Options in Plantation Point include lots, estate homes, single-family homes, and town-house communities in a range of prices—from around $125,000 for a modest town house to up to $4.5 million for an estate home.

PRESTWICK COUNTRY CLUB
1001 Links Rd., Myrtle Beach
(888) 250-1767, (843) 293-4100
www.prestwickcountryclub.com
Prestwick is situated around a semiprivate, $6 million Pete and P. B. Dye–designed golf course (see the Golf chapter). Prestwick Country Club also boasts one of the Strand's finest tennis complexes—11 clay courts and 2 hard-surface courts. You'll also find a health-club facility with a sauna, whirlpool, exercise areas, and indoor and outdoor pools. Security is provided 24 hours a day.

Prestwick features condominiums and homes, with direct fairway or lake views, ranging from $150,000 to over $1 million. Custom-built residences are also available. Homesites run from approximately $50,000 to $120,000. Patio homes are priced from $185,000 to more than $275,000.

SEAGATE VILLAGE
US 17 Business S., Myrtle Beach
(843) 267-2000
www.myrtlebeach.cc/seagate2.html
Seagate is an affordable, conveniently located community located immediately across the highway from Myrtle Beach State Park, on the sight of the former Myrtle Beach Air Force Base. Two-, three-, and four-bedroom homes are offered with a variety of different floor plans. Exterior features include carports, outside storage, and landscaping packages. The amenity package includes pools, cabanas, garden plots, boat and RV storage, exercise facilities, and miles of walking paths. Seagate is extremely convenient to shopping, restaurants, golf, and the beach. Condo ownership is also available at Seagate. Homes begin at $135,000, making this one of the area's most affordable communities.

SOUTHGATE IN CAROLINA FOREST
US 501, Myrtle Beach
Inquire through local Realtors
www.homesincarolinaforest.com
Southgate is located in Carolina Forest, Myrtle Beach's only master-planned community. International Paper Realty created Carolina Forest with areas for churches, schools, shopping, and a post office. The 11,000-square-acre community has the potential to accommodate a population of 40,000. Spacious three-bedroom homes include two-car garages and extra-large master bedroom suites. The community is literally minutes to numerous golf courses, restaurants, entertainment, shopping, and the award-winning Conway Hospital. In addition to Myrtle Beach's proximity, historic Conway and Coastal Carolina University are also close at hand. Three-bedroom homes start in the lower $200,000s.

South Strand
DEBORDIEU
US 17, Georgetown
(800) 753-5597, (843) 527-4321
www.debordieu.com
DeBordieu is a private oceanfront residential community encompassing 2,700 acres of age-old oaks and pines, tidal marshes, and creeks with access to the Atlantic Ocean. This might be the most prestigious address on the South Strand. Justifiably so, DeBordieu bills itself as a purveyor of "splendid isolation."

This community offers a variety of homesites and villas with ocean, forest, marsh, and fairway views, and all are served by central water and sewer systems and underground utilities.

DeBordieu Club's golf course has been nationally acclaimed as one of Pete Dye's best. The colonial-style clubhouse is spectacular. The Beach Club, with its lovely pool overlooking the ocean, offers superb dining. And the Tennis Center boasts eight composition courts and an excellent pro shop. Access to DeBordieu is controlled by a security entrance that is staffed 24 hours a day.

Living here is a pricey proposition, but if money is not an object and you don't mind the half-hour drive to Myrtle Beach, there's no prettier place or better investment. Homesites range from one-half acre to five acres, with forest, creek, golf, and ocean views. Prices range from $730,000 to more than $3 million.

i Unless you've lived along the Grand Strand for a while or visited often, don't jump into buying a home just because the market's hot and houses seem to sell quickly. Rent first to avoid making a hasty decision that you might later find difficult to live with. That will give you time to explore all the real estate opportunities here.

HERITAGE PLANTATION
US 17, Pawleys Island
Inquire through local Realtors
www.heritageplantation.com

Blessed with a unique combination of 300-year-old oaks, giant magnolias, scenic rice fields, and Waccamaw River vistas, Heritage Plantation features a clubhouse with a 75-foot heated pool and Jacuzzi, lighted tennis courts, a fitness center, card room, and a social area for entertaining.

Property owners enjoy abundant golfing opportunities, including special privileges on six of the Grand Strand's top-rated courses: Oyster Bay, Marsh Harbour, all three Legends courses, and the Heritage Club itself, where members get reserved tee times. The beaches of Pawleys Island are only 3 miles away.

Homesites at Heritage Plantation start at $170,000. Homes start at around $350,000.

INDIGO CREEK
9557 Indigo Club Dr., off US 17 Bypass S., Murrells Inlet
Inquire through local Realtors
www.indigocreekgolfclub.com

Indigo Creek is rich in natural beauty, thick with forest, and sprinkled with lakes. It's a breeze to reach Myrtle Beach on US 17 Bypass from Indigo Creek, which is less than a five-minute drive from restaurants, entertainment, shopping, medical facilities, and beaches.

Indigo Creek boasts the features of a community committed to preserving long-term value: privacy, attractive landscaping, well-lighted streets with curbs and gutters, underground utilities, and an architectural review board. Even when the local real estate market was sluggish and slow, Indigo Creek was setting sales records.

An 18-hole championship course designed by Willard Byrd offers an indisputably challenging game of golf. There's a private pool complex, too.

Indigo Creek homes begin at about $300,000.

LITCHFIELD BY THE SEA
US 17, Pawleys Island
(800) 476-2861, (843) 237-4000
www.thelitchfieldcompany.com

Since 1956 the Litchfield Company has been developing private seaside communities amid beaches, marshlands, and lush Lowcountry golf courses. Amenities include pools, spas, tennis and volleyball courts, bike paths, fishing opportunities, picnic areas, and three of the finest golf clubs in the Lowcountry.

Throughout this spacious resort, you can choose from homesites, single-family homes, and a variety of quality townhomes or villas overlooking miles of clean, white-sand beaches, marshland, lakes, or golf-course fairways. Prices range from around $250,000 to more than $7.5 million.

PAWLEYS PLANTATION
70 Tanglewood Dr., Pawleys Island
(843) 237-5050
www.pawleysplantation.com

Pawleys Plantation is a world-class golf and country club built on 582 acres of natural wetlands, salt marshes, lakes, and rolling green fairways. Bordered on the south by a 645-acre nature preserve, this private community offers homesites and golf villas for purchase as well as accommodations and golf packages for those who want to vacation in the country-club atmosphere. The Pawleys Plantation golf course is an 18-hole championship layout designed by Jack Nicklaus. Among its most unforgettable features are a tremendous double green, a dramatic split fairway, and breathtaking lake and marsh views. An antebellum-style clubhouse ranks with the finest club facilities in the Southeast. (See the Golf chapter for more detailed information.)

Neighborhoods of villas throughout the plantation offer comfortable year-round living or a perfect getaway house for the second-home buyer. Lots feature a variety of views. Homesites start at about $200,000, and villas start around $130,000.

PEBBLE CREEK AT THE INTERNATIONAL CLUB
Tournament Boulevard, off Highway 707, Murrells Inlet
Inquire through local Realtors

New three- and four-bedroom single-family homes with scenic lake views are available along this championship 18-hole golf course. Floor plans of 1,600 to 2,500 square feet are designed to buyer specifications and include spacious master suites, as well as something rare to the area— a walk-up basement. Pebble Creek is situated next door to the highly acclaimed Tournament Player's Club. This community is minutes from the ocean, the Intracoastal Waterway, Inlet Square Mall, Brookgreen Gardens, Huntington Beach State Park, and all the beauty of historic Georgetown. Homes are priced from about $250,000 to around $450,000.

PRINCE CREEK
Highway 707, Murrells Inlet
(800) 476-2861
www.thelitchfieldcompany.com

This community has gotten lots of press for being the last master-planned community on the Waccamaw Neck, a finger of land that extends from Winyah Bay in Georgetown to the edge of Horry County.

Just 15 minutes south of Myrtle Beach, Prince Creek bills itself as being "next to nature but in the middle of it all." The nearby fishing village of Murrells Inlet offers restaurants, shopping, schools, and state-of-the-art health-care facilities, including the Waccamaw Community Hospital.

Whether you are looking for a townhome, villa, single-family home, or mansion, Prince Creek is likely to have an option for you.

Highwood offers homesites surrounding the PGA-owned Tournament Players Club. Showcasing golf and wetland and woodland views, these custom sites offer a gated community and amenities including an on-site pool and cabana.

The Bays is a gated community that integrates a variety of neighborhoods within 400 acres of natural beauty. Each neighborhood is distinct but linked by the Greenway, a tree-lined boulevard designed for vehicles and pedestrians alike. All communities within the Bays have access to the Park—a shared 10-acre recreation area.

John's Bay of Prince Creek, located within the Bays, is a townhome community. With five floor plans, John's Bay delivers a low-maintenance lifestyle that leaves time for enjoying the community's pool, workout room, park, golf, and more. Prices start at $200,000 for townhomes and climb into the mulitmillion-dollar range for ocean- or riverfront homes.

i Rentals, whether weekly, monthly, or annual, are big business on the Strand. If you're house shopping, consider letting next year's vacationers pay a good chunk of your mortgage—look into multifamily structures.

WACHESAW PLANTATION
Wachesaw Road, Murrells Inlet
(800) 373-1263, (843) 357-1263
www.wachesaw.com

Wachesaw Plantation has an interesting history: It's built on the site of old Native American burial grounds that later became flourishing rice plantations. Ancient moss-draped oaks characterize this private community.

Amenities include a clubhouse, equestrian center, eight tennis courts, a swimming pool, and a Tom Fazio–designed private golf course. A beautiful dining facility offers expansive views of the Intracoastal Waterway. Homes are priced from $260,000; cottages from $255,000; homesites from the $40,000s.

WACHESAW PLANTATION EAST
US 17, Murrells Inlet
(888) 922-0027, (843) 357-5252
www.wachesaweast.com

Wachesaw Plantation East, a more recent development phase, offers a golf course, a private residential community, and a host of amenities. Homes are carefully situated to capture views of the golf course, lakes, and the natural beauty of the surrounding landscape. Though just a 15-minute drive south of Myrtle Beach, Wachesaw Plantation East remains worlds apart from Myrtle's fray yet is conveniently near shopping, dining, and medical facilities.

The Clyde Johnston–designed golf course, which opened for play in fall 1996, offers a hint of Scottish-links influence—accented by freshwater wetlands and lakes. (See the Golf chapter for details.)

The community features fitness and biking trails, and a clubhouse complex that includes a health club, swimming pool, guest inn, and conference center.

Homes of 1,700 to 3,500 square feet start in the mid-$200,000s and go as high as $1 million. Condominiums—1,100 to 1,800 square feet—are priced from around $155,000.

WILLBROOK PLANTATION
US 17, Litchfield Beach
(800) 476-2861, (843) 237-4000

The natural profile of Willbrook Plantation has changed little since it operated as three colonial rice plantations. Deer and fowl remain abundant, as do towering cypress trees, Carolina pines, and age-old oaks.

Half-acre lots, from about $240,000, are currently for sale throughout Willbrook Plantation. Single-family homes are available in a pleasant community called Allston Point.

Centex Builders developed the newest community within Willbrook built among centuries-old oak trees and around a Dan Maples–designed golf course. Several different floor plans are offered, starting at $500,000.

In addition to swimming, tennis, and the extensive clubhouse, all Willbrook residents can take advantage of the amenities at Litchfield By The Sea. Private beach access, a beach club, tennis, and bike trails set the stage for a lifestyle that's tough to beat.

REAL ESTATE AGENCIES

As you drive along the Strand, it might seem that there's a real estate office on every corner. Since you have a plethora of choices, you should give much time and consideration to choosing your agent. More often than with many other occupations, people enter the real estate field from widely disparate backgrounds. Consequently, the first salesperson you stumble across might or might not be a good fit for you. Scan first, then narrow down. Interview different people and choose someone with whom you're truly comfortable. After all, this is probably one of the biggest investments you'll ever make, and you deserve someone you can speak with honestly, confide in frequently, and respect without reservation. If you're coming from another area, speak with a real estate agent you know and trust back home. Often, agents have contacts in the industry that will help you zero in on the perfect person.

When looking for the perfect property, the *Sun News* can be a primary resource. In particular, every Sunday paper delivers a comprehensive insert called *Real Estate Plus*. It is estimated that at least a third of realty transactions begin with a newspaper ad. Realtors use it religiously—though not always to advertise their best buys. (Can't tip off the competition!) They usually advertise a broad and respectable selection of their listings, hoping to attract prospective buyers for the hidden bargains.

Listed below are some area real estate agencies whose brokers can help with the purchase of a new residence or an investment property. Please consider that the Strand has dozens and dozens of professional Realtors, many of whom are not detailed here. This list is in no way meant to reflect upon the qualifications of the real estate professionals not included here. If you'd like further information about other companies in the area, call the Grand Strand Board of Realtors at (843) 280-6250 or the Coastal Carolina Association of Realtors at (843) 626-3638.

North Strand

CENTURY 21 COASTAL LIFESTYLES
1908 US 17 S., North Myrtle Beach
(800) 568-9253, (843) 272-6754
www.c21myrtlebeach.com

Coastal Carolina Lifestyles was founded in August 1973 as a general brokerage and development agency. In 1978 a decision was made to concentrate on general brokerage, and Coastal Carolina Lifestyles joined the renowned Century 21 system. Originally operating under the name Coastal Carolina Properties, owners Swami and Nina Nash changed the name to Coastal Carolina Lifestyles in 2003, reflecting their belief that there is more to the real estate business than just real estate. It has grown to employ more than 80 agents and staffs a property management division. In 2003 and 2006, the company received the Century 21 Centurian Award, which recognizes agencies within the top 2 percent of Century 21 sales.

ELLIOTT REALTY/GMAC REAL ESTATE
401 Sea Mountain Hwy.,
North Myrtle Beach
(888) 280-5704, (843) 249-1406
204 South Ocean Blvd.,
North Myrtle Beach
(888) 280-5704, (843) 249-8307
1401 US 17 S., North Myrtle Beach
(888) 280-5704, (843) 272-2020
706 48th Ave. S., North Myrtle Beach,
(888) 280-5704, (843) 280-5704
www.elliottgmac.com

Since its founding as an independent agency in 1959, Elliott Realty has been a leader in the way real estate is sold along the Grand Strand. Almost 50 years later, the company still takes pride in offering clients and customers the most current and accurate information about the local real estate market. In 2000 Elliott Realty affiliated with GMAC Home Services, becoming Elliott Realty/GMAC Real Estate. Each of this agency's knowledgeable, well-trained real estate agents is a full-time Realtor. They have over 20 agents to serve you. The company's market area includes, but is not limited to, Little River, Cherry Grove, North Myrtle Beach, Atlantic Beach, Crescent Beach, Windy Hill, Loris, Longs, Chestnut Hill, Myrtle Beach, Surfside, Garden City, and Murrells Inlet.

RE/MAX SOUTHERN SHORES
100 US 17 S., North Myrtle Beach
(800) 729-0064, (843) 249-5555
www.myrtlebeachshores.com

With offices throughout North America, RE/MAX serves residential, commercial, and investment needs. The office, formed in 1988, has doubled in size since its founding. It is the oldest operating RE/MAX franchise on the Grand Strand. Currently, RE/MAX Southern Shores staff has nearly 20 agents.

Myrtle Beach

CENTURY 21 BOLING & ASSOCIATES
7722 North Kings Hwy., Myrtle Beach
(800) 634-2500, (843) 449-2121
www.century21boling.com

This Century 21 office opened for business in 1986. In five years Penny I. Boling, broker-in-charge, helped the company—at the time, one of the least productive in the region—become one of the leading Century 21 offices in South Carolina. Boling & Associates controls 200 or more listings at any given time, including condos and townhomes; residential, commercial, and multifamily structures; as well as land—all properties in various price ranges.

This agency thrives on a team-players concept. The majority of the sales associates have been with the company for more than five years. A property management division is available to coordinate annual rentals.

CENTURY 21 BROADHURST & ASSOCIATES INC.

3405 North Kings Hwy., Myrtle Beach
(800) 845-2055, (843) 448-7169
www.century21broadhurst.com
Century 21 Broadhurst & Associates, owned by Myrtle Beach City Councilwoman Rachel Broadhurst, is a full-service real estate company with almost 60 professionally trained property specialists. In business since 1974, this firm is one of the largest Century 21 offices in the Carolinas, with agents in Murrells Inlet and Calabash as well as Myrtle Beach. Serving clients in all phases of real estate, Broadhurst & Associates offers one-stop shopping for residential, vacation, commercial, and investment properties. Broadhurst has received the Centurian Award six times. This is the highest honor presented by Century 21 International.

COLDWELL BANKER CHICORA

Various Grand Strand locations
(843) 272-8700
www.chicora.com
Combining the two biggest companies on the Grand Strand, the Coldwell Banker Roberts Agency and Chicora Real Estate & Development, has created the largest company in the area. The two companies merged in 2000, and Coldwell Banker Chicora Real Estate was born. Today Coldwell Banker Chicora and affiliated companies have grown to more than 200 real estate professionals responsible for planning, development, sales, financial management, and property supervision of more than 60 communities with nearly 8,000 dwellings. More than 1,700 individual properties with a value that approaches $250 million are currently listed.

Coldwell Banker Chicora has 17 locations from North Myrtle Beach to Georgetown. Their "Blue Ribbon Preferred" program is based on the concept of creating a preapproved, buyer-ready home. Many tasks previously postponed until after the sale are now taken care of as soon as the property is listed. This means every sale is quick, professional, and hassle free.

i The city planning offices of Myrtle and North Myrtle Beach are vaults of information for prospective homebuyers and current homeowners. City planners and building inspectors are on hand to offer advice concerning everything from flood zones to future developments. These factors and many more affect everything from your insurance rates to future land values.

EXIT GRAND STRAND PROPERTIES

4600 Oleander Dr., Suite B, Myrtle Beach
(843) 449-3948
www.mbexit.com
Exit Grand Strand Properties bills itself as "Your Source for Exceptional Real Estate Service!" With more than 20 sales associates, executives, and specialists, Exit makes it easy for buyers to find the right property. Visit the company's Web site for a variety of listings, area information, and home-buying tips.

LITUS* PROPERTIES—JOE GARRELL & ASSOCIATES

1551 21st Ave. N., Suite 1, Myrtle Beach
(800) 285-5634, (843) 449-9000
www.litus.com
LITUS* Properties has been in business for more than 20 years, and its experience is renowned. LITUS* staffs more than 50 agents in numerous departments that handle commercial sales, business properties, resort properties, and general brokerage. The company is distinguished by a sales staff that collectively holds more certifications and accreditations in real estate and business-practice brokerage than any other agency in North America.

PAVILACK REALTY & RENTAL CORP.

603 North Kings Hwy., Myrtle Beach
(800) 868-9471, (843) 448-9471
www.pavilackrealty.com

Pavilack is a small company that offers clients personalized service in the sale or purchase of commercial real estate. Owner Harry Pavilack works closely with his associates, bringing his legal expertise to all transactions.

PRUDENTIAL BURROUGHS & CHAPIN REALTY INC.
7421 North Kings Hwy., Myrtle Beach
(800) 277-7704, (843) 449-9444
www.prudentialbc.com

Anyone who knows anything about the history of Myrtle Beach will recognize the names Burroughs and Chapin. The parent company has been around for more than a century. With 24,000 acres, this company is one of the largest landowners in Horry County. The firm owns numerous office buildings and retail complexes, including Broadway at the Beach, Coastal Grand Mall, Pine Lakes Country Club, and the Grand Dunes Resort.

Burroughs & Chapin has four real estate offices located in the Grand Strand area and offices located as far north as Carolina Beach, North Carolina. They like to say they represent more than 150 miles of the Carolina coastline.

South Strand

FITZGERALD REALTY INC.
900 Gilead Dr., Suite 101A,
Murrells Inlet
(800) 395-6610, (843) 651-0003
www.fitzgeraldrealty.com

Established in 1985, Fitzgerald Realty has approximately eight full-time and several part-time agents. This real estate firm specializes in residential and resort properties in the Grand Strand area and is available 24/7 to assist you.

The company prides itself on a "no surprises" sales process—from home selection through the final closing.

GARDEN CITY REALTY INC.
608 Atlantic Ave., Garden City Beach
(866) 427-7253, (843) 651-0900
www.gardencityrealty.com

Since 1973 Garden City Realty has been a focal point for South Strand real estate deals and has earned a reputation for scrupulously fair dealing. This comprehensive agency's 14 agents can handle a range of real estate needs—buying, selling, or renting. The experienced, well-trained staff has access to more than 4,500 listings of Myrtle Beach–area homes, condos, and land parcels.

PAWLEYS ISLAND REALTY COMPANY
88 North Causeway, Pawleys Island
(800) 937-7352, (843) 237-2431
www.pawleysislandrealty.com

Pawleys Island Realty's professional associates can answer any questions you might have about any property in Georgetown County, including all the developments. The specialty at this agency is the resort real estate market. Pawleys Island Realty also prides itself in being the largest vacation rental company in its area, with a large inventory of homes in Pawleys Island and Litchfield Beach.

ROSE REAL ESTATE
1711 US 17 S., Surfside Beach
(800) 845-6706, (843) 650-9274
www.rose-real-estate.com

Rose Real Estate is the exclusive property-management company of Tupelo Bay Golf Villas as well as the huge development known as Oceanside Village, a planned community of more than 900 modular beach homes and cottages. Half are occupied by owners, and the others are available as rentals. Like the Ocean Lakes community of Myrtle Beach, residents of Oceanside Village get around in golf carts and enjoy the safety and security of 24-hour, on-site security systems. Amenities include swimming pools, lakes stocked with game fish, tennis courts, a volleyball court, softball diamond, huge clubhouse, and planned activities. Tupelo Bay Golf Villas in Garden City is located on 165 acres, which include wetlands, ponds, and natural expanses. The villas offer two- and three-bedroom floor plans and are located right at the golf course. Rose Real Estate has been in operation since 1989.

SENIOR SCENE

The Grand Strand and retirees have a passionate love affair going. And this perfect coupling is not only compatible, but also seems to be intensifying every year as more and more active seniors come south to embrace the comfortable coastal lifestyle. In the past decade the number of adults age 65 and older has increased by almost 50 percent.

Who can blame them? They're finished with the workaday world but not with life. They come to get ultimate quality out of the golden years under the warm Carolina sunshine. Many of our retirees hail from colder regions to the north where they spent many a winter shoveling snow, wrapping kids in knitted scarves, and navigating icy roads. Here seniors can enjoy the freedom of a temperate climate, partake in the luxury of walking barefoot along a sandy coast, and, for the most part, get far more purchasing mileage out of their dollar.

In turn, they have wooed and won the hearts of Grand Stranders with the skills and experience they apply to local civic groups, churches, the arts, and governmental entities. Retirees have become and will remain an integral part of this community. As one 69-year-old widow put it, "I moved to Myrtle Beach . . . and have a busier schedule than ever before. No one needs to be lonely in Myrtle Beach. There's just too much to do."

OVERVIEW

The Myrtle Beach area has been named by *Money* magazine as one of the top 20 places to retire in America. The *Southeast Journal* edition of the *Wall Street Journal* also ranked the Grand Strand as one of the dozen hottest retirement spots in six Southeast states.

Many retired folks volunteer at area schools and hospitals. They serve on boards and councils, operate community projects, head up fund-raising drives, and participate in cultural programs. The Long Bay Symphony can credit its very existence to retirees who worked in the music business and performed with symphonies in larger cities. The over-55 set have their own acting troupe, the Grand Strand Players, which puts on three productions a year. The Waccamaw Carving Club, the Waccamaw Arts and Crafts Guild, the Grand Strand Concert Band, and the Long Bay Photography Club would all have slim membership rolls without retirees.

Horry's seniors have their own newspaper, *Fifty Plus;* their own annual trade show, the Life-

styles Expo, held each winter in the Myrtle Beach Convention Center (see the Annual Events chapter); and their own production company that puts together a 30-minute program each month for Cox Cable TV.

The Grand Strand also entices migrant retirees, usually referred to as "snowbirds," who follow the sunshine south to escape the harsh northern winters. They rent houses and apartments or stay in hotels, taking advantage of lower winter rates. Around March or April, when temperatures start to rise, they head home. No one seems to have a good grasp of just how many snowbirds winter along the Grand Strand, although estimates range upwards of 50,000.

The Carolinas are perfectly positioned to attract the new generation of retirees. Younger, more active seniors are choosing destinations like South Carolina because it is at least a day closer to their northern homes than Florida, offers a break from relentless heat and humidity, and provides plenty of activities beyond shuffleboard or a dip in the pool.

Jobs and entrepreneurial opportunity are also high on the list of desirable qualities, since many of today's retirees want to continue to work at least part time or wish to start their own businesses.

THE SINGLE SENIOR SET

A recent census report tells us that 9 percent of Horry County's population is over the age of 65 and living alone. Many of these single seniors are satisfied with their newfound life of freedom and take up traveling and rediscover lifelong passions that have lain dormant for years.

Of course, tried-and-true ways to meet new friends are through attending your church or synagogue, becoming a member of a local senior center, enrolling in special-interest courses, and joining volunteer organizations. But this section of the Insiders' Guide passes along some formal and informal settings guaranteed to put you in the mainstream of local, active seniors that you probably wouldn't find until you had lived here a while.

The VFW Post 10420, 4359 US 17 Bypass in Murrells Inlet, (843) 651-6900, is a hot spot for the older set when it comes to dining and dancing. It's open every day for lunch and dinner, with live bands performing on Friday and Sunday from 6:30 to 10:30 p.m. Music ranges from Big Band tunes to beach music, and the dance floor is usually packed.

Mall-walking clubs have become serious programs for health and socializing among the 50-plus circle. Before stores open at 10 a.m., the empty aisles are alive with the sounds of chitchat and padding Reeboks as hundreds of participants log in mall-miles. All of the Grand Strand malls offer a walking club, and all are thriving. The Myrtle Beach Mall Walkers operate out of Myrtle Beach Mall, 10177 North Kings Hwy., Myrtle Beach, and the group is in cooperation with the Loris Healthcare System. Applications and flyers can be picked up anytime at the guest services booth near JCPenney and the food court, or call the mall at (843) 272-4040. Coastal Grand also has its own Mall Walkers. More information can be found in the mall offices at 2000 Coastal Grand Circle or by calling (843) 839-9100.

Applications for the Inlet Square Mall Walkers, US 17 Business in Murrells Inlet, are available near the entrance to JCPenney or by contacting customer service at (843) 651-6990.

i If you're 55 years of age or older, always ask about available senior discounts whenever you shop, dine out, or purchase goods or services. Many Grand Strand businesses offer seniors special price reductions.

ACTIVE SENIOR CENTERS

To offer a central meeting spot and support to our ever-growing senior population along the Grand Strand, a number of centers have sprung up all along our shoreline. All are staffed by full-time activities personnel and operate Monday through Friday only. If you're a regular participant in these arenas of action, you'll need the weekends to rest up!

Myrtle Beach

GRAND STRAND CHAPTER OF H2U
Grand Strand Regional Medical Center,
809 82nd Parkway, Myrtle Beach
(843) 692-1645, (843) 692-1634
www.grandstrandmed.com
H2U is a not-for-profit organization for anyone beyond the age of 50. Its goal is to funnel social and health benefits and opportunities through a single source. The local sponsor for the Grand Strand chapter is the Grand Strand Regional Medical Center. Activities include a monthly Dutch-treat luncheon and chapter meeting, a bowling league and brown-bag movie, day trips and overnight trips, an annual convention, a member-guest cookout, a birthday party, and a Christmas dance. Many benefits and discounts are available to members through the medical center. Membership is reasonably priced at only $15 a year.

GRAND STRAND SENIOR CENTER
1268 21st Ave. N., Myrtle Beach
(843) 626-3991
www.seniornews.biz
The Horry County Council On Aging realized the fruits of its labor in 1995 when this senior center opened its doors. This $1.4 million project offers seniors 16,000 square feet of space, including an auditorium, kitchen, dressing rooms, and meeting chambers. Open Mon through Fri from 9 a.m. to 3 p.m., the senior center plays host to a dizzying schedule of events: arts and crafts, bridge, dance aerobics, yoga, mah-jongg (a game of Chinese origin similar to dominoes), bingo for prizes, health screening, ballroom dancing, art classes, chess, support groups, quilting . . . let us catch our breath . . . seminars, and tax-preparation instruction. You would have to have the energy of two preteens on summer vacation to keep up with all of the center's activities! The Seniors for the Performing Arts theatrical troupe performs in the auditorium full-production plays that have become very popular with senior-center members and locals alike. Regular luncheons are also part of the center's monthly agenda. There is no membership fee. New volunteers are always welcome.

South Strand
GEORGETOWN SENIOR CENTER
2104 Lincoln St., Georgetown
(843) 546-8539
The Georgetown center offers an agenda of things to do that includes crafts, exercise programs, quilting, card games, and day trips to such attractions as Brookgreen Gardens. There are about 30 active members. Lunch is served each day for a nominal fee. There is no fee to join this senior center. This program operates from 8:30 a.m. to 4 p.m.

SOUTH STRAND SENIOR CENTER
1032 10th Ave. N., Surfside Beach
(843) 238-3644
South Strand has 100 members with an average of 45 people coming to the center daily. A van service is available for seniors without transportation. A different roster of events is coordinated for each day, keeping things hopping with speakers, day trips, games, ceramics, and exercise. Hot lunches are served five days a week for donations. Membership is free. South Strand is open Mon through Fri from 9 a.m. to 3 p.m.

EDUCATIONAL PROGRAMS

Since the pursuit of knowledge spans every generation and one is never too young or too old to learn, the Grand Strand has enjoyed a proliferation of educational programs that enroll seniors by the hundreds. With time on their hands and minds as sharp as tacks, many of our older citizens have quit marking off days on the calendar—they're too busy organizing their lives by semester.

CLASS
Art Works/Litchfield Exchange
US 17, Litchfield Beach
(843) 235-9600
www.classatpawleys.com
Held year-round at Art Works in the Litchfield Exchange, CLASS (Community Learning About Special Subjects) is an exciting addition to senior life for students from Myrtle Beach to Georgetown. Taught by talented and well-qualified instructors, classes range from single-day workshops to eight-week courses that meet once a week during the day and evening. Whether you are a native or new to the area, CLASS provides a casual environment for meeting people with common interests and for exploring subjects seniors may have been interested about but never had time to pursue.

As research findings continue to emphasize the importance of exercising the mind as well as the body, CLASS offers many programs that combine mental, sensory, and social stimulation. Subjects include cultural appreciation (art, music, film, literature), history (local and beyond), hands-on learning (computers, bridge, genealogy, cooking, herb gardening, handwriting analysis, creative writing, interior design), art instruction for beginners and accomplished artists in a variety of media (drawing, painting, portraiture, photography, stained glass), and a variety of personal-growth opportunities. Capping each week is The Moveable Feast, a series of literary luncheons featuring accomplished authors and held at different Waccamaw Neck restaurants.

The fall, winter, and spring terms include approximately 60 courses. Around 30 courses are planned during the summer months for short-term visitors. A complete schedule is available on the Web site.

HORRY-GEORGETOWN TECHNICAL COLLEGE
Continuing Education
Conway Campus, 2050 US 501 E., Conway
(843) 347-3186

GRAND STRAND CAMPUS,
743 Hemlock Ave.,
Myrtle Beach
(843) 477-0808

GEORGETOWN CAMPUS,
4003 South Frasier St., Georgetown
(843) 546-8406
www.hgtc.edu

All campus locations of Horry-Georgetown Technical College, including the Grand Strand campus on the former Myrtle Beach Air Force Base, encourage and support a wide range of courses and special programs that attract senior students due to their scope, convenience, and affordability. Every semester, a good number of continuing-education courses are designated as senior-citizen specials. If you are at least 60 years of age, a South Carolina resident, and neither you nor your spouse is employed full time, you may qualify to receive a total tuition waiver to take a particular course or be eligible for a 50 percent discount of the tuition fee.

Continuing-education courses have included topics such as financial and business training, computers and the Internet, construction and home repair, health and wellness, arts and crafts specialties, and languages.

The cost and hours of each course do vary. Each campus of Horry-Georgetown Technical College is happy to send you its current schedule and updates if you give them a call.

Preregistration is required for all classes.

OSHER LIFELONG LEARNING
Coastal Carolina University, Conway
(843) 349-2665
www.coastal.edu/olli

University faculty and professionals from the community teach a variety of intellectual, cultural, and social classes. No formal papers or exams are required of the senior students. There is no membership fee to join the Osher Lifelong program; you are an automatic member if you have taken classes at Coastal. Membership entitles participants to use of the campus facilities and student rates to University cultural events and performances. Members also have the opportunity to attend special workshops, travel-study programs, and sessions at the university. Past course offerings have included literature and film, computer classes, political science, history of China, the Aztecs, heroes and villains in American History, and art and music. There are also courses in ecology, marine science, genealogy, foreign languages, folklore, creative writing, and philosophy.

Adult noncredit students pay course tuition, and anyone enrolled in at least one course will be considered a Lifelong Learning student. Lifelong Learning students may take courses at any or all of Coastal's four sites: the Coastal campus, the Waccamaw Center, the Myrtle Beach Center, and the Georgetown Center. Students may register at any of the sites or may register online. More than 200 courses are offered by 76 instructors.

INDEPENDENT-LIVING COMMUNITIES

Many retirees choose to live in residential communities not exclusively for seniors. Here is a listing we put together of beautiful, safe, active-adult communities for a wider range of age groups.

North Strand

COUNTRY LAKES

4353 Erie Street, Little River
(888) 716-9750, (843) 399-2333
www.jensencommunities.com

The Jensen family's Country Lakes in the north end of the county is smaller than its Garden City cousin. A small pool and clubhouse grace the grounds. For security, an electronic bar crosses the road to keep uninvited guests out and protect residents and their properties. There is an on-site sales office. Home costs run from the $90,000s to $145,000.

MYRTLE TRACE SOUTH

506 Sand Ridge Rd., East Conway
(800) 227-0631, (843) 357-6638
www.mbliving.com

As motorists pass the Myrtle Trace sign on US 501, they don't get a hint about the magnitude of what lies beyond that sign and the wooded area that buffers the community from traffic. But pull in and take a look around; you'll be stunned to find about 500 homes in three unique communities. Myrtle Trace is about 20 years old and has a maturity that some newer developments lack. It is immaculately manicured and features lakes, golf course lots, a clubhouse, and a swimming pool.

Most of the people who buy at Myrtle Trace move in while they're still in their late 50s or early 60s, and they give new meaning to the term "active retirement." Residents band together to plan activities that range from all kinds of card games to theatrical performances. There is a bowling league, and, of course, golf is king. Between 20 and 30 residents work several days a week at area golf courses as starters and rangers to earn a few dollars and, mostly, to secure golf privileges. About 50 of Myrtle Trace's women work as volunteers at nearby Conway Hospital.

Homes range from $160,000 to $195,000, depending on the location and floor plan selected. Myrtle Trace is within 1 mile of a shopping center off US 501, which offers a grocery store, pharmacy, shops, and restaurants.

Myrtle Beach

COVENANT TOWERS

5001 Little River Rd., Myrtle Beach
(843) 449-2484
www.covenanttowers.com

Covenant Towers offers a simple and unique opportunity for independent adult living in an upscale development. Located in the residential north end next to prestigious Pine Lakes golf course, the nine-acre campus has 159 independent-living condominium residences and even a few two-bedroom-plus-den/study residences.

Occupants must be 55 years old or older, and ownership is deeded fee simple. In addition to being equipped with an emergency call system, each residence boasts a balcony, full kitchen, and one, two, or three full baths. On-site amenities include a swimming pool, library, dining room, coffee shop, craft/game room, mail room, banking, beauty/barber shop, fishponds, and gardens/grounds with walking paths. Nestled in a quiet, established residential neighborhood, Covenant Towers enjoys easy access to the beach, shopping, golf, restaurants, and all the wonderful opportunities the Grand Strand offers.

Numerous services and activities are available to homeowners. Dinner is available in the dining room Monday through Saturday evenings, and a full brunch is available on Sunday. A full-time activities staff coordinates recreational activities—water aerobics, sittercise, bridge, bowling, golf, bingo, crafts, etc.—as well as opportunities to enjoy shows, concerts, lectures, shopping, and the many restaurants along the Grand Strand.

Residents also enjoy the convenience of housekeeping service, weekly linen service, water and sewerage, insurance coverage on the structure(s), and maintenance on the buildings and grounds included as well. The convenience of a small 30-bed, private, fully licensed, skilled nursing unit allows homeowners the comfort of a quick-skilled response to an emergency call or care by familiar professionals should a resident need respite or long-term care. Covenant Towers does not provide assisted-living services.

Homeowner residents elect the board of directors that governs the association with the guidance of a licensed administrator and professional property management company. They have proven themselves to be good stewards of their assets for two decades and bring a wealth of professional and life experiences to this democratic process. Residences range in price from the mid-$40,000s to approximately $150,000 for the largest floor plan. Information is available on-site Monday through Friday and by appointment on the weekends.

South Strand

GARDEN MANOR ASSISTED LIVING
11951 Grandhaven Drive, Murrells Inlet
(843) 357-7471

Garden Manor offers apartments for seniors who are still active but don't want to worry about maintaining a home. These senior apartments provide safety, comfort, and the availability of a community. One- and two-bedroom apartments are available from $1,600 to $2,500 a month, and the cost includes daily lunch and weekly housekeeping. Residents tend to be social, so there's always some kind of informal activity taking place.

OCEAN LAKES
6001 US 17 S., Surfside Beach
(800) 845-2229, (843) 238-5356
www.oceanlakes.com

Ocean Lakes is billed as the largest oceanfront campground on the East Coast, and although it serves as a typical campground during the tourist season, it also has about 500 year-round residents, mostly retirees. In 1999 the National Association of RV Parks and Campgrounds nominated Ocean Lakes as the No. 1 large RV park in the United States. In 2006 it won the South Carolina Governor's Cup, awarded to businesses that have a positive impact on the community. The campground is on the ocean and has a recreational building where residents can work on crafts or meet for a variety of activities. An indoor pool was added, and an activities director makes sure residents stay busy with everything from shopping and trips to miniature golf tournaments. A year-round chaplain works to meet residents' spiritual needs, providing Sunday worship services in an outdoor amphitheater when the weather permits and indoors when it doesn't.

Homes at Ocean Lakes are mostly small mobile units, some of which showcase a more permanent appearance with added rooms and porches. However, with the housing boom along the Grand Strand, a large number of two-story beach homes have been added to the landscape.

Ocean Lakes is a guarded community, and security staff stationed at the gate make sure only residents, their guests, registered campers, and people attending worship services get in. As added security, Ocean Lakes instituted a 24-hour patrol of the grounds.

Few people use their cars inside Ocean Lakes. Instead, you'll find their transportation much slower and more relaxed—golf carts work just fine, thank you! At any given time, there are about 130 sites for sale, ranging from $35,000 for a camper home to almost $300,000 for some oceanfront beach houses.

OCEAN PINES/MAGNOLIA GROVE
3196 Moonshadow Lane, Garden City
(800) 238-6565, (843) 651-2520
www.jensencommunities.com

In accordance with federal guidelines, Jensen's has restricted its manufactured-housing development to people age 55 and older. Initiated in the early 1970s, this development is currently home to about 575 families. At Jensen's, residents lease their lots and buy their own homes. A senior can move into a double-wide abode for between $85,000 and the low $100,000s. Jensen's is quiet and well manicured and bubbles with small lakes and canals. A clubhouse in the development has a pool. Residents plan their own activities through the Jensen's Activity Club (JAC), which distributes a monthly newsletter chock-full of things to do. There's a sales office on-site.

ASSISTED-LIVING COMMUNITIES

Myrtle Beach

MYRTLE BEACH ESTATES
3620 Happy Woods Court, Myrtle Beach
(843) 293-8888
www.myrtlebeachestates.net
Myrtle Beach Estates takes great pride in providing gentle care and trained assistance for every resident. The community's atmosphere is created through a combination of a like-home environment and a professionally trained staff capable of providing skillful assistance on a moment's notice. The staff also coordinates all services provided by outside health professionals.

Residents enjoy a comfortable environment that is also secure—an environment that enhances well-being and ensures peace of mind. A full-time activities director provides a full slate of activities; residents can choose to do as much or as little as they prefer. Diet, exercise, and wellness programs are followed closely and managed to fit each resident's needs.

An ideal choice for independent, assisted living, Myrtle Beach Estates requires no entrance fees, endowments, or long-term leases, just one low, affordable monthly fee. This fee covers all services, features, and amenities, including a staff nurse on call 24 hours per day; three daily meals, daily housekeeping, and personal laundry services; weekly worship services; and a host of social, recreational, educational, and cultural activities. Fees start at $1,600, depending on the facilities and services selected.

MYRTLE BEACH MANOR
9547 North Kings Hwy., Myrtle Beach
(843) 449-5283
Myrtle Beach Manor offers services for people in all phases of their senior years. There are 60 apartments, ranging from studios to one-bedroom units. These are rented on a monthly basis to people who want to live independently but like the security of knowing someone is nearby to watch out for them. The 104 beds in the health-care center are designed for those who need to be regularly looked in on. The manor also houses a secured Nursing Care Center and full rehabilitation department that includes occupational and physical therapy. An activities director makes sure that residents have something to do seven days a week. The 40-year-old establishment has six lovely manicured acres, and a sunny day will bring many manor residents outside to enjoy the scenery and a view of the Intracoastal Waterway. Monthly costs at Myrtle Beach Manor begin at about $2,000. A daily rate of $115 to $138 applies to residents who require substantial health-care services.

South Strand

THE LAKES AT LITCHFIELD
120 Lakes at Litchfield Dr.,
Pawleys Island
(800) 684-7866, (843) 235-9393
www.lakes-litchfield.com
The Lakes at Litchfield is much more than a place to live. Residents and families take comfort in knowing the community offers a continuum of care that meets needs and provides a seamless transition as needs change. It's a community that takes pride in offering the setting, support, and services necessary to ensure residents' comfort and security.

The Lakes at Litchfield features a range of elegant residential choices that offers every comfort and convenience. Lovely two- and three-bedroom homes feature bright Carolina sunrooms, fireplaces, 9-foot ceilings, and quality appliances. Each home has its own garage, a cart for community travel, and a 24-hour emergency call system for safety. Meals in the elegant Charleston Dining Room, maid service, all maintenance, taxes, insurance, utilities, scheduled transportation, and more are all included in a reasonable occupancy fee. Plus, should you ever decide to leave the Lakes at Litchfield, a substantial amount of your initial investment will be returned. Spacious one- and two-bedroom apartments (with no up-front investment) are also affordable options. And the community is thoughtfully designed to embrace the natural charm of Pawleys Island with lakes, courtyards, and fountains, as well as a gazebo and clubhouse with pool.

In addition to single-family homes, garden homes, and apartment homes, the Lakes at Litchfield Assisted Living and Special Care Communities provide state-of-the-art services for those needing special attention and care. Per-month costs start at around $3,000 and go up to around $4,500 for dementia care. Both centers offer incomparable care in a truly caring community. See for yourself what makes the Lakes at Litchfield so special.

SENIOR DAY CARE

Several area senior centers provide adult day care services. The Grand Strand Active Day Center at 3901 North Kings Hwy. in Myrtle Beach is a good option for those visiting the beach and in need of assistance. They are open Mon through Fri from 7:30 a.m. to 4:30 p.m. Call director Lesley Bass at (843) 626-8501.

IN-HOME HEALTH-CARE OPTIONS

When a parent, aunt, or other older relative becomes ill or infirm, it's not surprising that concerned family members look to a nursing home for care. But according to the South Carolina Budget and Control Board, Office of Insurance Services, a nursing home is often the most extreme option.

In order to keep loved ones in their own homes with their pride intact, there are other options to consider. We discuss some of those options in the following section, outlining the positive and negative aspects of each in a realistic manner.

Family Home Care

If you, your siblings, or other caring relatives live within reach, you could consider family home care. Modifications to the ailing person's home may be needed, such as installing a ramp near the entrance for wheelchair access and rearranging furniture to accommodate the chair or a walker. It might also be necessary to rent or purchase special equipment such as a hospital bed or oxygen tank. Everyone involved should decide who will do the cooking, cleaning, laundry, and shopping. And most of all, each helper must honestly evaluate his or her ability to do these chores.

The positive side to this arrangement is that it costs nothing but time, and in many cases, patients recover best in the comfort of familiar surroundings. It can also be a way to strengthen family relationships, providing the time required does not become a strain.

On the negative side, family members usually are not health-care professionals. Albeit with the best intentions, family members might tend to pamper a relative, rather than insisting, for example, on a prescribed daily walk.

Private Nursing

This arrangement intrudes the least on the lives of other family members, including a spouse. A private nurse can be hired to care for someone in the comfort of home. Private nurses can be found through nursing-placement services, home-health agencies, or discharge services of a hospital. Every hospital staffs a discharge nurse who can provide this information.

Some private nursing fees are covered by Medicare or the sick relative's supplemental insurance. For the most part, however, this is a very expensive care option since most private nurses charge by the hour.

Home-Care Services

Overall, this care option compromises between the relatively high cost of a private nurse and the difficult task of being sole caretaker of a sick relative.

Generally, you arrange for a nurse to stop in for a few hours, two or three times a week, depending on the person's needs. Along with this, a nurse's aide is hired to come in on a particular schedule to bathe and groom the relative. Physical or occupational therapists can also be attained. Discharge services at your hospital can usually provide you with a list of qualified professionals or, in some cases, make all of the arrangements for you.

Medicare covers the costs of an agency-approved visiting nurse, nurse's aide, and therapist for up to eight hours a day for 21 consecutive days or as long as the relative's doctor deems necessary. Medicare coverage stops when the doctor says the nurse is no longer needed for care. At that point, if you want the nurse's aide to continue, you foot the bill.

Care Management

This is a variation on home-care services, usually employed by relatives who don't live near the person requiring help. An elder-care agency or geriatric-care manager evaluates what the patient needs, develops an appropriate health-care plan, and hires the necessary personnel. The program is overseen by the manager, who is available 24 hours a day to handle problems or emergencies. Care managers usually receive $150 to $300 an hour for the initial consultation and to monitor the person's care regularly. You must also pay the fees for all personnel hired to care for the relative. Medicare and supplemental coverage does kick in for this service, but every condition is different.

Besides the Caregivers of South Carolina number listed in this chapter's subsequent "Senior Services Directory" section, you can also contact the National Association of Professional Geriatric Care Managers in Tucson, Arizona, (520) 881-8008 or www.caremanager.org. This association publishes a directory of geriatric-care managers nationwide. For additional information contact the local chapter of the AARP (refer to the "Senior Services Directory") and ask for the free booklet Care Management: Arranging for Long-term Care.

SENIOR SERVICES DIRECTORY

The following agencies and information clearinghouses could come in handy as resources for seniors.

North Strand

NORTH STRAND SENIOR HEALTH CENTER
4237 River Hills Dr., Little River
(843) 281-2778
www.grandstrandmed.com
As an outpatient department of Grand Strand Regional Medical Center designed to meet and simplify the health-care process for seniors, the North Strand Senior Health Center targets the needs of the senior population. The staff has been specially trained in the needs of senior citizens and will help patients assess, manage, and prevent health-related problems. On-site services include medical exams, lab work, and EKGs. The center welcomes Medicare assignments. Non-health services include assistance in locating community resources to addressing legal, financial, and housing concerns.

Myrtle Beach

GRAND STRAND RETIREMENT CLUB
(843) 448-5670, (843) 449-0345
For $10 a year, any permanent and retired resident living east of the Intracoastal Waterway can join this social club, which meets regularly for lunch. Members perform some charity work but primarily meet to network. Please call ahead for reservations.

i Coastal Carolina University has an online senior directory that has 27 categories of services ranging from adult day care and financial services to legal assistance and volunteer opportunities. For information call (843) 349-4115 or (843) 349-4116, or visit www.coastal.edu/caar/srservices.

SENIOR ADVISORY COMMITTEE OF MYRTLE BEACH
City Hall, 937 Broadway St.,
Myrtle Beach
(843) 918-1014
www.cityofmyrtlebeach.com/seniors.html

This committee was organized through the City of Myrtle Beach to address specific needs of senior citizens, such as larger print on road signs, longer crosswalk signals, and noise ordinances.

SENIOR GOLFERS ASSOCIATION AND *SENIOR GOLF JOURNAL*
3013 Church St., Myrtle Beach
(800) 337-0047, (843) 626-8100
www.seniorgolfersamerica.com
The Senior Golfers Association and its publication, *Senior Golf Journal,* include members and subscriptions from virtually every town and city across the United States. Golf tournaments and the journal are coordinated here, but interest is national.

SERVICE CORPS OF RETIRED EXECUTIVES (SCORE)
(843) 918-1079
www.mbscore.org
Calling all retired businesspeople and executives . . . . This volunteer corps offers free counsel to individuals who want to go into business as well as to businesses experiencing problems. Retired executives and professionals are encouraged to donate their skills and background to the cause.

South Strand

GEORGETOWN COUNTY COUNCIL ON AGING
2104 Lincoln St.
Georgetown
(843) 546-8539
www.scmatureadults.org
This agency can provide referral services for local seniors that will help them to continue being an integral part of their communities.

SURFSIDE BEACH FIFTIES-PLUS GROUP
Surfside Civic Center, 829 Pine Dr.,
Surfside Beach
(843) 913-6339
This active social group is for older couples and singles. Fifties-Plus members get together for a meeting on the third Monday each month. A potluck luncheon is held the first Monday of each month, and planned activities range from bowling and games to trips.

Beyond the Strand

AMERICAN ASSOCIATION OF RETIRED PERSONS (AARP)
(800) 424-3410
www.aarp.org/scsep
Devoted to needs of senior adults, AARP sponsors an employment program that includes job training and, in some cases, placement for older workers with limited incomes. Call the office nearest you and ask about the Senior Community Service Employment Program (SCSEP).

CAREGIVERS OF SOUTH CAROLINA, LLC
821 River Birch Dr., Conway
(843) 347-6440
www.caregiverssc.com
Caregivers is a locally owned company that can help you locate caregivers for senior adults, including those with Alzheimer's. They guarantee thorough background checks on all employees and can meet most needs. Rates start at $11.50 an hour, depending on the services needed, which range from helping to bathe and dress a patient to full-time live-in care.

ELDERHOSTEL
Coastal Carolina University, Conway
(877) 426-8056, (843) 349-2665
www.elderhostel.org
Participants in this exciting program get an opportunity to take up to three noncredit courses in liberal arts and sciences from a host institution in the United States or abroad. This program is offered at more than 1,600 locations internationally.

HORRY COUNTY COUNCIL ON AGING INC.
2213 North Main St., Conway
(843) 248-5523
The Council on Aging acts as an information and referral service for all senior citizens and their families. Staff provide up-to-date information on everything from home-delivered meals to living

wills. This agency also performs the daunting task of managing eight area senior centers.

HORRY COUNTY VETERANS AFFAIRS OFFICE
2830 Oak St., Conway
(843) 248-1291
www.horrycounty.org

This agency provides services to veterans and their dependents or survivors. It also operates as an intermediary between veteran patients and the VA hospital.

SENIORS HELPING SENIORS
(843) 449-0553
www.sos-healthcare.com

Seniors Helping Seniors is run by SOS, which stands for Save Our Seniors. SOS Health Care was founded in 1990 by Dr. Bill Davis as a grass roots effort to help provide assistance, in particular health-care assistance, to seniors who often fall through the cracks of the health-care system. Many of its volunteers are seniors themselves. The program trains lay counselors over the age of 50 to provide support for those in need. Open Mon through Thurs from 9 a.m. to 4 p.m., the SOS hotline is staffed to provide assistance in finding medications and treatments, and sometimes just lend an ear to seniors who need someone to talk to.

SOCIAL SECURITY ADMINISTRATION
1316 Third Ave., Conway
(800) 325-0778, (800) 772-1213,
(843) 248-4271
www.ssa.gov

This agency provides information on Social Security benefits, including Supplemental Security Income (SSI) and disability. As of this writing, if you are under normal (or full) retirement age (FRA) when you start getting your Social Security payments, $1 in benefits will be deducted for each $2 you earn above the annual limit. For 2009 that limit was $14,160, and for 2008 the limit was $12,560. Remember, the earliest age that you can receive Social Security retirement benefits remains 62 even though the FRA is rising. In the year you reach your FRA, $1 in benefits will be deducted for each $3 you earn above a different limit, but only counting earnings before the month you reach FRA. For 2009 this limit was $37,680; for 2008 the limit was $36,120. Starting with the month you reach FRA, you will get your benefits with no limit on your earnings. Office hours are 9 a.m. to 4 p.m. Mon through Fri.

SC EMPLOYMENT SECURITY COMMISSION COASTAL WORKFORCE CENTER
200-A Victory Lane, Conway
(843) 234-WORK
www.sces.org

Many Grand Strand companies readily employ older citizens. Contact the center about job opportunities and a variety of training and educational programs in both Horry and Georgetown Counties.

SOUTH CAROLINA SENIOR RESOURCES, INC.
(866) 818-6499
www.seniorresourcesinc.org

Any senior who endures the misfortune of being disabled should call this toll-free number. South Carolina Services provides information on a variety of specialized resources for those in need.

CHILD CARE AND EDUCATION

Grand Stranders take great pride in their reputation as a beach community where family concerns receive their full attention. For example, parents here take education very seriously. In fact, 99 percent of area parents had participated in a parent-teacher conference in 2005. In addition, the student attendance rate was 96 percent.

The fine schools of the Grand Strand—from private religious schools to technical academies—make good use of the amazing resources available in this area. For example, Horry Telephone Cooperative, a local connectivity provider, helped get the schools online. The tools are in place for the next generation of Grand Stranders to be able to read, write, and compete with their peers nationwide. As a result, Horry County school district was chosen to be a recipient of the "What Parents Want" award, as presented by School Match, an independent educational consulting firm. More than 60,000 parents were surveyed nationally to determine the criteria for this designation, and only 14 percent of schools nationwide qualified. The Horry County school system serves nearly 38,000 students. Horry County ranks first in the state for in-migration; in 2007 enrollment reached 36,142, representing a 15 percent increase from 1998. While South Carolina schools as a whole have not ranked very high in the nation, Horry County scholastic statistics rate higher and are improving.

The Horry County School District has been recognized as a national leader in technology. All classrooms are networked to the Internet, and the ratio of computers to students is just over 5 to 1. Wireless labs continue to expand. Since 2006, more than $3 million has been allocated for a laptop-computer initiative for teachers, giving them equipment and training to enhance the use of technology and instruction.

In 2004 a $240 million bond referendum was approved to provide for six new schools and additions, and renovations for 20 others.

The Horry County school district is the third largest of 85 state districts, and it still maintains a relatively low dropout rate of 1.5 percent, with 75 percent of graduates going on to higher education. Of the county's 2,073 classroom teachers, 1,616 hold advanced degrees. The board of education is elected democratically, hires a superintendent, and works with the National Education Association. Class sizes in grades kindergarten through eighth have been limited to 25 or less, and seven schools in the area have been named National Blue Ribbon Schools by the U.S. Department of Education. In 2008 the Horry County School District SAT scores were 12 points above the national average. In fact, HCS students outpaced the state in each of the subject areas tested in 2008. Efforts also include such practical measures as placing a school resource officer or a security guard on campus and full-time drug and weapon canine surveillance teams in all high schools, middle schools, and career centers.

The first portion of this chapter discusses child care for the youngest of your gang. Then we move on to discuss primary- and secondary-education options.

CHILD CARE

Day-Care Options

Although word of mouth has always been one of the best ways to zero in on reliable child care, newcomers don't have the benefit of an established network of reliable parents and other adults for advice. So if you're new to our area, we suggest you request information from Hands on Health—South Carolina. Hands on Health is affiliated with the Medical University of South Carolina and is a clearinghouse of information regarding day care, physicians, and even nutrition involving your child. The main resource Web page is www.handsonhealth-sc.org. Hands on Health also provides information for teens as well as seniors.

The South Carolina Department of Social Services is responsible for licensing all day-care centers in the state. The Conway office, 1951 Industrial Park Rd., (843) 915-4700, can provide you with a list of approved centers, including for-profit and nonprofit centers, as well as the names of individuals licensed to keep children in their homes. You can visit the Web site at www.state.us/dss.

Increasingly popular AuPairCare is an option. AuPairCare matches American families with childcare providers from all over the world, ages 18 to 26, who are interested in spending a year in the United States. Au pairs are thoroughly screened, and host families can choose for themselves a provider who best suits their personal needs and collective personality.

Unlike a paid employee for whom you have to report income, an au pair essentially becomes a member of the family: The individual lives in your home, participates in household chores, and shares your meals and your celebrations. In exchange for room, board, and a salary-like weekly allowance, the au pair offers constant care for one or more children. During the program year, local or regional AuPairCare counselors provide support to both the families and the au pair. For more information call (800) 428-7247 or visit www.aupaircare.com.

St. Philip's Lutheran Church in Myrtle Beach offers a Mother's Morning Out program that runs through May and June to supplement their extensive day-care program, which includes kinder-music and gymnastics. Contact Jeanie Stetzer, (843) 449-4322, for an application. Timberlake Baptist Church, 9850 Hwy. 707, also offers Mother's Morning Out. Call (843) 650-9509 for more information.

Be sure to read the Kidstuff and Attractions chapters for fun and educational activities to occupy your brood's time.

i The mall-size Barnes & Noble bookstore on US 17 Bypass is the perfect place to take the kids. In addition to a truly staggering collection of children's literature, there are frequent storytelling hours and other activities for tykes. Call (843) 444-4046 for details.

Babysitting Services for Visitors

With the heavy influx of families visiting this area, there are frequent inquiries about babysitting services available to nonresidents. After all, time-starved moms and dads deserve a break from the family rat race every now and again!

If you'd consider leaving your child with a sitting service, read on. The following businesses cater primarily to the tourist market but serve a few locals as well. Although they can sometimes accommodate parents on short notice, officials suggest calling at least 24 hours in advance, especially during the busy summer season. Most of the sitters are mature women, many of whom are age 30 or older. All are thoroughly screened. Sitters provide their own transportation and will accept jobs from North Myrtle Beach to Garden City Beach.

The Kiddie Park Learning Center in Myrtle Beach is a service that caters to shoppers, beachgoers, and partygoers. In business for more than three decades, Kiddie Park is open Monday through Saturday from 6:45 a.m. until 11:30 p.m. Patrons will pay $ to $5 an hour. A day rate is $30. Weekly service is also offered, and rates run from $80 to $100, depending on the age of your child. The 10-hour day includes a meal and a snack. The meal can be lunch or dinner, depending on the shift. Call (843) 488-3413 for an appointment.

Many hotels and resorts also provide babysitting. Ask about availability of services—and rates—when making reservations.

EDUCATION

Public Schools

The Horry County School District's student services begin with an early-childhood program for four-year-olds with developmental and learning difficulties. Kindergarten for five-year-olds is a standard part of the statewide school curriculum and is available throughout the district.

The Horry County School District Web site, www.hcs.k12.sc.us, offers activity calendars so families can help their children continue learning during the summer. Activities can be adapted to suit the age, learning style, and progress of each child.

Every elementary school offers the PELICAN program for gifted and talented students. PELICAN provides enrichment activities one day a week that foster critical-thinking skills and encourage creativity.

Middle schools offer basic classes as well as honors programs. Similarly, all seven Horry County high schools provide a basic curriculum plus college-preparatory and honors classes. Advanced Placement classes afford students who pass standardized tests possible exemption from certain introductory college classes.

One unique feature of the Horry County schools is Playcard Environmental Center, a nature preserve in the western portion of the county. The center gives urban and suburban kids a taste of rural life and also teaches all children a healthy respect for the earth's resources. Students learn about Native American and pioneer cultures and the ecosystems of a thriving black-water swamp. The pristine preserve features a collection of farm and domestic animals, a nature trail with labeled flora and fauna, an old rope swing in a forested area, and a real beaver dam.

School officials say that Playcard is unique in South Carolina and perhaps the United States. The 200-acre preserve also provides a site for observation and study in various scientific disciplines. The program is sponsored by both the community and the school district and is governed by an advisory board made up of representatives from Coastal Carolina University, Horry-Georgetown Technical College, and community and business members.

Conway is the district's largest high school, with almost 1,800 students. Carolina Forest High School ranks second with slightly more than 1,000.

The Aynor/Conway Adult Education Center; the Loris, Socastee, and North Myrtle Beach Adult Education Centers; and the Academy of Arts, Science and Technology collectively provide vocational, technical, occupational, and academic training. The Conway School of Nursing, housed at the Aynor/Conway Adult Education Center, is a two-year program that prepares students for careers as licensed practical nurses (LPNs). The Academy of Arts, Science and Technology offers instruction in programs such as graphics, video/audio technology, pre-engineering, golf course technology (that's right, the academic study of golf courses!), dance, and hospitality services (also known as hotel management).

For more information call Horry County Schools at (843) 448-6700.

Private Schools

With the exception of some day-care centers and preschools, all of Horry's private schools are church affiliated and basically Christian, reflecting a regional tradition of fundamental Christian morality, beliefs, and culture (see the Worship chapter).

North Strand

RISEN CHRIST LUTHERAN SCHOOL
10595 US 17 N., North Myrtle Beach
(843) 272-8163
www.risenchristmyrtlebeach.org
Risen Christ was established with the primary stated goal "of preparing each child for a happy and fruitful life." In keeping with their interpretation of such a lofty goal, a number of developmental categories are emphasized: intellectual, spiritual, emotional, social, and physical. Risen Christ staff believe that administering to students on these levels helps children grow into well-rounded and successful adults.

Risen Christ is dedicated to bringing up children "in the way of the Lord." Along with providing spiritual training, Risen Christ strives to maintain high academic standards. The school belongs to the Lutheran Education Association and is one of more than 2,000 Lutheran schools in the United States. Curricular areas of study include religion, English, spelling, writing, math, social studies, science, computers, art, music, physical education, and Spanish (grades 6, 7, and 8).

Risen Christ offers prekindergarten and kindergarten classes as well as primary grades 1 through 8. Additionally, it offers before- and after-school child care for prekindergartners through 5th graders. A summer camp also is offered for students.

Myrtle Beach

CALVARY CHRISTIAN SCHOOL
**4511 Dick Pond Rd. (Highway 544),
Myrtle Beach
(843) 238-0148
www.ccsmb.com**
A ministry of Calvary Bible Church, Calvary offers preschool programs for youngsters three through five years of age and regular classes for 1st through 12th graders in a distinctly religious setting. This is the Strand's oldest Christian school, although officially all denominations are welcome in a student body of more than 300. The elementary classes are known for their strong phonics program. According to standardized achievement test results, Calvary rates more than a year ahead of national grade-level averages. Similarly, SAT scores rank ahead of both the state and the national average.

CATHEDRAL HALL ACADEMY
**803 Howard Parkway, Myrtle Beach
(843) 238-0148
www.cathedralministries.org**
Sponsored by the Cathedral Bible College (also profiled in this chapter), Grand Strand Academy is a school with strong academics and a strong religious emphasis. The academy uses the advanced A Beka curriculum for four-year-olds through 12th graders. The school's active fine-arts program includes chorus, orchestra, art appreciation, and even Latin and Greek on the high-school level. In 2008 the school added a new building that features a science lab, computer lab, library, and state-of-the-art cafeteria.

CHABAD ACADEMY
**2803 North Oak St., Myrtle Beach
(843) 448-0035
www.chabadmb.com**
Chabad is the Grand Strand's only Jewish-affiliated private school. The student body totals almost 130 and features prekindergarten through 9th grade. Chabad's mission is to educate and unite a diverse Jewish community: children from well-to-do families with children whose parents are hourly workers; children from families stressing strong traditional religious backgrounds with children from secular families; children of American-born parents with children of recent immigrants. The synagogue meets twice a day every day and hosts a full house on the weekends, officiates for life-cycle events, and is most known for its warmth and closeness.

ST. ANDREW CATHOLIC SCHOOL
**3601 North Kings Hwy., Myrtle Beach
(843) 448-6062
www.standrewmb.com/school**
In November 2005, St. Andrew was named a Blue Ribbon School by the U.S. Department of Education. This school is supported by tuition and parish subsidies. Class sizes range from 25 to 30 students, and faculty positions total approximately 14. The program is enhanced by an active PTO and Mother's Club. Consequently, parent volunteers contribute significantly to the overall quality of their children's educational experience.

Christian education at St. Andrew is designed to educate the child as a whole—intellectually, morally, physically, emotionally, and socially. Students enjoy a high level of interaction with teachers and classmates. St. Andrew strives to develop leadership through classroom activities, school worship, liturgies, and extracurricular activities. The educational program is designed to foster academic excellence, emphasizing basic skills as a strong foundation. And the program's success is evident in standardized test results and in the number of students admitted to advanced-placement high-school programs.

Classes are offered from kindergarten (five-year-olds) through 8th grade, and after-school care is available for students.

South Strand

PAWLEYS ISLAND MONTESSORI DAY SCHOOL

236 Commerce Dr., Pawleys Island
(843) 237-9015
www.pawleysislandmontessori.org

Approximately 50 students, from 18-month-olds to 6th graders, attend Pawleys Island Montessori Day School. The curriculum, as the name indicates, is based on the world-renowned Montessori philosophy of education, where instructors respect each child's pace of learning and encourage students to follow their own interests. Emphasizing "concrete manipulations" (aka hands-on activities), the school has a student-teacher ratio of 10 to 1 or less. Established two decades ago, the school operates nine months of the year, has playground facilities, and welcomes new students. Call the listed number for an application.

Beyond the Strand

ATC CHRISTIAN SCHOOL

1672 Hwy. 905, Conway
(843) 365-6800

An affiliate of the Prayer Center, A Touch of Christ (ATC) Christian School offers A Beka classes for four-year-olds through 8th graders. A preschool program for two- and three-year-olds is also available. Education is administered in a Christian environment, which school officials believe is vital not only for developing character through moral training but also for reaching an outstanding level of academic excellence.

CONWAY CHRISTIAN SCHOOL

1200 Medlen Parkway, Conway
(843) 365-2005
www.conwaychristian.com

The primary goal of Conway Christian School is to provide quality education with a Biblical perspective in a distinctly Christian atmosphere of discipline. The school's academic priority is teaching fundamental skills. An affiliate of Grace Presbyterian Church, Conway Christian offers preschool classes for four- and five-year-olds and uses the A Beka curriculum, including French and Spanish, for students in the 1st through 12th grades.

Higher Education

Myrtle Beach

CATHEDRAL BIBLE COLLEGE

803 Howard Parkway, Myrtle Beach
(843) 238-4388
www.cathedralministries.org

Cathedral Bible College offers a master of theology degree, with majors in ministry, missions, Christian education, church administration, counseling, and music. The college, which occupies the site of a former U.S. Air Force base, enrolls approximately 100 students.

FORTUNE ACADEMY

734 Hemlock Ave., Myrtle Beach
(800) 922-2245, (843) 236-1131,
(843) 477-0808
www.fortuneacademy.com

Located with Horry-Georgetown Technical College, Fortune Academy's goal is to help train those seeking a profession in numerous areas of real estate. Fortune offers live and online courses in real estate licensing, home inspection, appraisal, mortgage lending, and real estate coaching. The school is considered one of the best real estate agent schools in South Carolina.

WEBSTER UNIVERSITY

4589 Oleander Drive, Myrtle Beach
(843) 497-3677
www.webster.edu

Webster University is an independent, nonde-nominational, multicampus international business college offering a graduate program at its Myrtle Beach campus. Webster prides itself on offering degree programs that many schools in the area do not, including management, human resources, and counseling. Classes are conveniently scheduled to attract students from up to two hours away as well as working professionals.

Graduate programs in business, human resources development, management, and clinical counseling are all accredited by the North Central Association of Colleges and Schools. Admission to the MA and MBA programs is open to all students who hold an undergraduate degree from a regionally accredited college or university.

In a nutshell, Webster offers education tailored to busy professionals. The distinction of Webster's whole approach is that of its commitment to education and to the community. This motto has created distinct advantages for adult students—fulfilling the wish list of anyone who wants to change careers, retool in the wake of cutbacks or closings, or advance in his or her current situation.

i Coastal Carolina's Center for Marine and Wetland Studies in the College of Natural and Applied Sciences is recognized nationally for its comprehensive research on beach erosion and marine geology. Coastal was one of only 10 universities to receive recognition from the National Science Foundation and receive a $500,000 grant to help in its continuous water-quality monitoring projects of the coast and the river systems of Horry and Georgetown Counties.

Beyond the Strand
COASTAL CAROLINA UNIVERSITY
US 501 E., Conway
(843) 347-3161
www.coastal.edu

Coastal Carolina is a comprehensive liberal arts institution offering baccalaureate degrees in more than 30 major fields of study as well as master's degrees in education. The university is committed to excellence in teaching, research, and public service.

Covering more than 300 wooded acres just minutes from the Atlantic Ocean and the resort area of Myrtle Beach, the Coastal Carolina campus is home to more than 8,049 students from South Carolina and 44 other states as well as 32 foreign countries.

A Coastal Carolina education offers a hands-on, personal educational experience. Approximately 240 faculty members bring impressive credentials from universities throughout the nation. Select faculty have been awarded Fulbright grants for research projects and study in such countries as New Zealand, Kenya, Colombia, Poland, and China. In addition, students can interact with worldwide experts on a variety of topical issues through the advanced technologies of long-distance education and online computer services.

Coastal Carolina's academic programs often are supplemented with field experiences and "real world" applications. Students have the chance to participate in faculty-led travel to a pristine barrier island on the South Carolina coast, the Grand Canyon, archaeological digs in surrounding historical settings, Fortune 500 companies, the marbled chambers of the U.S. Supreme Court, Oxford University, and East Africa. Coastal's many international partnerships make it possible for students to study in places such as Australia, Costa Rica, England, Ecuador, the Galapagos Islands, Germany, India, Japan, Russia, and Spain.

The university boasts many accreditations, including AACSB (the Association to Advance Collegiate Schools of Business) International, the National Council for Accreditation of Teacher Education (NCATE), the South Carolina State Board of Education, and the Accreditation Board for Engineering and Technology (ABET). Coastal is also an accredited institutional member of the National Association of Schools of Art and Design (NASAD).

The university's four applied-research centers help students realize the practical applications of classroom theory and the importance of university-community relations.

University programs that serve the community include continuing education; Lifelong Learning, an academic program for those age 50 and older (see the Senior Scene chapter); and cultural events including live arts performances.

Coastal Carolina athletes participate in NCAA Division I, with 17 varsity teams competing in the Big South Conference.

Coastal Carolina is accredited by the Commission of the Southern Association of Colleges and Schools to award the baccalaureate degree and the master's degree in education.

In 1954, when a group of concerned citizens met in the Horry County Memorial Library to discuss the creation of a local college, the foundation was laid for Coastal Carolina to provide quality education for its students. For more than 50 years, the university has been building a tradition of excellence. In 1994 it broke from the University of South Carolina system in a major political battle over endowments; it seems that Coastal officials felt that they were at the bottom of the priorities list for fund-raising expenditures. Since the split, Coastal Carolina has begun major expansion, and the Golf Course Management program has come to be recognized as one of the nation's finest.

i **Horry-Georgetown Technical College offers a degree in golf course management. The two-year program is highly acclaimed.**

HORRY-GEORGETOWN TECHNICAL COLLEGE
2050 US 501 E., Conway
(843) 347-3186
www.hgtc.edu

Horry-Georgetown Technical College, established in 1966, currently boasts an annual student enrollment of more than 5,400. Combined with the Continuing Education Division of HGTC, which provides skill enhancement and specialized job training, that number reaches 16,000. The college continues to grow and prosper while serving Horry and Georgetown Counties as well as surrounding communities.

HGTC is in the business of cultivating excellence across three campuses, with convenient sites in Conway, Myrtle Beach (now also on the former Air Force base), and Georgetown. The college offers more than 60 degrees, diplomas, and certificates—from associate in arts and associate in science to a varied technical and business curriculum. In addition to the two-year degrees, HGTC has several transfer agreements with other South Carolina colleges and universities that allow students to obtain four-year degrees. Furthermore, HGTC has more than 70 courses guaranteed to transfer for full credit to any public higher-education institution in South Carolina. Its thriving Continuing Education program and intensive on-site industrial training program—serving more than 75 businesses, industries, and organizations each year—round out HGTC's educational opportunities.

Horry-Georgetown Technical College is accredited by the Commission on Colleges of the Southern Association of Colleges and Schools.

HEALTH CARE

For the benefit of any visitor to the Grand Strand, this chapter will give you pertinent information about regional medical services, clinics, and hospitals. Health-care services listed here should be able to handle anything from a severe sunburn to debilitating pain.

The Grand Strand has witnessed an incredible growth in health-care services and specialists. Rapid growth, ideal locations for golf and attractions, and what one physician called "a doctor-friendly environment" have brought a weighty influx of medical expertise to the area.

The less-stressful lifestyle and heralded Southern hospitality are enjoyed by many of these practitioners. The need for doctors who practice geriatrics, rheumatology, and endocrinology has soared in direct proportion with the number of senior citizens relocating to the Grand Strand.

If you are about to become a resident or have just moved into our area, the referral services can quickly put you in touch with a new family doctor or specialist.

REFERRALS AND FREE ADVICE

PHYSICIAN REFERRAL SOURCE
(843) 692-1052
www.grandstrandmed.com

Especially if a medical specialist is needed, this service will give you all the necessary referral information, including a doctor's hours. Physician Referral represents more than 275 physicians on Grand Strand Regional Medical Center's staff and more than 30 medical specialties and subspecialties. This service is available 9 a.m. to 5 p.m., Mon through Fri.

PHYSICIANS REFERRAL SERVICE
(843) 716-7000, ext. 6410

Sponsored by Loris Community Hospital, this service provides referral to conveniently located physicians who meet a person's medical needs.

Physicans Referral Service is available Mon through Fri from 8:30 a.m. to 5 p.m.

REGIONAL HEALTH-CARE FACILITIES

Walk-in Clinics

Visitors who need to see a doctor but aren't sick enough to go to a hospital emergency room can save themselves time and money by seeking care at one of the Grand Strand's walk-in medical clinics.

These clinics take patients without appointments, but most of them don't take insurance, Medicaid, or Medicare, so be prepared to pay when you go. Costs run anywhere from $55 to $100 for an average visit, and some health-care providers accept traveler's checks, in-state personal checks, or credit cards as methods of payment (as noted in each write-up).

Clinic doctors routinely treat sunburn, heat rash, heat exhaustion, cuts, sprains, broken bones, jellyfish stings, and sore throats. And some facilities offer more complex services, including X-rays and stabilization of patients who have had heart attacks. Here is a listing of walk-in clinics representing each area of the Strand.

North Strand
ACCESS MEDICAL CARE
3816 US 17 S., North Myrtle Beach
(843) 272-1411

Access Medical Care offers minor surgery, X-rays, electrocardiograms, and complete laboratory services, as well as a pharmacy. With the exception of Blue Cross/Blue Shield, insurance is not accepted, but office workers will fill out Medicare and Medicaid papers for people who live in South and North Carolina. Access will file workers' compensation claims. The clinic is open Mon through Fri from 8 a.m. to 7 p.m., and on Sat and Sun from 9 a.m. to 3 p.m.

DOCTOR'S CARE NORTH MYRTLE BEACH
1714 US 17 S., North Myrtle Beach
(843) 361-0705
www.doctorscare.com
Doctor's Care medical clinic provides primary and urgent care, including X-rays, stitches, and stabilization of heart attack patients. The clinic accepts regular patients for family practice and can also handle minor lab work. Emergencies will be sent to the nearest hospital. The cost for a typical nonemergency office visit starts at $92. The North Myrtle Beach clinic is open extended hours seven days a week.

Myrtle Beach
DOCTOR'S CARE MYRTLE BEACH
1220 21st Ave. N., Myrtle Beach
(843) 626-9379
www.doctorscare.com
The Doctor's Care medical clinics provide primary and urgent care, including X-rays, stitches, and stabilization of heart attack patients. Doctors here accept regular patients for family practice. The clinics also handle minor lab work. Emergencies are sent to the nearest hospital. The center is open extended hours seven days a week. The cost for a typical nonemergency office visit starts at $92; if you return to the clinic, the cost is reduced. Doctor's Care dispenses common medications to its patients.

DUNES URGENT MEDICAL CARE
1410 South Kings Highway, Myrtle Beach
(843) 448-2228
Dunes Medical is located in a busy part of the southern section of Myrtle Beach. With one doctor and one nurse practitioner, Dunes can handle any minor emergency, as well as some minor surgeries and X-rays. The urgent care facility is open Mon through Fri from 9 a.m. to 4 p.m. They accept Visa and MasterCard as well as most insurance.

South Strand
DOCTOR'S CARE
Surfside Medical Center, 1600 US 17 N., Surfside Beach
(843) 238-1461
www.doctorscare.com
This Doctor's Care clinic, like its counterparts in North Myrtle Beach and Myrtle Beach (see previous entries for details), provides primary and urgent care and handles minor lab work. The Surfside Beach clinic is open seven days a week from 8 a.m. to 8 p.m.

LITCHFIELD MEDICAL CENTER
14866 Ocean Hwy., Pawleys Island
(843) 250-0760
The Litchfield Medical Center serves the South Strand community of Pawleys Island. The Center is a two-doctor family practice, treating regular patients in addition to emergencies. Among its services are wound care, pulmonary function testing, physical examinations, minor surgery and TRICARE. Most major insurance is accepted. They are open Mon through Fri 8:30 a.m. to 5 p.m.

MED PLUS SOUTH STRAND FAMILY CLINIC
2347 US 17 Business, Garden City
(843) 357-2443
www.medplussc.com
This walk-in clinic, across from Garden City Furniture, also serves regular patients by appointment. The clinic conducts allergy tests as well as bone-density tests to determine early signs of osteoporosis.

It is open Mon through Fri from 8 a.m. to 8 p.m., and on Sat from 9 a.m. to 1 p.m. The cost of a first-time urgent-care visit ranges from $85 to $120. Discounts are applied for subsequent visits.

Hospitals

It's heart-wrenching when you, a loved one, or friend needs hospital attention, but you can take comfort in the care and professionalism found at the following medical facilities. Scanning through this section, you should be able to get a good idea of the specialty services offered by each, just in case you need to make a quick decision about where to take someone for medical attention.

North Strand
LORIS HEALTHCARE SYSTEM
3655 Mitchell St., Loris
(843) 716-7000
www.lorishealthcaresystem.com

Some visitors at the northern end of the Grand Strand might find it quickest to visit Loris, an acute-care, nonprofit community hospital. Loris has a capacity of 105 patients, all in private rooms. The hospital also runs a separate 88-bed, skilled nursing assisted facility known as the Loris Healthcare System Extended Care Center.

Loris Hospital offers 24-hour emergency service, cardiac rehabilitation services, same-day surgery, a modern intensive-care unit, ultrasound, magnetic resonance imaging (MRI), a CT scanner, nuclear medicine, extensive outpatient services, an obstetrics unit with childbirth and breast-feeding classes, and nutritional counseling.

A 26,000-square-foot center for health and fitness houses cardiac rehabilitation, physical therapy, hydrotherapy, exercise programs, and meeting facilities. Regular classes focus on smoking cessation, weight loss, and low-fat cooking. Unlike other hospital-sponsored wellness programs, Loris Community offers use of its fitness facility to the public in an effort to keep people out of its beds through prevention.

The fitness center offers a variety of aerobic classes, including Seniorcize and water aerobics, plus cardiovascular and strength-building equipment. In fact, the center quickly earned a local reputation as an "unofficial" community spot, being selected by community members as the site for wedding receptions, gatherings, and programs.

Loris Healthcare System also operates Seacoast Medical Center. Located in Little River, this 24-hour emergency and same-day surgery facility makes health-care services more easily accessible to the communities of Longs, Little River, North Myrtle Beach, and Calabash.

Loris Healthcare System has also opened a full complement of medical offices, including Calabash Imaging and Diagnostic Center, Extended Care Center, Family Health Centers in Loris and Mt. Olive, and Rainbow Pediatrics in Loris and Little River. It offers extensive community outreach programs.

Loris Healthcare System continues to enhance health services in the region by providing new services and renovations to existing facilities, including the open MRI services conveniently available at Seacoast Medical Center and enhanced Women's Services with the addition of new labor, delivery, and recovery suites.

Myrtle Beach
GRAND STRAND REGIONAL MEDICAL CENTER
809 82nd Parkway, Myrtle Beach
(843) 692-1000
www.grandstrandmed.com

Grand Strand Regional Medical Center is a 219-bed acute-care facility that offers an array of medical services on both an inpatient and outpatient basis. The medical staff numbers more than 900, with more than 250 physicians on call.

Grand Strand Regional was named as one of the top 100 hospitals in the country for cardiovascular care, with two operating rooms dedicated solely to open-heart surgery, angioplasty, and other heart-related procedures. The hospital is noted for its state-of-the-art cardiac catheterization and diagnostic laboratory, stents, and cardiac rehabilitation. A rehabilitation center houses exercise equipment and supervised programs for cardiac patients that include fitness, nutritional counseling, education, and risk education.

In 2008, 400 cardiac surgeries were performed with success rates exceeding state and national averages. The need for local services was apparent: Heart disease is the leading cause of death in South Carolina and accounts for 40 percent of all deaths statewide. Grand Strand Regional Medical Center in Myrtle Beach answered that need by building a 14,600-square-foot, $5.9 million surgical addition to the hospital that includes an eight-bed surgical intensive-care unit and two operating suites. A satellite pharmacy services the operating rooms and the surgical intensive-care unit.

The emergency department is a designated

trauma center using electronic technology that includes a hyperbaric chamber commonly used in treating diving accidents, wounds, and burns. Emergency also offers Care Express to treat minor injuries and illnesses for anyone without a local physician. Care Express is open to new residents and visitors alike. Grand Strand Regional emergency services is also the proud owner of HeartLink, a cardiac transport ambulance for those in need of acute care. All of Grand Strand's emergency department physicians are board certified in emergency medicine. For added convenience, an outpatient pharmacy is open to the public from 7 a.m. to 7 p.m. every day of the week.

Grand Strand Hospital operates an accredited community cancer program in Horry and Georgetown Counties. It is also a member of the National Consortium of Breast Centers, and oncology physicians and nurses are board certified. Mammography is available at the hospital and at diagnostic centers in Little River and Surfside Beach. Radiation therapy is available at a nearby facility, and a cancer registry is employed to track patient treatments and follow-up through a national data bank. Grand Strand Medical utilizes minimally invasive breast biopsy (MIBB) and a sentinel node biopsy program.

Grand Strand Regional Medical Center has six affiliates throughout the Grand Strand to provide quality, convenient health care. These affiliates are at the Grand Strand Regional Diagnostic & Women's Center, South Strand Ambulatory Care Center, Grand Strand Regional Medical Center Wound Care Program, North Strand Diagnostic Center, North Strand Senior Health Center, and the South Strand Senior Health Center on the campus of Community Medical Center–South Strand.

Hospital officials work especially hard at preventive care and community education through an annual health fair held on the first Saturday in February and a cardiac wellness program that includes the Mall Walkers Club, the Cardiac Lifelong Program, and ongoing community cholesterol screenings.

Other community programs include prostate cancer screening and a teddy bear clinic for children—an annual event at Grand Strand Regional aimed at allaying children's fears of hospitals. Preschoolers bring their "injured" teddy bears into the emergency room, where doctors and nurses apply bandages, splints, stitches, and the odd button.

> **i** Nearly all Grand Strand hospitals have impressive wellness centers with exercise equipment, aerobics classes, swimming pools, and a host of health-related programs. Membership is open to the public, making them an alternative workout spot to gyms, aerobics studios, and fitness venues. Trained, professional staff is a must for all hospital wellness programs.

South Strand

GEORGETOWN MEMORIAL HOSPITAL
606 Black River Rd., Georgetown
(843) 527-7000, (843) 626-9040
(from Myrtle Beach)
www.gmhsc.com

This is a private, nonprofit acute-care medical facility that is currently licensed for 131 beds. More than 50 physicians representing 20 areas of specialty practice are members of the active medical staff.

Medical services include ambulatory surgery; birthing suites; cardiac diagnostics, catheterization, and rehabilitation; full emergency and lab services; MRI; pathology; radiology; renal dialysis; and respiratory therapy. The hospital also offers cholesterol screenings, dietary consultation, and discharge planning. Throughout any given year, Georgetown Memorial holds various educational programs and events.

Established in 1950, Georgetown Memorial has consistently expanded services to keep up with the needs of the community. More recently the hospital added pre-op bays, a fifth surgical suite, and a diagnostic imaging center.

WACCAMAW COMMUNITY HOSPITAL
4070 US 17 Bypass, Murrells Inlet
(843) 357-5100
www.gmhsc.com

The newest member of the Georgetown Hospital Family opened its doors in late 2002. Waccamaw Community Hospital, a 40-bed inpatient facility, accommodates the needs of a growing population in northern Georgetown County and southern Horry County. The three-story building is composed of nearly 187,000 square feet of interior space. Twenty-four-hour emergency services, obstetrics, inpatient and outpatient surgery, and medical/surgical units are offered at the new hospital. In addition, a 29-bed acute-care rehabilitation facility is located on the same site. It is designed to serve as a short-term, interim step for patients who have been discharged from an inpatient facility. Rehabilitation therapy services, including physical, occupational, and speech therapy, are available to acute rehab inpatients.

Beyond the Strand
CONWAY MEDICAL CENTER
300 Singleton Ridge Rd., Conway
(843) 347-7111
www.conwayhospital.com

Conway Medical Center, a private, nonprofit institution, was in downtown Conway for more than a half century before a large, modern facility was built outside the city limits between Conway and Myrtle Beach.

The medical center opened in 1982, and today approximately 200 physicians make rounds among 160 modern, private rooms. The building itself has three stories, with patient rooms occupying the top two floors. Conway Medical Center has 80 medical/surgical beds, 16 obstetrical/gynecological beds, 23 pediatrics beds, and 10 beds equipped for intensive and coronary care.

Services include 24-hour emergency and urgent care, one-day surgery, chemotherapy, CT scanning, MRI, lithotripsy, maternity care, pediatric care, mammography, cardiac rehabilitation, nuclear medicine, physical therapy, respiratory therapy, home health care, surgical care, ultrasound, intensive care, and progressive care. A new generation of echocardiographic equipment, as well as CT scanning, MRI, digital substraction angiography, blood gas analysis, impedance plethysmography, advanced telemetry techniques, and cardiac catheterization allows for state-of-the-art diagnostic and treatment capabilities. The hospital is also certified as a Level III trauma center as well as Level II perinatal center.

Conway Medical Center was the world's first to receive the Spectron Hip Reconstruction system. In August 1996 Dr. James Yates performed the sixth autologous chondrocyte transplant in the United States at Conway Medical Center. The procedure is noted for producing remarkable results for young patients suffering from knee cartilage injury.

Patients requiring dialysis during their hospital stay are served at the facility through an inpatient dialysis unit. In addition, the adjoining Medstar subacute care building provides care to individuals in transition from intensive services to home, at a significantly reduced cost.

Adjacent to Conway Medical Center is Kingston Nursing Center, an 88-bed long-term nursing home owned and operated by the medical center. And, through the efforts of a joint venture, Conway Medical Center works with American Home Patient, a company that supplies home infusion services, home respiratory services, and home medical equipment.

In spring 1996 Conway Medical Center opened its 39,000-square-foot wellness and fitness center. This center includes a swimming pool, racquetball courts, an indoor track, basketball court, weight room, his and hers saunas, and locker rooms. Aerobics classes are scheduled as well. Memberships to the wellness facility are open to individuals, patients, and corporations, and a variety of rate packages is available. For more information call (843) 347-1515.

Conway Medical Center has developed a mobile health service program called HEALTHREACH, which provides free mobile health screenings to those in the community without access to adequate primary health care services. HEALTHREACH's mobile unit has been designed to provide screenings for early detection of heart disease, cancer, stroke, and chronic lung disease, which are the leading causes of death in Horry County.

Other Regional Facilities

McLEOD REGIONAL MEDICAL CENTER
555 East Cheves St., Florence
(843) 777-2000
www.mcleodhealth.org

About 75 miles from Myrtle Beach is McLeod Regional Hospital, a regional referral center for 12 counties in southeastern South Carolina. McLeod was established in 1906 as a small infirmary; today it's a large high-tech medical center, with 331 beds and a variety of services. Many Horry County residents depend on McLeod's neonatal intensive-care unit to tend to premature babies and full-term babies born with special problems.

The hospital's breast-imaging center helps doctors detect breast cancer in its early stages. McLeod had the state's first permanent MRI system, a high-tech machine that uses a magnetic field to see into the body in a much clearer way than other scanning machines allow.

McLeod also provides comprehensive inpatient, outpatient, and diagnostic facilities, including an extensive 24-hour laboratory, computerized tomography, angiography, computer-enhanced nuclear medicine, ultrasound, echocardiography, mammography, EEG, EKG, a vascular laboratory, osteoporosis screening, a sleep center, and 24-hour emergency care. The Florence hospital is the state-designated regional trauma center.

The facility added a five-story freestanding Women's Pavilion connected to McLeod. The pavilion houses a mammography unit, outpatient surgery rooms, and a special section for labor and delivery or Caesarean section.

McLeod Children's Hospital provides the highest level of pediatric care and technology available in the region. Nearly 100 of McLeod's beds are dedicated to serving the needs of children. The Child Life Activity Center offers a place for relaxed play and distraction from illness or injury, and Child Life Specialists are assigned to work with children and their families to make the hospital stay easier. In 1994 McLeod opened the region's only five-bed Pediatric Intensive Care Unit (PICU). In 1997 the PICU was upgraded to a six-bed unit and is under the direction of two board-certified pediatric specialists. McLeod has five pediatric subspecialists of pediatric cardiology, endocrinology, gastroenterology, and critical care.

A range of support departments buttress the hospital's services. These include rehabilitative services, pain management, cardiac rehabilitation, respiratory services, counseling and discharge planning, hospice, infection control, pastoral services, patient representatives, volunteer services, computer services, and marketing.

Mental Health/Addictions
South Strand
THE WACCAMAW CENTER FOR MENTAL HEALTH
525 Lafayette Circle, Georgetown
(843) 546-6107
164 Waccamaw Medical Park Dr., Conway
(843) 347-4888
www.waccamawmentalhealth.org

The Waccamaw Center is a public, nonprofit agency that handles any sort of mental-health issue on an outpatient basis. Fees are established on a sliding scale; you pay only what you can afford based on income and expenses, and most insurances are accepted. Staff is on call 24 hours a day, seven days a week to respond to emergencies and crises. Both clinics offer adult services, child and adolescent therapy, alcohol and drug abuse counseling, programs for the chronically mentally ill, and emergency stabilization.

The center is continuously developing special community programs to institute prevention of growing mental-health problems. The school-based program operates out of a number of Grand Strand schools, offering on-site help to children and their families. An Employee Assistance Program offers mental-health services to business and industry on a contractual basis. The Waccamaw Center also will refer clients to an appropriate inpatient facility if it is necessary.

Beyond the Strand
SHORELINE BEHAVIORAL HEALTH SERVICES
2404 Wise Rd., Conway
(843) 365-8884
www.shorelinebhs.org
Shoreline Behavioral Health Services works with the South Carolina Department of Alcohol, other drug abuse services, and numerous local individuals, agencies, and organizations to reduce and control problems related to the use of alcohol and other drugs. They accomplish this through a variety of primary prevention, intervention, and treatment services. The agency strives to provide affordable and accessible quality services to the general public, as well as to special and high-risk populations. Services include a 10-bed Psychoactive Substance Abuse Dependency facility (PSAD), day and evening counseling services, employee assistance programs, a DUI education program, and lots more. Fees are based on services received, and a variety of payment plans are available.

Health-Related Associations and Support Groups
ALCOHOLICS ANONYMOUS
(843) 445-7119
www.area62.org
Vacations tend to be a big temptation for alcoholics to slip, so there are numerous support groups in the Grand Strand area sponsored by Alcoholics Anonymous. The South Carolina region is AA's Area 62, and the Grand Strand falls under District 81. There are 22 support groups in the region with daily meetings at 11 locations. Some start as early as 6:30 a.m., and most have their last meeting at 8 p.m. The Myrtle Beach 12 Study Group offers a midnight meeting on Saturday at the Alano Club at 910 67th Avenue North in Myrtle Beach.

ALZHEIMER'S SUPPORT GROUP OF MURRELLS INLET
Belin Methodist Church, 4182 US 17, Murrells Inlet
(843) 651-9711

ALZHEIMER'S SUPPORT GROUP OF GEORGETOWN
Prince George Episcopal Church, 301 Broad St., Georgetown
(843) 237-2845
Cosponsored by the Alzheimer's Association Palmetto Chapter, the groups offer care and support for individuals affected by Alzheimer's disease, as well as teaching coping techniques and offering general information. The Murrells Inlet chapter meets the second and fourth Wed of every month at 10 a.m. at Belin Methodist Church. The Georgetown support group meets every first Mon at noon at Prince George Episcopal Church.

ARTHRITIS FOUNDATION
1330 West Peachtree St., Atlanta, GA
(800) 283-7800
www.arthritis.org
The Arthritis Foundation provides a toll-free number to answer questions about various types of arthritis and, when appropriate, refers callers to community organizations. The foundation is also prepared to help clients and their families with financial support.

BETTER BREATHERS CLUB
Grand Strand Regional Medical Center
809 82nd Parkway, Myrtle Beach
(843) 692-1885
www.grandstrandmed.com
This group, supporting individuals who suffer from breathing difficulties, meets on the third Thurs of each month at 3 p.m. Meetings are free and open to the public. The group usually meets in the Cardiac Rehabilitation classroom. To be sure, please call the number listed to confirm the location.

CANCER SUPPORT GROUP
Georgetown Memorial Hospital
606 Black River Rd., Georgetown
(843) 527-7448
www.gmhsc.com
The Cancer Support Group is open to anyone affected by cancer. The group meets monthly at the Georgetown Hospital Education Center.

Other area groups include Breast Cancer Support, (843) 213-0333, and Grand Strand Prostate Cancer support group, (843) 272-1537.

COMMUNITY SEMINAR
5046 US 17 Bypass, Myrtle Beach
(843) 839-6162
Informative, educational community-health seminars are presented monthly, usually at a 10 a.m. meeting, at the South Strand Senior Health Center Community Room, Suite 101. Seminars feature local health-care professionals discussing a variety of health topics. The community health-care seminars are free and open to the public. Call ahead for a schedule.

DEPARTMENT OF HEALTH AND ENVIRONMENTAL CONTROL
53 Lafayette St., Georgetown
(843) 546-5593
2830 Oak St., Conway
(843) 365-3126
DHEC provides pregnancy tests, blood tests, immunizations, family planning, and tuberculosis screening. The agency can provide health care to the homebound, depending upon the particular circumstances. This department is always happy to provide the larger community and schools with health promotion and educational programs.

DEPARTMENT OF SOCIAL SERVICES (DSS)
330 Dozier St., Georgetown
(843) 546-5134
1951 Industrial Park Rd., Conway
(843) 915-7400
www.state.sc.us/dss
The mission of the South Carolina Department of Social Services is to ensure the health and safety of children and adults who cannot protect themselves, to help people in need of financial assistance reach their highest level of social and economic self-sufficiency, and to help parents and caregivers provide nurturing homes. In short,

the agency states its goal as helping people to live better lives. From child support services to elder care, DSS provides a wealth of health- and human-services information.

DIABETES EDUCATION GROUP
Grand Strand Senior Center
1268 21st Ave. N., Myrtle Beach
(843) 692-9526
www.grandstrandmed.com
This group meets on the fourth Tues of each month at 6:30 p.m. for the purpose of educating diabetes patients and their family members. Special diabetes management programs and speakers from health-care providers are featured. Time is also allotted for question-and-answer sessions. Meetings are free and open to the public. For more information call Grand Strand Regional Medical Center's Diabetes Management Program coordinator at the number listed above.

DIABETIC OUTREACH
300 Singleton Ridge Rd., Conway
(843) 347-8108
A registered nurse and dietician are on hand for this group's monthly meetings, held the first Thursday of every month at 2 p.m. in the Finlayson Classroom of Conway Medical Center. A gastric bypass support group meets the second Tuesday of each month at 7 p.m. at the Conway Medical Center Wellness and Fitness Center.

MENDED HEARTS SUPPORT GROUP
Grand Strand Regional Medical Center
809 82nd Parkway, Myrtle Beach
(843) 692-1885
www.mendedhearts.org
Individuals with heart problems—heart attack, angioplasty, or bypass—can attend this meeting on the second Thurs of the month at 7 p.m. Meetings are held in the Grand Strand Regional Medical Center Cardiac Rehabilitation classroom and are free and open to the public.

MEDIA

Grand Stranders could not live without the media. Literally. When Hurricane Hugo thundered into town in September 1989, the radio became our nearest, dearest, and most trusted friend. We found ourselves again beholden to the radio during fall 1996 with stormy visits from Hurricanes Bertha and Fran. Even when power outages shrouded us in darkness and rudely shut off the television set, local radio stations such as WYAV-FM and WYAK-FM kept us informed. A number of local radio and television newscasters braved the swirling, high winds on Ocean Boulevard to give us up-to-the-minute reports, while newspaper reporters left the safety of their own homes to get the story from shelters and police outposts.

Besides comforting us through natural disasters, the media help us digest the burgeoning amount of local goings-on. The Grand Strand has become a veritable boomtown. Without media reports and newspapers, we would have one heck of a time keeping up with the daily opening and closing of businesses, entertainment venues, new housing developments, and retailers.

In an area that is frenetically attracting national franchises, recording artists, and movie stars, the sense of the Grand Strand as a community would be lost in the shuffle without media stories about the people we know—our neighbors.

One thing is sure: The Grand Strand media will keep you in touch and up-to-date. Figuring out where to go on the weekend is easy when you pick up a copy of the **Sun News** on Friday and rifle through the "kicks!" insert. Every festival, arts event, feature movie, new restaurant, entertainer, and venue is listed.

You can even start making plans while driving into town by surfing the channels of your car radio. Especially from March through September, radio airwaves are packed with announcements from nightclubs, restaurants, and shops. Nightclubs generally advertise what's happening that evening for entertainment, plus food and drink specials. In fact, your night's itinerary can be set even before you check into your hotel room.

With that in mind, get in touch with the Grand Strand by lending your eyes and ears to the local media.

NEWSPAPERS

Dailies

SUN NEWS
914 Frontage Road E., Myrtle Beach
(843) 626-8555
www.thesunnews.com
Established in 1961 with the merger of the *Myrtle Beach News* and the *Myrtle Beach Sun* newspapers, the *Sun News* is the only daily newspaper along the Grand Strand. It provides comprehensive local and international news, stock market reports, weather forecasts, and a classified advertising section. On Friday the paper includes the "kicks!" section, which offers information about upcoming entertainment as well as reviews. In 1997 the *Sun News* began a Saturday insert magazine, rotating the subjects of Health & Fitness, Senior Living, Outdoors, Technology & Computers, and Homes & Gardens. The Sunday edition is chock-full of extras, including a separate real estate section, TV guide, coupons, and *Parade* magazine. Daily circulation is nearly 50,000. The McClatchy Company owns the *Sun News*.

Daily delivery subscriptions for a full year are $171 or $124 if you just want delivery on Friday,

Saturday, and Sunday. A 13-week daily subscription runs $49; for weekend editions only, the cost is $31.

ℹ The McClatchy Company, which publishes the *Sun News,* is the third-largest publishing company in the United States. It was founded by James McClatchy in 1857 during the California Gold Rush. The company acquired the *Sun News* in 2006 when it bought renowned publisher Knight-Ridder, Inc.

Non-dailies

COASTAL OBSERVER
97 Commerce Dr., Pawleys Island
(843) 237-8438
www.coastalobserver.com
This weekly newspaper hits the streets on Thursday and covers the region known as the Waccamaw Neck: DeBordieu, Pawleys Island, Murrells Inlet, Litchfield Beach, and Garden City Beach. The *Observer* has been the recipient of numerous awards presented by the South Carolina Press Association for feature writing, sports coverage, layout, and design. It can be found in businesses and boxes throughout the Waccamaw Neck region at a cost of 35 cents per issue. Subscriptions are $27 a year.

GEORGETOWN TIMES
615 Front St., Georgetown
(843) 546-4148
www.gtowntimes.com
A well-established local newspaper, the *Georgetown Times* is published on Monday, Wednesday, and Friday and covers events in Georgetown and its surrounding communities. Special and favorite sections that come out in the Times at least once a year include the "Newcomer's Guide," "Bridal Guide," and "Hunting Guide." You'll find copies in news racks throughout the county for 50 cents apiece. Local subscriptions run $39 per year.

MYRTLE BEACH HERALD
3364 Huger St., Myrtle Beach
(843) 626-3131
www.myrtlebeachherald.com
Found mainly in area bookstores and grocery stores, this broadsheet newspaper comes out every Thursday morning. Editorial coverage investigates the Grand Strand from Little River to Murrells Inlet. A newcomer to the area, the *Herald* started rolling the presses in 1994. Individual issues are 50 cents a copy. Subscriptions are $30 for Horry and Georgetown Counties, with other South Carolina counties paying $35. Elsewhere in the United States, it costs $40.

NORTH MYRTLE BEACH TIMES
203 North Kings Hwy., Myrtle Beach
(843) 249-3525
www.nmbtimes.com
Published on Wednesday, the *Times* attempts to zero in on Grand Strand–related issues, such as the local option sales tax and further development of the local transportation infrastructure. You can find it at bookstores and in brochure racks at local restaurants and businesses for 50 cents each. Subscriptions are $35 for Horry and Georgetown Counties, with other South Carolina counties paying $40. Elsewhere in the United States, it costs $50.

MAGAZINES

ALTERNATIVES NEWSMAGAZINE
721 Seaboard St., Myrtle Beach
(843) 444-5556
www.myrtlebeachalternatives.com
Alternatives is considered a magazine by content only, since an issue is actually slightly smaller and glossier than a broadsheet newspaper. The magazine focus more on ideas or concepts than on reporting news. Local cultural events are always listed thoroughly in *Alternatives*. The publication features a roster of eclectic columnists who give opinions on various subjects. *Alternatives* is a freebie and is available all over the Grand

Strand—in offices, businesses, magazine racks, and restaurants. It's published twice a month, every other Thursday.

GRAND STRAND MAGAZINE
1111 48th Ave. N, Suite 116,
Myrtle Beach
(843) 449-8640
www.gsmagazine.net
As the premier lifestyle publication of the Grand Strand, *Grand Strand Magazine* represents the best of Lowcountry style, culture, and fine living. For the latest subscription rates, contact the magazine.

LOWCOUNTRY COMPANION
Hagley Center, Pawleys Island
(843) 237-3899
www.elowcountry.com/home/lc_companion .cfm
Lowcountry Companion is a free distribution, tabloid-size publication devoted to showcasing the South Carolina Lowcountry. It has featured a wide variety of articles exploring all sorts of unique subjects that relate to the rich historic and natural heritage of the region. The magazine strives to promote eco-friendly tourism—tourism that utilizes natural resources without depleting them. Each of three annual issues includes the area's most comprehensive calendar of events, as well as a restaurant guide, a golf guide, and a comprehensive directory of eco-friendly things to do. Annual subscriptions are available for $12.

RADIO STATIONS

As in most any area with a largely tourism-driven economy, the Grand Strand's world of radio is an ever-changing, volatile industry. Local radio personalities are in a constant state of flux: in and out of town, changing stations, switching formats, and showing up at different time drives. On any given day your favorite country-music DJ might disappear from the airwaves, only to be heard further down the dial hawking the latest rap tunes.

But if you're here long enough, you can place a face to almost every voice you hear on the radio. Businesses, restaurants, nightclubs, and entertainment theaters are always booking radio personalities to perform on-site "remotes." These are hardworking people, ladies and gentlemen. Many local radio personnel start their days on-air at 5 a.m., then spend the evening promoting a club act.

A 1997 study independently conducted by Young & Rubicam found that radio rules in the Myrtle Beach and Florence markets. The analysis set out to determine how much time American adults spend watching television, reading newspapers and magazines, and listening to the radio. Out of the 211 markets across the nation used in the study, Myrtle Beach and Florence ranked No. 7 for radio loyalty. Apparently, our adult population listens to the radio an average of 3 hours and 26 minutes each day. The national average for tuning into the radio is 3 hours and 9 minutes each day.

We are confident that you will find the music that you love to listen to on at least one of the stations listed here.

ADULT CONTEMPORARY
WMYB-FM 92.1 (Soft rock)

ADULT URBAN CONTEMPORARY
WXJY-FM 93.7
WDAI-FM 98.5

BEACH MUSIC
WODR-FM 105.3
WVCO-FM 94.9

CONTEMPORARY HITS
WWXM-FM 97.7

COUNTRY
WEGX-FM 92.9
WYAK-FM 103.1
WGTR-FM 107.9
WLSC-AM 1240

EASY LISTENING
WEZV-FM 94.5 and 105.9
WJYR-AM 1450

GOSPEL
WMBJ-FM 88.3
WLPG-FM 96.7
WPJS-AM 1330

JAZZ
WBAN-FM 90.9

OLDIES
WNMB-AM 900WGTN-FM 100.7
COOL-FM 104.9
WSYN-FM 106.5

ROCK
WKZQ-FM 101.7
WYAV-FM 104.1
WWSK-FM 107.1

TALK RADIO
WHMC-FM 90.1 (NPR)
WRNN-FM 99.5
WLMC-AM 1470

TELEVISION STATIONS

First things first. In order to find your favorite program on a particular network, you need to know which cable company is servicing your area. TV guides will give you a lineup of what channel you should turn to, in accordance with the designated cable delivery company you're hooked up to. This listing should set your remote control straight. Warning: If you're a channel surfer, ignore this section and simply proceed as usual.

North Strand

HORRY TELEPHONE COOPERATIVE
3480 Hwy. 701, Conway
(843) 365-2151
www.htcinc.net
This cable provider jumps around Horry County, but it exclusively services the northern Longs

region and its surrounding communities, including Carolina Forest, Little River Inn, the Spa at Little River, the Preserve, and Colonial Charters.

Myrtle Beach

TIME WARNER CABLE
1901 Oak St., Myrtle Beach
(843) 913-7941
www.twcsc.com
You are in Time Warner country if you are living or staying in Myrtle Beach proper, Little River, Atlantic Beach, North Myrtle Beach, Briarcliffe, or any Myrtle Beach hotel or condominium. TV guides use "TG" to designate the Time Warner service in the areas of Georgetown and Andrews.

Time Warner officially acquired Jones Intercable in mid-1998. This cable company serves three-fourths of all customers in Horry and Georgetown Counties. At the same time, its delivery system was upgraded, at a cost of $15 million, to install fiber-optic cable and new converters. To the customer this means greater channel capacity, improved picture and sound quality, and increased reliability. High-speed cable modems offer Internet access.

Network Affiliates and Local Satellites

ABC Affiliates
WWAY-TV 3 (WILMINGTON)

WCIV-TV 4 (CHARLESTON)
Local Satellite: WPDE–TV 15
1194 Atlantic Ave., Myrtle Beach
(843) 234-WPDE
(843) 946-6689 (Weather Center)
www.carolinalive.com
News channel 15 boasts an impressive weather and environmental team and offers newscasts at 5:30 a.m., noon, and 5 and 11 p.m. Chief Meteorologist Ed Piotrowski has been voted the state's No. 1 weathercaster by the Associated Press of South Carolina and was nominated for the National Hurricane Center's media award for outstanding efforts to educate and inform the

public about hurricanes and hurricane preparedness. WPDE is the only area station to broadcast line lottery drawings nightly at 6:58 p.m. All of our ABC stations bring you *Good Morning America* at 7 a.m. and air soaps from 1 through 4 p.m. Other ABC programming varies from channel to channel during the time blocks of morning talk shows and evening sitcoms.

Subscribers to Time Warner Cable can access ABC programming on channel 9. TV 4 is on channel 4. Horry Telephone service is on channel 9 as well. Cablevision airs channel 4 on channel 57; channel 9 stays the same.

CBS Affiliates

WCSC-TV 5 (CHARLESTON)
Local Satellite: WBTW-TV 13
101 McDonald Court, Myrtle Beach
(843) 293-1301
www.wbtw.com

Like the weather team of WPDE-TV 15, WBTW chief meteorologist Frank Johnson has received accolades from public and press alike for his outstanding coverage of weather conditions. Johnson joined the weather team in 2003, having previously covered tornadoes in Oklahoma and hurricanes in Louisiana. TV 13 offers a local segment during its morning news broadcast that is one of the best venues for exposure in town. Approximately 40,000 viewers from the Grand Strand and as far away as Florence, South Carolina, tune in regularly. All CBS affiliates air the news at 5 and 6 p.m. Between 12:30 and 4 p.m., CBS offers an impressive lineup of soaps. CBS carries tried-and-true shows, such as *60 Minutes*, as well as hit programming such as *Survivor* and *CSI*.

TV 13 has originated news and programming from the Myrtle Beach area for more than two decades now and prides itself on being an integral part of the Grand Strand community. During Halloween, the station works with local Holiday Inns to provide barrier-free trick or treating to special-needs children. WBTW TV-13 also sponsors a Senior Fair each year and projects that honor outstanding local teachers, students, and athletes.

All CBS programming is found on channel 13 for Time Warner customers and Horry Telephone viewers. HTC customers may select either channel 5 or 13.

NBC Affiliates

WECT-TV 6 (WILMINGTON)
www.wect.com

WIS-TV 10 (COLUMBIA)
www.wistv.com

WCBD-TV 2 (CHARLESTON)
www.wcbd.com

These NBC stations offer a popular programming roster. *Days of Our Lives, Dr. Phil,* and *Oprah Winfrey* round out daytime viewing from 1 to 5 p.m. Two hours of award-winning news follows, and then the NBC lineup. These affiliates also bring you the *Tonight Show* every night of the week after local news.

Time Warner Cable gives you NBC on channels 6 and 10, as does Horry Telephone. The network is found on channels 6 and 62 with Cablevision.

Fox Affiliates

WFXB-TV 43(MYRTLE BEACH)
www.wfxb.com

WTAT-TV 24 (CHARLESTON)
www.wtat24.com

Home of the ever-popular *American Idol*, Fox's programming includes *The Simpsons, 24,* and *House*. Fox programming can be found on Time Warner channel 4. Cablevision airs Fox on channels 24 and 26, and Horry Telephone subscribers need to switch to channel 7.

CW Affiliate

WWMB-TV 21
www.cwtv21.com

No matter what local cable service you subscribe to, WWMB programming is found on channel 16.

This is the only network affiliate on the Grand Strand that airs the popular series *Gossip Girl, America's Next Top Model,* and *One Tree Hill*.

Educational

WITV-TV 7
www.scetv.org

WHMC-TV 23
www.scetv.org

WUNJ-TV 39
www.unctv.org

All of these education-oriented stations offer programming for the entire family. All are good morning channels for kids; catch *Arthur* and *Clifford the Big Red Dog*.

The *NewsHour with Jim Lehrer* airs every evening at 6 p.m., followed by a variety of instructional and investigative programming.

Time Warner customers can find TV 7 and TV 23, while WUNJ-TV 39 is on channel 3. If you're staying in a Myrtle Beach hotel, the channel will be 21. The Horry Telephone channel is 8.

Scroll Channels

TIME WARNER CABLE AND
WACCAMAW CABLE

Scroll channels offer a constant listing of local information and public-service announcements accompanied by easy-listening music. These channels are widely accessed by hotel guests since they supply Grand Strand visitors with plenty of updated information and complete community calendars.

Local Feature Shows

The talk show *Southern Style* has featured local guests since its inception in 1985. "Hostess with the mostest" Diane DeVaughn Stokes invites a variety of people with stories and passions to her hour-long program, which airs twice daily at 10 a.m. and 7:30 p.m. on Time Warner Cable, channel 5. Diane's spots are always upbeat, like the hostess herself—whether on or off the air.

WFXB Fox 43 produces several local shows, including its daily morning show *Carolina People*. The 30-minute television talk program airs at 7 a.m. weekdays and is jointly produced by the Local Newspaper, Inc. and Lucky Dog TV Productions. Sponsored by the *Myrtle Beach Herald*, it is hosted by WFXB owner Greg Everett. The show focuses on the lives and activities of people living and working in the Carolinas. At 8 a.m. Jack Murphy hosts the community-oriented *River Talk*. *Myrtle Beach Homes Today* airs weekly on WFBX as well and is hosted by Penny Mohney and Miranda Fuller. The two travel around the Grand Strand, visiting some of the area's most beautiful golf courses and area businesses.

WFBX also airs a 30-minute weekly show called *Myrtle Beach TV*, which it refers to as Grand Strand reality television. The show does candid, on-location interviews with people around the Grand Strand. Each new program airs Sunday morning and then is simulcast 24/7 on the Web at www.myrtlebeachtv.com.

VOLUNTEER OPPORTUNITIES

Want to get the pulse on a seemingly erratic resort area in a hurry? Become a volunteer! We highly recommend a volunteer pastime as one of the best ways to become entrenched in the community. Whether you're a newcomer to the Grand Strand or have chosen this sandy coast as your retirement home, joining a volunteer corps can open an insightful window to local politics, culture, and people.

For those who are coming into town to tackle a new job assignment or career, a number of area businesses encourage volunteer activity by paying club membership dues for their employees. Civic, which means "of citizenship," organizations can often plug you right into a networking circuit of business contacts. Even *Fortune* magazine cites volunteer experience as a highlight many American corporations look for on resumes.

On a purely social level, civic involvement in a specific club will serve you up a slice of local life. Each organization presents its own microcosm or cross section of Grand Strand citizenry, where you're bound to meet an interesting friend or two and, perhaps, the man or woman of your dreams. For singles, we can assure you that meeting locals through volunteer activities will beat a werewolf lifestyle of moonlight bar stalking.

Volunteer opportunities abound up and down the Grand Strand strip and in its pockets of subcommunities. To get a fairly comprehensive listing of volunteer outlets, we suggest dropping into the main office of the Myrtle Beach Area Chamber of Commerce on Oak Street to pick up the free-to-the-public guide *Civic & Service Organizations of the Myrtle Beach Area.* You can also get updated volunteer information from the *Sun News:* Civic and support-group meetings are announced in Sunday's "Coastal Living" section.

Included here are some volunteer organizations we know would gratefully welcome your help and/or participation.

COUNTYWIDE

BIG BROTHERS AND BIG SISTERS OF HORRY COUNTY
(843) 248-0164
www.bbbsa.org

Big Brothers and Big Sisters is a nationwide, not-for-profit youth service organization. The mission of Big Brothers and Big Sisters is to "make a big difference, one child at a time" in the lives of at-risk children through professionally supported, primarily one-to-one mentoring relationships with caring adults, and to assist the children in achieving their highest potential as they grow to become confident, competent, and caring indi-viduals. Big Brothers and Big Sisters of America has matched millions of children in need with caring adult mentors since 1904. Research shows that children with Big Brothers and Big Sisters are less likely to use drugs and alcohol, skip school, or exhibit violent behavior.

Big Brothers and Big Sisters are caring adults who are mentors to children, often from single-parent homes. Men and women from all backgrounds help guide their little brothers and little sisters toward bright futures by sharing life experiences. "Bigs" and "Littles" enjoy schoolwork, sports, recreational activities, movies, museums, and just talking together. In a nutshell, a "Big" is a friend.

GIRL SCOUTS, CAROLINA LOW COUNTRY
(843) 669-5174

www.girlscoutsofeasternsouthcarolina.org

Girl Scouts is the world's preeminent organization dedicated solely to girls. Girl Scouts aims to provide an accepting and nurturing environment where girls can build character and skills for success in the real world. Girl Scouting would not be possible without a league of dedicated adult volunteers. Opportunities exist for those willing and able to help once a week, once a month, or once a year. Volunteer opportunities include troop leader or committee member, trainer/workshop coordinator, mentor/advisor, chaperone, fundraiser, camp staff, event director, nature consultant, cultural awareness instructor, and more.

HORRY-GEORGETOWN COUNTY GUARDIAN AD LITEM PROGRAM
Horry County Offices, Third Avenue, Conway

(843) 248-7374

www.govoepp.state.sc.us

Volunteers in this program are specially trained to become advocates for abused and neglected children, representing the child's best interests through the Family Court system. This is interesting, viable work and a wonderful opportunity to learn the legal system firsthand while helping a child in need.

Virtually anyone over the age of 21 who has an interest in children and the desire and time to serve can become a Guardian Ad Litem. Volunteers come from all professions and backgrounds, from stay-at-home moms to corporate executives. They conduct interviews with the child and other sources deemed necessary to a case, collect records and documents, seek recommendations and advice from experts, and monitor agencies and persons who provide care or service to the child. All of this data is reported as findings to the court.

We must tell you that the situations guardians encounter are often not at all pleasant, and cases of abuse and neglect are downright ugly.

This program asks for a one-year commitment from its volunteers to handle one or more cases at a time, depending on your available time to give. You must apply and undergo a criminal check through the State Law Enforcement Division and the central registry at the Department of Social Services. Volunteers initially receive 30 hours of free training and must observe a court hearing. Ongoing training is constantly in the works.

LITERACY COUNCIL OF HORRY COUNTY
(843) 248-6140

http://horrycountyliteracycouncil.org

How can you measure the contribution to a life when you teach someone who is illiterate how to read? The Literary Council is always eager to recruit volunteers to this task and offers a comprehensive training program. Teaching materials are given to every volunteer, and placement with a wishful reader is almost immediate. Literacy tutor training is held almost every other month at different locations around the county.

MERCY HOSPICE OF HORRY COUNTY
(843) 347-5500

www.mercyhospice.org

Hospice volunteers lend an extra pair of hands to help, extra ears to listen, and a heart to love and console. A training course is required to become a hospice volunteer since you will be working with a person suffering from a terminal, incurable condition and with his or her family. Volunteers are considered to be dedicated, loving friends who often provide relief for the caregiver. Volunteers also assist Mercy hospice with office duties and fund-raising activities. The program is sponsored by Conway Medical Center, Grand Strand Regional Medical Center, and Loris Healthcare System.

MOBILE MEALS
(843) 997-6199

http://mowhc.org

"Waste not, want not" is the motto of this group, and its active volunteers don't believe in squandering a minute when it comes to delivering food to hungry people in need. Dozens of volunteers race hot lunches every day of the week—regardless of weather—to homebound citizens from the state line in Little River as far south as Brookgreen

Gardens in Murrells Inlet. More than 40,000 meals are delivered. These volunteers are so dedicated, they even make deliveries on Christmas Day and New Year's Day. With so many meals to deliver to so many needy folks, Mobile Meals more than welcomes another pair of helping hands.

OPTIMIST CLUBS
(800) 500-8130

www.optimist.org

If you are searching for an outlet to help the community and the opportunity to develop and demonstrate your own leadership skills, you'll find what you're looking for in your local Optimist Club. Optimist Clubs conduct many exciting youth-oriented special events and promotions, including a youth safety program, childhood cancer campaign, and an "Always Buckle Children in the Back Seat" auto safety program. The Grand Strand club meets in Myrtle Beach, and the North Strand chapter meets in North Myrtle Beach.

VOLUNTEER RESCUE SQUADS
In Myrtle Beach

(843) 626-7352

In Murrells Inlet

(843) 651-5143

In North Myrtle Beach

(843) 280-5510

www.horrycountyfirerescue.com

The Grand Strand emergency ambulance service is run by a combination of career and volunteer staff. Operating 24/7, they respond to emergencies from 11 different fire stations. Horry County is the fourth largest county east of the Mississippi. That means they cover over 1134 square miles. You must be 18 or older to volunteer. Applications are available at the Web site.

MYRTLE BEACH

AMERICAN RED CROSS
2795 Pampas Dr., Myrtle Beach

(843) 477-0020

http://horrycounty.redcross.org

537 Lafayette Circle, Georgetown

(843) 546-5422

If you prefer hands-on, in-the-trenches work, volunteering with the Red Cross could be just the ticket. This national community-assistance organization needs people to teach CPR courses, assist with Bloodmobiles, work in hurricane shelters, train for emergency disaster relief, and help coordinate the annual Community Christmas Dinner.

CITY OF MYRTLE BEACH
921-A Oak St., Myrtle Beach

(843) 918-1000

www.cityofmyrtlebeach.com

If you want to get right in the thick of things, consider volunteering for the city. Take surveys, coach a youth sports team, or perform a number of office duties. Volunteer positions are available in the departments of planning, construction, police, finance, engineering, public services, and parks and recreation. The city of Myrtle Beach also recruits active volunteers by the score for Chapin Library. Each department and facility accepts, screens, and trains volunteers to its specifications.

GRAND STRAND HUMANE SOCIETY
3241 Mr. Joe White Ave., Myrtle Beach

(843) 448-5891, (843) 448-9151

www.grandstrandhumanesociety.com

This is definitely the right place for animal lovers to donate time and energy. People are needed to assist in the care of animals and to help with fundraising and community-awareness programs.

GRAND STRAND REGIONAL MEDICAL CENTER AUXILIARY
809 82nd Parkway, Myrtle Beach

(843) 692-1634

www.grandstrandmed.com

Volunteers are used in every department and on every floor of this major hospital. An orientation session is held monthly, at which time all guidelines, rules, and regulations are discussed. Individuals are matched to particular positions at the hospital according to their backgrounds and skills. Orientation and training are provided. Talk to Gay Cooke, CDVS, to get involved.

GRAND STRAND YMCA
904 65th Ave. N., Myrtle Beach
(843) 449-9622
www.gsfymca.org
YMCA volunteers are the lifeblood of the Grand Strand Family YMCA. As a volunteer in programs—a volunteer position aptly known as a VIP—you can spearhead activities, act as a role model for a variety of young people, serve in the office, provide care for infants and toddlers, assist with special events, coach youth sports, chaperone trips, serve on various committees, and so much more. What you offer will be determined by your own interests and expertise. No matter how you help, you can make a big difference. In recognition of your time, support, and commitment, all VIPs are provided with special training, equipment, fellowship, and privileges.

HABITAT FOR HUMANITY OF HORRY COUNTY
(843) 916-8815
www.habitatmb.org
Dedicated to providing adequate housing for needy families, this local chapter of Habitat for Humanity works in partnership with people in need to build and renovate decent, affordable housing. Volunteers for Habitat assist in a variety of ways: The entire construction of a home is done by volunteers and the soon-to-be-homeowners; others help to raise money for the organization through Habitat's thrift shop, concession stands at major events, and gift wrapping at local malls during the Christmas shopping season. All Habitat committees, including Site Selection, Family Selection, Legal Affairs, and Surveying, are composed of volunteers. The only restriction is that a volunteer must be at least 14 years of age to work on a construction site. Call the number above if you want to pick up a hammer and join.

KIWANIS INTERNATIONAL
(843) 448-5123
www.kiwanis.org
A group for men and women age 18 and older, Kiwanis clubs worldwide are mandated to serve their communities. They run four or five major fund-raisers each year, and all monies raised must be donated or spent in the hometown. The group does a fine job supporting many area services, such as Helping Hand and Meals on Wheels.

SOUTH STRAND

SURFSIDE BEACH FIRE DEPARTMENT
115 US 17 N., Surfside Beach
(843) 913-6366

MURRELLS INLET FIRE DEPARTMENT
3641 US 17 S., Murrells Inlet
(843) 651-5143
www.migcfd-ashift.com
Here's your chance to live out that childhood dream of riding along in a screeching fire engine, wearing a shiny red hat and big boots, with your arm slung around a Dalmatian . . . OK, it's not really all fun and games. But volunteer firefighters are always needed, and the department requires no previous experience; training is provided.

UNITED WAY
515 Front St., Georgetown
(843) 546-6317
www.unitedwayhcsc.org
Nationally, United Way of America is dedicated to making a measurable impact in every community across America. The United Way movement includes approximately 1,400 community-based United Way organizations. Each is independent, separately incorporated, and governed by local volunteers. Volunteers are needed to assist with such office duties as typing, mail coordination, and filing. Volunteers are also needed to assist with various special events and activities. The Georgetown-area United Way is especially active and well respected. Year after year some of the community's most powerful businesspeople take a pivotal role in this local chapter—which makes this United Way a great opportunity for networking and making a difference in the lives of others.

WORSHIP

One local, albeit cynical, restaurant owner once commented to us, "Visitors don't come here to think, they don't come to read, and they certainly don't come here to go to church." He, of course, was alluding to the party-all-the-time image so often associated with Myrtle Beach. But despite his analysis and pronouncement, the Grand Strand is part of, and the vast majority of its visitors are from, the heart of the God-fearing Bible Belt. And one thing about Southerners is that regardless of how hard they party, they tend to be spiritual with the same vigor.

The denominational makeup of the area traditionally has been largely Protestant and more than a little fundamentalist in nature; South Carolina voters elected the only Christian Coalition–affiliated governor in the nation. Furthermore, this region's churches reflect its history: All Saints Episcopal Church on Pawleys Island celebrated its 240th birthday in 2007, and Prince George Winyah Church in Georgetown is one of South Carolina's few original colonial church buildings still in use. Conway's historic district is home to two more distinctive churches—Kingston Presbyterian and First United Methodist.

Nonetheless, with the large numbers of northern retirees and a more diverse population becoming year-round Grand Strand residents, the religious scene has come to include plenty of players in addition to Presbyterians, Methodists, and Baptists. Longtime resident, newcomer, or visitor, you can be assured of finding almost any congregation of your religious philosophy on the Grand Strand. Here's an abbreviated list of choices: Charismatic, interdenominational, nondenominational, Apostolic, Assemblies of God, Bible Church, Free Will Baptist, Independent Baptist, Southern Baptist, Catholic, Christian Nondenominational, Christian Science, Church of Christ, Community Church, Disciples of Christ, Episcopal, Evangelical, Jewish, Jehovah's Witnesses, Antiochian Orthodox, Greek Orthodox, Russian Orthodox, Latter-Day Saints (Mormon), Lutheran-ELCA, Lutheran-LCMS, Methodist, United Fellowship of Metropolitan Community Church, African Methodist Episcopal Zion, Nazarene, Pentecostal Holiness, Presbyterian-ARP, Presbyterian-PCA, Presbyterian-USA, Religious Society of Friends (Quakers), Salvation Army, Spirit-Filled Evangelical, Unitarian, and Unity.

So diverse has the area become, it serves as home to a 1,000-seat Charismatic Christian church, as well as an Indian-mysticism retreat, Meher Spiritual Center, on the oceanfront just to the north of Myrtle Beach (a retreat often visited by well-known rock 'n' roll musicians from the United States and England).

For the tried-and-true, born-and-raised Grand Strander, church is often at the center of social, family, and political life. And a large number of locals find it hugely important to be considered "Christian," however nebulous the term might be. Allegiance to a particular place of worship is not demonstrated merely by regularly attending Sunday services or tithing. Your children attend the church's day-care program. You are dedicated enough to serve as director of a church-sponsored board. You or your spouse teach Sunday School classes. And you would never consider playing in a softball league that is not sanctioned by your church. Indeed, for many native Stranders, the church weaves the very fabric of their lives.

There are simply too many churches to mention them all, so please check a phone book to find listings and worship times. The Myrtle Beach Area Chamber of Commerce, (843) 626-7444, also prints a free list of area churches and synagogues, and the *Sun News* runs a church directory every Saturday.

INDEX

ABOUT THE AUTHOR

Janice McDonald grew up in the house her grandparents built when they came to Myrtle Beach in the 1930s. She and her sisters spent their days combing the beach and their evenings listening to the ocean outside their bedroom windows. Janice left to become a producer and sometimes reporter for CNN, where she garnered numerous awards, including eight Emmy nominations. She currently owns her own Atlanta-based production company, J-Mac Productions, and has produced material for the Travel Channel, ABC, NBC, CBS, and VH-1, among others. She also is a contributing editor for *travelgirl* magazine and writes for numerous publications, such as *Atlanta Style and Design, South Carolina Homes and Interiors,* and *Delta Sky.* As a writer and producer, she continues to travel the world, but she considers herself a Carolina girl in every sense of the words and calls Myrtle Beach her true home.